> Dedicated to
Morgan and Cameron

May 2003

A de.MO Project

RETHINK

CAUSE AND CONSEQUENCES OF SEPTEMBER 11

EDITED BY GIORGIO BARAVALLE

de.MO

PREFACE

USEFUL INFORMATION

RETHINK is a word that requires introspection and a certain mind disposition, a reinterpretation of standard thinking. That does not mean that we need to be super human to read this book; we just need to be open-minded. So that by reviewing all the opinions and issues contained in these pages, one might emerge with a new perspective and personal ideology

RETHINK is an important book to me. I am worried for my children and their future. Worried that the world will be a very hard place for them to grow up and live in.

My love for my family drives this book.

What is this book about? It is a book about history and politics, a book about our life and about our world and what we are trying to accomplish on it. It is a book that confronts our diversities, our stupidity and cleverness, our preoccupations and rage, our laughter and desperate tears, our need for justice and love, our thirst for blood and power, our need to nourish and be nourished, our need to breath, close our eyes, and dream.

This book can be used as a weapon or as a treasure so I invite readers to handle it carefully.

Giorgio Baravalle

HOW TO READ THE CAPTIONS

< Previous pages   ◊ This page   > Following pages

LOCATION 1

WHAT THE ESSAYS TALK ABOUT

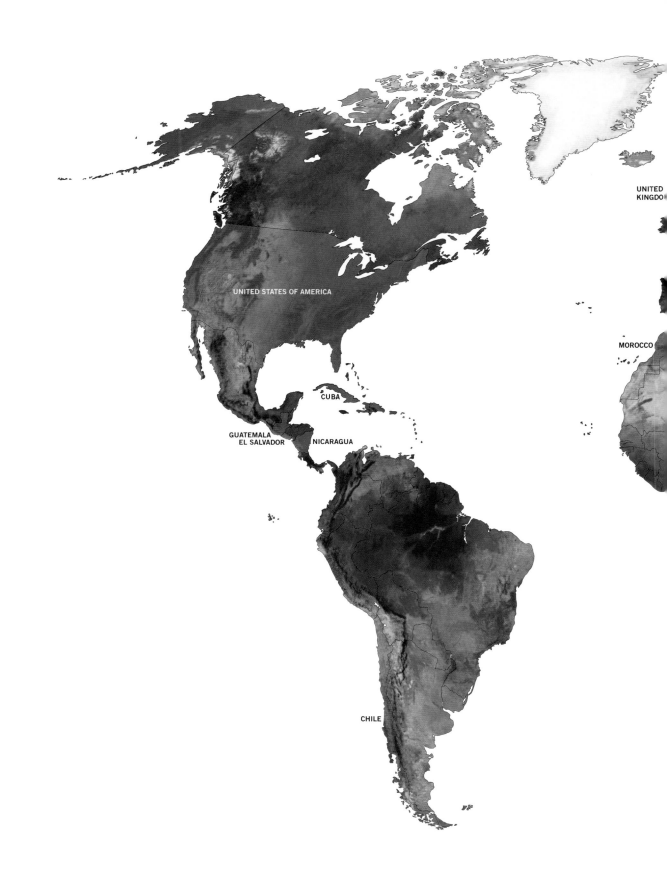

LOCATION 2

WHERE THE ESSAYS ARE IN THE BOOK

RETHINK

001

KOFI A. ANNAN

FIGHTING TERRORISM ON A GLOBAL FRONT

SEPTEMBER 21 2001

The terrorists who attacked the United States on September 11 aimed at one nation but wounded an entire world. Rarely, if ever, has the world been as united as it was on that terrible day. It was a unity born of horror, of fear, of outrage and of profound sympathy with the American people. This unity also reflected the fact that the World Trade Center, in this uniquely international city, was home to men and women of every faith from some 60 nations. This was an attack on all humanity, and all humanity has a stake in defeating the forces behind it.

As the United States decides what actions it will take in defense of its citizens, and as the world comes to terms with the full implications of this calamity, the unity of September 11 will be invoked, and it will be tested. I have expressed to President Bush and Mayor Rudolph Giuliani - and to New Yorkers at services in churches, synagogues and mosques - the complete solidarity of the United Nations with Americans in their grief. **In less than 48 hours, the Security Council and the General Assembly joined me in condemning the attacks and voted to support actions taken against those responsible and states that aid them. Of this solidarity, let no one be in doubt.**

Nor should anyone question the worldwide resolve to fight terrorism as long as is needed. The most eloquent global answer so far to last week's attacks has been the commitment of states from every faith and region to act firmly against terrorism.

The international community is defined not only by what it is for, but by what and whom it is against. The United Nations must have the courage to recognize that just as there are common aims, there are common enemies. To defeat them, all nations must join forces in an effort encompassing every aspect of the open, free global system so wickedly exploited by the perpetrators of last week's atrocities.

The United Nations is uniquely positioned to advance this effort. It provides the forum necessary for building a universal coalition and can ensure global legitimacy for the long-term response to terrorism. United Nations conventions already provide a legal framework for many of the steps that must be taken to eradicate terrorism - including the extradition and prosecution of offenders and the suppression of money laundering. These conventions must be implemented in full.

Essential to the global response to terrorism is that it not fracture the unity of September 11. While the world must recognize that there are enemies common to all societies, it must equally understand that they are not, are never, defined by religion or national descent. No

people, no region and no religion should be targeted because of the unspeakable acts of individuals. As Mayor Giuliani said, "That is exactly what we are fighting here." To allow divisions between and within societies to be exacerbated by these acts would be to do the terrorists' work for them.

TERRORISM THREATENS EVERY SOCIETY. AS THE WORLD TAKES ACTION AGAINST IT, WE HAVE ALL BEEN REMINDED OF THE NEED TO ADDRESS THE CONDITIONS THAT PERMIT THE GROWTH OF SUCH HATRED AND DEPRAVITY. WE MUST CONFRONT VIOLENCE, BIGOTRY AND HATRED EVEN MORE RESOLUTELY. THE UNITED NATIONS' WORK MUST CONTINUE AS WE ADDRESS THE ILLS OF CONFLICT, IGNORANCE, POVERTY AND DISEASE.

Doing so will not remove every source of hatred or prevent every act of violence. There are those who will hate and who will kill even if every injustice is ended. But if the world can show that it will carry on, that it will persevere in creating a stronger, more just, more benevolent and more genuine international community across all lines of religion and race, then terrorism will have failed.

On September 9, 2001, Ahmad Shah Massoud, commander of Afghanistan's Northern Alliance and legendary hero of the Mujahadeen rebellion against the Soviet invasion, was assassinated by two Arab suicide bombers posing as journalists.

002

REZA

LETTER TO THE LIGHT BEARER
OCTOBER 1 2001

You leave us mown down by a bomb. Shortly before this death, which we all expected and feared so much, in front of your relatives you told your son Ahmad:

"IF I SHOULD EVER DIE FOR THE IDEAS I HAVE DEFENDED MY LIFE LONG, I DO NOT WANT YOU TO CRY, NOR DO I WANT YOUR HEART TO TREMBLE."

How can we not be overwhelmed with sadness when a man of truth is murdered?

In this world where calculation, perversion, economic interests, and power conflicts mingle, the bearers of light seem to occupy little room. They upset the order, or rather the **disorders** of the world. Didn't Socrates or Gandhi die in the name of the truth which went against obscurantism?

Child of a culture, of a rich and misunderstood civilization, you were part of that limited number of beings who put their actions and thoughts in the service of humanity at the risk of attracting the animosity of the powers in place.

Poet at heart, you were forced to take the disguise of a war head in order to drive off the Red Army that came to crush your people under its destructive boot to the detriment of the country's independence.

You are the only one who were able to wrestle against this dreaded war machine of the West when the Cold War was at its height. It is you alone who brought down the Berlin Wall which cut the world in two before it fell down one year after the Russian soldiers left. As for the Westerners, they cowardly turned their backs on you. Remembering, I see it again, that scene. We were both squatting down on top of a map of the region laid out on the ground. I still hear your words:

"THE AMERICAN OIL COMPANIES WANT TO CONTROL THE PIPELINES AND THE GAS PIPELINES JOINING THIS NEW ELDORADO OF ENERGY ON THE EDGE OF THE CASPIAN SEA. UNSURE OF AN IRAN IN THE HANDS OF THOSE WHO THREW OVER THEIR

VASSAL, MOHAMMAD REZA SHAH PAHLAVI, THEY NEED AFGHANISTAN AND PAKISTAN. THE CIA AND THE PAKISTANI ARMY HAVE ESTABLISHED A PRECISE PROGRAM OF MILITARY AND IDEOLOGICAL FORMATION OF THE CHILDREN OF MISERY, OF WAR, OF EXODUS, WHO CROWD THE REFUGEE CAMPS IN PAKISTAN. THE INDOCTRINATION IN THE NAME OF A CONQUERING ISLAM, FAR FROM THE MYSTICAL ISLAM OF MOLANA, IS AT THE VERY BASE OF THE POWER OF THOSE WHOM THEY CALL THE TALIBAN. DO NOT FORGET THAT BIN LADEN WAS AN AGENT OF THE CIA. THEY RECEIVED FROM THAT INSTITUTION LOTS OF WEAPONS AND INFORMATION. THE FUNDS CAME FROM ONE OF THE GREAT ALLIES OF THE UNITED STATES, SAUDI ARABIA."

Between a Soviet Empire at the twilight of its influence-wounded by its failure-and a West sold out to economic interests, you attempted the impossible, again alone, to establish not your power, but the peace and independence of your country. How many times did you call out? How many times did only the echo of your words that seemed to hit the sides of the mountains return to you?

Life is beautiful, my friend. I believe it strongly. One can kill a man, crush his body, destroy his flesh, but one cannot annihilate his thoughts. You are that noble soul who dreamed for your country, for the world:

"I SEE A FREE, INDEPENDENT AFGHANISTAN. A COUNTRY WHOSE PEOPLE WILL ELECT A COUNCIL OF THE WISE, A LOYA JIRGA COMPOSED OF HUNDREDS OF REPRESENTATIVES. A COUNTRY WHOSE GOVERNMENT WILL BE ELECTED AND WHERE WEAPONS WILL BE GIVEN UP. I SEE THE MOUDJAHEDDIN, THE FIGHTERS, COMPRISE AN ARMY OF RECONSTRUCTION AND AN ARMY OF EDUCATION. I SEE GIRLS GO TO SCHOOL JUST LIKE BOYS. I SEE THE TRADITIONAL AGRICULTURAL SYSTEM, BURIED IN OUR SOIL, REGAIN ITS PLACE. I SEE OUR CULTURAL AND HISTORICAL PATRIMONY PRESERVED AND VALUED; IT IS OUR MEMORY. FINALLY I SEE ALL OF ABRAHAM'S CHILDREN LIVE IN PEACE ON OUR SOIL."

He continued with a pensive and candid look:

"I STARTED TO CREATE THAT IN PANDJSHIR AND ONE DAY I WILL HELP EXTEND IT THROUGHOUT AFGHANISTAN. MAYBE THE WORLD WILL BE INTERESTED BY SUCH A MODEL."

And when I told you naively:

"DEMOCRACY EXISTS IN THE WEST WITH SUCH PRINCIPLES AND A SIMILAR ORGANIZATION,"

You replied:

"NO. THESE ARE NOT TRUE DEMOCRACIES. A DEMOCRACY DOES NOT PUT IN POWER TALIBANS, PEOPLE SO FAR REMOVED FROM ITS PRINCIPLES, IN THE NAME OF ECONOMIC INTERESTS. IT IS NECESSARY TO IMAGINE AND APPLY A TRUE DEMOCRACY."

You were the flame on the arduous road to peace. My friend, I strongly believe that life is beautiful when I see other torch bearers following the path that you have outlined for us.

Remember the old Persian proverb I quoted to you one day:

"ALL THE DARKNESS IN THE WORLD CANNOT SUFFOCATE THAT LIGHT OF A SINGLE LITTLE CANDLE."

003

SURAYA SADEED

FROM HEROES TO TERRORISTS
OCTOBER 10 2002

I have lived in the United States for the past twenty years.

It is my second home.

I was born and raised in Afghanistan.

My heart is still there.

On September 11, when I heard that Bin Laden was behind the crime that had shaken the world, the fear that I had for years was realized. I knew that Afghanistan would have to pay for having Bin Laden as its unwanted guest.

For the past ten years, I have traveled twenty-four times to different cities of Afghanistan and the refugee camps in neighboring Pakistan to deliver emergency aid. I have seen the unspeakable pain and agony of millions who have been terrorized and spent years in constant fear, living a powerless, shackled existence where even learning and a woman showing her face in public was outlawed.

AFGHANISTAN HAS BEEN A FORGOTTEN LAND, A SMALL NATION THAT PAID A HEAVY PRICE FOR FIGHTING A WAR FOR FREEDOM AGAINST THE INVADING SOVIET UNION THAT HELPED BRING AN END TO THE COLD WAR. AND WHILE THE INTERNATIONAL COMMUNITY ENJOYED THE NEW WORLD ORDER, AFGHANISTAN, A SILENT NATION WITH ENORMOUS PAIN, WAS DROWNING IN HER SORROWS. IN THE ABSENCE OF A CENTRAL GOVERNMENT AFTER YEARS OF WAR AND LAWLESSNESS, THE COUNTRY BECAME A SAFE HAVEN FOR TERRORISTS.

In November of 2001, in the midst of the U.S. bombardment, I went back to Afghanistan to deliver emergency aid to thousands who had been stranded in the middle of nowhere and caught in yet another war. I was not sure if people knew why the U.S. was bombarding their country, so I asked a young man, and he answered:

"Oh yes, because of the two tall buildings, it was a tragedy, but why they are dropping bombs on us? What did we do? Are they blaming it on Afghans? This is crazy. Do they know how much this nation suffered? Let me tell you, first Russians came and killed hundreds of thousands of Afghans, poisoned our wells, burned our homes and destroyed everything in their way. Then, the bloody civil war started. The warlords, the Taliban, Pakistanis, Arabs, you know the story. And now Americans? What on earth do people want from us? Over one million of my people gave up their lives to defend this country against the invading Russians who wanted us to become Communists, just like themselves. We defeated them. Can you imagine? A small poor nation like us defeated that giant ugly bear? But we are a brave nation. My uncle told me that the Americans were very happy when Russians were defeated by us, and called us 'heroes.' Now we are terrorists? Please tell Americans that Bin Laden is an Arab, not an Afghan. The whole world knows this, how come they don't know? Why are they blaming everything on us? Do they think that we sent an invitation to Bin Laden?" I am asking you, whom do you think we should blame for our destroyed country? For our tens of thousands of amputees? For our widows? For our over one million orphans? For our children paralyzed because of the use of chemical weapons? For millions of landmines? Do you want more? I have a long list."

The young man started crying in despair and continued:

"Do you want to know what happened to my life? I was only five years old when my father was murdered. I was ten years old when my mother was raped and tortured in front of my eyes. Look at me; I am living in a plastic tent in this freezing weather with my four sisters. How should I feed them? I lost one of my hands when I was a kid because I picked up something that looked like a butterfly, but it was a landmine. Look around, what do you see? Countless numbers of people; most of them are children and women. They are hungry, many of them are sick and have no place to hide. Their homes were burned down. They are constantly looking to the skies in fear of America's huge planes coming everyday and dropping bombs. I have never had a normal family life. I have never seen peace and love in my life. Everybody, including America, benefited from our war and forgot we existed. Do you think that America became the only superpower just by accident? Now go and tell America that I am angry at the world, but I am not a terrorist."

It was over a year ago when the U.S. started its military campaign against Al-Qaeda and the Taliban in Afghanistan. Thousands of innocent children and civilians lost their lives caught in the midst of the war on terrorism, became the cost of the war: collateral damage, the characteristic phrase of our age. All we saw on CNN or FOX News was smoke rising from behind the mountains of Afghanistan, as if nobody ever lived in that country. I don't argue the political wisdom of the American military response in Afghanistan. Was it Justified? Was it Successful? We will let politicians answer these questions.

Perhaps one of the most distressing issues regarding the civilian deaths in Afghanistan is that nobody seems to really care. Is it because it might not suit the purpose of the war to bring to light what really happens? There has not been one single official investigation by governments or the independent sector to assess the number of civilian casualties in Afghanistan. How many people died while searching for a safe shelter from the bombing and a night's meal? I don't think we will ever know.

Today, Afghanistan is more destroyed than ever. Afghans know how the Americans feel looking at ground zero in New York, because Afghanistan itself is one giant ground zero. The international community's commitment to help rebuild that country is extremely slow, and I am fearful that Afghanistan will once again be yesterday's problem since our focus has now shifted towards Iraq.

Afghanistan's future lies in the hands of a new generation of underprivileged, illiterate, and impoverished children. The educational system has suffered a double blow — war and fundamentalism. According to the Pentagon, the cost of the U.S. military operations, for the first several months, against terrorists in Afghanistan was estimated at one billion dollars each month. If we invest a fraction of that to help rebuild Afghanistan's infrastructure, and educate the future generation of that country, they will be able to address the country's needs within its own context. They will embrace values that would defeat terrorism, and promote a civil society. Only then, can Afghanistan become a productive member of the global community.

I BELIEVE THAT OUR INVESTMENT IN CHILDREN'S EDUCATION CAN PREVENT THE NEXT WAR.

004

ANTONIN KRATOCHVIL

THE BEAR THAT OVERSTAYED
AFGHANISTAN 1978 - 1988

If you weren't there you'd never know. Even if you were you'd never make sense of it. Man, those Ruskies, the superpower who one day checked the map and saw a warm port for its cold war, and a little Yankee containment. "Here," they said, "we go here, to Indian Ocean through Afghanistan. Da, piece of cake."

In **1978**, Nar Mohammed Teraki was Moscow's marionette … head of the People's Democratic Party of Afghanistan. Talk about predicament … dangling by your Soviet strings above the newly formed Mujaheedin waiting below. You had to be either crazy, or just screwed. The place was a pressure cooker, alright. Red Army advisers scouting the lay of the land, and the Mujah -- waiting, planning, and sliding the bolt on their Enfield rifles shut. Teraki didn't last long. By the time 1979 rolled around, he'd buried his head so deep in his pillow it had killed him — you have to hand it to the KGB: they took people out in style.

So here it was, the late seventies version of the early seventies Apocalypse Now going down. Mercenaries, a few journos, and every spook you could have dreamt of mixed up in the espionage, adding to the tension and smoking a shit load of hashish … a ton of it, in fact. Everybody was on hashish. From the little Red Army garrison stuck on a rock waiting for all hell to break loose, to every home grown Rambo that was hell-bent on making certain that that was what exactly happened, people in Afghanistan were busy sucking down Allah's wonder woo-woo night and day.

One photographer used Rolling Stone as his horse to ride to Afghanistan on. The magazine had lost Antonin Kratochvil's precious slides … oops. They gave him five grand … even got him a taxi to the airport and a hash brownie to go — this was the seventies man, although by the time he'd arrived at JFK with only brownie crumbs left he told me he wasn't so sure.

Before he got bumped, Teraki's government granted Kratochvil permission to travel the northern routes along the Soviet border — only with no guarantees. At that time guarantees came in three forms: a good chance of being killed anytime, anywhere; no sex with the opposite sex; and a civil war of major proportions about to erupt — inshallah. Up in the north, things were wild. Tribal leaders were in charge here. And the levels of discontent brewing among the people carried as far as the call to prayer. People seethed. Women could now drop their veils, wear slacks and join the communist party — how about that? The Mullahs were losing their grip. These Ruskies with their programs and ideology had to go. The Mujaheedin thought Kratochvil was an adviser for these foreign agitators. According to them it said so in his U.S. passport — and it may well have; English read upside down says many things to the average Uzbek speaker. Kratochvil was lucky his driver, Khalid, was dialed in. Khalid pleaded for his passenger's life and lo and behold the bemused Muja released the man with the cameras and the upside down passport … he could live. But the pressure grew. With each day, small raids on the Soviet backed Afghan army upped the ante. A garrison here, a patrol party there … with weapons and clothing going to the victors. The Russians were right: these Afghanis were nothing but bandits, "Dushman." Now what would they wear?

At his hotel Kratochvil got a visit from a guy in a Brooks Brothers suit … wanted to know what he'd had seen up there in the north … told him it was his patriotic duty to cough up any info seeing as he was on the good guys side. Kratochvil described his ride, the surreal rock formations of this dusty frontier, the bright sunlight and the crisp air, along with the fact he'd had an army soldier stand beside him each day with a gun as he took his daily dump. "That's how dangerous it was," he said. "No shit," the quiet American said and left.

Atop a truck smoking Afghan's finest, Kratochvil remembers watching a hawk tethered to the vehicle fly above him like a kite. The mumblings of the fighters who were in tow … their stares, and the secrecy of their communication signaled what was to come. Kratochhvil left too that day, traveling the Khyber Pass bound for Peshawar and didn't make it back until 1986 when Afghanistan's pressure cooker had exploded and the mess was there for all to see.

With President Reagan's new-and-improved foreign policy of screw-this-cold-war-containment-shit-let's-turn-up-the-heat, the Mujaheedin now held Kalashnikovs and fired Stinger missiles. The Soviets had dumped their local help. They were now fighting this war … fully engaged, and at the same time in the crosshairs of the Mujah's new ground to air rockets. For these freedom fighters the mountains were what the jungle had been for the Viet Cong. Scores of Red Army choppers hit the ground each day as a little man would stand up from behind a rock and unload the contents of what sat on his shoulder at an attack chopper less than a hundred feet away. The Romans couldn't do it. The British couldn't do it. What made the Ruskies think they could now do it? Take control of this desolate place where Feudalism remained supreme and where the invading army had little choice but play hide and seek with a bunch of partisans who'd been told by God it was o.k. to die?

With Kratochvil's return, the war against the same enemy that had stuffed Czechoslovakia, his country of birth, back into its union, was now in full swing. He couldn't help cheering for the local guerillas. The Czechs had battled the Soviets almost twenty years before as their close encounter with freedom had been crushed that spring. The Brezhnev Doctrine was simple: stay in the Union or we will fuck you up! That meant

< **Mazaar-e Sharif**
Communist demonstration 1978.

> **North West Frontier**
Mujahadeen 1986.

> **Afghanistan**
Afghan refugee camp 1988.

> **Afghanistan**
Shrine to Martyrs
Afghan border near Quetta 1988.

Afghanistan as well. So, for Kratochvil, this war, the one he now vicariously took part in, was the war his motherland had been unable to fight. In keeping with Brezhnev's edict, hearts and minds would be won like this, by fear. The KGB unleashed the Afghan version of itself, KHAD, to stir it up. KHAD brought terror to rock the boat that was already capsizing. Car bombs were becoming as popular as the dope everyone smoked, and throughout Pakistan's tribal territories, and in Peshawar especially, you could set your watch by the regularity and frequency of the blasts. Pakistan was the Mujaheedin's base of operations, the place weapons were getting in, money was coming through, and where Uncle Sam's aid program was having some really impressive results. Like they say, one infidel's Cold War is another Islamist's Jihad. Kratochvil's hotel got a taste … blew the lobby out … covered everything in dust and rubble, and in the process screwed up the guests' bills ... happy days. Terror gripped everybody … someone had to give. Inside Afghanistan the sounds of boomerangs filled the air around the North West Frontier Province, the Khyber Pass, and the supply routes used by the freedom fighters as Red Army choppers peppered the terrain with butterfly mines — a gift that years later would continue giving, ripping apart an estimated one million Afghanis. It was a bitter legacy.

1988. KHAD's reign of terror was heading down the plughole fast … Najibullah, its top goon, now ran the de-facto Afghani government. Glasnost had been declared in Moscow, and Gorbachev's grip on the Union's "open wound" was loosening. Perestroika and its cut backs were the way out, and the way home for these tired, wobbling, godless lot. Kratochvil wanted to catch up on the war … wanted to visit the tribal territories again around Miram Shah, one of the most lawless places to have existed in the past few hundred years. Here, kidnapping was their game, trading captives from one tribe to another, or when foreigners showed up, them too. This place was where the hardcore fighters had been based when Kratochvil left two years before. He got lucky, traveling there with a Pakistani official. What he saw wasn't the swells of a liberating army waiting to deliver its final and decisive blow, but warehouses full of opium, whiskey, and guns. Container loads of Soviet air conditioners and fridge-freezers piling up to the sky. Yeah, this place was chilling out alright, with gallons of booze and a full metal jacket for every man to protect his booty with. The unity of the Mjuaheedin had reverted … turned back to the old clannish customs and scams of out-fucking rival tribes. Commerce ran this war now -- dollars and cents and nothing more. His Muslim hosts offered him whiskey; it was what they were drinking, kicking back and ogling a painting of an unveiled woman hanging from the wall. The men drooled over her neck, exposed, brazen and, unfortunately for them, only in oil and sadly on canvas. Out here things were growing stranger and scarier … you never knew who anyone was. Before you could tell between friend and foe, your head was in a sack and bye bye.

Inside Afghanistan's perforated border with Pakistan, the burnt out hardware of fried tanks and barbequed choppers had men all over them salvaging scrap, cutting up the remains like crows picking over carrion. The image of these scavengers was something Kratochvil would never forget. One Pakistani official boasted that another year's worth of kickbacks and he could return home a rich man. Afghanistan had revealed itself. It was nothing more than a country for rent, a bazaar, and only then when it suited its volatile warlords who sat at its eastern edge tallying the profit. All bets could be off in a split second, money gone, and the air full of rockets and bullets heading your way ... that's how things were here. It was a trap, operated by hundreds of leaders working for themselves, and no one understood, least of all the duking superpowers. The Red Army was busy packing, and the CIA's clever plans of training guerillas to dislodge their commie adversary were slowly creating another monster that years later would turn, flying two fully-loaded jetliners into the heart of its creator's financial capital. The good guys always do that in their Frankenstein workshop … train contras and freedom fighters, install puppets and strongmen, topple governments when they shouldn't, prop-up dictatorships when they should know better, eventually doing it all over again in order to clean the mess they left in the first place, or, as of recently, scraping it up off their own sidewalks.

On February 15, 1989 at 10.00 am, Lieutenant General Boris Gromov walked across the Amu Darya Bridge, heading north … the last Soviet soldier to leave Afghanistan. Above him sat the Mujaheedin as he shepherded the last of his tanks, trucks, and hardware that had entered this rock to take charge, but had met resistance stiffer than its own intent. Kratochvil saw it on television, watching the foreign press ambush the retreating soldiers with questions and close-ups, looking at the dazed young men who'd done their best against an invisible enemy and with no help from an empire that was on its knees. Eight months later the Soviet Union would no longer exist, and in two years Afghanistan would be under the control of the Taliban. For the Soviets, their war was over. The general had promised them "rodina" — home. For Afghanistan it was never over. The conflict would just shift, from one hopeful invader to another, who'd come, conquer, think themselves invincible, then die.

> **Afghanistan**
Afghan refugee camp 1986.

> **Afghanistan**
Afghan refugee camp 1986.

> **Baluchistan**
Afghan refugee camp 1988.

004 Antonin Kratochvil
The Bear that Overstayed

Page 29

< **Afghanistan**
Field hospital Afghan border 1988.

◊ **North West Frontier**
Afghan refugees 1986.

> **Gareyz**
Afghanisytan 1988.

> **Afghanistan**
Mujahadeen base
Afghan border 1988.

> **Afghanistan**
Bushkashi game Afghan
refugee camp 1988.

◊ **Afghanistan**
Afghan war wound 1988

> **Baluchistan**
Military fort 1988

> **Miram Shah**
Political officer in charge of gun
smuggling sector 1988

> **Miram Shah**
Miram Shah tribal territory
Mujahadeen base 1988

> **Afghanistan**
Mujahadeen 1988

> **Gareyz**
Mujahadeen returning
from battle 1988

004 Antonin Kratochvil
The Bear that Overstayed

Page 51

< Gardeyz
Soviet cluster bombs near
Gardeyz 1988.

◊ Afghanistan
Making hashish Afghan border 1986.

> Afghanistan
Salang Tunnel
guarded by government soldiers
1979.

> Kabul
Afghanisyan December 1978.

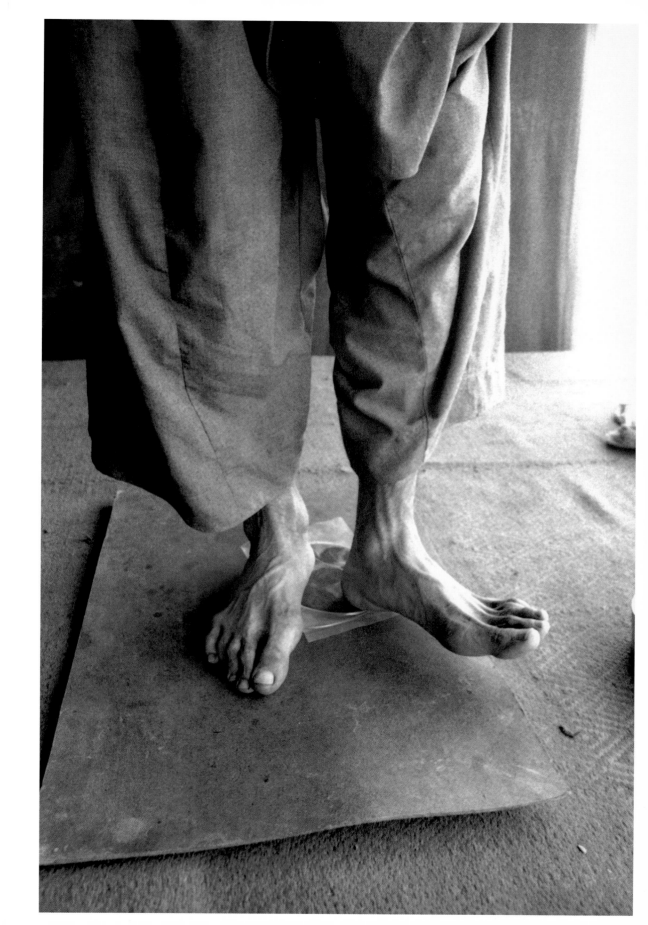

005

RICHARD MEDLEY

NEW YORK
SEPTEMBER 14 2001 - MAY 5 2003

As with all tragedies, the memories and emotions of September 11th fade — and in fact shift — with time. What happened, where we were, how we felt, all erode somewhat as we tell our own stories and listen to others. This is how gemeinschaft evolves and how the individual stories of the lives lost that day and since then in two wars merge with our own lives.

But this very process makes the texts and explicit reactions of that moment, in that moment, all the more important as historic documents. Only by brutally revisiting those times through direct access can we keep the memories from fading into a comfort zone.

My company was in a unique position that day. First, because of location: a few blocks north of Ground Zero in TriBeCa and right on Greenwich Street. In fact, before the first television images flashed I knew there was tragedy when my assistant reached me in a London hotel room to tell me that a missile had flown directly over our building and smashed into the World Trade Center. That was how the plane sounded at full throttle. Second, because of what we do: our job is to tell private clients how to react to and anticipate political and geopolitical events around the world. **We are different than a standard news organization in that we get paid explicitly for being able to see around the corner and to be able to see around that corner with significant accuracy.** Traders, corporations, oil companies, and a small group of global individuals are our clients and they do not pay us for what they can read in the Times.

On September 11th, the power went out at our office. We had two back-up computer systems. Unfortunately one of them was in the World Trade Center itself; the other was in Jersey City, but the lines ran through the PATH tunnels at Ground Zero. For three days we struggled to bring our service back up and to find a route of communication with clients who needed us then more than ever.

By Friday, September 14th our tech team had created mirror groups through yahoo and other mailing lists, and our content team had managed to contact and report from a wide variety of American administration, military, and Federal Reserve sources. That Friday — as I raced down the Zurich hill from the Dolder Grand to get to my brother's wedding in Long Island (and made it) — we put out the first report since September 11th. It was a comprehensive look at the policy choices most likely to be taken in the coming days, months, and years, and it stands as an outstanding contemporary document, very raw, very emotional, much more right than it was wrong, but wrong in interesting ways.

What follows is the full note we sent to clients on Friday, September 14th, looking ahead through the rest of the year and beyond. Not a word has been changed. **I hope it sends that same chill of reality and recognition to you that it still does to us.**

US REACTION TO TUESDAY:
MONETARY, FISCAL, OIL AND MILITARY FRONTS

Our hopes and prayers go out to all our friends and neighbors, colleagues and clients, acquaintances and strangers, all the innocents who perished or who are still missing. As we told you in our message yesterday, this is coming to you in a temporary format because our offices are only a few blocks from the devastation at the WTC and remain without power and cordoned off. Our backup systems were damaged as well. We hope to be back in our offices sometime early next week, but until that time we will operate from remote facilities and contact you through this format. Please feel free to contact us to discuss the current situation or anything else at all — you can simply reply to this email (medleyadvisors@yahoo.com) and we will get back to you as soon as we can. Alternately, specific contact details for several of our relationship managers are contained at the end of this email as well.

US reaction to Tuesday's terrorist attack is forming on several fronts.

MONETARY POLICY – Federal Reserve, ECB and Bank of Japan officials are trying to accomplish two main tasks: (1) provide a zone of stability through direct liquidity injections, quiet intervention on the currency front and intense discussions with senior banking and trading participants; and (2) conduct monetary policy as appropriate to the economic and market conditions of each country and not in response to the terrorist attacks. Because of the severe impact of Tuesday's events on US economic growth there is pressure from senior officials for an inter-meeting rate cut.

In addition, the pace and eventual depth of rate cuts (which we already thought was destined for sub -3% levels) has widened dramatically. The markets are right about this. However, the combined impact of all the forces at work here may add up to a deeper drop followed by a sharper rise in economic growth than Federal Reserve officials had been forecasting.

FISCAL POLICY – Obviously all spending limits are off. There is no more discussion about the surplus — social security or otherwise.

Congress' doubling of the administration's initial request for rescue and recovery funding ($40 billion approved) is just the start of a spending campaign whose size depends more on what the administration can think of to spend money on than anything else. Combined with the likely impact of forced corporate and long-bond selling by beleaguered insurance companies, the impact should steepen the yield curve even if all rates come down

ENERGY POLICY – The United States is putting substantial and sustained pressure on its major allies within OPEC to allow prices to drop through the bottom of the $25-30 per barrel range that they have maintained this year. Middle Eastern governments report "dramatic pressure" and a very clear message from this administration: you are with us or you are against us – there are no shades of gray. The combined impact of diplomatic, economic and military events will send oil prices into an extremely volatile state. The US wants prices down now, fast so if they spike, as the military action gets under way, it does so from a lower base. However, the weight of the global recession will make that spike short-lived.

MIDDLE EAST POLICY – The days of the Bush administration having no Middle East policy are now over. Bush officials expect their normal allies to respond aggressively and immediately to their energy, basing, material and intelligence needs. In addition, they are making it clear to less obvious friendly states (such as Iran and Syria) that this is a time for them to make a choice about which side of they support. This is not Islam versus Christianity, but it is the G-7 versus Terrorism and there are no neutral states in that battle (sorry Switzerland).

But some of closest allies in this region are pushing the administration back hard, demanding two conditions for cooperation — first, that the US commit itself to sustained and consistent pursuit of a very clearly drawn policy (when it starts fighting this time it has to finish the job unlike 1990-1) and second, that they take a tougher stance with Israel's Prime Minister Sharon and prevent him from turning this into a Bin Laden/Hamas/Islamic Jihad/Syria conspiracy that justifies occupation or blockade of the West Bank.

MILITARY POLICY – There can be no doubt that we are moving to a sustained war footing. The decade long obsession with avoiding any casualties in a war has been wiped out by the realization that the United States has suffered more casualties to terrorism in one day than Israel and Ireland in 50 years. The only thing that has prevented Congress from a formal declaration of war is the seeming constitutional requirement to name a specific enemy in such a declaration. Give Congress a name and they will pass the resolution. Invoking Pearl Harbor, "acts of war," NATO's article 5 provisions and — if they can arrange it — a declaration by the UN that Tuesday's events were a "crime against humanity" are all designed to give the US a completely free hand when it decides to begin actions, most likely within the next week.

Here are the details behind each of those bullet points.

> MONETARY AND FISCAL POLICY

In brief, both throttles of government economic policy will be pushed to fast forward with the prospect building that a sharp spending downturn in the next few weeks and months could be followed by an equally sharp recovery by early next year at the latest. In other words, the "v" may be here after all.

Federal Reserve officials tell us they "are ready to do whatever it takes, but we do not want to respond directly to the terrorist attack except by creating conditions that maximize market stability." Fed officials will be helped by the sense among market professionals that pushing down stock or currency markets would be tantamount to lining up with the terrorists.

But the main concern among Fed officials is not with speculators, it is with American consumers who — aside from American flags — appear likely to use this as one more reason to pull back from shopping, buying cars and new houses. As you know, we have been telling you consistently that the Fed has worried that consumers would not sustain their buying binge long enough to let industrial and business investment return. This week's new and deeper drop in the Michigan Consumer Confidence Survey (completed before the WTC bombing) will only add to that concern.

All of this could easily trigger an inter-meeting rate move as Fed officials get back to business after completing their anecdotal survey of each reserve bank district. Of course, the early results of that survey have been horrific in all the ways you may suspect, but particularly with respect to the willingness of major credit organizations to extend significant new credit lines before they are able to assess the total impact of insurance company, bank lending and counter-party risk factors can be assessed.

In our own survey we have heard a drumbeat of extreme caution from the credit community. One mid-size, solid-credit developer told us. "One of our lenders just told us that all loan commitments we had are now void unless already signed and sealed. These (very large) lenders happen to have loans outstanding on the WTC, but we are afraid we will be hearing this from everyone. They just do not want to do anything until they see how things shape up. It does not help us if bond yields are at 4.6% but our credit spreads go out to 800 basis points."

Despite the terrible news from real time surveys these past few days, officials have reasons to hope that when the world begins to function again next week there will be significant moral and social pressure to get back to buying. In other words, at least for the first few days of trading there could even be a substantial bounce in stocks. This could especially be the case if there is forceful response on the military and political front to get the nation's confidence recharged.

This prospect has led to a major debate among Federal Reserve officials. The question is whether the US will suffer a "hurricane effect" from these attacks or a prolonged and more devastating "uncertainty effect." This debate will not impact immediate rate-cutting decisions which will be made to stabilize the sharp drops in confidence that go with either scenario, but the differences will turn out to be substantial for the fourth quarter of this year and into next.

The way Fed officials think about these two scenarios, a "hurricane effect" implies substantial immediate pullbacks in spending, lending and investment. As one senior official put it, "this could be just like what we saw in the Gulf war. When people feel uncertain they freeze up; they disengage. When you walk into a dark room, your first instinct is to hesitate, you freeze." However, if it is only this first "shock impact" then the combined force of fiscal and monetary stimulus from the government joined with the obvious demand generated by the need to rebuild the private sector provides a major boost to consumer and business spending. In other words, after a short drop in GDP, there is a positive external shock to growth.

The other model in Fed thinking is that the "uncertainty effect" dampens consumer spending, business investment, housing and other activities for a prolonged period of time. As one official put it, "we are worried that consumers will rein in because they are afraid. Can you imagine buying a house or car right now?"

For at least the next few weeks, Fed officials are certain that under either scenario, we will have "an acceleration of the deceleration." And that makes rate cuts a no-brainer. One advantage of tying the cut, even if only indirectly, to the immediate systemic issue is that it gets the Fed off the hook of looking like it was panicky about the real economy, even the Fed would be aiming to reverse a sharp consumer pullback through swift rate cuts.

Before all of this, we had already told you the Fed was preparing to adjust the market to the idea of sub-3% interest rates. That is now obvious. But if there is no financial market seizure or immediate signs of economic collapse, be cautious with the most extreme knee-jerk

rate cut scenarios. The Fed is therefore us, but will not show panic and if the hurricane effect prevails the surprise could be that the economic "u-turn" they have been dismissing would emerge from the wellspring of massive fiscal and monetary stimulus. We could turn out to be in the final months of the economic downturn.

> ENERGY, MID-EAST, AND MILITARY POLICY

Middle Eastern officials are collectively holding their breath as the days pass. They cannot believe the audacity, timing and insanity of the terrorist attacks and more than one leader from that region has told us that they are terrified the US will simply wage war on the Middle East without making distinctions. This attitude reflects part sheer fear and in part sheer horse shit as they maneuver to lineup with the United States but to get certain conditions understood as they do it.

The basic deal appears to be that in return for cooperation on oil prices, intelligence cooperation, and other specific avenues of joint action the US musts take out a clear and consistent strategy and then carry it out to the end. The failure of US administrations to do that have long been the most important impediment to cooperation and this time, with the stakes so high, Middle Eastern officials want to make sure things are different.

Early indications from US and Middle Eastern officials are that there are three main targets for policy action following this week's events. First, of course, is the Bin Laden network and deeply associated terrorist groups. These will be the targets of a very sustained and brutal military assault and the US will expect countries in the region to understand that American forces will be used on the ground in countries that are host to these groups.

Second is Iraq. The early thinking is that Bin Laden could not have carried out these raids by himself and that Saddam is an active participant. At the very least this means sanctions, blockades and massively increased pressure on his regime. Whether it eventually means more forceful military action has yet to be decided.

Third is Pakistan. This is the trickiest for three reasons. First, the Pakistani government is not in control of huge portions of its territory and warlord conditions obtain in most of those areas. This is particularly true in its northern frontiers on the Afghan border. Thus getting the cooperation of the Pakistani government is less helpful than it might seem. Second, because the Pakistanis have nuclear weapons and the United States has been aggressively pursuing warmer relations with their mortal enemy, India. The prospect of setting off regional aftershock wars because of US action has to be taken seriously. Third, because the Pakistani government is deeply divided about how much it can afford to cooperate with the United States (particularly if that means it has to allow troops on its territory). The US does not want to force Pakistan in to the Iraqi camp as an opponent, but it has to demand as much cooperation as that weak government is capable of providing.

A fourth target for US attention is Russia, but in a very positive sense. Early gushing enthusiasm for Vladimir Putin may be paying off for George Bush here, since the Russians have been very cooperative both behind the scenes and in public (including calling off some long-planned military exercises at the US request). American officials believe they have Russia's support for resolutions of action against terrorism in the UN, although not to be part of any multi-national force.

One interesting note on that front, Russian leaders have not been able to keep themselves from reminding American officials that this kind of terrorism is exactly what happened to them from the Chechens. "Maybe now there will be more sympathy for what we have had to deal with from our own terrorists."

> OIL PRICES

The most important point to emphasize from a markets perspective on this front is that US officials are putting sustained and substantial pressure on our OPEC allies to get the price of oil down now. Although they recognize that prices may get "spiky" as the military part of this equation evolves, they want these spikes to occur from lower levels.

US officials do not believe that the OPEC pricing strategy will survive the developments stemming from Tuesday's terrorism and that prices are on the way down. We have been consistently telling you that crude prices would stay higher than expected and have obviously been right. We are now changing our call on this front for several reasons:

> Our discussions with Middle Eastern officials convince us that the Bush administration will get their way with Saudi and other moderate Arab leaders and the current price targeting strategy will not survive.
> The global downturn in demand that was already underway will accelerate dramatically as travel, consumption and daily energy use declines sharply.
> US and European officials have already discussed tapping into the American and IEA strategic petroleum reserves. President Bush's "war-time footing" language and invocation of NATO's Article 5 provisions clear the way for using these reserves at anytime, although

they will probably hold off for now in the belief that oil prices are on their way down.

> ISRAEL AND US POLICY

There are two conditions to this price reversal.

First, heating oil may not decline in the same pace as other oil and crude products both because of the impending heating season in the global north and because the fuel used by military jets, tanks and other heavy ground equipment has the same crack structure as heating oil.

Second, if the United States mis-handles Israeli Prime Minister Sharon and allows a larger scale Middle Eastern conflict centered on this conflict to erupt supplies may be vastly more disrupted than just pulling Iraqi oil off the market. One of the most frequently asked questions by Middle Eastern officials (and Russian leaders) in the past few days is whether the Bush administration will use these events to step up their involvement in the Israeli-Palestinian battle by reining in Sharon the way his father and Jim Baker reigned in the Israelis during the Gulf War. If so, it will buy the administration substantial new credit with a range of moderate (and some not so moderate) Arab states. Of course, if the administration aligns more tightly with Sharon, particularly with his desire to paint Tuesday's events as part of a grand Hamas/Fatah/Iraq/Taliban/Iran/Bin Laden alliance that justifies more aggressive action on the West Bank then — in the understatement of the century — one Middle Eastern official said, "This thing could get out of control." Time and again we heard from these sources that "we are very willing to help, but if every organization that Sharon hates gets lumped together with Bin Laden and Iraq, our ability to help effectively becomes severely compromised." This will be one of the most crucial decisions for the administration in coming days and it is not clear at this writing how the Administration is going to play this or who is exerting the most influence.

In the end, US foreign policy is now being defined by a single guiding principle that every country in the world must face: you are either with me or against me. Choose. Nowhere is this truer than in OPEC and the middle east right now. The US wants the price of crude oil down. Period. It will not be done publicly, and the US pressure will not be applied publicly. But the price of crude oil will come down. These views have been conveyed to the Saudis. The choice is a simple one, either let OPEC go or go down together. There is little doubt that most countries in the region will opt for the former.

006

ADMIRAL STANSFIELD TURNER

A BRIEF BUT IMPORTANT IDEA
AUGUST 8 2002

THE MOST PRESSING LESSON FROM 9/11 IS THAT WE MUST HAVE BETTER INTELLIGENCE ABOUT TERRORISM.

IT IS NOT SUFFICIENT TO FIND OUT AFTER THE FACT WHO COMMITTED A TERRORIST ACT. WE MUST KNOW IN ADVANCE AND BE ABLE TO CUT THEM OFF. THAT IS A FORMIDABLE CHALLENGE. IT CAN ONLY BE MET IF WE IMPROVE THE OVERALL COORDINATION OF OUR INTELLIGENCE COMMUNITY.

A PROBLEM HERE IS THAT THERE IS NO ONE IN OVERALL CHARGE OF INTELLIGENCE IN OUR COUNTRY. THAT NATIONAL SECURITY ACT OF 1947 CREATED THE OFFICE OF DIRECTOR OF CENTRAL INTELLIGENCE TO COORDINATE ALL OF THE FOURTEEN INTELLIGENCE AGENCIES OF OUR GOVERNMENT.

UNFORTUNATELY, THAT ACT DID NOT GIVE THE DIRECTOR OF CENTRAL INTELLIGENCE AUTHORITY TO CARRY OUT THAT FUNCTION. IT IS URGENT THAT WE PLACE SOMEONE IN CHARGE TODAY BECAUSE THERE CLEARLY IS A LACK OF COOPERATION BETWEEN THESE FOURTEEN AGENCIES. THAT PERSON HAS TO BE THE DIRECTOR OF CENTRAL INTELLIGENCE AND HE/SHE SHOULD BE SO EMPOWERED IMMEDIATELY.

THAT EMPOWERMENT CAN BE DONE BY PRESIDENTIAL FIAT, THOUGH IT WOULD BETTER BE ENACTED IN LAW ALSO. THE PRESENT LEGISLATION FOR A DEPARTMENT OF HOMELAND SECURITY DOES NOT EVEN ADDRESS THIS PROBLEM. IT IS AN URGENT ISSUE, AND MUST BE ATTENDED TO IMMEDIATELY.

007

JONATHAN BELKE

TRYING TO MAKE SENSE FROM THE SENSELESS:
9/11 FROM MY PERSPECTIVE

The streets of Cairo were eerily silent the evening of September 11, 2001 and for days afterwards.

Even the normally loud and chaotic traffic was muted. All humanity had been deeply moved by the images of destruction in the United States. During the early afternoon of September 11, Central Cairo had been teeming, as Tahrir Square was filled with riot police squaring off against tens of thousands of angry protestors calling on both the Egyptian and United States governments to take some kind of meaningful action to halt the escalating violence in the West Bank and Gaza Strip. Amidst the tight and unflinching security, the enraged protestors were corralled in front of the Egyptian government's mammoth Soviet-styled central registry building known as the Mugamma and prevented from reaching the nearby U.S. Embassy. It was late afternoon Cairo local time and the crowds of demonstrators had already been broken up when news started to trickle in shortly to be followed by live television images of the events unfolding in the eastern United States.

LIKE MOST PEOPLE AROUND THE WORLD WATCHING THE MASS DESTRUCTION OCCUR LIVE ON TELEVISION SO FAR AWAY,

WITHOUT REALIZING IT MY SUBCONSCIOUS STARTED A PROCESS OF CONFUSED SELF-EXAMINATION.

IT'S THROUGH SUCH INTERNAL AND MORE FORMAL QUESTIONING THAT OUR INDIVIDUAL AND NATIONAL POLITICAL, CULTURAL, AND HISTORICAL RATIONALIZATIONS COME TO THE SURFACE. RATIONALIZATIONS THAT TEAR US APART THROUGH OUR DIFFERENCES OF OPINION, THAT CUT THROUGH THE EMOTIONAL AND MORAL QUALITIES THAT CONTINUE TO UNITE US ALL AS HUMANS, RATIONALIZATIONS FOR SUPPORT OF AGGRESSIVE MILITARY ACTION IN RESPONSE TO SEPTEMBER 11 SQUARING OFF AGAINST RATIONALIZATIONS OF WHY THE ATTACKS TOOK PLACE.

Like the most Americans, millions around Egypt and the Middle East stayed glued to their television sets for hours and hours through the night of September 11, and in the days that followed I received countless phone calls and emails from friends and colleagues throughout the region expressing their condolences for the attack on my country. Later we were all surprised to see televised images of Palestinians, Iraqis, Egyptians and others celebrating the events of September 11 with dancing, passing out sweets, and shooting automatic weapons in the air. Rumors swirled that American television broadcasters were deliberately using old news footage of celebrations to discredit Arabs and Muslims. The same people who passed on their condolences later asked me why America didn't seem to be interested in the candlelight vigils and blood donations for the victims taking place throughout the region, and that even Palestinian leader Yasser Arafat donated blood while the American government-labeled "terrorist states" such as Sudan, Syria, Libya, and Iran condemned the attacks. People I never met before stopped me on the street to express their grief and outrage, and stated their opposition to the killing of innocent civilians anywhere in the world.

As weeks passed, the streets of Cairo returned to their normal buzz of life. Throughout the Middle East, instead of the "normal office talk" and "voices from the street" about the never-ending Israeli-Palestinian situation and struggle for peace, the new topics focused on the looming American retaliation for the September attacks.

Unfortunately in a region that knows about terrorism and violent attacks on civilians firsthand, I was asked time and again if the lives of innocent Americans were worth more than the lives of others.

I too wondered if an American "victory over terror" would come at a price of even greater innocent casualties around the world (what Washington calls 'collateral damage' when civilian casualties don't hold U.S. citizenship). Around the world, critics of American retaliation asked if greater innocent civilian casualties caused by the American military would serve the purposes of extremist groups by intensifying hatred against Washington, leading to even more unthinkable attacks.

As an American fortunate enough to live and work in several different regions of the world, I've come to see that people of all religions and backgrounds share the same hopes and dreams of living reasonable lives in which to raise their children. Cultural and historical differences, often times shaped by religious values, mean that not all people share "Western values" of democracy, freedom, and prosperity. I and others like me, with access to both American mainstream media and international media, find it appalling to see the misleading portraits of American foreign policy in action.

Despite all the patriotic jingoism, America doesn't uphold democracy when helping depose democratically elected governments, or by supporting despotic monarchies and one-party governments aligned with Washington. Freedom and tolerance are in short order in many of these aligned countries, whose jails are full of political prisoners, and where prosperity remains in the hands of the few.

FOR PERHAPS THE FIRST TIME, THE CONSEQUENCES OF AMERICAN FOREIGN POLICY, WHETHER REAL OR IMAGINED BY THE PERPETRATORS OF SEPTEMBER 11, WERE SEEN AND FELT BY THE MAJORITY OF THE AMERICAN PEOPLE. HOWEVER, IN THIS TIME OF GLOBALIZATION, SUCH A RIPPLE EFFECT HAS TO BE LOOKED AT FROM ADDITIONAL PERSPECTIVES. CAN THE ACTIONS OF SEPTEMBER 11 BE COMPARED TO OTHER ATROCITIES?

Many observers in the Middle East and around the world have pointed out that in the years prior to September 11, 2001, the United States and U.S.-led NATO bombed Serbia and Iraq, launched cruise missiles at Sudan and Afghanistan, enforced crippling sanctions against Iraq, supported despotic regimes around the world that rule by corruption and torture, and overlooked human rights atrocities committed by allied countries. The list goes on. While this doesn't justify September 11, it helps highlight the fine line between what Washington may call operation "Enduring Freedom" and others would label state terrorism, or a true demonstration of "real politick cause and effect." Regardless, the historical contexts resulting from years of the American government's arrogant dismissal of differing views from the rest of the world are the "excess baggage" people outside of America have seen and remember.

Many non-Americans see the United States as standing alone against a world unified in efforts aimed at making the world a safer and better place. Highlighting moves to limit weapons of mass destruction and warfare one can look at Washington's failure to sign, ratify, or comply with 1972's "Anti-Ballistic Missile Treaty," overturned by President Bush, 1996's "Comprehensive Test Ban Treaty," voted down by the U.S. Senate and opposed by President Bush, 1998's "Chemical Weapons Convention," crippled by Washington's limits on what may be inspected on American soil, 2001's "Biological Weapons Convention," signed by 144 countries but rendered useless by Washington's refusal to sign the "verification protocol," and 2002's "International Criminal Court," backed by 74 countries but fiercely opposed by the U.S. unless American citizens are given immunity from war crimes prosecution.

Non-military or security-prompted conventions and protocols Washington has refused to ratify continue to raise international indignation. These include: 1966's "International Covenant on Economic, Social, and Cultural Rights," that was unanimously approved by the UN General Assembly, 1979's "Convention on the Elimination of Discrimination Against Women" ratified by more than 150 governments, 1989's "Convention on the Rights of the Child," ratified by 187 governments, and more recently, the notorious 1997 "Kyoto Protocol" which set targets for emissions which cause global warming.

Other American government actions such as walking out of the International Conference on Racism, continued operation of Fort Benning's notorious School of the Americas, and withholding payments from the United Nations as punishment for not following Washington's every demand, all reinforce a spirit of the US's selfish, self-centered policies. Do any of these actions warrant the events of September 11, 2001? Clearly the answer is no! But without intending to imply support in any way, shape, or form for 9-11, to better understand the perceived reasoning behind such attacks is essential.

SEPTEMBER 11, 2001 WAS NOT ONLY A DATE OF HORRENDOUS AND VILE ACTS OF TERROR BUT ALSO A REAL DEPARTURE POINT THAT WILL DEFINE OUR COLLECTIVE FUTURE.

THIS DATE HAS ACTED AS A REBIRTH FOR ALL, SHOWING HOW HISTORY AND OUR HUMANNESS CAN SO QUICKLY BE RESHAPED.

AT THE SAME TIME, WE NEED TO REFLECT AND LEARN FROM THESE EVENTS IN AN EFFORT TO BEST STAVE OFF SUCH ACTIONS IN THE FUTURE. ALL CAN BENEFIT FROM THE WORK OF BERKELEY PHYSICIST FRITJOF CAPRA WHO EXPLAINED, **"THE MORE WE STUDY MAJOR PROBLEMS OF OUR TIME, THE MORE WE COME TO REALIZE THAT THEY CANNOT BE UNDERSTOOD IN ISOLATION. THEY ARE SYSTEMIC PROBLEMS, WHICH MEANS THAT THEY ARE INTERCONNECTED AND INTERDEPENDENT."**

Indeed, it is time for the United States to learn what has been apparent among the people of the Middle East for decades. Worldviews which isolate people and nations from a globally interconnected world are obsolete and inadequate. The current realities and problems of the world need to be looked at from newer angles, from imaginations that are wider and more open to various perceptions, while thinking and values need to allowed and encouraged to change if we are ever to live in real security.

008

TAKIS MICHAS

IT SERVED THEM RIGHT !
REACTIONS IN GREECE TO THE SEPTEMBER 11 ATTACKS

Popular reactions in Greece to the September 11 attacks were unique for a western country.

According to opinion polls, Greece was the only NATO and European Union member state in which, following the tragedy of September 11, the majority of the population expressed feelings of dislike for the United States and disagreed with the Alliance's decision to attack the Taliban. In a poll published in a Greek newspaper a few days after the tragic events of September 11, only 18.9% of the respondents expressed positive feelings about the United States and its inhabitants. A separate poll revealed that 25% of respondents said they felt "satisfied," and believed that "justice had been served." Moreover, 30% of respondents said that the attacks were a justified reaction to U.S. policies. Another poll found that only 6% of Greeks, the lowest number in Western Europe, supported a U.S. campaign against countries that harbor terrorism (a similar poll taken among the Palestinians showed that 7% supported America's anti-terror campaign). Moreover, in a poll published in the Greek daily To Vima on December 29 under the headline "Greeks declare (they are) unhappy with the USA's victory in Afghanistan," 61% of respondents said they felt unhappy about the coalition's victory, while only 29% expressed happiness with the outcome of the military campaign.

> POLITICAL AND MILITARY SINS

The view that somehow American was to blame for the terrorist attack dominated public discourse from the start. In learning about the terrorist attack, the immensely popular Archbishop Christodoulos of the Greek Orthodox Church stated that the terrorist act was the result of the "injustice and inequality" pervading the world. The media, too, joined in the fray. As ASS Press reported, television broadcasting in Greece was consumed by discussions "over whether America brought this event upon itself for perceived political and military sins."Not long thereafter, the Center for New Policy Pavlos Bakoyannis - named after the Greek terrorists' most prominent victim - invited the citizens of Athens to participate in a memorial service for the victims of terrorist attacks. Only about five hundred people turned up. By contrast, the next day nearly five thousand participated in a communist-led demonstration against the U.S., denouncing the CIA.

Meanwhile, allegations that the Jews were responsible for the September 11 attacks were so prominent in sections of the Greek media that the Israeli Embassy took the unprecedented step of denouncing those allegations as constituting "criminal, racist, anti-Semitic propaganda resembling that of the Nazis."

But perhaps the most outrageous incident happened during a soccer match between a Greek and a Scottish club on September 13.

Fans of the Greek soccer club tried to burn the American flag before the start of the game and booed during a moment of silence for the victims of the terrorist attacks in the United States.

"What went on in Athens disgusted me," the coach of Scotland's team said in a statement to the Associated Press. "What badly disappointed me was that there was no effort made by anyone, the police included, to do anything about it. I could not believe such anti-American feeling in a European country."

While feelings of sorrow and outrage marked the response of most observers in the rest of Europe, the reactions in Greece were at best extremely subdued: "Instead of reacting with the shock grief and outrage that every Greek-American felt," wrote Nikos Konstandaras, the editor of the English-language edition of Kathimerini, "the Greeks were seen - on satellite television and in editorials and too many comments by people in the street - to be analyzing the event with their trademark, 'Yes, but.' The expressions of support for America were drowned out by the inevitable anti-Americanism that was once confined to the Communist Party but in the last ten years, in the dearth of public statements to the contrary, appears to have become the only opinion on view."

According to Richardos Someritis, a writer for To Vima, the four main ideas that dominate Greek explanations of the terrorist attack are:

> That it was an act of the Jews, who wanted to promote their own interests.

> That Osama bin Laden is the creation of CIA propaganda.

> That terrorism is part of the struggle of the repressed against U.S. imperialism.

> That Greece is not threatened by terrorism, but by the fight against terrorism.

Such views seem to have more in common with public opinion in Cairo or Damascus than in Berlin or Rome. From where do they spring?

Since at least the mid-1970s, the perception that has dominated the political left is that Greek national aspirations required a break with the U.S. and its policies. Anti-Americanism based on real and perceived wrongs relating to the rise of the Greek military junta (1967-1974) and the Cyprus issue became the common denominator of political thinking. Cyprus has been divided into a Turkish-Cypriot and a Greek Cypriot part since 1974, after a Turkish military invasion of the island followed an attempted coup against President Makarios of Cyprus, instigated by the military regime in Athens The international community recognizes the Greek Cypriot government as the legal government of the island. Greeks accuse the U.S. of failing to force Turkey to comply with various UN resolutions asking the Turkish government to withdraw its troops from the island.

Thus, throughout the 1980s, the governing Pasok socialist party under Andreas Papandreou made it a cardinal point to antagonize Western, and especially American governments. It supported the Jaruzelski dictatorship in Poland, refused to condemn the suppression of dissidents in the Soviet Union and the 1983 shoot-down of a Korean airliner, harbored organizations perceived as terrorist by the West, and opposed the Reagan administration's deployment of cruise and Pershing missiles in Europe.

Then too, following the collapse of communism in Eastern Europe, the anti-American narrative came to be adopted by the political right. According to recent polls, over 50% of Greek conservatives dislike the U.S. Much of this owes to events in the Balkans over the last decade.

AMERICAN POLICIES IN BOSNIA AND KOSOVO WERE WIDELY SEEN AS AIMING TO DESTROY EASTERN ORTHODOXY ITSELF.

The war in the former Yugoslavia was not perceived, as in the rest of Europe, as caused by the expansionist ideology of a Greater Serbia, but as a conflict pitting an Orthodox nation - the Serbs - against the Muslims (Bosnians, Kosovo Albanians) and Catholics (Croats). The religious factor (both countries are overwhelmingly Orthodox Christian) thus played a major part in Greece's decision to support Milosevic's Serbia morally, economically, politically, and militarily.

Feeble attempts by the present government of Costa Simitis to lessen the identification of church and state in Greece were immediately attacked as being directed by the "Jewish lobby" in Washington, while the overthrow of Slobodan Milosevic - celebrated all over the world - was seen as a sinister CIA plot.

Today Greek nationalism, encompassing large sections of all political parties, has become identical with anti-Americanism. Seen as a system of ideas, the new anti-American narrative in Greece has little in common with critiques of American policies and social structures that were prevalent in the 1960s and early 1970s. The latter were rights-based discourses and had as their goal liberal emancipation. Current anti-Americanism, on the other hand, is suffused with xenophobia, irrationality, and plain hatred. Earlier forms of anti-Americanism attacked what America did. Present forms attack what America is.

Such attitudes did not go unnoticed, both in the Western news media and especially by the large and influential Greek-American community in the U.S..

In an avalanche of letters to the English-language edition of the Greek daily Kathimerini, Greek-Americans expressed their outrage at the behavior of their ethnic cousins. Greece had reached "the bottom of the swamp," wrote one. "It is truly shameful" wrote another, "that the mainstream press of a civilized nation would find ways to justify the terrorist attack on innocent civilians." But perhaps the strongest emotional reaction to the events in Greece came from Stephen Miller, a professor of classical archeology at Berkeley. After pointing out that considerable archeological work in Greecewas carried out by private donations of American citizens, he questioned whether this flow of funds would continue as donors became aware of Greek responses.

"After the attempted U.S. flag burning, after the anti-American editorials in so many Athenian newspapers ... how can I approach those American donors and ask them to continue support of the work? How can I ask them to take money and contribute it to a place where Americans are hated?"

> VIRULENT ANTI-AMERICANISM

The leaders of Greece's two main parties expressed their grief for the terrorist attack and pledged their support for U.S. attempts to fight terrorism. Nevertheless, as the polls showed, their ability to influence public opinion is minimal. Having for so many years tolerated attacks by their colleagues against U.S. policies on terrorism, economic globalization, the Balkans, human rights, and so forth, they suddenly found themselves in the unenviable position of having to argue against the (Balkan) version of tiersmondisme that constitutes Greece's dominant ideology.

THROUGHOUT THE LAST DECADE NOT A SINGLE MAJOR GREEK POLITICAL FIGURE HAD THE WILL, THE COURAGE, OR THE INCLINATION TO CHALLENGE THE POPULIST ANTI-AMERICANISM. ON THEY CONTRARY, THEY HAVE DONE EVERYTHING IN THEIR POWER TO ENCOURAGE IT.

As the following incident demonstrates:

In the summer of 1999 the popular Greek composer Mikis Theodorakis said during an interview: "I hate Americans and everything American. I hope that youth will begin to hate everything American." At the time he also advocated the formation of a nuclear alliance between Greece, Belarus, Serbia, and Russia directed against Greece's erstwhile allies - and the United States in particular.

During the same period Mr. Theodorakis was nominated as Greece's candidate for the Nobel Peace Prize. Theodorakis' candidacy was supported by leading Greek politicians and intellectuals from across the spectrum, including Premier Costas Simitis, Foreign Minister George Papandreou, and the leader of the conservative opposition New Democracy Party, Costas Karamanlis.

Theodorakis' views did not seem to faze those supporting his candidacy precisely because such views had by then become part of the mainstream opinion in Greece.

009

GARETH EVANS

CONFRONTING THE CHALLENGE OF TERRORISM: INTERNATIONAL RELATIONS AFTER 9/11

WHAT HAS CHANGED SINCE 9/11

Whether the world changed quite as much on September 11 last year as most of us thought and said at the time is something I want to explore in this essay.

BUT THERE IS ABSOLUTELY NO DOUBT THAT SOME THINGS CHANGED.

The first is that we all have a horrifying new sense of vulnerability. If this is the kind of damage that could be done by a handful of people willing to commit suicide, employing creative imagination but zero primary technology, what would be the impact of a truly full-scale chemical, biological or even nuclear attack? In an instant, the concept of "asymmetric" security threats moved from abstraction to alarming reality. In America the shock of losing both the physical and psychological protection of the two-ocean cocoon has been particularly acute, but the shock of 9/11 has been felt everywhere around the world. We've never known in peace time – and rarely in war – a sense of insecurity as pervasive as this one, and this is certainly affecting the way governments are behaving toward each other.

Secondly, we all understand much more about the interconnectedness of the world: for many people "globalization" moved for the first time from abstraction to reality. 9/11 made abundantly clear that no country can immunize or isolate itself entirely from external events; grievances bred elsewhere can have catastrophic consequences half a world away, and the ease of transport, international communications, and personal movement in and out of countries, has made it easier that ever before in history, not only to plot evil, but to deliver it. People in developing countries have long had the sense that their future was in the hands of other continents, but it's come as a shock to the citizens of New York and London and Brussels that decisions directly and immediately affecting their own security can be made in the Hindu Kush. We may not have seen the end of unilateralism in U.S. foreign policy, but we can wave goodbye to isolationism.

Thirdly, we know that we can no longer treat with erratic neglect the problems of the Arab and Islamic world, with its democratic vacuum from Morocco to Pakistan, ignoring those problems except when oil supplies appear threatened. The 9/11 terrorists weren't themselves poor, but they were supported by millions of people who are – those who resent perceived U.S. support for their own corrupt and insensitive regimes, resent perceived U.S. indifference to concerns affecting their political and social injustices (including those of the Palestinians), who want more economic opportunity and a bigger slice of the pie, and resent those who seem so effortlessly to have so much of it already and to be so unwilling to share.

Part of the resentment is obviously also fueled by a distaste for modernity, not least, Western cultural currents encouraging greater freedom and opportunity for women. But hostility to the West is not a matter of anything inherent in Islamic civilization — something I learned living alongside Indonesia for so long, by far the biggest Islamic country in the world, modern in its aspirations and now struggling hard to consolidate its democracy.

The debate about how to respond to these Arab-world problems is still very confused, particularly in the U.S., where any call to address, not just the symptoms of terrorism, but also some of the underlying political, economic, and social factors that breed and sustain it, tends to be greeted with cries of: "You're rewarding them!" But there is a huge difference between rewarding terrorists and addressing the problem they present, and policy makers ignore that difference at their peril.

The fourth impact of 9/11 is that it does seem to have made some old problems easier to solve, and some difficult relationships easier to manage. Whatever cynicism might have contributed to the warming of hearts in Moscow and Beijing – with Chechnya and Xinjiang turned into even more open free fire zones – there is no doubt that relations between the U.S. and Russia and China are on a more stable and substantial basis since 9/11 that they have been for some time.

In Sudan, the new obligation to demonstrate good international anti-terrorist behavior has concentrated the government's mind on the virtues of a settlement more than at any time in the two-decade history of this nation's horrible conflict. With some focused leadership from the U.S. and others, there's a big window of opportunity to now climb through. Again in Sri Lanka, a terrorist leadership has been having second thoughts about its sustainable future, and as a result of a new government and some effective Norwegian mediation, peace is closer at hand than it has been for years. For a time it seemed that even the Israeli-Palestinian conflict could benefit from the new atmosphere, with the Palestinian leadership being very quick to ally itself with the anti-terrorist cause. But with Ariel Sharon having a very different view of the opportunities presented by 9/11, the peace opening all too rapidly closed.

Finally, and conversely, 9/11 may have made a number of old problems harder to solve. The certain diversion of attention and the likely diversion of resources away from the job that remains to be done in the Balkans is causing a good deal of anxiety; certainly the winding down of American military involvement in Bosnia and Kosovo would be a particularly unhappy and destabilizing development. The diversion of diplomatic resources into the all encompassing war on terror is, again, of real concern across sub-Saharan Africa – from Liberia to the Congo and Zimbabwe and beyond – where there are a legion of problems and where strong American leadership (of the kind foreshadowed by Secretary Powell before 9/11) would be enormously helpful.

There are, moreover, some other problems that are in danger of reigniting in the new post-9/11 atmosphere. To the bemusement of most of the world outside Washington, North Korea and Iran have been lumped in with Iraq as co-axial evildoers, causing concern that this will only make things harder for the faltering moderate cause in Tehran, and prejudice the steady, albeit painfully slow, progress that was being made to bring Pyongyang back to planet Earth.

In the case of Iraq, it is widely acknowledged that urgent international attention through the U.N. is required, and that eventual reignition may not be possible to avoid, given that Saddam Hussein is not only reasonably suspected of rapidly acquiring new weapons of mass destruction, but also has an established track record of using them. But that does not translate into any support at all in the rest of the world for the emerging new U.S.doctrine that it is entitled to act preemptively, and if necessary, unilaterally, to deal with states emerging as possessors of weapons of mass destruction because of the temptations to which such states might succumb to deliver such weapons to terrorists. If 9/11 eventually results in the accepted rules of international behavior being turned inside out and upside down to this extent, its impact will indeed have been world-changing.

What is perhaps most disconcerting about these post-9/11, and in particular, post-Axis-of-Evil, developments, is the way they seem to be translating into a growing estrangement between the U.S. and its NATO allies in Europe, with even Britain being much more cautious about military adventurism in Iraq than a casual reading of Tony Blair's one-liners might suggest. Hard-line Americans (although being given some pause, both chronologically and in policy terms, by the disastrous impact of West Bank events on what might otherwise have been tacit moderate Arab support) argue that a war against Iraq is the logical next step in the war against terror, that it is winnable with or without allies in Europe and the region, and that victory over Saddam will unlock things elsewhere – making clear that nothing is to be gained by supporting terrorism, extremism, or authoritarianism. The Europeans argue, simply, and I think plausibly, that all this wildly understates the risks and overstates the potential benefits of such action. These disagreements are the most important and serious to have emerged since NATO was founded, and it may not be farfetched to suggest they may ultimately put the very existence of the organization at risk.

WHAT HAS NOT CHANGED SINCE 9/11

All that said, if one stands back a little, there is a lot that has not changed at all in the world as we find it after 9/11.

One is the endless capacity of individual leaders to create havoc, miss opportunities, and generally undermine the best-laid theories of academics as to how the world works. In all my years of international public life, I have never ceased to be amazed at the capacity of individuals to make a difference, for better or for worse. So much seems to depend merely on the luck of the draw, whether at a time of fragility and transition you get a Mandela or a Milosevic, a Rabin or a Sharon, an Arafat or an Ataturk, an Obasanjo or a Mugabe. That has always been so, and I suspect it will always remain so.

A second thing that hasn't changed since 9/11 is the underlying reality of the distribution of power in the world. The U.S. was neither more nor less a hyperpower, compared with everyone else, when September 12 dawned, although the further increase in defense expenditure, at least partly prompted by 9/11, makes the disparities even starker: the increase of $48 billion requested by President Bush is itself larger that the total military budget of any other country in the world, and will bring U.S. military spending to 40 per cent of the global total, double its share of global GDP, and eight times its share of global population.

Elsewhere, the rise of China and decline of Japan continues apace; Indian and Pakistan continue to maintain the world's most fragile and — because of their nuclear armories — dangerous relationship; one much affected by terrorist activity, but not especially changed by 9/11; and Europe's struggle to build a coherent common foreign and security policy capable of reflecting its economic weight in the world continues to limp along more or less unaffected by the travails of 9/11. Intergovernmental institutions like the United Nations continue to have no more and no less power to change the world than their member states will allow, with member states being overwhelmingly driven, in turn, by the same old perceptions of national interest and the same old power relativities.

Thirdly, the security fundamentals have not changed. Most of the security problems the world will have to deal in the years ahead are exactly the kinds of problems it had to deal with in the past – some involving conflicts or potential conflicts or unresolved grievances between states, but more involving conflicts within states, the product of greed or grievance or state failure, or all of the above. Each has its own dynamic and each requires to be tackled on its own terms. Some cross border conflicts will require full-scale international action of the kind clearly mandated by the U.N. Charter and set in train against Iraq a decade ago; some internal crises will involve such catastrophic human suffering — and such government incapacity or abdication of responsibility — as to cry out for international military intervention. All of them will require more intelligent and committed preventive action than the international community has so far been able, or willing, to provide.

With the understandable post-9/11 preoccupation with terrorism, it is worth reminding ourselves how little the fundamentals of conflict have actually changed. The great dangers come from political problems – some with underlying economic and social causes – that are unresolved, unaddressed, incompetently addressed, or deliberately left to fester until they become so acute they explode. Part of the fallout of such explosions can be terrorism, including international terrorism, but terrorism is not, in and of itself, a self-driving concept, the "enemy." It is not even an ideology — as anarchism was in the 19th century. Rather it is a tool or a tactic resorted to, in particular, by the weak against the strong – weak individuals, weak groups, weak states.

Since power relativities have changed to the point where virtually everybody is weak in comparison to the U.S., and since 9/11 has shown the way, there is more risk today that those in serious dispute with Washington will use terror as a tactic to compensate for that weakness. But the core problems go back to political issues. Military force is part of the answer, and was legitimately used in Afghanistan for punitive, retaliatory, and, in effect, self-defense purposes, but – whether in the hands of the U.S., Israel, or anyone else – it can never be an effective substitute for the traditional hard work of dealing politically with those core problems.

Part of the problem of characterizing the global security task ahead in President Bush's favored language of a "war on terrorism" or a "war on evil" is that it conceals the complexity of the issues and the necessity to accompany grand principles with detailed case-by-case strategies and tactics for dealing with each situation on its own merits. As others have pointed out, a war against evil is, almost by definition, unlimited and interminable. The concept doesn't help us much in identifying points of entry, and there is certainly no obvious exit strategy.

In terms of Isaiah Berlin's famous dichotomy, there's a place for hedgehogs – those consumed by one big idea – when it comes to global security issues, but most of the time the most productive work is done by foxes – those who know many things, and understand the need for endlessly varied approaches to solve endlessly variable problems. There are big risks in ignoring those problems – like many in Sub-Saharan Africa and the Balkans – which are not easily subsumed under the mantle of a war against terror, and perhaps even bigger risks in wrapping in that mantle security problems, like those in Iraq, Iran, and North Korea, which are at best only marginally connected to it.

Fourth, and finally under this heading, if the character of most of the world's security problems hasn't much changed since 9/11, the economic, social and equity problem fundamentals have not changed either. Secretary General Kofi Annan made the point succinctly in his end of year press conference last December:

"FOR MANY PEOPLE IN THE WORLD, 2001 WAS NOT DIFFERENT FROM 2000 OR 1999. IT WAS JUST ANOTHER YEAR OF LIVING WITH HIV/AIDS, OR IN A REFUGEE CAMP, OR UNDER REPRESSIVE RULE, OR WITH CRUSHING POVERTY."

The developing world is slowly beginning to show signs of having understood how comprehensively it has abdicated its responsibility, in terms of development assistance, to redress the fearful deprivation – starting with basic health, housing, and education – that exists in so much of the developing world. But the recent Monterrey Conference on Finance for Development hardly changed anything in terms of serious commitments made. Even the very welcome announcement by the Bush Administration of a significant increase in the U.S. aid commitment, won't do much to lift the U.S. out of the cellar division internationally: the one cent in every $10 of GDP going to Official Development Assistance will become just one and a half cents — still a long way from the seven cents set years ago as the appropriate international standard.

RESPONDING TO TERRORISM AND THE WORLD AS WE NOW FIND IT
How then should policy makers be responding to terrorism and the other security problems of the world as we now find them after 9/11?

MY SHORT ANSWER IS THAT WE SHOULD BE RESPONDING

COMPREHENSIVELY,

COOPERATIVELY,

DECENTLY,

AND ABOVE ALL

INTELLIGENTLY.

> Acting comprehensively means addressing security problems in a way that recognizes that they are not one-dimensional, and that social, economic, and cultural factors can be at least as important as political and military ones in explaining why people and governments act as they do, and in persuading them to act otherwise.

> Acting cooperatively means recognizing that in the real contemporary world, however big you are, most international problems are only solvable with the help of others, and that acting together rather than in splendid isolation in addressing security threats is what for the most part is required by the UN Charter – the only dominant system of security law we have, and which we would have to invent if it didn't exist.

> Acting decently is something that should, on the face of it, come naturally to those of us who spend so much of our time telling others how indecently they are behaving when it comes to democracy, fairness, openness, and respect for human rights. But our performance hasn't always lived up to our rhetoric, and I'm referring not just to the policy problems the U.S. keeps on experiencing with almost any kind of treaty commitment – the International Criminal Court being just the most recent example – which might limit its own absolute freedom of action.

During the Cold War years there were all too many examples – acceptance of the Khmer Rouge in Cambodia pre-eminent among them – when the West's worldwide struggle against Soviet-led communism created extraordinary bedfellows and led to a distortion of the values which the West itself claimed to be defending. But the double standards didn't stop with the end of the Cold War. Perhaps the most chilling of all recent examples is what happened not so long ago in Rwanda. In the words of Samantha Power, in her just-published "A Problem from Hell: America in the Age of Genocide": "In 1994, Rwanda, a country of just eight million experienced the numerical equivalent of more than two World Trade Center attacks every single day for one hundred days. On an American scale this would mean 23 million people murdered in three months. When on September 12, 2001 the United States turned for help to its friends around the world, Americans were gratified by the overwhelming response. When the Tutsis cried out, by contrast, every country in the world turned away."

> Maybe it's offensive to prevailing realist norms to ask that governments behave decently, but it can hardly be inappropriate to urge them to behave intelligently – and at the end of the day that's the most important of my set of adjectives, not least because it subsumes so many of the others. Behaving intelligently will usually mean acting comprehensively, because that's the only way to get at the roots of a problem and solve it with any hope of permanence. Behaving intelligently will usually also mean behaving cooperatively and decently, because it will involve recognizing that states' national interests – the only currency in which realists ever trade – are not exhausted by listing security interests and economic interests.

Intelligent states recognize, I have long argued, that they have a third national interest: their interest in being, and being seen to be, good international citizens. In a world where multiple problems are beyond the capacity of any government to fix by itself – terrorism, unregulated population flow, health pandemics, narcotics and other organized crime, certain environmental catastrophes – it just makes good common sense to make, and to be seen to make, common cause with others: I'll help you with your consuming problem today, you help me with mine tomorrow.

But behaving intelligently means some other things as well. It means acting preventively – before, rather that after, the event, when the cost in lives, money, property, and human misery are bound to have grown dramatically. It means following through: recognizing that the job in Afghanistan, for example, is only half done if you don't make a commitment to provide the military security necessary for any kind of serious institution-building to occur (the unwillingness to extend the role and reach of the international protective force ISAF beyond Kabul is almost incomprehensible in this respect), and if you don't make a serious and generous commitment to massive reconstruction assistance (despite the orgy of self-congratulation at the Tokyo Donors' Conference last January, less than half the amount identified as necessary by the World Bank and UNDP was pledged). Acting both preventively and effectively after conflict involves an unequivocal commitment to nation -building, and it is gratifying that the Bush Administration has now, at least in principle, recognized the force of that argument. Reference to the Marshall Plan may have become something of a clichÈ in international discourse, but it was music to a great many ears around the world to hear President Bush invoke so warmly the shade of the great General.

There's one more important dimension to acting intelligently that needs to be mentioned, and that is the need to act productively and not counter-productively. A constant theme of the International Crisis Group's reporting on Central Asia has been the risk of buying support for the anti-al Qaeda and Taliban operation at too high a price, in the sense of encouraging, or at least allowing, repressive leaders to go on being so repressive that they turn opposing moderates into extremists – and with the door of the mosque often the last one left open, Islamist extremists at that.

It is unhappily the case that signing up for the fight against terrorism has allowed authoritarian leaders to cleanse themselves of past sins, with Islam Karimov of Uzbekistan lauded in Washington for his help and given new funds; with Askar Akaev of Kyrgyzstan feeling freer to jail opposition members and curb the press; and with Nursultan Nazarbayev of Khazakstan also free from pressure to open up politics and deal with corruption. We have moreover seen Pakistan's Pervez Musharraf not just rehabilitated, but lauded, his history of undercutting institutions and democracy in Pakistan, not just being ignored, but encouraged, heedless of the history of military rulers and their nurturing of extremism. And particularly galling, if not as significant in regional security terms, we have seen Dr. Mahathir welcomed in Washington for the first time since 1994, using the specter of 'terrorism' to undercut the remaining opposition to his rule from PAS and the supporters of his disgracefully jailed former deputy, Anwar Ibrahim.

How does all this translate into prescriptions for the kind of policy the U.S. and wider international community should be following in response to 9/11 itself, the particular problem of Iraq, and the disastrously escalated Israeli-Palestinian conflict – all of which have now become almost inextricably entangled?

RESPONDING TO THE ATTACKS OF 9/11

In relation to the attacks of 9/11, I would argue that there are five separate objectives which have to be simultaneously pursued if the response is to be adequate, if short term objectives are not to work against longer term ones, and if the tightrope between over-reaction (in the sense of counter-productive action) and under-reaction is to be walked.

> The first: strengthening internal security, essentially a domestic matter, but one involving big issues of principle about how much liberty can

be sacrificed in the name of security without losing the very identity and character of the nation that the attackers have set out to destroy. There is also an external dimension in the sense that policy makers have to remember — as to their credit those in Washington overwhelmingly have — that any legitimate war is one against deeds, not beliefs, and that there are huge downside risks, in terms of winning the sustained cooperation of other countries, in engaging in any form of negative religious or racial profiling.

> The second is bringing the perpetrators to justice. There can be no doubt about America's moral and legal right to take robust action, as it has, against those responsible for the September 11 crimes, and those who aid or harbor them; in international law, the self-defense provision in Article 51 of the UN Charter is itself sufficient justification. But as a matter not only of law and morality, but of hard-headed national self-interest, there are several constraints which should nonetheless continue to apply to such action:

THERE SHOULD BE STRONG EVIDENTIARY FOUNDATION FOR IT, WITHOUT WHICH THE SUPPORT OF FRIENDS AND ALLIES WILL FALL AWAY. THIS CONDITION WAS PRETTY WELL SATISFIED IN AFGHANISTAN, BUT THE JURY IS STILL OUT ON THE SIGNIFICANCE OF AL QUAEDA LINKS WHEN IT COMES TO IRAQ, YEMEN, SOMALIA, THE PHILIPPINES, AND INDONESIA. THE KILLING AND MAIMING OF THE INNOCENT HAS TO BE AVOIDED AT ALMOST ALL COSTS. IF THAT HAPPENS, A WHOLE NEW GENERATION OF PEOPLE FEARING AND HATING THE WEST AND EVERYTHING IT STANDS FOR IS CREATED, A NEW BREEDING GROUND FOR A WHOLE NEW GENERATION OF FANATICS. YOU HAVE TO FOLLOW THROUGH PUNITIVE ACTION IN A PRINCIPLED WAY, IN THE PROCESSES FOR DETENTION, TRIAL, AND PUNISHMENT OF THOSE APPREHENDED – ALL OF WHICH CONTINUE TO BE CONTROVERSIAL IN THE PRESENT CASE. AND YOU HAVE TO MAKE A COMMITMENT TO FULLY REBUILD THE COUNTRIES IN QUESTION, AND NOT MAKE THE MISTAKE OF AFGHANISTAN LAST TIME ROUND OF WALKING AWAY WHEN THE IMMEDIATE PROBLEM HAD BEEN RESOLVED.

> The third objective must be building front line defenses against future attacks in the terrorists' countries of origin. The CIA, FBI, and U.S. military can never be as effective as the Taliban — or Saudi Arabia or the Sudan before them — in dealing with Osama bin Laden; just as neither the Indians or anyone else can possibly be as effective as the Pakistani government and military in curbing, if they chose, the terrorist fanaticism that continues to tear Kashmir apart. To strengthen these international defenses, the capacity and, above all, the will for these countries and authorities to act, both internally and in close cooperation with the wider international community, has to be built. Intelligence has to be supplied, financial supply lines broken, logistic support offered, and common strategies systematically pursued over time.

Building capacity means, in the first instance, building basic physical capacity – once again a question of generous development support. Building the will means essentially building political support. But there are two important constraints to bear in mind here. The first is that such support not be bought at too counterproductively high a price. The second is that it must be recognized that, whatever the will, political support is impossible without the capacity to deliver that support. If we want, as we must, strong local action against terrorism, we have to go all out to create environments in which there is more local support for cracking down on terrorism, and in which insecure governments will feel more confident doing so. And that in turn leads to the forth and fifth objectives I want to mention.

> The fourth objective is addressing the conflicts and policy issues that generate grievance. I have already made clear my view that to drain some of these swamps, as the approved metaphor would have it, is not to reward terrorism but to address it. Maybe my judgment here is a little affected by my role as head of the International Crisis Group, an organization dedicated to preventing and containing deadly conflict. But it is our strong belief that the task of fighting terrorism cannot be separated from the task of preventing, containing, and ending conflict. All too often the places that generate terrorism – along with drug trafficking, health pandemics, refugee outflows, and international environmental disasters – are shattered societies where grievance, greed, repression, poverty, and prejudice have, in various combinations, fed violence, utter despair, and extremism. Think not only of the Middle East and Central Asia, but of Northern Ireland, the Sudan, Columbia, the Caucasus. In none of these conflicts, or a dozen others, has the conflict remained local.

> The fifth objective must be the companion one to addressing the underlying social, economic, and cultural issues that generate grievance. Any comprehensive response to terrorism has to address the reality that not all the festering grievances that breed it have a rational, or semi-rational, foundation in unresolved or badly-resolved conflicts, or other policy issues of this kind. The unhappy reality is that the U.S. is the

natural international target for the resentment of those who feel themselves deprived. This country's role in the global economy, its perceived political influence, and above all its perceived cultural influence everywhere, mean that trouble is bound to follow, through whatever walls its citizens may be tempted to build around themselves.

There are no easy answers to this, but part of the response must be to try to gradually diminish the envy and sense of both absolute and comparative economic disadvantage that are significant parts of the problem; to make a sustained effort to improve social conditions, reduce disparities of wealth, create more and more economic opportunity; and above all, to create more and more educational opportunity. The madrassas of Pakistan continue to flourish because they offer a low cost education which millions of poor families simply cannot obtain for their children in any other way. There is no iron law that wealth or education will diminish fanaticism or hatred of the West – Osama bin Laden is himself living proof of that – but there is every reason to believe it would help, as would efforts both internal and external to improve the quality, and responsiveness, of national governance.

THE CHALLENGE OF IRAQ

On Iraq I have already made clear my own concern about some of the ways this issue is being handled in the U.S. — a certain indifference to international process, a certain over-confidence about the ease with which Saddam might be overthrown, and a certain overestimation of the positive regional benefits that would flow from that event.

However much Iraq is detested by its Arab neighbors and Iran, it still has an extraordinary capacity to win support if it can paint itself as oppressed — as we have seen in the playing out of the sanctions issue. And the recent developments on the West Bank have consolidated that support as nothing else could. Moreover, so far as the West is concerned, it cannot be assumed that even with active or tacit Arab-neighbor support, any military victory would be easily won. The assumption of a Shiite revolutionary guard to be decimated by American firepower while the population waits enthusiastically for the liberators to arrive is, to say the least, simplistic. So too is the notion that all this would result, not only in the collapse of the Saddam regime, but of anyone likely to be as bad — and would be sustainable without massive and highly risky ongoing military occupation.

All that said, it is high time to demand some better behavior of Iraq. But the way to deal with the whole issue is through the UN Security Council, which exists and is fully mandated to respond to precisely the threat Iraq represents. A big responsibility lies, in this respect, with those Security Council members who say they are committed to multilateral processes and find deeply distasteful, understandably enough, the U.S. tendency toward unilateralism. The need to put their money where their mouths are, to support the ultimatum demanding the return of fully-empowered weapons inspectors, and to follow that through. If some major powers are not prepared to make such hard calls, they will have to accept that others may make them unilaterally.

THE ISRAELI-PALESTINIAN CRISIS

One of the most depressing features of U.S. policy on the Israeli-Palestinian situation is that it seems to have been driven less by the merits, than by a combination of domestic political pressures on the one hand, and a desire to clear the ground for an assault on Iraq on the other. Hearing multiple voices, the Administration has wobbled backward and forward between unequivocal support for Ariel Sharon and distaste for his excuses; support and condemnation of Yasser Arafat; pressure and no-pressure on Israel; and support for an incremental security-first approach and support for a substantial up-front political initiative.

The truth of the matter is that violence – however ugly, however extreme and however protracted – cannot itself secure victory for either side; that Sharon's vision of a Palestinian state divided into impotent and cowed shreds and patches is totally illusory; and that the only possible way out of the present morass is to rebuild the political center on both sides, and find a way of offering both sides simultaneously – because they are not now likely to be able to negotiate it themselves – a final political settlement which is just and fair and balanced enough to give each side something to believe in, something to argue for, and something to justify restraint. Just as the issue of Iraq ought to be approached coolly and objectively on its own merits, and not in any crusading spirit, so, too, must the Israeli-Palestinian issue.

One of the most unforgettable conversations I ever had as Australian Foreign Minister was with Yitzhak Rabin, just three months before his assassination in 1995 at the hands of an Israeli extremist. Making a pitch on a particular issue to do with the peace process, I finished a little mischievously by saying, "Of course I know I'm preaching to the converted." Rabin looked at me with a little half-smile, paused, and replied: "To the committed, not the converted."

One of the many tragedies of the present situation is that one just can't imagine Ariel Sharon uttering any such words. And yet it's exactly that capacity to make choices from the head rather that the heart that is the key to salvaging something from the present appalling wreckage. In any rational analysis, the violence now being perpetrated by both sides is going to breed nothing but further hatred and killing. With neither absolute victory nor absolute defeat conceivable for either side, sooner or later a settlement will have to be reached. The only questions are when, and after how much more misery?

How can you negotiate with those you know, or believe, have committed appalling atrocities? The answer is: in the same way peacemakers always have when further suffering becomes intolerable. How else could peace have had a chance in Sri Lanka today, or Bosnia in the mid-90s, or in Cambodia a decade ago? It was chilling beyond description to sit across tables for meeting after meeting with Pol Pot's right-hand men. I still shudder to recall it. But we did it because all the other options were worse.

Both the Israelis and Palestinians have been let down by their leaders. At Camp David in 2000, and much more so in Taba in early 2001, a just settlement was almost there for the taking. As published insider accounts now make depressingly clear, peace became a victim, not of any congenital incapacity on either side to be a partner, but a deeply depressing series of misperceptions, miscalculations, and misjudgments, not only by Arafat, but by Barak and, to some extent, Clinton as well.

The only way out of the present mess is to turn the old incrementalism on its head, for the international community, led by the U.S., to show the way. What used to be thought of as the political endgame, built on foundations of security and growing trust, has to be brought back to the beginning. There will be no incentive or capacity to end violence and terror until majorities on both sides see within reach a settlement that fairly addresses all the issues. But, given all that's now happened, it won't be drafted by the parties themselves anytime soon.

To kickstart the process, a coherent, comprehensive, and credible plan has to be drafted in consultation with cool heads on both sides – there are some still around – and put on the table by the so-called "Quartet" group (U.S., EU, Russia, UN) together with the three key Arab countries (Egypt, Saudi Arabia, and Jordan). It can be done, but the only country with the clout to pull the process together is the U.S. If it continues to shy away from the necessary leadership role – with Colin Powell counting for less in Washington than Ariel Sharon – all the horrors so far will pall beside those yet to come.

In all this swirl of events in the world as we find it after 9/11, it is not easy for anyone to keep their bearings. The temptation is to respond in a piecemeal, ad hoc fashion, taking each separate problem as it comes and not worrying too much about the connections between them. If the alternative is to subsume everything into some single conceptual or ideological straitjacket – as part of the war on terror or the war on evil – maybe a piecemeal approach is not such a bad thing. But in international relations, as in life itself, there are principles that give coherence and meaning to the individual decisions we make. What is ultimately required is a decent approach and an intelligent approach, which are, I have argued, essentially the same thing.

010

VAIRA VIKE-FREIBERGA

REFLECTIONS
MARCH 7 2003

Before September 11 2001, we all thought that we had seen every conceivable form of blind, random, senseless, unprovoked murder and destruction. We had not. Never before had we seen evil in this particular guise.

September 11 will mark all who experienced it for the rest of their lives. For me personally, it revived painful memories from my childhood. As the end of the Second World War drew near, my parents and I fled our home in Latvia to escape communism and Soviet occupation. We arrived in a Germany being reduced to rubble by month after month of Allied bombings.

I still remember the threatening drone of waves of approaching bombers. I remember the high-pitched whistle of bombs hurtling down, each sounding as if it was falling directly towards the top of your head. I remember the sound of collapsing buildings; the sight of a neighbor covered in plaster to the whites of his eyes, yelling even before the all-clear had sounded for people to come to help his wife who was buried and screaming in pain under the rubble. Since then, bombs, exploding buildings and rubble have been a daily spectacle on the world's TV screens. Even so, September 11 was something unprecedented and different.

The Twin Towers had been a symbol of America, of its upward thrust of success, ambition, and pride. Even in a city synonymous with skyscrapers, the Twin Towers rose twice as high as the surrounding buildings - bigger and taller than the rest. They pierced the skyline in arrogant confidence, monuments to American know-how, engineering skill, prosperity and imagination. Like the Tower of Babylon, they defied the gods by reaching up into their domain.

After the fact, one had to start fathoming the reasons for the attacks and the choice of the terrorists' targets. The aim in striking at the Twin Towers would be no less than to strike at the heart and soul of America. Reducing these buildings to piles of dust would deal a hard blow to the image of the United States as impregnable and as invincible. Add to that an attack on the Pentagon, America's seat of military power, add to this a possible attack on the White House, the seat of political power, and you get the picture of a carefully thought-out assault on three symbols of American strength and power. Independently of their tactical goals, the attacks would certainly serve to appease the boundless rage and blind hatred of those who felt helpless and impotent to advance their cause through any other means, those who certainly felt unable to compete with America on any equal footing.

It was a stroke of evil genius to accomplish in peace-time, within the territory of a foreign country, and without the use of any military hardware whatsoever, the sort of attack that otherwise had been seen only in war-time and with the use of conventional military weapons. By using a commercial airplane as a rocket, strategic air defence was bypassed and rendered useless. By using something that was an ordinary, everyday part of normal life as a weapon, there was no need to smuggle anything into the country and bypass border controls. All that was needed were people ready to die for their cause and to take as many lives with them as possible.

The aim was to strike terror into the heart of every American, to create a sense of total vulnerability, a paralysing insecurity, the feeling that no place was safe and that there was nowhere to hide. This, thought the terrorists, would spread like a cancer across the land and undermine the very source of American success - the character and the values of the American people.

The towers did crumble into dust, one after the other, under our very eyes, as the whole world gasped in disbelief and horror. Thousands perished, and the world saw them die. We understood from those very first moments that many thousands more would be left with a legacy of irreparable loss, a lifetime of grief and of sorrow. We knew from the start that the economic impact would be enormous, the losses staggering. What we could not know from the start was how far the terrorists had achieved their goals and how far they had failed. This only unfolded in the days and weeks that followed.

Predictably, there was a lot of fear and anxiety and insecurity in many people's hearts. There was anger and bitterness, as might be expected. But over and above all there was courage. America coped with the shock, the surprise, and the losses with dignity, authority and grace. The world rallied around America in sympathy, grief and support. **What had been the World Trade Center now became the World Center for the Reevaluation of Basic Human Values**. Who can forget the images of the policemen and firemen of New York rushing into the doomed buildings, risking - and losing - their lives in the faint hope of saving others? Who can forget the moving testimonials of those had been personally touched by the tragedy? The attacks had been in defiance and renouncement of everything that we hold of value in civilized society. The reaction of the people of New York, the reaction of America as a whole, gave us all a lesson in bravery, resilience and nobility of spirit. This reaction was what spelled the utter and dismal failure of all that the terrorists had hoped to achieve.

My country, Latvia, is no stranger to loss and sorrow. There is hardly a Latvian alive who has not lost some family member to war or to mass deportations during the last century. This very experience of suffering caused a great outpouring of sympathy for the victims of September 11 among our people. Latvia knows the value of freedom, having lost if for half a century - first to a Nazi German, then to a Soviet Russian occupation. That is why we admired the gallantry of the American people when all that they hold dear was being threatened.

The aim of terrorism is terror. The best way to combat it is not to give in to fear. The whole world has to be united in this thought: We will not let them destroy our spirit.

The root of terrorism is hatred. How can we reach something that lies so deeply buried in so many people's hearts? How can we reach out to those who detest and abhor so many things that are an essential part of our own civilization? How can we extend a hand without renouncing what we ourselves stand for? How can they accept it without renouncing the values that have been drilled into them?

I think it can be done. It will need time and patience, but it can be done. If we manage to break down the barriers to communication that exist between continents and between civilizations. If all of us reexamine how our actions fit our words and our deeper principles and ideals. If we start teaching all children about tolerance and understanding, instead of teaching hatred and putting weapons into their hands - be they toy guns or real ones. If more of us start believing that there is more than one way of being righteous, but that there is only one way of being truly human. The day we all agree that every single human life is of intrinsic and irreplaceable value, that day we will have moved closer to a better world for us all.

011

JOHN BERGER

WAR AGAINST TERRORISM
OR A TERRORIST WAR?

Now that the number of innocent civilian victims killed collaterally in Afghanistan by the U.S. bombardments is equal to the number killed in the attack on the twin towers, we can perhaps place the events in a larger, but not less tragic perspective, and face a new question:

IS IT MORE EVIL OR REPREHENSIBLE TO KILL DELIBERATELY THAN TO SYSTEMATICALLY KILL BLINDLY?

(Systematically because the same logic of U.S. armed strategy began with the Gulf War.) **I don't know the answer to the question.** Perhaps on the ground among the cluster bombs dropped by B52s or amongst the stifling smoke in Church Street, Manhattan, perhaps ethical judgments cannot be comparative.

When on September 11th I watched the videos on television, I was instantly reminded of August 6th 1945. We in Europe heard the news of the bombing of Hiroshima on the evening of the same day.

The immediate correspondences between the two events include a fireball descending without warning from a clear sky, both attacks being timed to coincide with the civilians of the targeted city going to work in the morning, with the shops opening, with children in school preparing their lessons. A similar reduction to ashes, with bodies, flung through the air, becoming debris. A comparable incredulity and chaos provoked by a new weapon of destruction being used for the first time - the A-bomb sixty years ago, and a civil airliner last autumn. Everywhere at the epicentre, on everything and every body, a thick pall of dust.

The differences of context and scale are of course enormous. In Manhattan the dust was not radioactive. In 1945 the United States had been waging a full-scale, three-year-old war with Japan. Both attacks, however, were planned as announcements.

Watching either, one knew that the world would never again be the same; the risks everywhere, to which life was heir, had been changed on the morning of a new unclouded day.

The bombs dropped on Hiroshima and Nagasaki announced that the United States was henceforth the supreme armed power in the world. The attack of September 11th announced that this power was no longer guaranteed invulnerability on its home ground. The two events mark the beginning and end of a certain historical period.

Concerning President Bush's riposte to September 11th, his so-called "War against terrorism," which was first baptised Infinite Justice, and then renamed Enduring Freedom, concerning this riposte the most trenchant and anguished comments and analyses I have come across,

011 John Berger
War Against Terrorism or a Terrorist War?

Page 97

during the last six months, have been made and written by United States citizens. The accusation of "anti-Americanism" against those of us who adamantly oppose the present decision-makers in Washington is as short-sighted as the policies in question. There are countless anti-American U.S. citizens, with whom we are in solidarity.

There are also many U.S. citizens who support these policies, including the 60 intellectuals who recently signed a statement which set out to define what is a "just" war in general, and why in particular the operation Enduring Freedom in Afghanistan, and the ongoing war against terrorism, are justified.

They argued that the moral justification for a just war is when its purpose is to defend the innocent against evil. They quoted St. Augustine. They added that such a war must respect as far as possible the immunity of non-combatants.

If their text is read innocently (and of course it was not written either spontaneously or innocently), it suggests a patient gathering of erudite, quietly-spoken experts, with access to a great library (and perhaps, between sessions, a swimming pool) who have the time and quiet to reflect, to discuss their hesitations, and finally to come to an agreement and offer their judgment. And it suggests that this meeting took place somewhere in a mythic 6 Star hotel (access only by helicopter) in its own spacious grounds, surrounded by high walls with guards and checkpoints. No contact whatsoever between thinkers and the local populations. No chance meetings. As a result, what really happened in history and what is happening today beyond the walls of the hotel is unadmitted and unknown. Isolated De Luxe Tourist Ethics.

Return to the summer of 1945. Sixty-six of Japan's largest cities had been burnt down by napalm bombing. In Tokyo a million civilians were homeless and 100,000 people had died. They had been, according to Major General Curtis Lemay, who was in charge of the fire bombing operations, "scorched and boiled and baked to death." President Franklin Roosevelt's son and confidant said that the bombing should continue "until we have destroyed about half the Japanese civilian population." On July 18 the Japanese emperor telegraphed President Truman, who had succeeded Roosevelt, and once again asked for peace. The message was ignored.

A few days before the bombing of Hiroshima, Vice Admiral Radford boosted that "Japan will eventually be a nation without cities - a nomadic people."

The bomb, exploding above a hospital in the centre of the city, killed 100,000 people instantly, 95% of them civilians. Another 100,000 died slowly from burns and the effects of radiation.

"Sixteen hours ago," President Truman announced, "an American airplane dropped one bomb on Hiroshima, an important Japanese army base."

One month later the first uncensored report - by the intrepid Australian journalist Wilfred Burchett - described the cataclysmic suffering he encountered after visiting a makeshift hospital in the city.

General Groves, who was the military director of the Manhattan Project for planning and manufacturing the bomb, hastily reassured congressmen that radiation caused no "undue suffering" and that "in fact, they say it is a very pleasant way to die."

In 1946 the U.S. Strategic Bombing Survey came to the conclusion that "Japan would have surrendered even if atomic bombs had not been dropped ...."

To describe a course of events as briefly as I have, is of course to over-simplify. The Manhattan Project was started in 1942 when Hitler was triumphant and there was the risk that researchers in Germany might manufacture atomic weapons first. The U.S. decision, when this risk no longer existed, to drop two atomic bombs on Japan, needs to be considered in the shadow of the atrocities committed by Japanese armed forces across Southeast Asia, and the surprise attack on Pearl Harbor in December 1941. There were U.S. commanders and certain scientists working on the Manhattan Project who did their best to delay or argue against Truman's fateful decision.

Yet finally, when all was said and done, the unconditional surrender of Japan on August 14th could not have been, and was certainly not, celebrated as the longed-for victory. There was an anguish at the centre of it, and a blindness which blinded.

I tell this story to show how far even from the reality of their own history were the 60 American thinkers in their 6 Star mythic hotel. I tell it also as a reminder of how the period of U.S. armed supremacy which began in 1945, began for all those outside the U.S. orbit, with a blinding demonstration of a remote and ignorant ruthlessness. When President Bush asks himself "why do they hate us," he might ponder on this - except that he is one of the directors of the 6 Star hotel and never leaves it.

011 John Berger
War Against Terrorism or a Terrorist War?

Page 99

012

JOHN STANMEYER

MOVING THROUGH THE WRINKLES OF GOD'S HAND PAKISTAN AND AFGHANISTAN 2001 - 2002

◊ **Peshawar**
Anti-US demonstrators in Pakistan burn
an effigy of President Bush during a rally
outside a mosque. October 9 2001.

> **Taliqan**
A family heading home with all their
possessions on mules a day
after the Taliban fell in Afghanistan.

> **Chaghatay Ridge**
U.S. fighter jets circle Chaghatay Ridge, Afghanistan, waiting for targeting information
from U.S. Special Forces on the ground as the Northern Alliance open up a second major front
against Taliban forces.

> **Kunduz**
Northern Alliance troops take a moment
to lay down their guns and pray towards Mecca
at the front lines.

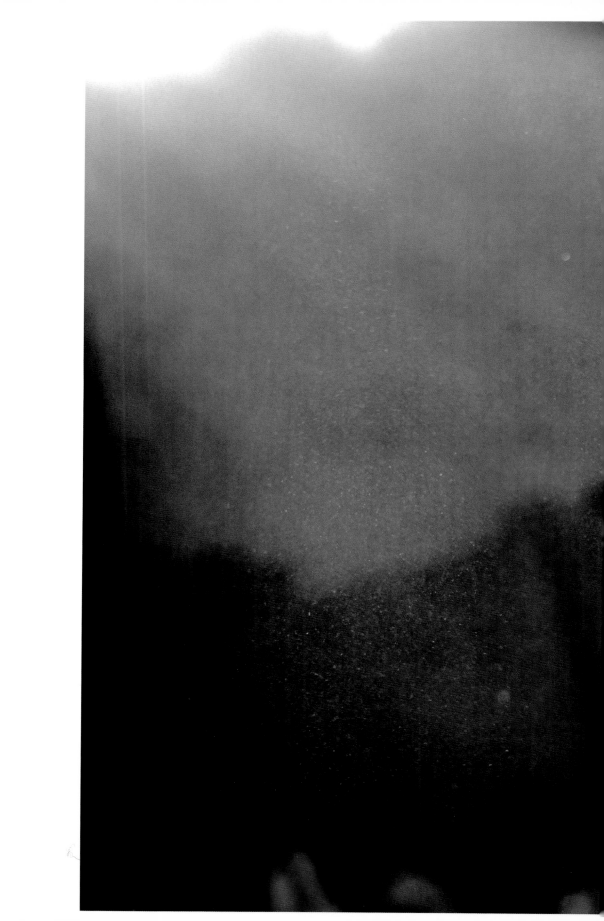

< Herat
Gullshan, 60 years old, sick due to the lack of food at the Rowzabagh Refugee Camp in Herat, western Afghanistan.

< Herat
Hundreds of men carry the body of Abdulha Habib to the Jamay Mosque. Habib was murdered when driving his truck near the Iranian border.

◊ Kabul
Woman in a traditional burka heading to her home within the ruined city sections of Gada-e-Mawaind, Kabul.

> Kabul
Demolition of building in the Jad-i-Maywand Reckakhana area of Kabul City.

> **Kabul**
Children's graffiti on a wall in
Kabul, depicting a war scene of
tanks, bombs and bullets.

> **Kabul**
Gournan-i-Darmak Sikh School for Sikh's
located in central Kabul. For 5 years the Taliban
never paid the teachers.

> **Kabul**
Child laborers weaving carpets at the
Charhi Sarsabzy Carpet Factory in Kabul. It takes
the boys 3 months to make the carpet.

O12 John Stanmeyer
Moving Through the Wrinkles of God's Hand

Page 113

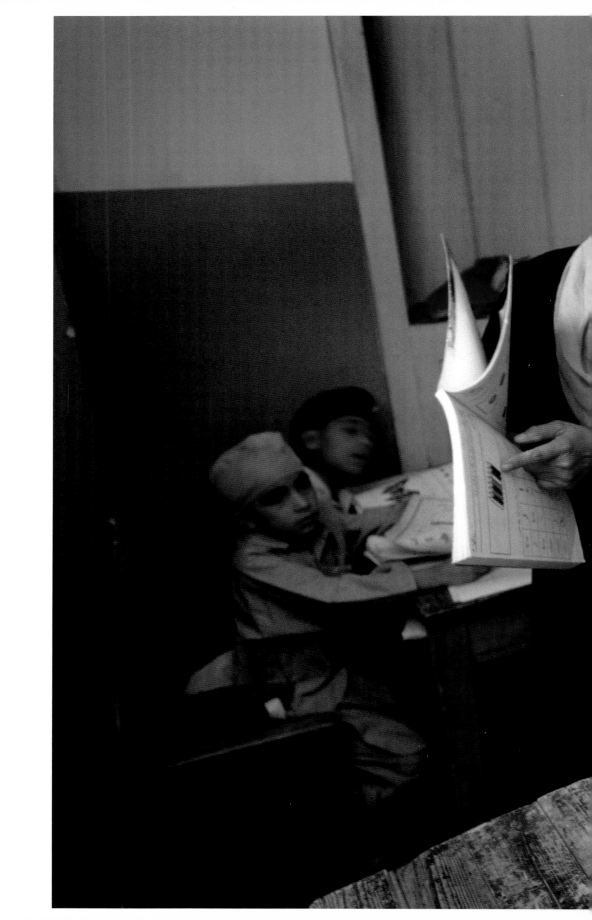

< Kabul
Covered in burqa's, mother's fight in line
to receive medicine for their sick children outside
the Indira Ghandi Children's Hospital.

◊ Kabul
A women in ankle chains. Nasrin, 22 years old, came to the Marastoon Mental Hospital in the
Afshar area of Kabul in 1995. At that time Nasrin returned to her home and found most of her family killed
by the Taliban. Since that day Nasrin has been committed to the mental hospital.

There is a truly overwhelming physical essence to the terra firma of Afghanistan. That can also be said for its people. For years I'd envisioned working in the country, one of my mind's favorite stans of the region (Kurdistan, Tajikistan, Pakistan, etc.). I'd been an avid collector of world music since my early 20's, allowing my mind to touch upon cultures and peoples through the universal language of music. Even though I only speak one language well, through these musical discs the vast and paradoxical Stan region revealed itself, words I could not speak, but was able to hear; voices morphing into sorrow and longing in songs by Afghani exiles living in Europe or America, yearning for their homes, their families, their land; then on another disc, one made in the early Seventies, joyful and romantic, with songs like "My Beloved Walks in the Garden, Love Songs from Mazar Region" and "Laili and Madjunun, Ballad from Kunduz" -- a collection made even more luminous by its title: "A Journey to an Unknown Musical World."

Tragically, I could never have expected that my first trip to the stan of my dreams would be brought about through an event such as September 11, 2001.

More often than not, the mind really does play tricks on you. Entering into Afghanistan from neighboring Tajikistan meant moving through a land literally stopped in time. The surrounding landscape of mountains dwarfed me to the point of reminding myself that I was but a speck within the universe, and the sheer staggering beauty of the people around me brought weighted measure to the sounds I had heard on the audio box back home.

I was where I had never been before, moving through a terrain that could only be expressed as traveling through the wrinkled creases of God's knuckles.

Everything beyond scale.

Everything beyond proportions.

Beyond human.

For decades, the suffering of Afghanistan's people has likewise been beyond human. Inner conflicts and numerous invasions helped create an almost perfect sanctuary for the likes of Al-Qaeda. But what helped most in this incubator of disaster was the lack of attention toward a group of people who have, through their voices, been screaming for assistance and guidance in an endless struggle to survive.

What happened on 9/11 in the country of my birth was epic unto itself. One seeks unutterable words to express the anguish. In more developed nations we listen and sometimes act upon that call. In Afghanistan, the call was rarely heard.

In the hospitals I visited upon arrival in Kabul, one day after the Taliban-held capital fell, the reality was clear. Not only did much have to be done — everything needed to done. Women were bleeding to death during childbirth. Children were dying from lack of food. Men were dying from landmines. Doctors with no equipment and little medicine were trying to treat thousands. At Ali Abad Hospital in central Kabul, doctors told me there was no pain medicine during operations. Like a makeshift hospital at the front lines of the American Civil War, patients would simply scream in ragging anguish. Being an Islamic nation, no alcohol was available to numb the body. One simply shoves a cloth in the mouth to muffle the cries.

In a mental hospital, women were chained like slaves. One I met, Jamila, would eat like an animal crouched upon a urine-covered foam floor mat in a room more like a cage for a forgotten circus animal than for a human being. Like many who went mad from years of witnessing death upon death in their families and villages, Jamila had been there ever since her parents brought her to the hospital in the Eighties during the war.

Sadly, like many of my colleagues, I'd seen this all before in other forgotten nations — from Haiti to southern Sudan, countless fellow human beings screaming and few, if any, listening.

But the world is now, or at least was, focused on the forgotten land of Afghanistan. There is hope where none was. There is a chance for change. Unfortunately it took the death of nearly three thousand on September 11, a few billion dollars' worth of bombs, and a few thousand more lives lost in Afghanistan for the world to finally begin paying attention.

As the world moves deeper into this War on Terrorism, one can only be guardedly optimistic that we don't again forget this vast and beautiful unknown land.

The Afghanis are truly in God's hands … as well as ours.

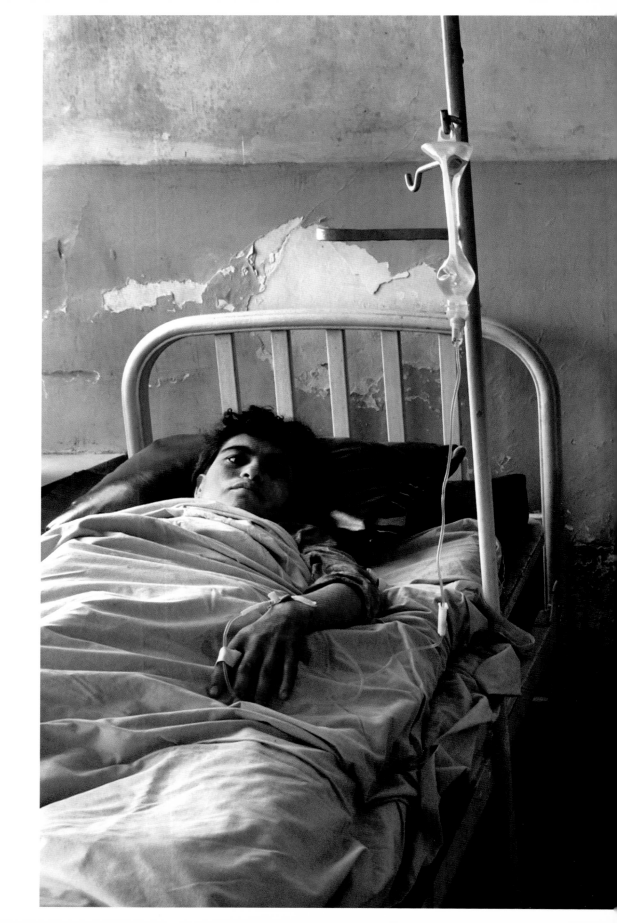

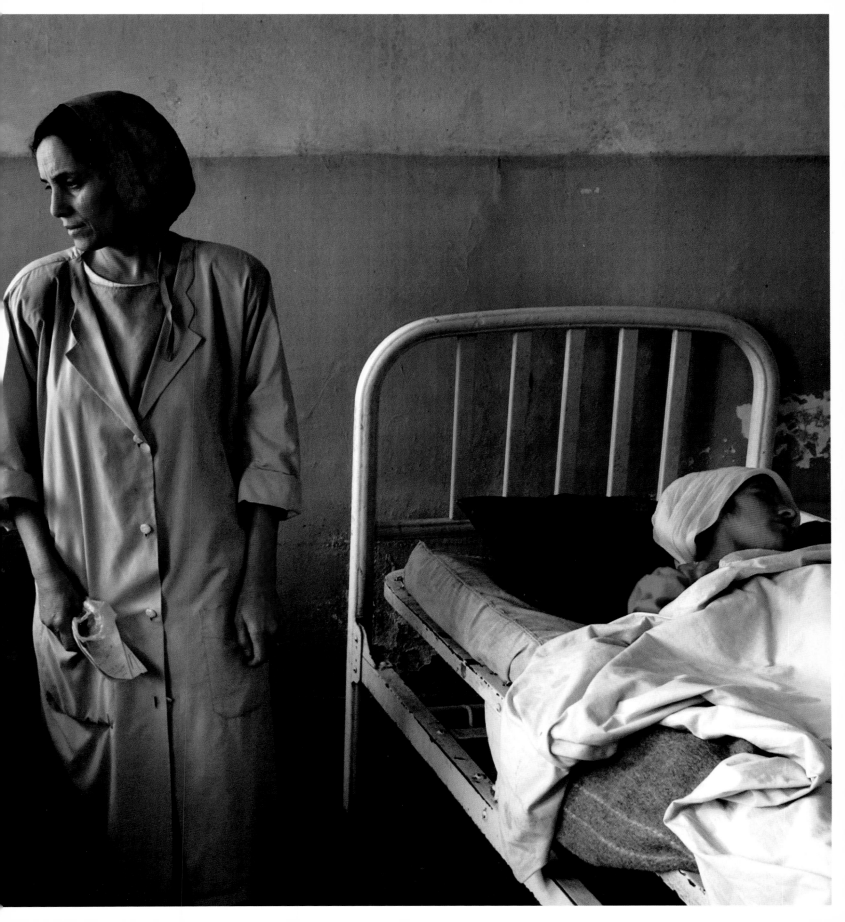

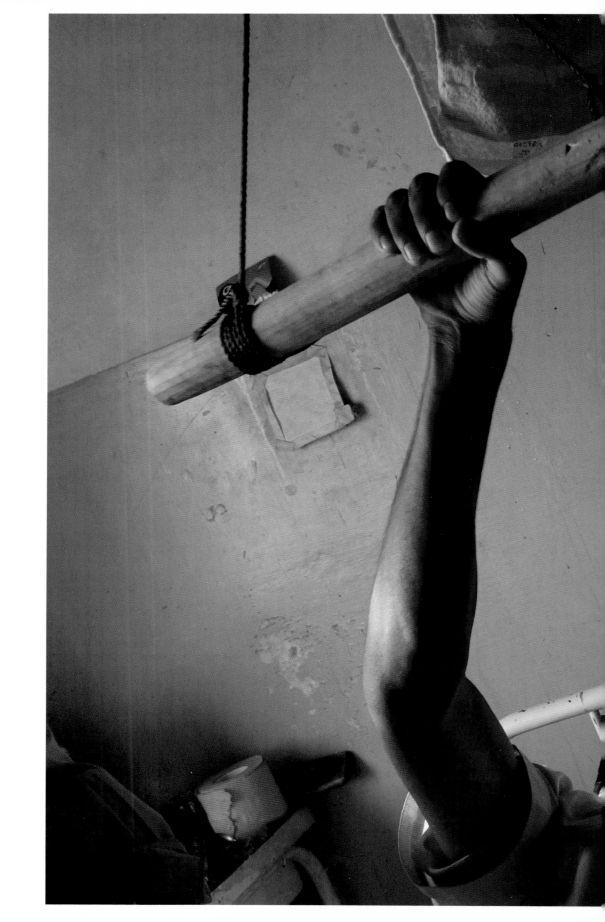

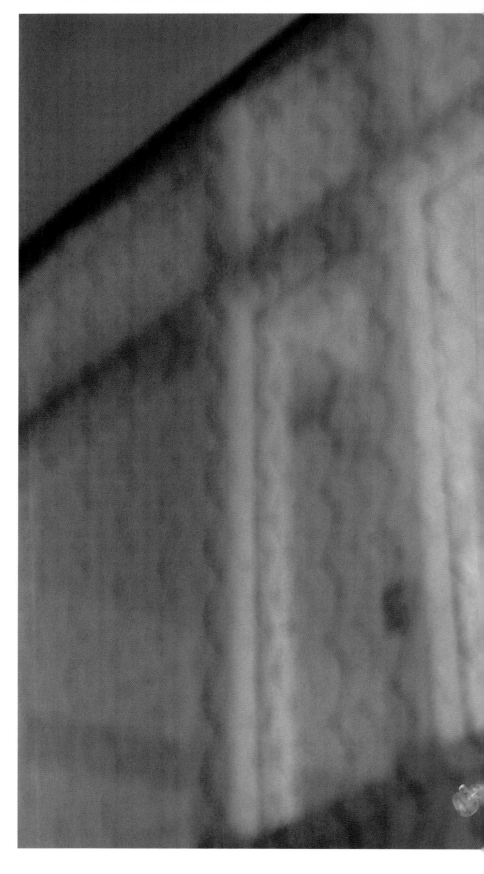

< **Kabul**
A nurse can do very little for the sick women
at the Malalia Maternity Hospital since there are
little to no medical supplies.

< **Kabul**
A man screams "Allah" while a doctor washes an open wound on his leg at the Wazir Akber Khan
Hospital. Without money patients can not afford medicine like pain killers nor can
the hospital provide them other than through a private pharmacy located near the hospital.

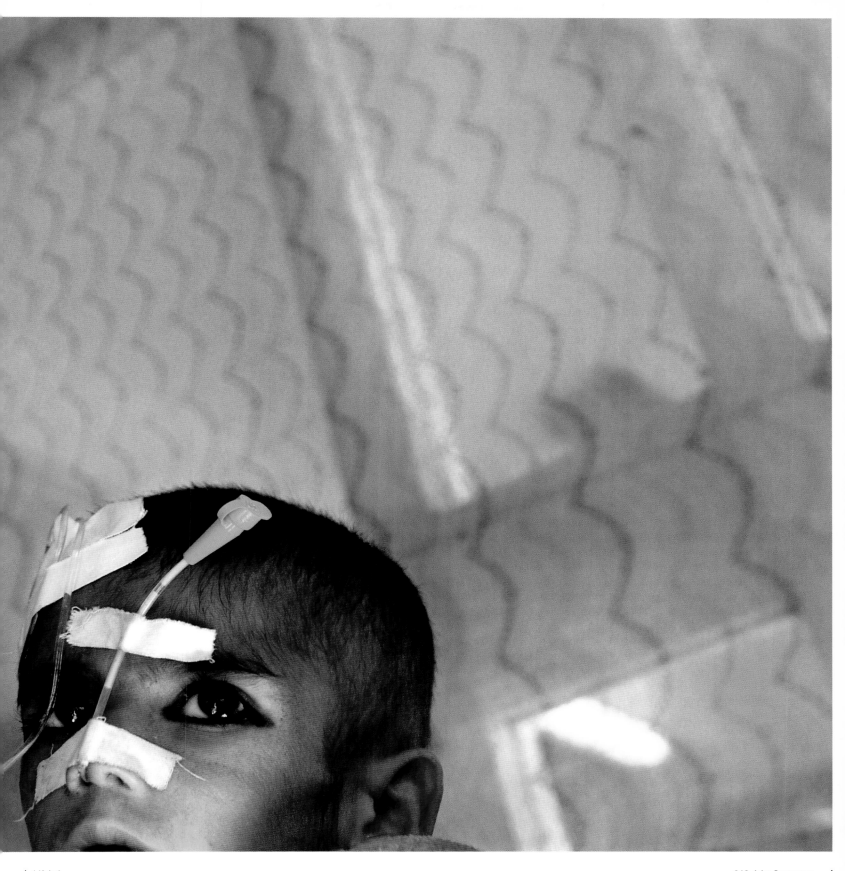

◊ **Kabul**
Shkerullha, 6 years old, in the malnutrition ward at the Indira Ghandi Children's Hospital. Hunger and malnutrition is one of the
leading causes of death among children in Afghanistan after 20 years of war and years of drought. Shkerullha's mother is a widow who's
husband was killed while fighting against the Taliban five years ago.

012 John Stanmeyer
Moving Through the Wrinkles of God's Hand

Page 131

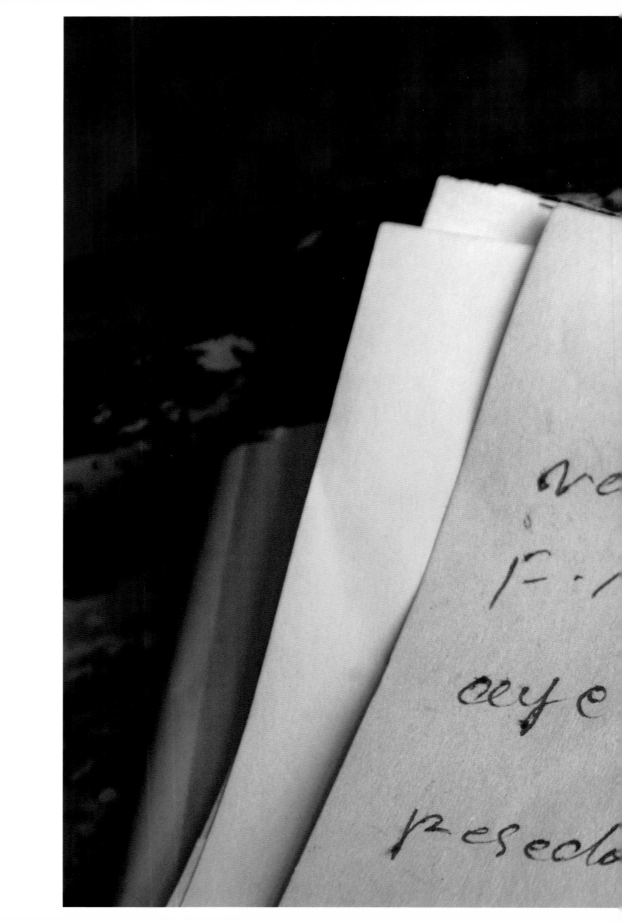

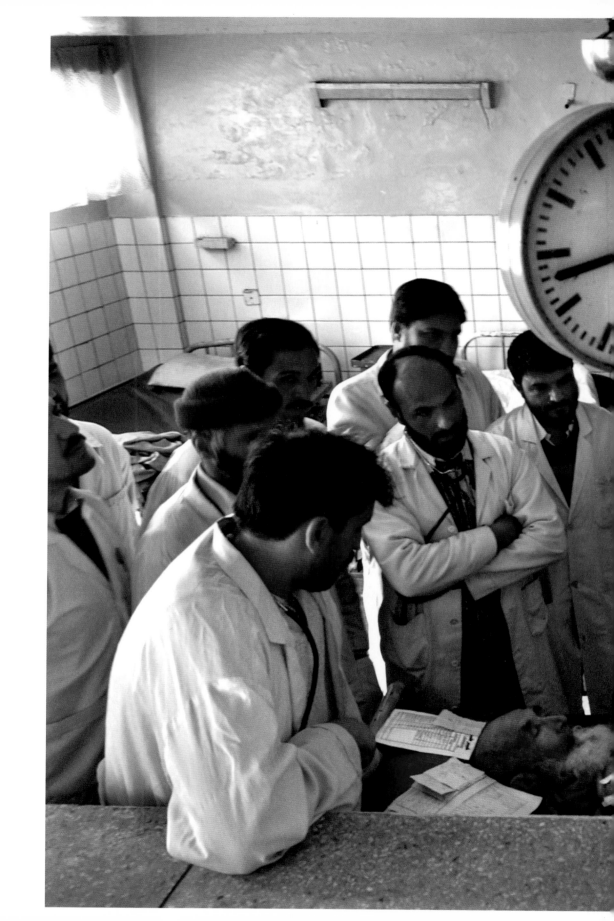

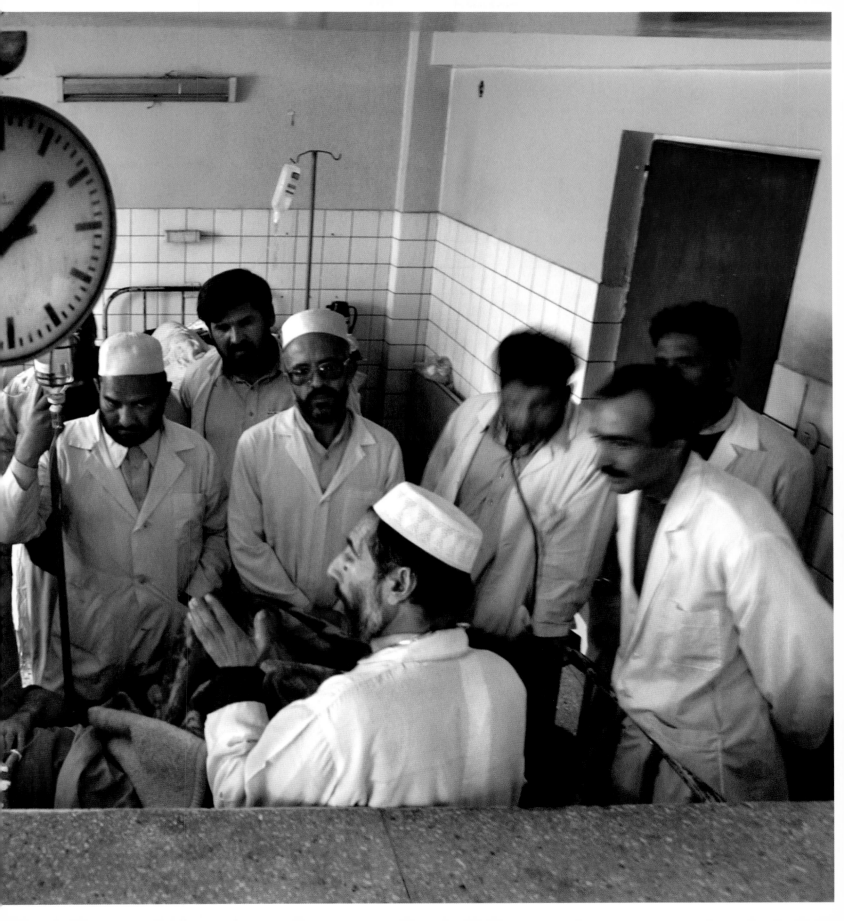

< **Kabul**
Doctors need to use used hypodermic needles
as a pin to hold a patients medical
records together due to a total lack of funding.

< **Kabul**
Medicines left about and electrical wiring in
shambles as doctors enter to check on patients at
the Rabia Balkhy General Hospital.

< **Kabul**
At 9 o'clock each morning 19 doctors make
their daily rounds at the Jamheret Hospital and
debate how to treat patients.

◊ **Kabul**
At the Wazir Akber Khan Hospital, Ghulam Sakhi
places his foot in an old bucket filled with a medical
solution in order to try and help heal his foot.

> **Kabul**
Doctor visiting a patient at the
Wazir Akber Khan Hospital.

> **Kabul**
Getting weighed in malnutrition ward at the
Indira Ghandi Children's Hospital.

> **Kabul**
Brought in by her parents due to shock during the
civilwar in the 80's, Jamila, 30, has spent eighteen years
living in the Marastoon Mental Health Hopsital.

012 John Stanmeyer
Moving Through the Wrinkles of God's Hand

Page 139

013

DR. ALBERTO CAIRO

THE VINEYARD
AFGHANISTAN OCTOBER 9 2002

When he was 22 years old, Anar Gul decided to get married. A farmer, he had often heard people say, "The sooner you get married and have children, the sooner you will have grown kids to help you with the work." In Afghanistan, children are your old age insurance.

The bride-to-be was his cousin. His father chose her for him. It was fine that way. She would leave her village and go to live with his parents. He would work his father's land with his brother. One day his sisters would marry and leave home. His mother would miss them and cry awhile, but she would soon console herself with his children, who would arrive just on time.

With the mine that exploded in the vineyard right behind the house, these plans were all blown away. His brother died, and Anar Gul lost both legs. It was September 11, 2001.

It is written on his medical record, documented when he arrived at the INTERNATIONAL COMMITTEE OF THE RED CROSS Center of Rehabilitation in Kabul four months later.

In the hospital he underwent four surgeries. Skinny and pale, he does not speak much. The physiotherapy to prepare him for the prostheses is intensive. Anar Gul exercises with precision and constancy, but you can see that he is there only because they brought him. He quickly learns to walk with the prostheses, and goes up and down inclines, even steep ones. A man who repairs watches at the bazaar took him in and teaches him the trade. It doesn't pay much, but Anar Gul doesn't mind. Any job is okay now that he can no longer be a farmer, now that his cousin will marry him from pity — if they don't give her to somebody else — and now that his father will have to work the land by himself until old age. Anar Gul will be one of the many disabled in Kabul, without even a brother to help him home when he is older. He will not be able to work and live in his village because few people there use watches. When you lose your legs or your arms, you lose much more than a limb. You lose a piece of your heart, a piece of your mind.

Your world changes forever, rehabilitation or not.

Hate, incapability to communicate, fanaticism, a desire to hit the masses. That is what links Anar Gul's September 11 to the one in New York — with a difference. In New York, evil wanted to make itself visible, to become a horrible spectacle. In Afghanistan there is a more discreet, subdued routine: the mines. Manufactured somewhere else in the world and brought here. But always hate. And while we hope that nothing like this ever happens again in New York, in Afghanistan we know for sure that it will, every day, for the next twenty years, at least ten more Anar Guls.

014

SIMA WALI

A YEAR WITHOUT GRACE:
THE FIRST ANNIVERSARY

For more than two decades I have struggled with enormous anguish to convey the horror visited upon my people. Now, in addition to all they have withstood, in the aftermath of September 11 they bear the additional burden of being unjustifiably suspect in the eyes of many Americans.

There is nothing comparable to being driven to the brink of despair. Yet many in the long-suffering Afghan community are now confronted by a new kind of horror.

Over the last 23 years, Afghans have occupied the annals of history primarily as "collateral damage" in the U.S.-led war on the 'evil empire' of the former Soviet Union.

Now, as an advocate who has long called for justice and peace for war-traumatized Afghans, my grief has taken a new dimension. As I witness Afghans caught up in the midst of this new war, I have lost any real hope that the world will alleviate the horrors visited upon many innocent people.

My immediate fear is that those of us who led the struggle for freedom and democracy, freedom from the ongoing holocaust — and yes, a holocaust has occurred against the Afghan people — have been once again silenced. My fears have been compounded by the realization that the very war which I had fled from in my home country has now followed me here to my home of exile.

I have watched in horror as the aspirations of freedom-loving Afghans were once again torn asunder as many came to view Afghanistan as a state synonymous with terrorist activities: Al Qaeda, Bin Laden, Mullah Omar — a haven for terrorist cells. Often, the media promoted this misconception and failed to recognize that the Afghan people were themselves hostages of these same invading terrorists while the world paid scant attention.

The ensuring accusatory propaganda, which equated a majority of the Afghan people with extremist Islamic militants, was unfair and groundless. Many in the compatriot Afghan-American community often feel defenseless against the rising tide of a hatred, which we see as misdirected. Often we are at a loss to explain that we too have fled flagrant, systematic acts of violence by many of these same terrorists, and that many Afghans have been U.S. allies, and sought asylum on U.S. soil.

This immense distortion was often fueled by wide misinformation among the American public. I fear that not only will the world remain intransigent to the misery of the Afghan people — in particular its women — but that after having endured years of heinous crimes against their humanity, they will be subject to further hate crimes. Such distortion is an affront to every Afghan woman and man yearning for social justice, peace, and a decent standard of life.

Is it too much to ask, Afghans contend after 23 years of violence and the total destruction of their homeland, to aspire to freedom from violence, torture, rape, hunger, want? Is any individual Afghan life lost — and millions have perished — any less significant than any individual American life?

At a time when the Afghan people most need the international community to come their aid, they are often depicted in an undignified light as a result of the September 11 atrocity. With more than two million dead, twelve million women living in abject poverty and subjected to the gender apartheid of the Taliban, one million handicapped by land mines, and 500,000 war widows, the threshold of pain in Afghanistan has reached its limit.

Just as our lives here in the United States changed on September 11, Afghans have undergone dramatic changes in their lives since the Soviet Union's invasion of their homeland on December 27, 1979.

Twenty-four million Afghan citizens were affected by this foreign intrusion and the subsequent brutalities of war. If there is a common thread in the fabric of American and Afghan lives, it would be this common bond of grief over the colossal loss of life and property, and the ensuing economic downfall.

Long before September 11, the common Afghan reaction toward the United States was that Afghanistan had been unceremoniously abandoned by the U.S. following its role as ally in the fight to thwart communism. But by writing off Afghanistan after importing, training, supporting and financing a "Jihad" against the Soviet Union, the U.S. and its allies delivered Afghanistan as a breeding ground for Al Qaeda and other terrorist activities.

Some of these very forces, originally recruited for war against the Soviet Union, continued operations once the U.S. abandoned Afghanistan in 1989. The conditions to incubate terror became possible just as Afghanistan had started to embark on the path to peaceful transition.

Nation-building was sacrificed to the short-term goal of declaring victory over communism when Afghanistan most needed U.S. support to root out of the forces of terror.

Prior to September 11, relentless acts of violence against the Afghan people were treated as a phenomenon distinct from U.S. foreign policy.

BUT THE VERY CONDITIONS WHICH SPAWNED THE ATTACK ON AMERICA LAST SEPTEMBER 11 TOOK ROOT AS A DIRECT RESULT OF THOSE FOREIGN POLICIES FROM WHICH MOST AFGHANS CONTINUE TO SUFFER DISPROPORTIONATELY.

This is the reward for Afghanistan's assistance in the defeat of the "Evil Empire." This is the reward for sparing the United States the burden of the loss of American life.

Prior to September 11, the role the U.S. played in Afghanistan went unheeded by policy makers and the Western media. Following the Soviet defeat, there was little questioning of the origins of the Afghan tragedy, the untold suffering for a majority of Afghans, or the most brutal aspects of the repressive policies against its female population. Unprecedented and heinous crimes were committed against women during these years of conflict while the world looked away.

The only groups that initially came to the aid of Afghan women were women's and human rights' groups. Subsequently, the practices of gender atrocities germinated into a new term describing these crimes against Afghan women as 'gender apartheid.' As a result, the world community slowly and painfully became familiarized with the colossal tragedy visited upon the women of Afghanistan, and with it the realization that women as war victims bear the harshest consequences of the decades-old war and misguided U.S. foreign policies.

With the advent of the Taliban and the introduction of edicts barring women from public life, education, and health care, these gender-specific edicts extended this declaration of war from the country's female citizenry to moderate Muslim Afghan males in support of women's liberty and freedom from male domination.

During this period, two U.S. administrations attempted to address the horrors imposed by the Taliban regime by introducing legislation concerning "gender-apartheid." The legislation, however, remained at the rhetorical level, focusing on the symptoms of the war rather than on the strategies needed to understand its origins.

Understanding the origins of the war is critical to developing sustainable solutions for conflict resolution and reconstruction efforts rather than providing short-term band-aid type solutions. As a side-effect of this approach, women's groups inadvertently began addressing the dress code imposed by the Taliban, rather than the causes of the problems facing Afghan women.

BY NOT FOCUSING ON THE CAUSAL EFFECTS OF THE WAR, BY NOT FOCUSING ON THE U.S. ABANDONMENT OF AFGHANISTAN, BY NOT FOCUSING ON THE DISEMPOWERMENT OF THE AFGHAN PEOPLE, OR THE EMPOWERMENT OF THE WARLORDS THROUGH MONEY AND ARMS, OR THE FAILURE TO HALT THE ARMS FLOW INTO AFGHANISTAN, AND BY IGNORING THE IMPACT OF THE US'S ARAB ALLIES, AFGHANISTAN'S ENEMIES WERE FREE TO WREAK HAVOC ON THE LIVES OF THE AFGHAN PEOPLE.

Such shortsightedness led Afghan women to decry the lack of sanctions against its Arab and Pakistani allies for their destructive policies in Afghanistan. But no further mention of the decades-long build-up or transfer of weapons of mass destruction by extremists from militant Arab countries, including Pakistan, could be found in media coverage.

Now let me turn to dispelling the myths about the Afghan people and of women's hopes of revealing their true nature.

During the weeks immediately following September 11, I began to receive calls from Afghan women inquiring about my own safety as an Afghan and a Muslim living in the U.S. coupled with great empathy for the American people who had suffered such colossal damage. Afghan women had an immediate and profound understanding of the pain caused by those heinous acts. As innocent civilians caught in the depravity of war, they felt the deep pain of American women: mothers, wives, sisters, daughters, grandmothers, and aunts. It is the humanity of Afghan women, who themselves had lost all to war, that they were now reaching out with such immense grief, and it was this that led me to share their wishes with "war-affected" American women.

This unprecedented and historic campaign is the first one of its kind led by war-affected Afghan women living as destitute refugees in neighboring Pakistan and as internally displaced women in Afghanistan. To date, Afghan women have themselves been the subject of US-led campaigns to portray their suffering to the outside world. These are women who have lost children to war, land mines, poverty, starvation, human trafficking, and disease.

These are women who have witnessed the brutal torture of their family members. They are women who have been driven to the brink of despair and madness from witnessing relentless human brutality. They are women whose voices until now remain fractured in the free world. They are women who lost the opportunity to educate themselves or their children. They are women who cannot read or write. They are women who cannot sign their names. They are women who lived under the Taliban rule but took grave risks to themselves and their families to reach those affected by September 11. And they are women who, despite all, found the courage to affix their thumb prints to a letter of condolence to American women.

I am resorting to sharing the contents of this letter and the background surrounding this historic campaign by some of the world's most severely impoverished women to raise awareness in the U.S.. My hope is to correct misunderstandings and to reveal the profound humanity and dignity of the Afghan people.

> BACKGROUND OF AFGHAN WOMEN'S CAMPAIGN POST-9/11

Soon after the 9/II attacks, prior to the downfall of the Taliban, Afghan women refugees and internally displaced women with whom I had worked over the years began contacting me to convey their wishes to their "American sisters." These women initiated an unprecedented campaign of collecting signatures and thumb prints from women inside Afghanistan and Pakistan. A letter describing their heartfelt emotions emerged from women who held a meeting addressing this subject despite Taliban edits forbidding women to congregate. The letter which appears below has been translated from Dari into English by my agency, Refugee Women in Development (RefWID). We attempted to keep the spirit and intent of the message. The letter was written and clandestinely carried inside Afghanistan while the Taliban were still in power. Two female escorts secretly crossed the border into Afghanistan and collected approximately 500 signatures. Many women knew they were risking their lives by signing this letter. Many opted to sign in pseudonyms. Those who were not literate affixed their thumb prints. I, in turn, spent many sleepless nights anxiously waiting for the messengers to safely cross the border, terrified they would be intercepted, the list exposed, and lives lost. Luckily, the letter and signatures arrived safely, but I could not reveal the list, for fear of exposing the women who had signed, until the downfall of the Taliban during the U.S. war on terrorism.

> CONCLUSION

I sincerely hope that at this first anniversary of 9/11, the humanity manifested in these acts will prevail.

In order for Afghanistan to embark on the path to a peaceful democracy it is essential that the U.S. remain true to its promise of rebuilding Afghanistan. President Bush's commitment for a Marshall Plan for Afghanistan is vital to restore the institutions necessary to build a sustaining democracy. Funds pledged at the Tokyo Conference in January 2001 must be released for the reconstruction of Afghanistan. Nation-building must be viewed and financed separately from the war to eliminate Al Qaeda and the Taliban. Afghanistan must be helped to peacefully transition from a nation at war, besieged, battered and betrayed, to a peaceful democracy. Anything less than this will result in risking America's own ideal of democracy and freedom, as well as its security. It will taint America's image in the Muslim world. The entire Muslim world is gauging America's actions in Afghanistan as a measure of its policy toward the Islamic world. It is critical America deliver its promises to the new Afghan government, as well as put forth the true story behind Afghanistan's devastation. The public must educate itself about America's role in Afghanistan and explore the origins of the Afghan predicament so that sustainable strategies are devised to resolve the longstanding conflict. Not only will this be beneficial to Afghanistan, but it will be beneficial to the U.S. and go a long way to end the threat of terrorism in the new century. America must deliver that for which the Afghan people have long sacrificed: peace, freedom, security, and democracy. To regain the trust of the Afghans, America must respond by delivering what it promised in Tokyo, and post-9/11.

> IN THE NAME OF THE ONE GOD

ON BEHALF OF THE MILLIONS OF LONG-SUFFERING WOMEN OF AFGHANISTAN WHO HAVE FOR YEARS BORNE UNTOLD OPPRESSION, OF THE SEPTEMBER 11 CALAMITY TO YOURSELF AND THE PEOPLE OF AMERICA.

THE DEFENSELESS AFGHAN WOMEN WHO HAVE BEEN PRISONERS OF DARKNESS AND SAVAGERY SHARE IN THE PAIN AND AGONY BURIED UNDER TONS OF DEBRIS. WE HEAR THE AGONIZED CRIES OF OUR AMERICAN SISTERS WHO HAVE LOST THEIR LOVED ONES. ARE BOUND BY THE LEGACY OF THEIR LOSS WITH THAT OF THE WOMEN IN YOUR COUNTRY.

WE HOPE YOU AND OUR AMERICAN SISTERS ACCEPT OUR DEEPEST CONDOLENCES AND PUREST SENTIMENTS OF SYMPATHY FOR AFGHAN WOMEN JOIN HANDS TO BRING A TRUE MESSAGE OF HOPE AND PEACE TO OUR TROUBLED HUMANITY. MAY NO WOMAN

COME, SHARE SINCERITY AND SOLIDARITY WITH US.   WITH MUCH LOVE

THE WOMEN OF AFGHANISTAN

GRIEF, AND OUTRAGE, WE WISH TO CONVEY A MESSAGE OF SINCERE CONDOLENCES AND HEARTFELT SYMPATHY ON THE OCCASION

OF YOUR PEOPLE. WE ARE INDEED AN ECHO OF THE SCREAMS OF THE THOUSANDS DYING, THE INNOCENT VICTIMS WHO STILL LIE
WE KNOW THEIR TERRIBLE PAIN BECAUSE FOR THE PAST TWO DECADES, WE TOO HAVE SUFFERED AS THEY DO NOW. AFGHAN WOMEN

THEY ARE AS PURE AND IMMACULATE AS THE HONOR OF MARY THE MOTHER OF JESUS. WE ARDENTLY DESIRE THAT AMERICAN AND
OR MAN ENDURE SUCH PAIN AND SENSELESS LOSS. MAY NO MOTHER GRIEVE FOR A LOST CHILD.

015

ZBIGNIEW BRZEZINSKI

CONFRONTING ANTI-AMERICAN GRIEVANCES
SEPTEMBER 1 2002

Nearly a year after the start of America's war on terrorism, that war faces the real risk of being hijacked by foreign governments with repressive agendas. **Instead of leading a democratic coalition, the United States faces the risk of dangerous isolation.** The Bush administration's definition of the challenge that America confronts has been cast largely in semireligious terms. The public has been told repeatedly that terrorism is "evil," which it undoubtedly is, and that "evildoers" are responsible for it, which doubtless they are. But beyond these justifiable condemnations, there is a historical void. It is as if terrorism is suspended in outer space as an abstract phenomenon, with ruthless terrorists acting under some Satanic inspiration unrelated to any specific motivation.

President Bush has wisely eschewed identifying terrorism with Islam as a whole and been careful to stress that Islam as such is not at fault. But some supporters of the administration have been less careful about such distinctions, arguing that Islamic culture in general is so hostile to the West, and especially to democracy, that it has created a fertile soil for terrorist hatred of America.

Missing from much of the public debate is discussion of the simple fact that lurking behind every terroristic act is a specific political antecedent. That does not justify either the perpetrator or his political cause. Nonetheless, the fact is that almost all terrorist activity originates from some political conflict and is sustained by it as well. That is true of the Irish Republican Army in Northern Ireland, the Basques in Spain, the Palestinians in the West Bank and Gaza, the Muslims in Kashmir and so forth.

In the case of 9/11, it does not require deep analysis to note — given the identity of the perpetrators — that the Middle East's political history has something to do with the hatred of Middle Eastern terrorists for America. The specifics of the region's political history need not be dissected too closely because terrorists presumably do not delve deeply into archival research before embarking on a terrorist career.

RATHER, IT IS THE EMOTIONAL CONTEXT OF FELT, OBSERVED OR HISTORICALLY RECOUNTED POLITICAL GRIEVANCES THAT SHAPES THE FANATICAL PATHOLOGY OF TERRORISTS AND EVENTUALLY TRIGGERS THEIR MURDEROUS ACTIONS.

American involvement in the Middle East is clearly the main impulse of the hatred that has been directed at America. There is no escaping the fact that Arab political emotions have been shaped by the region's encounter with French and British colonialism, by the defeat of the

Arab effort to prevent the existence of Israel and by the subsequent American support for Israel and its treatment of the Palestinians, as well as by the direct injection of American power into the region.

This last has been perceived by the more fanatical elements in the region as offensive to the sacred religious purity of Saudi Arabian custodianship of Islam's holy places and as hurtful to the welfare of the Iraqi people. The religious aspect adds fervor to their zeal, but it is worth noting that some of the 9/11 terrorists had non-religious lifestyles. Their attack on the World Trade Center had a definite political cast to it.

Yet there has been a remarkable reluctance in America to confront the more complex historical dimensions of this hatred. The inclination instead has been to rely on abstract assertions like terrorists "hate freedom" or that their religious background makes them despise Western culture.

TO WIN THE WAR ON TERRORISM, ONE MUST THEREFORE SET TWO GOALS:

FIRST TO DESTROY THE TERRORISTS.

SECOND TO BEGIN A POLITICAL EFFORT THAT FOCUSES ON THE CONDITIONS THAT BROUGHT ABOUT THEIR EMERGENCE.

That is what the British are doing in Ulster, the Spaniards are doing in Basque country and the Russians are being urged to do in Chechnya. To do so does not imply propitiation of the terrorists, but is a necessary component of a strategy designed to isolate and eliminate the terrorist underworld.

Analogies are not the same as identity, but with that in mind one might consider the parallels between what the United States faces today in regard to Middle Eastern terrorism and the crises that America confronted domestically in the 1960's and 70's. At that time, American society was shaken by violence undertaken by groups like the Ku Klux Klan (often in semi-autonomous klaverns), White Citizens' Councils, the Black Panthers and the Symbionese Liberation Army. Without civil-rights legislation and the concomitant changes in America's social views on race relations, the challenge that those organizations posed might have lasted much longer and become more menacing.

The rather narrow, almost one-dimensional definition of the terrorist threat favored by the Bush administration poses the special risk that foreign powers will also seize upon the word "terrorism" to promote their own agendas, as President Vladimir Putin of Russia, Prime Minister Ariel Sharon of Israel, Prime Minister Atal Bihari Vajpayee of India and President Jiang Zemin of China are doing. For each of them the disembodied American definition of the terrorist challenge has been both expedient and convenient.

When speaking to Americans, neither Mr. Putin nor Mr. Sharon can hardly utter a sentence without the "T" word in it in order to transform America's struggle against terrorism into a joint struggle against their particular Muslim neighbors. Mr. Putin clearly sees an opportunity to deflect Islamic hostility away from Russia despite Russian crimes in Chechnya and earlier in Afghanistan. Mr. Sharon would welcome a deterioration in United States relations with Saudi Arabia and perhaps American military action against Iraq while gaining a free hand to suppress the Palestinians. Hindu fanatics in India are also quite eager to conflate Islam in general with terrorism in Kashmir in particular. Not to be outdone, the Chinese recently succeeded in persuading the Bush administration to list an obscure Uighur Muslim separatist group fighting in Xinjiang province as a terrorist organization with ties to Al Qaeda.

For America, the potential risk is that its nonpolitically defined war on terrorism may thus be hijacked and diverted to other ends. The consequences would be dangerous. If America comes to be viewed by its key democratic allies in Europe and Asia as morally obtuse and politically naïve in failing to address terrorism in its broader and deeper dimensions — and if it is also seen by them as uncritically embracing intolerant suppression of ethnic or national aspirations — global support for America's policies will surely decline. America's ability to maintain a broadly democratic antiterrorist coalition will suffer gravely. The prospects of international support for an eventual military confrontation with Iraq will also be drastically diminished.

SUCH AN ISOLATED AMERICA IS LIKELY TO FACE EVEN MORE THREATS FROM VENGEFUL TERRORISTS WHO HAVE DECIDED TO BLAME AMERICA FOR ANY OUTRAGES COMMITTED BY ITS SELF-APPOINTED ALLIES.

A victory in the war against terrorism can never be registered in a formal act of surrender. Instead, it will only be divined from the gradual waning of terrorist acts. Any further strikes against Americans will thus be a painful reminder that the war has not been won. Sadly, a main reason will be America's reluctance to focus on the political roots of the terrorist atrocity of 9/11.

016

HIS HOLINESS THE DALAI LAMA

MESSAGE OF COMMEMORATION OF THE FIRST ANNIVERSARY OF SEPTEMBER 11

The 11th September 2001 terrorist attacks on the World Trade Center and the Pentagon were deeply shocking and very sad.

I regard such terrible destructive actions as acts of hatred, for violence is the result of destructive emotions. Events of this kind make clear that if we allow our human intelligence to be guided and controlled by negative emotions like hatred, the consequences are disastrous.

How to respond to such an attack is a very difficult question to answer.

Of course, those who are dealing with the problem may know better, but I feel that careful consideration is necessary and that it is appropriate to respond to an act of violence by employing the principles of non-violence. This is of great importance. The attacks on the United States were shocking, but retaliation that involves the use of further violence may not be the best solution in the long run.

We must continue to develop a wider perspective, to think rationally and work to avert future disasters in a non-violent way. These issues concern the whole of humanity, not just one country. We should explore the use of non-violence as a long-term measure to control terrorism of every kind. We need a well-thought-out, coordinated long-term strategy. I believe there will always be conflicts and clash of ideas as long as human beings exist. This is natural. Therefore, we need an active method or approach to overcome such contradictions.

In today's reality the only way of resolving differences is through dialogue and compromise, through human understanding and humility. We need to appreciate that genuine peace comes about through mutual understanding, respect, and trust. Problems within human society should be solved in a humanitarian way, for which non-violence provides the proper approach.

Terrorism cannot be overcome by the use of force because it does not address the complex underlying problems. In fact the use of force may not only fail to solve the problems, it may exacerbate them and frequently leaves destruction and suffering in its wake. Likewise, acts of terrorism, especially involving violence, only make matters worse. We must condemn terrorism not only because it involves violence but also because innocent people fall victims to senseless acts of terrorism such as what the world witnessed on September 11th.

In today's world expectations of war have changed. It is no longer realistic to expect that our enemy will be completely destroyed, or that victory will be total for us.

Or for that matter, can an enemy be considered absolute. We have seen many times that today's enemies are often tomorrow's allies, a clear indication that things are relative and very inter-related and inter-dependent.

OUR SURVIVAL, OUR SUCCESS, OUR PROGRESS, ARE VERY MUCH RELATED TO OTHERS' WELL-BEING. THEREFORE, WE AS WELL AS OUR ENEMIES, ARE STILL VERY MUCH INTERDEPENDENT. WHETHER WE REGARD THEM AS ECONOMIC, IDEOLOGICAL OR POLITICAL ENEMIES MAKES NO DIFFERENCE TO THIS. THEIR DESTRUCTION HAS A DESTRUCTIVE EFFECT UPON US. THUS, THE VERY CONCEPT OF WAR, WHICH IS NO LONGER RELEVANT.

Similarly, as the global economy evolves, every nation becomes to a greater or lesser extent dependent on every other nation.

The modern economy, like the environment, knows no boundaries. Even those countries openly hostile to one another must cooperated in their use of the world's resources. Often, for example, they will be dependent on the same rivers or other natural resources. And the more interdependent our economic relationships, the more interdependent must tour political relationships become.

What we need today is education among individuals and nations, from small children up to political leaders to inculcate the idea that violence is counterproductive, that it is not a realistic way to solve problems, and that dialogue and understanding are the only realistic way to resolve our difficulties.

The anniversary of the tragic events of September 11, 2001 provides us with a very good opportunity. There is a worldwide will to oppose terrorism. We can use this consensus to implement long-term preventive measures. This will ultimately be much more effective that taking dramatic and violent steps based on anger and other destructive emotions. The temptation to respond with violence is understandable but a more cautious approach will be more fruitful.

017

THOMAS L. FRIEDMAN

NOAH AND 9/11
SEPTEMBER 11 2002

Over the past year several friends have remarked to me how much they still feel a pit in their stomachs from 9/11. One even said she felt as if this was the beginning of the end of the world. And no wonder. Those suicide hijackings were such an evil act that they shattered your faith in human beings and in the wall of civilization that was supposed to constrain the worst in human behavior. There is now a jagged hole in that wall.

What to do? For guidance, I turned to one of my mentors, Rabbi Tzvi Marx, who teaches in the Netherlands. He offered me a biblical analogy. "To some extent," said Tzvi, "we feel after 9/11 like we have experienced the flood of Noah - as if a flood has inundated our civilization and we are the survivors. What do we do the morning after?"

The story of Noah has a lot to offer. "What was the first thing Noah did when the flood waters receded and he got off the ark?" asked Tzvi. "He planted a vine, made wine and got drunk." Noah's first response to the flood's devastation of humanity, and the challenge he now faced, was to numb himself to the world.

"But what was God's reaction to the flood?" asked Tzvi. "Just the opposite. God's reaction was to offer Noah a more detailed set of rules for mankind to live by - rules which we now call the Noahite laws. His first rule was that life is precious, so man should not murder man." (These Noahite laws were later expanded to include prohibitions against idolatry, adultery, blasphemy and theft.)

It's interesting - you would have thought that after wiping out humanity with a devastating flood, God's first post-flood act wouldn't have been to teach that all life is precious. But it was. Said Tzvi: "It is as though God said, 'Now I understand what I'm up against with these humans. I need to set for them some very clear boundaries of behavior, with some very clear values and norms, that they can internalize."

And that is where the analogy with today begins. After the analogy with today begins. After the deluge of 9/11 we have two choices: We can numb ourselves to the world, and plug our ears, or we can try to repair that jagged hole in the wall of civilization by insisting, more firmly and loudly than ever, on rules and norms-both for ourselves and for others.

"God, after the flood, refused to let Noah and his offspring indulge themselves in escapism," said Tzvi, "but he also refused to give them license to live without moral boundaries, just because humankind up to that point had failed."

The same applies to us. Yes, we must kill the murderers of 9/11, but without becoming murderers and without simply indulging ourselves. We must defend ourselves - without throwing out civil liberties at home, without barring every Muslim student from this country, without forgetting what a huge shadow a powerful America casts over the world and how it can leave people feeling powerless, and without telling the world we're going to do whatever we want because there has been a flood and now all bets are off.

Because imposing norms and rules on ourselves gives us the credibility to demand them from others. It gives us the credibility to demand the rule of law, religious tolerance, consensual government, self-criticism, pluralism, women's rights and respect for the notion that my grievance, however deep, does not entitle me to do anything to anyone anywhere.

It gives us the credibility to say to the Muslim world: Where have you been since 9/11? Where have your voices of reason? You humbly open all your prayers in the name of a God of mercy and compassion. But when members of your faith, acting in the name of Islam, murdered Americans or commited suicide against "infidels," your press extolled them as martyrs and your spiritual leaders were largely silent. Other than a few ritual condemnations, they offered no outcry in their mosques; they drew no new moral red lines in their schools. That's a problem, because if there isn't a struggle within Islam - over norms and values - there is going to be a struggle between Islam and us.

In short, numbing ourselves to the post-9/11 realities will not work. Military operations, while necessary, are not sufficient. Building higher walls may feel comforting, but in today's interconnected world they're an illusion. Our only hope is that people will be restrained by internal walls - norms and values. Visibility imposing them on ourselves, and loudly demanding them from others, is the only viable survival strategy for our shrinking planet.

Otherwise, start building an ark.

018

ROBERT FISK

A YEAR ON:
A VIEW FROM THE MIDDLE EAST

September 11 did not change the world. Indeed, for months afterwards, no one was allowed even to question the motives of the mass murderers. To point out that they were all Arabs and Muslims was fair enough. But any attempt to connect these facts to the region they came from - the Middle East - was treated as a form of subversion; because, of course, to look too closely at the Middle East would raise disturbing questions about the region, about our Western policies in those tragic lands, and about America's relationship with Israel. Yet now, at last, President Bush's increasingly manic administration has spotted the connection - and is drawing all the wrong conclusions.

For, as the days and weeks go by, it is becoming increasingly difficult to recognise in the words of Americans - and in their newspapers - the Middle East, the region in which I have lived for 26 years. While cocooned within the usual assurances that Islam is one of the world's great religions and that the United States is only against "terrorists", not Muslims, a brutal and cruel fate is being concocted for Arabs, a world in which more than a score of nations are being fingered as "terrorists" or "haters of democracy" or "kernels of evil". Richard Armitage, the US Deputy Secretary of State, last week decided to include the Lebanese Hizbollah. With a vague, though unspecific, reference to the 291 American servicemen killed in the suicide bombing of the US Marine base in Beirut in 1983, he announced that "they're on the list, their time will come, there's no question about it. They have a blood debt to us ...".

List?

Is that what it is now? A list as unending as Mr Bush's so-called "war on terror"? Does Hizbollah come above al-Qa'ida on the list these days? Or after Iraq? Or maybe after Iran? "They have a blood debt to us" is a remark as frightening as it is infantile; it suggests that what the United States is embarking upon, far from being a titanic battle of good vs evil, is a series of revenge attacks. One wonders what Tony Blair thinks of all this. Does he, too, have a blood debt owed to him? And what - a question that is never asked - do Muslims make of this nonsense?

I have to say that I have yet to meet a Muslim who has expressed anything but horror about September 11. But I have yet to meet a Muslim who said they were surprised. Indeed, after so long in the Middle East, I have to say that I wasn't surprised when, high over the Atlantic, the pilot of my America-bound plane told his astonished passengers that four commercial airliners had been crashed into the United States. Stunned by the awesome nature of the crime, yes. Appalled by the sheer cruelty of the mass killings, of course.

But surprised?

For weeks I had been waking up each morning in Beirut, wondering when the explosion would come. So had most Arabs I have talked to during the past year. How and when the explosion would take place, they had no idea - but that the detonation would occur was never in question. And in a part of the world so steeped in blood, it was perhaps understandable that both the intellectual and the public response to September 11 was somewhat less emotional than in the rest of the planet.

FOR EXAMPLE, IF YOU TALK TO A PALESTINIAN IN LEBANON ABOUT THE SEPTEMBER MASSACRE, HE WILL ASSUME YOU ARE REFERRING TO THE SLAUGHTER, AT THE HANDS OF ISRAEL'S MILITIA ALLIES, OF 1,700 PALESTINIANS IN BEIRUT IN SEPTEMBER OF 1982. JUST AS CHILEANS, WHEN HEARING THE PHRASE "SEPTEMBER 11" - AS THAT FINE JEWISH WRITER ARIEL DORFMAN POINTED OUT - WILL THINK OF 11 SEPTEMBER 1973, WHEN AN AMERICAN-SUPPORTED COUP D'ÉTAT LED TO THE OVERTHROW OF THE ALLENDE GOVERNMENT AND THE DEATHS OF THOUSANDS OF CHILEANS. TALK TO SYRIANS ABOUT A MASSACRE AND THEY WILL THINK FIRST OF ALL - THOUGH THEY WILL NOT SAY THE WORDS - OF THE KILLING OF UP TO 20,000 SYRIANS IN THE ISLAMIST UPRISING AT HAMA. TALK ABOUT MASSACRES TO THE KURDS AND THEY WILL TELL YOU ABOUT HALABJA; TO THE IRANIANS AND THEY WILL TELL YOU ABOUT KHORRAMSHAHR; TO THE ALGERIANS AND THEY WILL THINK OF BENTALHA AND A WHOLE SERIES OF OTHER VILLAGE ATROCITIES THAT HAVE COST THE LIVES OF 150,000 ALGERIANS.

The truth is that the Arabs - like Chileans and other people far from the new centre of total world power - are used to mass killing. They know what war is like, and quite a number of Lebanese asked me in the days after September 11 - our September 11, that is - if George Bush really did think America was at war. They weren't doubting the nature of the attacks. **They were just wondering if the US President knew what a real war was like**. In Lebanon, you have to remember, 150,000 men, women and children were killed in 16 years; 17,500 of them - almost six times the total of dead of September 11, and almost all of them civilians - were killed in just the summer of 1982, during Israel's bloody invasion of their little country, an invasion to which the US had given a green light.

And in many cases, of course, the dead - particularly in Lebanon, and ever more frequently in the Israeli-occupied territories - are being killed by American weapons. In the Palestinian town of Beit Jala, for example, almost all the missiles fired into Palestinian houses were made by the Boeing company. Only in the Arab world has a terrible irony been noted: that the very same company that proudly made those weapons - "all for one and one for all" is the logo for Boeing's Hellfire missile - also produced the airliners that were used to attack the United States. Having endured the company's weapons, Arabs turned their airplanes into weapons as well.

IT DOES NOT EXCUSE THE SEPTEMBER 11 KILLERS THEIR HIDEOUS CRIME AGAINST HUMANITY TO RECORD THAT IN THE MIDDLE EAST, YOU DO OFTEN HEAR THE THOUGHT EXPRESSED THAT NOW THE US KNOWS WHAT IT IS TO SUFFER. IT'S NOT INTENDED TO SUGGEST THAT THE UNITED STATES DESERVED SUCH HORRORS; MERELY A FAINT HOPE THAT AMERICANS WILL NOW UNDERSTAND HOW MUCH OTHERS HAVE SUFFERED IN THE MIDDLE EAST OVER THE YEARS. I HAVE TO SAY, OF COURSE, THAT THIS IS NOT THE LESSON THAT AMERICANS ARE IN ANY MOOD TO LEARN.

Indeed, one of the most extraordinary - and patently absurd - elements of post-September 11 America is the way in which the Bush administration has steadily transformed a hunt for international criminals into a biblical struggle against the Devil incarnate. The Devil started off with a beard and a propensity to live in Afghan caves. Then it turned out that he wore a military beret and had a hankering for poison gas and weapons of mass destruction. And by last week, when Richard Armitage was claiming that Hizbollah may be the "A-team of terrorists" - al-Qa'ida being demoted to the "B-team" - the Devil had apparently moved residence from Baghdad to Beirut. Add to all this Iran and the non-Muslim Dear Leader who lives in North Korea and really does have nuclear weapons - which is why we will not bomb him - and a very odd picture of the world emerges. In general, however, that world, however distorted, is a Muslim world.

Now, along with this transformation has come a whole set of policies intended to show the superiority of our Western civilisation - centred on the need for the Arab world to enjoy "democracy". It isn't the first time that the US has threatened the Arabs with democracy, but it's a dodgy project for both parties: first, because the Arabs don't have much democracy; second, because quite a lot of Arabs would like a bit of it; and third, because the countries where they would like this precious commodity include Saudi Arabia, Egypt and other regimes that the Americans would like to protect rather than destroy with democratic experiments. The Palestinians, President Bush has told us, must have a democracy. The Iraqis must have a democracy. Iran must have a democracy. But not, it seems, Saudi Arabia, Jordan, Egypt, Syria and the rest. Naturally, all these ambitious projects have set off a good deal of discussion in the Arab world - perhaps one of the few fruits of September 11 that hasn't yet turned sour.

A recent study in the United States - by Pippa Norris at Harvard and Ronald Inglehart of the University of Michigan - demonstrated convincingly that Samuel Huntington's grotesquely overrated "clash of civilisations" is a load of old baloney. Muslims, the study discovered, were as keen on democracy as Westerners - there presumably being no Christians left - and in some cases even more enthusiastic than Americans and others. The differences between the two emerged on social issues; on homosexuality, women's rights, abortion and divorce. Norris and Inglehart concluded that it would be a gross simplification to suggest that Muslims and Westerners hold fundamentally different political values.

Over the past few weeks, Arab intellectuals have been adding their own gloss to this, especially in Egypt. They have been challenging Huntington. Egyptians and Moroccans and even Saudis have been trying to make a cultural defence of Arabism, rejecting the idea of "globalisation" - a word I hate but which turns up in Arabic as awalameh (literally "world inclusivity") - and the notion that to be for globalisation is to be pro-Western and to be against it is to be against development. But development is not democracy, and the question remains: **why is there no serious democracy in the Arab world?** Although Ayatollah Khomeini created the theological machinery to emasculate Iranian social democracy, Iran's elections, and the repeated victories of President Mohammad Khatami, were undoubtedly fair; Mr Bush's remarks about how he wants to "bring democracy to Iran" are thus off course.

But it is the Arabs who have never developed a modern political state. If they had, might September 11 have been avoided? This was certainly an initial Bush suggestion; the suicide killers, he informed the world, had attacked America because they "hated democracy". The trouble is that the 19 murderers wouldn't have known what democracy was if they had woken up in bed with it. But let's not avoid the question: why only police states and torture chambers in the Arab world?

A HISTORIAN MIGHT GO BACK CENTURIES. WHEN THE CRUSADERS REACHED THE MIDDLE EAST IN THE 11TH CENTURY, IT WAS THE ARABS WHO WERE THE SCIENTISTS; THE WESTERNERS - THE "FRANJ" - WERE THE POLITICAL AND TECHNOLOGICAL NUMBSKULLS. AND WHEN THE ARABS DID DEVELOP A KIND OF SOCIAL ORDER UNDER THE REMNANTS OF THE ABBASIDS IN MEDIEVAL SPAIN, IN THE ANDALUSIA OF EL CID, THE ARABS - ALONG WITH THEIR CHRISTIAN AND JEWISH BROTHERS AND SISTERS - EXPERIENCED SOMETHING LIKE A CULTURAL RENAISSANCE.

In the Middle East, however, the Arabs felt they were under pressure from the West - from Western military prowess and economic power - and went on to the defensive. To question your caliph - or, even worse, to advance in theological philosophy - was a form of subversion, even treachery. When the enemy is at the gates, you don't question authority. Rather like the Americans after September 11 - when to seek the motives for the massacres was regarded as something akin to a thought crime - any intellectual enquiry was suppressed.

THE WESTERN POWERS DID MUCH THE SAME TO THE ARABS AFTER THE 1914-18 WAR. THEY CHOPPED UP THE OTTOMAN EMPIRE, SPRINKLED DICTATORS AND KINGS ACROSS THE MIDDLE EAST, AND THEN - IN EGYPT AND LEBANON, FOR EXAMPLE - LOCKED UP ANYONE EXERCISING THEIR DEMOCRATIC OPPOSITION TO THE REGIME. IF THE OPPOSITION WAS NOT GOING TO GAIN POLITICAL POWER DEMOCRATICALLY... WELL, IT WOULD STAGE A COUP D'ÉTAT. AND THIS HAS LARGELY BEEN THE FATE OF THE MIDDLE EAST SINCE: A SERIES OF COUPS - RATHER THAN REVOLUTIONS ON THE IRANIAN MODEL - WHICH HAD TO BE BACKED UP WITH ARMIES AND SECRET POLICEMEN AND TORTURE CHAMBERS.

To a patriarchal society - and to one in which there had been no theological development comparable to the European Renaissance - was added our own Western determination to support undemocratic regimes. **If we had democracy in the Middle East, the people who live there**

might not do what we want. So we supported the kings and princes and generals who did our bidding, unless they suddenly nationalised the Suez Canal, set off bombs in Berlin discos or invaded Kuwait, in which case we bombed them. Not by chance has Osama bin Laden raked over these historical coals. He wants the downfall of the Saudi regime - how he must have loved the Rand corporation's lecturer who called Saudi Arabia the "kernel of evil" - and he wants the downfall of the pro-Western Arab dictators.

Amid the twisted rhetoric now coming out of Washington - a linguistic barrage sounding more and more like the authentic voice of bin Laden - it is becoming ever more difficult to believe that Mr Bush is planning any kind of democracy in Iraq. Nor in "Palestine". After all, Yasser Arafat was not rejected because of his failure to create a democracy; he was rejected because he didn't do the job of a dictator well enough. He failed to create law and order in the small portions of land awarded to him in return for his putative good offices.

But something much bigger is going on today.

ALMOST EVERY ARAB NATION IS BEING LINED UP BY THE UNITED STATES, EAGERLY ENCOURAGED BY ISRAEL. PALESTINE MUST HAVE "REGIME CHANGE"; IRAQ MUST HAVE "REGIME CHANGE"; IRAN - MOST RECENTLY ACCUSED, WITHOUT ANY PROOF, OF SHIPPING AL-QA'IDA GOLD TO SUDAN - MUST HAVE DEMOCRACY; SAUDI ARABIA IS A "KERNEL OF EVIL"; SYRIA IS NOW TO BE SANCTIONED FOR "SUPPORTING TERRORISM"; LEBANON IS ACCUSED OF HARBOURING AL-QA'IDA MEMBERS - A PATENT UNTRUTH, BUT ONE THAT IS ALREADY FINDING ITS WAY INTO THE NEW YORK TIMES; AND JORDAN MAY HAVE TO SERVE AS A LAUNCH PAD FOR AN IRAQI INVASION (WHICH, POSSIBLY, WOULD MEAN GOODBYE TO OUR PLUCKY LITTLE KING). THE UNITED STATES ENDS EXTRA FINANCIAL SUPPORT FOR EGYPT BECAUSE IT LOCKS UP AN AMERICAN EGYPTIAN FOR STATING THE TRUTH - THAT EGYPTIAN ELECTIONS ARE A FRAUD. WHAT, ARABS ARE ASKING THEMSELVES, ARE THE AMERICANS UP TO? ARE THEY PLANNING TO RESHAPE THE MAP OF THE MIDDLE EAST? IS THIS TO BE ANOTHER EXERCISE IN COLONIAL PLANNING, AKIN TO THE ONE THE BRITISH AND FRENCH WROUGHT AFTER THE FIRST WORLD WAR? ARE WE PLANNING TO TOPPLE ALL THE ARAB REGIMES?

In other words, are we now trying to turn Huntington's third-rate book into a success story? Are we actually now in the process of starting a clash of civilisations? Never before have Muslims and Westerners been so polarised, their conflicts so sharpened - and Arab hopes so fraudulently raised. We are no more planning to give those Arabs "democracy" than we planned to honour our promise of independence at the end of the 1914-18 war. What we want to do is to bring them back under our firm control, to ensure their loyalty. If the House of Saud is collapsing of its own volition, the Americans seem to be saying, then let it collapse. If Jordan's King Abdullah won't play ball on the Iraqi invasion plans, what's he worth anyway? In the Arab press, there is a slow but growing suspicion that "regime change" might turn out to be Middle East change.

But let's remember two things; that the killers of September 11 were Arabs. And they were Muslims. And the Arab world has held no debate about this. There have been plenty of stories to the contrary: that the 19 murderers were working for the Americans or the Israelis; that hundreds of American Jews were warned not to go to work on the day of the attack; even that the planes were remotely controlled and had no pilots at all. This childish and sometimes pernicious rubbish is widely believed in parts of the Middle East. Anything to duck the blame, to avoid the truth.

And it's a strange thing that is happening now. The Americans want the world to know that the killers were Arabs. But they don't want to discuss the tragedy of the region they came from. The Arabs, on the other hand, do want to discuss their tragedy - but wish to deny the Arab identity of the killers. **The Americans have created a totally false image of the Arab world, peopling it with beasts and tyrants. The Arabs have**

adopted an almost equally absurd view of the US, believing its promises of "democracy" but failing to grasp the degree of anger many Americans still feel over the attacks.

Yet still there are double standards at work here. George Bush can rightly condemn the killing of Israeli university students as making him "mad", but blithely brush off the slaughter of Palestinian children by a bomb dropped from a US-made Israeli plane as "heavy handed". Yet it's not just the pitiful remarks of President Bush, but the double standards of whole peoples. Here's what I mean. Today, 11 September, our newspapers and our television screens are filled with the baleful images of those two towers and their biblical descent. We will remember and honour the thousands who died. But in just five days' time, Palestinians will remember their September massacre of 1982. Will a single candle be lit for them in the West? Will there be a single memorial service? Will a single American newspaper dare to recall this atrocity? Will a single British newspaper commemorate the 20th anniversary of these mass killings of 1,700 innocents? **Do I even need to give the answer?**

019

Samarra is a town in Iraq 125 kilometers north of Baghdad on the east bank of the middle Tigris. Capital of the Muslim world under the Abbasid Caliphs in the 9th century, Samarra expanded to occupy an area of 57 kilometers, making it one of the largest cities of the ancient world. Now a vast archaeological site, its collapsed pisé and brick walls are still visible.

How would people be discussing the issue of "regime change" in Iraq if the question were not being forced upon them by the Administration? In other words, is the American and European and international audience for this debate no more than just that — an audience, complete with theater critics and smart-ass reviewers? Or to put the matter in still another way, would the topic of "regime change" be dropped if the Bush White House were not telegraphing all its military intentions toward Iraq while continuing to make an eerie secret of its political ones?

I approach this question as one who has been in favor of "regime change" in Iraq for quite a long time, and who considers himself a friend of those Iraqis and Iraqi Kurds who have risked so much to bring it about. I don't feel that I require official permission or exhortation to adopt the argument, but I do feel that it's a relinquishment of responsibility to abandon it. Unlike the chronically enfeebled and cowardly Democratic leadership in Congress, I don't beg like a serf for the President to "make his case" about weapons of mass destruction. Nor do I feel comfortable waiting like a mendicant for him to speak out about the Kurds, or demanding that he pronounce in a less or more scary way about Saddam Hussein's underhanded friendship with the dark world of the international gangsters. I can make inquiries of my own, thanks all the same, and even form some conclusions.

The other day I was on some show with Senator Alan Simpson of Wyoming, a leading member of Washington's black-comedy troupe, who said that unless — like him — you had actually met Saddam Hussein you could have no conception of the reality of stone-cold evil. I reminded the Senator that on the occasion of his meeting with the Iraqi leadership, he had actually emerged to say that Saddam was getting an unfairly bad press, and recommended that he invite more reporters to record the achievements of the Baath Party. That was before the invasion of Kuwait, to which George Herbert Walker Bush and James Baker demonstrated an initially indulgent attitude. During the subsequent bombing of Baghdad, Senator Simpson was to the fore in denouncing Peter Arnett of CNN for being in Iraq at all, and later in circulating the allegation that Arnett had once had a brother-in-law who might have been a sympathizer of the Vietcong.

One can play this simple game, of hypocrisy and "double standards," indefinitely. I have played it myself and with better-seeded contestants than Senator Simpson. But a few nights ago I had a long conversation with my friend Dr. Barham Salih, the prime minister of the autonomous Kurdish region of Iraq, and thus one of the very few politicians in the area who have to face an election. He recently survived an assassination attempt by a gang that he is convinced is ideologically and organizationally linked to Al Qaeda. Salih is for a single standard: a democratic Iraq with a devolved Kurdistan.

He doesn't like it when the Administration talks about Saddam Hussein gassing "his own people," because the Kurds are by no means Saddam's property.

Salih speaks of a war "for Iraq" and not "on Iraq." He doesn't believe that the population can remove the dictator without outside help, but he also thinks the Turks are being given too much official consideration — partly because of their military alliance with Israel — in determining the outcome.

This is a serious dilemma for a serious person, who is being asked to stake his own life and the relative freedom of his people on the outcome. It's also a dilemma for us. Is the Bush Administration's "regime change" the same one the Iraqi and Kurdish democrats hope for? Rather than use the conservative language — of the risks of "destabilizing" the Middle East — liberals and radicals ought to be demanding that the Administration and Congress come clean about this. Meanwhile, one sees constant photo-ops of the President making nice with the Saudis, who have reasons of their own to worry about destabilization, while Kurdish leaders are met with in secret and at a much lower level.

"I am very disappointed with the left,"Salih told me. In the past the Kurdish cause was a major concern of the internationalist, human rights and socialist movements, but now a slight shuffling and evasiveness seems to have descended. Some of this obviously arises from a general reluctance to be identified with President Bush, but that, one hopes, is too paltry to explain much.

The other concern is more immediate. Since it is estimated by the Pentagon hawks that a war with Saddam Hussein (not, please, "with Iraq") might well bring about the fall of the Hashemite monarchy in Jordan, and since we also know that there are those around General Sharon who are looking for a pretext to cleanse the Palestinians from the West Bank and expel them onto Jordanian soil, there exists the possibility that a serious moral and political disaster is in the making. Here, then, is a proposal that ought to command broad and deep support, including from the European "allies":

The government of Israel should be required to say, in public and without reservation, that it has no such plans and would never implement such a scheme. It should be informed in public by the President that this undertaking is required on penalty of regime change in case of default. This, after all, is no more than is regularly required from the Palestinians. And it is not just a matter of moral equivalence but of self-interest.

Sooner or later the Saddam Hussein regime will fall, either of its own weight or from the physical and mental collapse of its leader or from endogenous or exogenous pressure. On that day one will want to be able to look the Iraqi and Kurdish peoples in the eye and say that we thought seriously about their interests and appreciated that, because of previous interventions that were actually in Saddam's favor, we owed them a debt. It's this dimension that seems to me lacking in the current antiwar critique.

020

SUSAN SONTAG

OF COURAGE AND RESISTANCE
MARCH 30 2003

Allow me to invoke not one but two, only two, who were heroes — among millions of heroes. Who were victims — among tens of millions of victims.

The first: Oscar Arnulfo Romero, Archbishop of San Salvador, murdered in his vestments, while saying mass in the cathedral on March 24, 1980 — twenty-three years ago — because he had become "a vocal advocate of a just peace, and had openly opposed the forces of violence and oppression."

The second: Rachel Corrie, a 23-year-old college student from Olympia, Washington, murdered in the bright neon-orange jacket with Day-Glo striping that "human shields" wear to make themselves quite visible, and possibly safer, while trying to stop one of the almost daily house demolitions by Israeli forces in Rafah, a town in the southern Gaza Strip (where Gaza abuts the Egyptian border), on March 16, 2003. Standing in front of a Palestinian physician's house that had been targeted for demolition, Corrie, one of eight young American and British human-shield volunteers in Rafah, had been waving and shouting at the driver of an oncoming armored D-9 bulldozer through her megaphone, then dropped to her knees in the path of the supersized bulldozer ... which did not slow down.

Two emblematic figures of sacrifice, killed by the forces of violence and oppression to which they were offering nonviolent, principled, dangerous opposition.

Let's start with risk. The risk of being punished. The risk of being isolated. The risk of being injured or killed. The risk of being scorned. We are all conscripts in one sense or another. For all of us, it is hard to break ranks; to incur the disapproval, the censure, the violence of an offended majority with a different idea of loyalty. We shelter under banner words like justice, peace and reconciliation that enroll us in new, if much smaller and relatively powerless, communities of the like-minded. That mobilize us for the demonstration, the protest and the public performance of acts of civil disobedience — not for the parade ground and the battlefield.

To fall out of step with one's tribe; to step beyond one's tribe into a world that is larger mentally but smaller numerically — if alienation or dissidence is not your habitual or gratifying posture, this is a complex, difficult process. It is hard to defy the wisdom of the tribe, the wisdom that values the lives of members of the tribe above all others. It will always be unpopular — it will always be deemed unpatriotic — to say that the lives of the members of the other tribe are as valuable as one's own. It is easier to give one's allegiance to those we know, to those we

see, to those with whom we are embedded, to those with whom we share — as we may — a community of fear.

Let's not underestimate the force of what we oppose. Let's not underestimate the retaliation that may be visited on those who dare to dissent from the brutalities and repressions thought justified by the fears of the majority. **We are flesh. We can be punctured by a bayonet, torn apart by a suicide bomber. We can be crushed by a bulldozer, gunned down in a cathedral. Fear binds people together. And fear disperses them**. Courage inspires communities: the courage of an example — for courage is as contagious as fear. But courage, certain kinds of courage, can also isolate the brave.

THE PERENNIAL DESTINY OF PRINCIPLES: WHILE EVERYONE PROFESSES TO HAVE THEM, THEY ARE LIKELY TO BE SACRIFICED WHEN THEY BECOME INCONVENIENCING. GENERALLY A MORAL PRINCIPLE IS SOMETHING THAT PUTS ONE AT VARIANCE WITH ACCEPTED PRACTICE. AND THAT VARIANCE HAS CONSEQUENCES, SOMETIMES UNPLEASANT CONSEQUENCES, AS THE COMMUNITY TAKES ITS REVENGE ON THOSE WHO CHALLENGE ITS CONTRADICTIONS — WHO WANT A SOCIETY ACTUALLY TO UPHOLD THE PRINCIPLES IT PROFESSES TO DEFEND.

The standard that a society should actually embody its own professed principles is a utopian one, in the sense that moral principles contradict the way things really are — and always will be. How things really are — and always will be — is neither all evil nor all good but deficient, inconsistent, inferior. Principles invite us to do something about the morass of contradictions in which we function morally. Principles invite us to clean up our act, to become intolerant of moral laxity and compromise and cowardice and the turning away from what is upsetting: that secret gnawing of the heart that tells us that what we are doing is not right, and so counsels us that we'd be better off just not thinking about it.

The cry of the anti-principled: "I'm doing the best I can." The best given the circumstances, of course.

Let's say, the principle is: It's wrong to oppress and humiliate a whole people. To deprive them systematically of lodging and proper nutrition; to destroy their habitations, means of livelihood, access to education and medical care, and ability to consort with one another. That these practices are wrong, whatever the provocation. And there is provocation. That, too, should not be denied.

At the center of our moral life and our moral imagination are the great models of resistance: the great stories of those who have said no. No, I will not serve. What models, what stories? A Mormon may resist the outlawing of polygamy. An antiabortion militant may resist the law that has made abortion legal. They, too, will invoke the claims of religion (or faith) and morality against the edicts of civil society. Appeal to the existence of a higher law that authorizes us to defy the laws of the state can be used to justify criminal transgression as well as the noblest struggle for justice.

Courage has no moral value in itself, for courage is not, in itself, a moral virtue.

Vicious scoundrels, murderers, terrorists, may be brave. To describe courage as a virtue, we need an adjective: We speak of "moral courage" — because there is such a thing as amoral courage, too.

And resistance has no value in itself. It is the content of the resistance that determines its merit, its moral necessity.

Let's say: resistance to a criminal war. Let's say: resistance to the occupation and annexation of another people's land.

Again: There is nothing inherently superior about resistance. All our claims for the righteousness of resistance rest on the rightness of the claim that the resisters are acting in the name of justice. And the justice of the cause does not depend on, and is not enhanced by, the virtue of those who make the assertion. It depends first and last on the truth of a description of a state of affairs that is, truly, unjust and unnecessary.

Here is what I believe to be a truthful description of a state of affairs that has taken me many years of uncertainty, ignorance and anguish to acknowledge:

A WOUNDED AND FEARFUL COUNTRY, ISRAEL, IS GOING THROUGH THE GREATEST CRISIS OF ITS TURBULENT HISTORY, BROUGHT ABOUT BY THE POLICY OF STEADILY INCREASING AND REINFORCING SETTLEMENTS ON THE TERRITORIES WON AFTER ITS VICTORY IN THE ARAB-ISRAELI WAR OF 1967. THE DECISION OF SUCCESSIVE ISRAELI GOVERNMENTS TO RETAIN CONTROL OVER THE WEST BANK AND GAZA, THEREBY DENYING THEIR PALESTINIAN NEIGHBORS A STATE OF THEIR OWN, IS A CATASTROPHE — MORAL, HUMAN AND POLITICAL — FOR BOTH PEOPLES. THE PALESTINIANS NEED A SOVEREIGN STATE. ISRAEL NEEDS A SOVEREIGN PALESTINIAN STATE. THOSE OF US ABROAD WHO WISH FOR ISRAEL TO SURVIVE CANNOT, SHOULD NOT, WISH IT TO SURVIVE NO MATTER WHAT, NO MATTER HOW. WE OWE A PARTICULAR DEBT OF GRATITUDE TO COURAGEOUS ISRAELI JEWISH WITNESSES, JOURNALISTS, ARCHITECTS, POETS, NOVELISTS, PROFESSORS — AMONG OTHERS — WHO HAVE DESCRIBED AND DOCUMENTED AND PROTESTED AND MILITATED AGAINST THE SUFFERINGS OF THE PALESTINIANS LIVING UNDER THE INCREASINGLY CRUEL TERMS OF ISRAELI MILITARY SUBJUGATION AND SETTLER ANNEXATION.

Our greatest admiration must go to the brave Israeli soldiers, represented here by Ishai Menuchin, who refuse to serve beyond the 1967 borders. These soldiers know that all settlements are bound to be evacuated in the end. These soldiers, who are Jews, take seriously the principle put forward at the Nuremberg trials in 1945-46: namely, that a soldier is not obliged to obey unjust orders, orders that contravene the laws of war – indeed, one has an obligation to disobey them.

The Israeli soldiers who are resisting service in the occupied territories are not refusing a particular order. They are refusing to enter the space where illegitimate orders are bound to be given — that is, where it is more than probable that they will be ordered to perform actions that continue the oppression and humiliation of Palestinian civilians. Houses are demolished, groves are uprooted, the stalls of a village market are bulldozed, a cultural center is looted; and now, nearly every day, civilians of all ages are fired on and killed. There can be no disputing the mounting cruelty of the Israeli occupation of the 22 percent of the former territory of British Palestine on which a Palestinian state will be erected. These soldiers believe, as I do, that there should be an unconditional withdrawal from the occupied territories. They have declared collectively that they will not continue to fight beyond the 1967 borders "in order to dominate, expel, starve and humiliate an entire people."

What the refuseniks have done — there are now more than 1,000 of them, more than 250 of whom have gone to prison — does not contribute to telling us how the Israelis and Palestinians can make peace, beyond the irrevocable demand that the settlements be disbanded. The actions of this heroic minority cannot contribute to the much-needed reform and democratization of the Palestinian Authority. Their stand will not lessen the grip of religious bigotry and racism in Israeli society or reduce the dissemination of virulent anti-Semitic propaganda in the aggrieved Arab world. It will not stop the suicide bombers.

It simply declares: enough. Or: there is a limit. Yesh gvul. It provides a model of resistance. Of disobedience. For which there will always be penalties.

None of us have yet to endure anything like what these brave conscripts are enduring, many of whom have gone to jail. To speak for peace at this moment in this country is merely to be jeered (as in the recent Academy Awards ceremony), harassed, blacklisted (the banning by one powerful chain of radio stations of the Dixie Chicks); in short, to be reviled as unpatriotic.

Our "United We Stand" or "Winner Takes All" ethos: The United States is a country that has made patriotism equivalent to consensus. Tocqueville, still the greatest observer of the United States, remarked on an unprecedented degree of conformity in the then-new country, and 168 more years have only confirmed his observation.

Sometimes, given the new, radical turn in American foreign policy, it seems as if it was inevitable that the national consensus on the greatness of America, which may be activated to an extraordinary pitch of triumphalist national self-regard, was bound eventually to find expression in wars like the present one, which are assented to by a majority of the population, who have been persuaded that America has the right — even the duty — to dominate the world.

The usual way of heralding people who act on principle is to say that they are the vanguard of an eventually triumphant revolt against injustice. But what if they're not? What if the evil is really unstoppable? At least in the short run. And that short run may be — is going to be — very long indeed.

My admiration for the soldiers who are resisting service in the occupied territories is as fierce as my belief that it will be a long time before their view prevails. But what haunts me at this moment — for obvious reasons — is acting on principle when it isn't going to alter the obvious distribution of force, the rank injustice and murderousness of a government policy that claims to be acting in the name not of peace but of security.

The force of arms has its own logic. If you commit an aggression and others resist, it is easy to convince the home front that the fighting must continue. Once the troops are there, they must be supported. It becomes irrelevant to question why the troops are there in the first place.

The soldiers are there because "we" are being attacked or menaced. Never mind that we may have attacked them first. They are now attacking back, causing casualties. Behaving in ways that defy the "proper" conduct of war. **Behaving like "savages," as people in our part of the world like to call people in that part of the world.** And their "savage" or "unlawful" actions give new justification to new aggressions. And new impetus to repress or censor or persecute citizens who oppose the aggression the government has undertaken.

LET'S NOT UNDERESTIMATE THE FORCE OF WHAT WE ARE OPPOSING. THE WORLD IS, FOR ALMOST EVERYONE, THAT OVER WHICH WE HAVE VIRTUALLY NO CONTROL. COMMON SENSE AND THE SENSE OF SELF-PROTECTIVENESS TELL US TO ACCOMMODATE TO WHAT WE CANNOT CHANGE.

It's not hard to see how some of us might be persuaded of the justice, the necessity of a war. Especially of a war that is formulated as a small, limited military action that will actually contribute to peace or improve security; of an aggression that announces itself as a campaign of disarmament — admittedly, disarmament of the enemy; and, regrettably, requiring the application of overpowering force. **An invasion that calls itself, officially, a liberation.**

Every violence in war has been justified as a retaliation. We are threatened. We are defending ourselves. The others, they want to kill us. We must stop them. And from there: We must stop them before they have a chance to carry out their plans. And since those who would attack us are sheltering behind noncombatants, no aspect of civil life can be immune to our depredations.

Never mind the disparity of forces, of wealth, of firepower — or simply of population. How many Americans know that the population of Iraq is 24 million, half of whom are children? (The population of the United States, as you will remember, is 290 million.) Not to support those who are coming under fire from the enemy seems like treason.

It may be that, in some cases, the threat is real. In such circumstances, the bearer of the moral principle seems like someone running alongside a moving train, yelling "Stop! Stop!" Can the train be stopped? No, it can't. At least, not now. Will other people on the train be moved to jump off and join those on the ground? Maybe some will, but most won't. (At least, not until they have a whole new panoply of fears).

The dramaturgy of "acting on principle" tells us that we don't have to think about whether acting on principle is expedient, or whether we can count on the eventual success of the actions we have undertaken. Acting on principle is, we're told, a good in itself. But it is still a political act, in the sense that you're not doing it for yourself. You don't do it just to be in the right, or to appease your own conscience; much less because you are confident your action will achieve its aim. You resist as an act of solidarity. With communities of the principled and the disobedient: here, elsewhere. In the present. In the future.

Thoreau's going to prison in 1846 for refusing to pay the poll tax in protest against the American war on Mexico hardly stopped the war. But the resonance of that most unpunishing and briefest spell of imprisonment (famously, a single night in jail) has not ceased to inspire principled resistance to injustice through the second half of the twentieth century and into our new era. The movement in the late 1980s to shut down the Nevada Test Site, a key location for the nuclear arms race, failed in its goal; the operations of the test site were unaffected by the protests. But it led directly to the formation of a movement of protesters in faraway Alma Ata, who eventually succeeded in shutting down the main Soviet test site in Kazakhstan, citing the Nevada antinuclear activists as their inspiration and expressing solidarity with the Native Americans on whose land the Nevada Test Site had been located.

The likelihood that your acts of resistance cannot stop the injustice does not exempt you from acting in what you sincerely and reflectively hold to be the best interests of your community.

Thus: It is not in the best interests of Israel to be an oppressor.

Thus: It is not in the best interests of the United States to be a hyperpower, capable of imposing its will on any country in the world, as it chooses.

What is in the true interests of a modern community is justice.

It cannot be right to systematically oppress and confine a neighboring people. It is surely false to think that murder, expulsion, annexations,

the building of walls — all that has contributed to reducing a whole people to dependence, penury and despair — will bring security and peace to the oppressors. It cannot be right that a President of the United States seems to believe that he has a mandate to be President of the planet — and announces that those who are not with America are with "the terrorists."

Those brave Israeli Jews who, in fervent and active opposition to the policies of the present government of their country, have spoken up on behalf of the plight and the rights of Palestinians are defending the true interests of Israel. Those of us who are opposed to the plans of the present government of the United States for global hegemony are patriots speaking for the best interests of the United States.

Beyond these struggles, which are worthy of our passionate adherence, it is important to remember that in programs of political resistance the relation of cause and effect is convoluted, and often indirect. All struggle, all resistance is — must be — concrete. And all struggle has a global resonance.

If not here, then there. If not now, then soon. Elsewhere as well as here.

To Archbishop Oscar Arnulfo Romero.

To Rachel Corrie.

And to Ishai Menuchin and his comrades.

021

EYAD SARRAJ M.D.

THEY NEVER PROMISE HEAVEN
REFLECTIONS ON SEPTEMBER 11

The world becomes a cold and lonely place when people such as Bin Laden, Bush and his entourage of Rumsfeld, and Sharon enter the scene — each with a bang. Collectively they represent failure. **Bin Laden is a representation of Arab Muslims who failed to enter the modern times of democracy and the rule of law, and continue to be held hostage to demagogy, slogans, police states, and tribalism.** Muslims failed to protect their religion from being hijacked by a few extremists. The Zionist project failed, too. Instead of turning Palestine into a safe haven for Jews, Israel became just another ghetto, a slaughterhouse for Jews and others. The failure of Israel is due partly to its military dictatorship, arrogance of power, and paranoia.

EXTREMISM IS AN EXPRESSION OF PARANOIA. IN THE PARANOID EYES OF PEOPLE LIKE BIN LADEN AND RUMSFELD, THE WORLD IS DIVIDED BETWEEN GOOD AND EVIL. ACCORDING TO BIN LADEN, YOU HAVE TO BE A MUSLIM TO BE GOOD, AND ACCORDING TO RUMSFELD, YOU HAVE TO BE PRO-AMERICAN, PREFERABLY WHITE AND CHRISTIAN. **THEY ARE MIRROR IMAGES OF EACH OTHER.** SHARON'S WORLD WAS ALREADY DIVIDED: BETWEEN JEWS AND GOYIM.

Colonialism, racism, and slavery are the most painful shames in the history of mankind. They are still practiced in the name of civilization or under the veil of Christianity. Britain, for example, left a wake of destruction behind everything it touched during its glorious empire. It contributed, through its mandate over Palestine, to the ethnic cleansing of Palestinians and consistently failed to address its brutal colonial past.

The tragedy of our time is that it is the Bin Ladens, Rumsfelds, Blairs, and Sharons who decide our future and the future of our children.

Extremism flourishes in an environment of poverty and hopelessness. Palestinians have failed in liberating their land, for they never had the right education, powerful friends, or needed leadership. Their desperate resort to violent suicide bombings only served to strengthen Sharon and his extremist allies, and to cost the Palestinians the morality of their cause. Earlier failures were just as spectacular, "Black September" to Lebanon to the second Gulf War to the Oslo process. The Palestinian leadership never understood the Israeli Jewish psychology or their political environment. Arafat is not an extremist, and may not be a terrorist. He is impotently squeezed between extremists who decide his fate and ours. As in the rest of the Arab world — with the exception of Sadat — Arafat has failed in war and in peace.

It is open to speculation if he ever had a strategy for either. In state-building he performed badly, as his Palestinian Authority blocked the path to democracy, abused the law, exploited the tribal structural, and encouraged nepotism and corruption. The intifada that erupted two years ago was an expression of the failure of Arafat, Israel, and the world powers. It was a long-awaited opening for militant groups to reenter the scene. The struggle for freedom took an ugly turn with the use of suicide bombings inside Israel. The fatal mistake was they never comprehended the significance of the horrors of the September 11. With their ruthless campaign of terror, they gave Sharon a seal of legitimacy and a renewed American blessing. A year on, America is still in the grips of paranoia and patriotism. It is in such critical times that nations need leadership. The tragedy is that the U.S. failed to provide itself and the world with a moral leadership equal to its economic and military power.

It is truly sad that ultra-Zionist Christian fundamentalists like Rumsfeld are in control of the only super power of this world. Such people threaten hell and death, but never promise heaven. I have no problem understanding that Saddam is a dangerous and brutal dictator, but I am concerned about people forced to have custom-made leadership. Violence can only breed violence, even when it is committed in the name of God, liberty, or civilization. Killing more Arabs, Americans, or Afghanis will never solve problems. It will only create more killing and more hell.

God has given us such a beautiful world, and it is in the name of God that they are destroying it.

022

ALEXANDRA BOULAT

TERROR AGAINST TERROR
PALESTINE APRIL 2002

◊ **Ramallah**
2:00 pm. Under full curfew.
A Palestinian ambulance
is being checked by Israeli soldier.

> **Ramallah**
Israeli army take over parts of
Yasser Arafat compound.

> **Jenin**
A tag left by Israeli Army on one a
door of the Jenin Refugee Camp.

> **Jenin**
Israeli army tags on one of Jenin
refugee camp door.

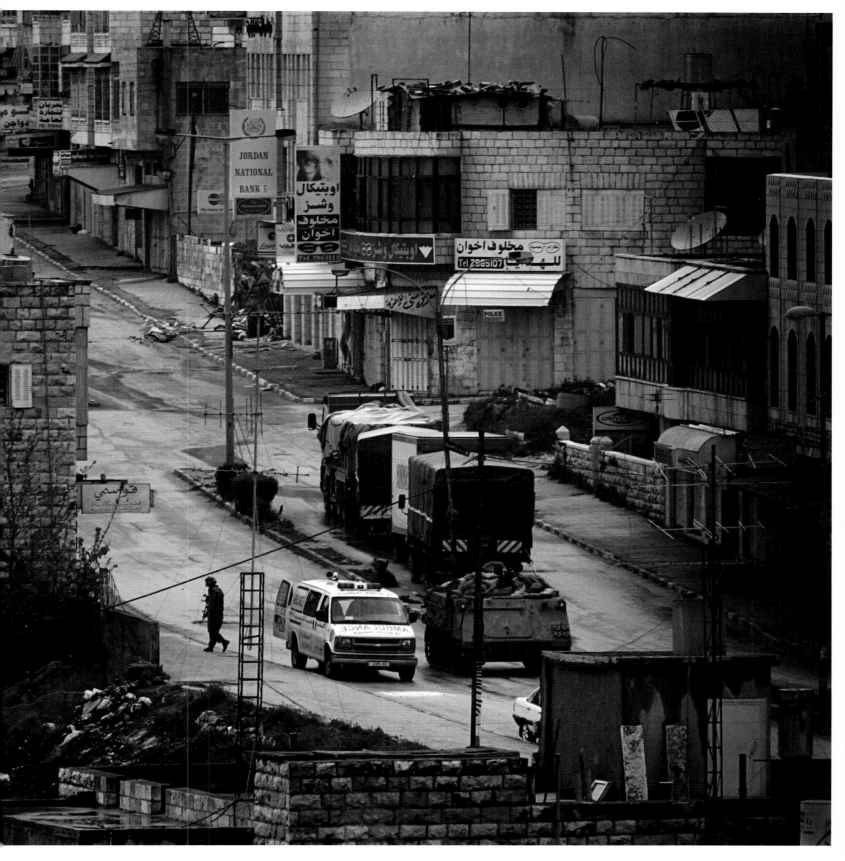

022 Alexandra Boulat

Terror Against Terror

Page 177

> **Jenin**
Israeli soldiers patrol in Jenin
Refugee Camp, West Bank, Israel.

> **Ramallah**
Palestinians who were detained by Israeli soldiers walk back into the besieged West Bank city of Ramallah past
a group of Israeli soldiers, lifting their shirts to show they were not carrying any explosive devices. A group of 40 men
was released from detention in the nearby town of Kalandia and walked back to Ramallah.

ISRAEL: OPERATION "WALL OF PROTECTION"

IN THE BEGINNING OF THE YEAR 2002, BIN LADEN'S MEN ARE NOT THOSE WHO CONTRIBUTE TO THE PRESENT-DAY EVENTS, BUT RATHER THE PALESTINIAN SUICIDE BOMBERS.

THE COVER OF TIME MAGAZINE SHOWS THE PICTURE OF A GRADUATE YOUNG PALESTINIAN WOMAN, A SUICIDE BOMBER WHO KILLS AN ISRAELI IN JERUSALEM BY BLOWING HERSELF UP IN A BUS IN JANUARY 2002. A FEW DAYS LATER, ANOTHER PALESTINIAN BLOWS HIMSELF UP IN AN ISRAELI RESTAURANT DURING PASSOVER CAUSING THE DEATH OF 26 PEOPLE.

IN REACTION TO THIS NEW WAVE OF PALESTINIAN ATTACKS, THE ISRAELI GOVERNMENT OF ARIEL SHARON LAUNCHES OPERATION "WALL OF PROTECTION" IN THE PALESTINIAN TERRITORIES.

From the roof of the house, with a telephoto lens, one can see Jenin, far in the distance, and imagine the intensity of the fighting. A country-man points to a camp of Palestinian refugees, above the city, backed against the side of the hill. In spite of blinding unfavorable light and clouds of black smoke produced by explosions that cover certain parts of the city, one can distinguish the movements of Israeli tanks in the street that climbs along the camps on the ridge and downwards, towards the exit of the city. High in the sky, a combat helicopter prowls around like a vulture, untouchable and despairing.

A few days later I manage to enter Jenin. The little streets are deserted. Behind the walls of the houses one can distinguish shouting of young children which supposes the presence of entire families. 20,000 Palestinians live in these camps, locked up and terrified.

The center of the city is unrecognizable. On a surface of thousands of square meters, houses are razed to the ground and their ruins are being leveled by bulldozers. Here and there, under the rubbish and the exploded concrete, one notices a foot, a hand or a decomposing body. The little streets are now only rocky paths which stink of death and are lined with holes like after an earthquake.

The Israeli soldiers occupy the Mosque and its minaret, transforming Jenin in a gruesome track. They patrol by groups of ten. Map in hand, they search, break in the doors with grenades, pierce the walls with pickaxes, line up the prisoners and execute those who attempt to resist.

The United Nations do not receive the right to investigate the crimes which have been committed in Jenin. Only the Palestinians will be able to quality these as war crimes.

◊ **Jenin**
A Palestinian activist poster
stuck on a door destroyed by
the Israelis.

< Ramallah
Israeli army killed one
and detain few Palestinian men.

< Jenin
Palestinian women weeping
in Jenin narrow streets.

◊ Jenin
Distraught Palestinians discover
the destruction of their home and the
rubble of the Jenin Refugee Camp.

◊ Jenin
Distressed Palestinians during the
lifting of the first curfew after the Israeli Army
operation Wall of Protection.

< **Jenin**
Palestinians in the rubbles of the
Jenin Refugee Camp.

< **Jenin**
Burrial of 30 dead Palestinians
killed in the Jenin Refugee Camp after
the Israeli Army raid.

< **Jenin**
Palestinian search for bodies in the
Jenin Refugee Camp.

◊ **Jenin**
A Palestinian woman collapses
as she discovered the rubble of her
home in Jenin.

◊ **Jenin**
A Palestinian women collects
some clothes out of the rubble
of her home.

> **Jenin**
A Palestinian woman sits on what
used to be her home
in Jenin Refugee Camp's rubble.

> **Jenin**
The foot of a dead Palestinian
in the rubble of his home in the
Jenin Refugee Camp.

022 Alexandra Boulat
Terror Against Terror

Page 203

023

URI SAVIR

GLOCALIZATION:
A NEW BALANCE OF POWER

At a time when multiple developing nations are on the verge of crisis, global environmental problems proliferate, markets slide, and terrorism threatens to never disappear, the Bush Administration's penchant for uni-dimensional foreign policy is by no means quieting hostile sentiments from the international community. America's determination to win the fight against terrorism, both in Afghanistan and Iraq, has resuscitated the unsavory perception that America is acting as the international watchdog. Yet changes in American policy which respond to a new dimension of anti-western terrorist warfare are not the only factors driving international change and struggle. It is also in the more fundamental process where we must look for answers to international stability.

Until fairly recently, globalization - or "Americanization" to many - was thought of as a global gift to humanity. Some went so far as to dedicate the possibility of world peace to globalization. With the fall of the Soviet Bloc and the passing of free-trade agreements, globalization was viewed by many in the world as a process that would create a common belonging and dissolve national boundaries in favor of peace and prosperity - a promising "Pax Americana."

BUT THE REPORTS FROM THE NEW MILLENNIUM INDICATE THAT GLOBALIZATION HAS NOT LIVED UP TO ITS NAME. AND CONSIDERING THE PAST YEAR'S EVENTS - PARTICULARLY THE WORSENING SITUATION IN THE MIDDLE EAST AND OTHER CONFLICT AREAS - THIS DREAM OF A NEW JOINT DESTINY SEEMS TO HAVE BEEN SHATTERED.

Globalization has left too many in its shadow both within and between societies, and the unprecedented, increasing division of wealth is no longer sustainable, nor humane. In developed regions, technology has made enormous progress in communication, space exploration, genetics and other specialized fields, while in the last decade in the developing world, ethnic strife, violence, and lack of access to food, water and medicine have resulted in hundred of millions of deaths. According to UN reports, at a time of record global prosperity nearly half of the least developed countries get less to eat than they did ten years ago and 840 million people live with daily hunger and an uncertain food supply. According to UNICEF, almost a third of children in developing countries under age five are malnourished, and in the past decade alone, more than two million children have been killed in armed conflict. Possibly as tragic are the sense of desperation and lack of hope which inevitably lead to terrorism and further degradation that have darkened the horizon.

According to a recent study published in the January 2003 Economist ("Living with a Superpower"), anti-American sentiment is growing, and it is not only due to differences in policy-making, but is deeply rooted differences in cultural values. It reports that though many countries support the "war on terrorism," more than half of forty-four countries polled think that America does not take other countries into account (while more than seventy-five percent of Americans think their government does). Further, more than fifty percent of the population of nearly all the countries polled by the Pew Research Center think "the spread of American ideas and customs is a bad thing" (with France registering 71%, Italy 58%, Egypt 84%, Pakistan 81%, Indonesia 73%, Germany 67%, Russia 68%, and Turkey 78%). This by no means sets the stage for international coherence.

There is no doubt that we are in urgent need for the development of a more complex approach to international stability - one which contends with the effects and nature of globalization, and addresses socio-economic imbalances and cultural differences. The solutions do not lie simply in anti-globalization - which is, to a large degree, "anti-Americanism" - because globalization will continue to spread resources and openness across boundaries, insufficient though it may be. And the backlash to moving from globalization to "good ole nationalism" would be a grave mistake when there is a need to redress the balance of interest between the strong and weak in a profound manner. For those who do not believe in the need for equity, it is enough to understand that in the post-global era the weak threaten the powerful on a very real level. Though it is surely not the interest of many indigent, there are too many have-nots left out of the global revolution who can destabilize markets through political turmoil and espouse dangerous fundamentalist ideology which can bear weapons of mass destruction and international terrorism.

It is the precise moment for powerful proponents of a global society to enact fundamental reforms to injustice and outmoded systems, and even more crucially, to concretely demonstrate a change of heart and true empathy towards the deeply suffering millions. This is the challenge that must be led by the White House in conjunction with local leaders and civil populations around the globe. Further, the challenge is not about making America better understood through a slick public relations campaign, it is about more fundamental changes of attitude, process and policy by the U.S. and its main global partners.

Such a shift needs a political-economic anchor for new, more humane intentions to materialize and be successful. It begins with the creation of a meeting point among representatives of global and local interest, and opens a joint analysis of opportunities and dangers on an international scale. Global governance is not a realistic response and existing forms of national governance barely effect change on a global scale when acting alone. Paradoxically, in the era of the global, the one socio-political unit growing in power is the city.

If unified and networked, major cities can be essential players in reforming globalization. The demographic growth of cities and their contribution to national economies suggest that cities can be at the core of innovative models. It has been estimated that in developing countries cities contribute an average of sixty percent of the GDP. Today there are more than five hundred cities with a population of more than one million people. Cities are growing in influence in both developing and developed worlds; city governments and their leaders - the mayors - are constantly expanding their span of responsibilities in relation to their citizens, but many lack a common organizational infra-structure to support these new responsibilities in the inter-city domain.

A reformed globalization of a very strategic nature which relies on cities as the core socio-political anchor is something we define as glocalization - a reform placing a strong emphasis on social equity as the basis for international stability. **The focal point of this balance is local government in both developed and developing countries.** By definition more pragmatic than its national big brother, local government is responsive to social and cultural needs. Mayors and local political activity are closer to citizens than are national leaders and policies. This new balance can be developed not only within cities, but more im-portantly between them, using a framework built on city-to-city relations.

Local government should play an operational role in developmental and post-conflict situations. Wealthy cities should support deprived cities in the realm of governance, infrastructure development, rural-urban integration, youth and education, information technology, cultural heritage, tourism and peace-building. There is no reason that New York or Rome should not assist Kabul or Kigali in the same way that the United States and Italy are aiding Afghanistan and Rwanda.

Closer to the needs of the people than national governments, city government can harness the strengths of civil society for capacity building. Civil society should replace the duties of national aid bureaucracies to a degree - contributing, in conjunction with municipal governance, technical know-how to projects. Peace-building activities can become a reality within a local framework: Barcelona can, and indeed is, working with Gaza and Tel Aviv on people-to-people reconciliation; Athens and Ankara have signed an agreement on cooperation, probably more effective than anything Greece and Turkey would have ever created.

Financing for such city-to-city initiatives (at least five percent of international aid) should be allocated by national governments and the private sector, as well as by international institutions such as the World Bank and the United Nations. In particular, these two institutions should 'localize' their efforts by significantly expanding support and encouraging inter-city relations, a trend which has already begun. They should make efforts to form an operative "United Cities" framework as a form of city diplomacy in which cities can easily interact on socio-economic and cultural issues for the sake of development and peace-building, while peacemaking should remain in the realm of national governments.

Glocalization requires the development of socio-economic trends that take into consideration the interests of local communities, small and medium size business, as well as give greater consideration to local labor. More resources should be turned from national government to local government for city diplomacy efforts. One role of a participatory civil society should be the private sector investing a fraction - at least one percent of their pre-tax profits over an extended period of time - into 'social venture capital' for the sake of investing in local communities around the world. Glocalization can contribute important benefit in both the developed and developing worlds, and it can set a balanced trend in the socio-economic sphere, as well as offer integration and respect to conflicting or widely differing cultures.

A central need for reform pertains to the respect for local culture and its link to development. Global players who are mainly proponents of American culture, have to work with local counterparts to expand economic opportunities for local cultural expression and to diversify cultural and informational tools in relation to language and cultural sensitivity. Sixty percent of today's Internet content is in English when only six percent of the world's population speaks English, serving mostly to increase the digital gap; global companies, as well as public institutions, must be attuned to and invest in local languages and cultures in all sectors.

The challenge now is finding a new meeting point between New York and "New Athens," followed by the development of innovative trends leading to a greater sense of equal opportunity. Various organizations are making tremendous efforts to establish such trends of decentralized diplomacy. Among them are: 1) WACLAC, formed in 1996 and composed of the International Union of Local Authorities, the United Towns Organisation, METROPOLIS - World Association of Major Metropolises, and the Summit Conference of the World's Major Cities, 2) Cities Alliance, launched in 1999 with the World Bank and UN-Habitat in an effort to combat urban poverty, 3) Sister Cities International, a nonprofit citizen diplomacy network creating and strengthening city to city partnerships between U.S. and international communities, and 4) the Glocal Forum, established in Rome in 2001 and partnered with numerous mayors and the World Bank, expanding city diplomacy efforts in the areas of peace-building and development, and focusing on the involvement of civil society and sectors involving ICT, youth, culture, sports, and tourism.

024

JOSEPH S. NYE

AMERICA IS NOT AN EMPIRE
SEPTEMBER 2 2002

How powerful is the United States, and how should it relate to the rest of the world?

Can we go it alone without friends and allies?

Is America a new version of the Roman Empire?

These questions are increasingly debated in Washington today.

Some neo-conservative columnists such Charles Krauthammer argue that the United States is so much stronger than other countries that it can afford to go it alone. He urges what he calls "a new unilateralism." The United States should do as it pleases, and others will simply have to fall in line. He notes that the word "empire", long banished in American foreign policy, is now gaining a new respectability. Others such as John Ikenberry disagree, and warn against a nascent neo-imperial grand strategy that threatens to rend to fabric of the international community. And a number of academic writers have compared the United States to the Roman and British empires.

The temptation to make such comparisons is strong. As I point out in The Paradox of American Power, not since Rome has one country been so large compared to all other nations as the United States is today. Our defense expenditure is equal to the next eight countries combined; our economy is larger than the total of the next three countries, and American culture — from Hollywood to higher education — has greater global reach than any other. The United States, like ancient Rome, is less likely to succumb in battle with another empire than to suffer a death of a thousand cuts by hordes of new barbarians. Despite fears that China or a revived Russia will challenge us for global primacy, it is difficult to see another country developing military strength equal to ours in the next few decades.

But the temptation to see ourselves as the new Romans should be resisted, Primacy should not be confused with empire. Empire involves supreme control over other peoples. The United States is more powerful compared to other countries than Britain was at its imperial peak, but the U.S. has less control over what occurs in other countries than Britain did. For example, when I lived in East Africa in the waning days of the British empire, Uganda's schools, taxes, laws and elections - not to mention external relations - were controlled by British officials. The United States has no such control outside our borders today. Historically, we have shunned it, except for the anomalous period at the beginning of the last century when we took Puerto Rico and the Philippines from Spain.

DEVOTEES OF THE NEW IMPERIALISM SAY NOT TO BE SO LITERAL. "EMPIRE" IS MERELY A METAPHOR. BUT THE PROBLEM WITH THE METAPHOR IS NOT MERELY THAT IT DISTORTS AMERICAN HISTORY. MORE IMPORTANTLY, IT DISTORTS THE PERCEPTIONS OF THOSE WHO SHAPE AMERICAN FOREIGN POLICY TODAY. IT IMPLIES A CONTROL FROM WASHINGTON THAT IS UNREALISTIC, AND REINFORCES THE PREVAILING STRONG TEMPTATIONS TOWARDS UNILATERALISM IN THE ADMINISTRATION AND PARTS OF THE CONGRESS.

The paradox of American power in the 21st century is that the strongest country since Rome cannot achieve many of its goals by acting alone. In the economic area, international financial stability is important for our prosperity, but we need the cooperation of others to achieve it. The United States cannot achieve its objective of a new trade round without the cooperation of Europe, Japan and other countries. The information revolution and globalization are creating issues that are inherently multilateral. Global climate change will affect the quality of life in the United States, but three-quarters of the problem arises outside our borders. Diseases originating in distant parts of the globe like AIDS or West Nile fever penetrate our borders with ease, and must be attacked in cooperation with other countries.

The war on terrorism illustrates my point. The American military easily toppled the Taliban government in Afghanistan, but it destroyed only a small part of the Al Qaeda network with its cells in more than fifty countries - including our own. In most of these countries, unilateral military solutions are out of the question. We are not about to bomb Italy or Spain. Success in the war on terrorism will require years of patient civilian cooperation with others in intelligence sharing, police work, and tracing of financial flows. We cannot win this war unilaterally with orders from imperial headquarters.

American primacy means the U.S. will often have to take the lead — witness the campaign in Afghanistan. But our preponderance of power will be generally be more acceptable and legitimate in the eyes of other countries when we embed our policies in multilateral frameworks where their views are taken into account. Sometimes the largest country must take the lead because it is difficult for others to do so, but when we act unilaterally, it matters whether we appear to be acting on narrow self interest or a broad approach that incorporates the interests of others.

We are far more likely to attract others to our cause if we consult them and incorporate their concerns in ours.

The ability to attract others - our soft power - will play an important role. American success will depend not just on our military and economic might, but on the soft power of our culture and values, and on pursuing policies that make others feel that they have been consulted and their interests taken into account. Hard power - the ability to get others to change through the use of carrots and sticks - will remain crucial, but soft or attractive power will be become increasingly important.

Power today is distributed among countries in a pattern that resembles a complex three-dimensional chess game. On the top chessboard, military power is largely unipolar. The U.S. is the only country with both intercontinental nuclear weapons and large state of the art air, naval, and ground forces capable of global deployment. But on the middle chessboard, economic power is multi-polar, with the U.S., Europe and Japan representing two-thirds of world product, and with China's dramatic growth likely to make it a major player early in the century. On this economic board, the United States is not a hegemon or empire. For example, even though the U.S. Justice Department approved, GE was unable to merge with Honeywell when the European Commission objected, and the administration has to accommodate others to reach a trade agreement.

The bottom chessboard is the realm of transnational relations that cross borders outside of government control. This realm includes actors as diverse as bankers electronically transferring sums larger than most national budgets at one extreme, and terrorists transferring weapons or hackers disrupting Internet operations at the other. On this bottom board, power is widely dispersed, and it makes no sense to speak of unipolarity, hegemony, or empire. Instead, the distribution of power is chaotic, and governments will need to cooperate to be able to cope.

Those who recommend a unilateralist American foreign policy based on purely military descriptions of American power are relying on woefully inadequate analysis. When you are in a three dimensional game, you will lose if you focus only on the military board and fail to notice the other boards and the vertical connections among them. For example, as the Administration seeks to persuade British Prime Minister Tony Blair to support a campaign against Saddam Hussein in Iraq, the British press reports that Blair has been weakened by our recent unilateral impositions of tariffs on European steel imports, and our efforts to undercut the International Criminal Court.

The United States will likely remain the world's single most powerful country well into this new century. While potential coalitions to check American power could be created, it is unlikely that they would become firm alliances unless the United States handles its hard coercive power in an overbearing unilateral manner that undermines our attractive or soft power. As the German editor Joseph Joffe has written, "unlike centuries past, when war was the great arbiter, today the most interesting types of power do not come out of the barrel of a gun ... Today there is a much bigger payoff in 'getting others to want what you want,' and that has to do with cultural attraction and ideology and agenda setting and holding out big prizes for cooperation, like the vastness and sophistication of the American market. On that gaming table, China, Russia and Japan, even the West Europeans, cannot match the pile of chips held by the United States." The United States could squander this soft power by heavy-handed unilateralism.

The new challenge for Americans in this three dimensional power game of the 21st century, is that there are more and more things outside the control of even a superpower - such as international financial stability, controlling the spread of infectious diseases, cyber crime and terrorism. Although the United States does well on the traditional measures, there is increasingly more going on in the world that those measures fail to capture. The true lesson of September 11 is that we are not an empire able to rule the world from Washington. Rather than succumb to the temptations of the new unilateralism, we must mobilize international coalitions to address new threats and challenges.

025

WILLIAM F. SCHULZ

I DON'T EVEN WANT TO SPEAK ENGLISH AGAIN:
TERRORISM AND THE CHALLENGE TO HUMAN RIGHTS

Not one of those good people who lost their lives on September 11, 2001 asked to be part of a drama. Not one of them knew that their deaths would trigger a worldwide struggle. Not one could have imagined all that their dying has come to mean.

For some it has come to mean almost no end to anxiety. For others it has spurred hatred of a debilitating intensity. For many it has given birth to suspicions of the stranger. And for almost all of us it has spawned inconvenience and a certain unsettledness in our lives.

But out of the ashes of that terrible day have emerged other revelations. That our lives here in the United States are inextricably linked to the fates of others. That terrorism has a multitude of causes. And that our security is tied profoundly to the pursuit of justice. Justice for the victims of the attacks and justice for the world at large.

For the human rights movement, the aftermath of September 11 has brought a special set of challenges. What happened that day was nothing less than a crime against humanity. Despite all the controversies that have marked the ensuing months, we must never forget that. The people who lost their lives were victims of a horrific human rights crime. Our job as human rights activists is to save people from such ill fortune. And we, among others, failed. It is in our own interest as much as any one else's to do everything we can to see that such crimes do not happen again. We are unalterable adversaries of all those who would use the violation of other people's human rights as a means to accomplish their ends.

Human rights are designed to make the world a safer place.

To do that, however, means respecting the human rights of all. Here of course is where the controversy sets in. But here is where we have to say that protecting even the most despised among us from things like torture or the denial of due process is why we have human rights in the first place. If virtue were a universal human trait, power distributed evenly, and guilt or innocence a given, the human rights movement could go out of business immediately.

But this is the paradox (and, granted, it is a hard faith to abide by when we are feeling frightened and justifiably angry): the more respect we extend to other peoples' rights, the more likely we are to convict the guilty, absolve the innocent, discourage antagonism, cultivate

friendships, win the admiration of the world, and secure our own country's future.

The United States does not exist in a vacuum. It may well be the most powerful country in the world, but one of the things that means is that our every action is subject to extra scrutiny. For good or ill, we have long been a model for the rest of the world. The question now is, a model of what?

THE ANSWER FOR WHICH WE ADVOCATES OF HUMAN RIGHTS HAVE BEEN PLEADING IS: "A MODEL OF RESPECT FOR THE RULE OF LAW IN THE NAME OF WHICH THE STRUGGLE AGAINST TERRORISM IS BEING WAGED. A MODEL OF COMPLIANCE WITH THE HIGHEST PRINCIPLE OF THE AMERICAN TRADITION-EQUITABLE TREATMENT OF ALL CITIZENS. A MODEL OF GENEROSITY TO THOSE WHO SUFFER DEPRIVATION AROUND THE WORLD. AND A MODEL OF GOOD SENSE WHEN IT COMES TO THE STRANGERS AMONG US-THE RECOGNITION THAT IF WE HARM THE MULTITUDE WHO WOULD DO US NO HARM TO STOP THE TINY FRACTION WHO WOULD, WE END UP INCREASING THAT FRACTION BEYOND IMAGINING".

When I was growing up in Pittsburgh, I was truly afraid of only two things: nuclear war and Tony Santaguido. I was afraid of nuclear war because our teachers had assured us that Pittsburgh's steel factories would be the first thing the Russians bombed in a nuclear attack. Of course since we were taught how to duck and cover under our desks to protect us from radiation, I soon relegated nuclear war to a lower spot on my litany of worries. That left Tony Santaguido, the neighborhood bully. I spent a lot of time trying to avoid ever running into Tony Santaguido. And once, when my guard was down, he caught me with a left hook that persuaded me on the spot to go into the ministry. But I happened to notice something we all know about bullies: Tony was far less fierce when he was by himself and not surrounded by his retinue of admirers. Over the years I even got to know one or two of Tony's friends and gradually they convinced him to leave me alone, if not exactly to hold me in his affection.

I worry that the United States has failed to learn that simple lesson I learned so long ago. Not that you don't sometimes have to stand up to bullies. Of course you do. But that equally as important is to strip them of their retinue. Casey Stengel once said, "The secret of a great manager is to keep the two guys who hate your guts away from the three guys who are undecided." And that's part of the way we fight terrorists, too. The war against terrorism will be won or lost in the moderate Arab community-among moderate Arab leaders and citizens in Jordan and Pakistan and Uzbekistan and Indonesia. They are the ones who will decide whether or not to make up the retinue of the extremists, to hide them, encourage them, support them, finance them, and provide them cannon fodder. If the United States is seen as propping up corrupt Arab regimes, if it is seen as acting with hostility to the legitimate demands of the Palestinian people even as it insists, as it must, that Israel be allowed to live in peace-the moderate Arab community will have fewer and fewer reasons not to opt for at least a passive form of extremism.

And what is true of our human rights practices abroad is equally as true of them at home. The United States has held hundreds of foreign nationals rounded up in the days following September 11 in our prisons without any criminal charge having been lodged against them. Not one of them has been determined to have anything to do with terrorism; they have been held on minor visa violations which, were they not of Middle Eastern or South Asian descent, would previously have resulted either in their deportation or an extension of time to correct the problem. One of the lucky ones who got out, the son of a Mauritanian diplomat who was held for forty days without criminal charge and finally released, said, "I used to love the United States, but now I don't understand it. I used to want to learn to speak English, but now I don't want to ever speak English again." Does that young man pose a greater or lesser threat to America than he did when he went to prison?

We in the human rights movement have no sympathy for the guilty prisoners held at Guantanamo Bay. We spoke out against the atrocities committed by the Taliban and Al Qaeda long before the U.S. government recognized the dangers. But the Geneva Conventions require that whether or not they be considered prisoners of war or so-called "illegal combatants" must be decided not unilaterally by the President but by an independent tribunal such as a U.S. civilian court. By violating the Geneva Conventions, we put at risk the life of every American serviceman or woman. For President Bush has said that this will be a long and complicated war, and if that is so, it is almost inevitable that some Americans will be captured. The Geneva Conventions are no guarantee, of course, that they will not be mistreated, but as Secretary of State Powell has made clear, the Geneva Conventions

are our best hope to protect our own, and if we ourselves have violated them that hope is no more than a pipedream and their chances no better than dust.

Every time, then, the United States violates human rights, every time we threaten to use military tribunals that allow no avenues of appeal, every time we hold U.S. citizens in prison and deny them access to attorneys, every time we threaten to torture a detainee to extract information, we risk the loyalty of our allies; we hand fodder to our adversaries, and we give those who are undecided about us one more reason to mistrust our word and disdain our values.

FAR FROM UNDERMINING NATIONAL SECURITY, RESPECT FOR HUMAN RIGHTS IS IN FACT ONE OF ITS STAUNCHEST PILLARS. DURING THE LAST CAMPAIGN FOR U.S. PRESIDENT, CONDOLEEZA RICE, NOW THE NATIONAL SECURITY ADVISER, WROTE THIS REMARKABLE SENTENCE IN FOREIGN AFFAIRS MAGAZINE: "FOREIGN POLICY IN A REPUBLICAN ADMINISTRATION," SHE SAID, " ... WILL ... PROCEED FROM THE FIRM GROUND OF THE NATIONAL INTEREST, NOT FROM THE INTERESTS OF AN ILLUSORY INTERNATIONAL COMMUNITY." AN "ILLUSORY INTERNATIONAL COMMUNITY." I WAS STRUCK DUMB BY THAT SENTENCE WHEN I FIRST READ IT ALMOST TWO YEARS AGO AND I HAVE THOUGHT OF IT FREQUENTLY SINCE SEPTEMBER 11 AS DR. RICE AND PRESIDENT BUSH HAVE ARDUOUSLY WORKED TO BUILD A COALITION OF COMMON INTERESTS OUT OF WHAT THEY APPARENTLY PREVIOUSLY REGARDED AS LITTLE MORE THAN AN ILLUSION. I CAN ONLY PRESUME THAT THEY, LIKE MANY OTHERS OF US, WERE TAUGHT A TOUGH, SAD LESSON BY THE EVENTS OF LAST SEPTEMBER. I CAN ONLY HOPE THAT THEY NOW HAVE AT LEAST ONE VERY GOOD REASON TO UNDERSTAND THAT OUR INTERESTS AND THOSE OF THE REST OF THE WORLD ARE INEXTRICABLY LINKED. AND THAT RESPECT FOR HUMAN RIGHTS IS AT THE HEART OF THOSE INTERESTS.

In 1965, in the midst of the Vietnam war, the great Buddhist monk Thich Nhat Hanh wrote these words to inspire young people whose lives were at risk every day: "Promise me, promise me this day, promise me now ... " he asked. "Even as they strike you down, you will remember: humanity is not our enemy. The only thing worthy of you is compassion ... Hatred will never let you face the beast in human beings. One day, when you face the beast alone, with your courage intact, your eyes kind ... out of your smile will bloom a flower. And ... on the long, rough road, the sun and the moon will continue to shine."

Perhaps Thich Nhat Hanh's vision is too much to ask. But we in the human rights community don't believe so. In the months since September 11 we have mourned the dead, comforted the living, stood up for the vulnerable, and waded deep in the waters of justice. I like to think that our actions are borne of compassion. I know that they are a repudiation of hatred. And I am certain that, as long as we and others tread this road, the sun and the moon will continue to shine.

026

JONATHAN SCHELL · KENZABURO OE

A LETTER EXCHANGE
OCTOBER 2002

Dear Jonathan Schell,

I have learned a great deal from your writings, which are always founded on scrupulous research and to the point. In particular, I have found The Gift of Time (Henry Holt, 1998) extremely important. It has relieved me of the suspicion, which I shared with the anti-nuclear campaigners in Hiroshima, that your alternative of gradual control of nuclear armament might postpone the complete abolition of nuclear weapons.

I have also been greatly enlightened by your serial, "Letter from Ground Zero," contributed to The Nation after September11th. You wrote these series of letters with your awareness that in actual fact no letter would be sent from the ground zero brought about by the terrorism in New York, nor from the ground zero of the whole world which is likely to be brought about by nuclear weapons.

In reading your article I was reminded of the words of a woman who paid a visit to the site in New Mexico where the first nuclear bomb was detonated. She herself had been worried by "the internal radiation" of the nuclear materials which infiltrated her body in Nagasaki.

Kyoko Hayashi has written a series of books, bringing into each of them her own experience of the atom bomb and her periodically renewed recognition of it. As she wrote: "When I stood in front of the monument, I experienced a genuine exposure to nuclear explosion."

"Until that moment when I stood at 'Trinity Site,' I thought the first victims of atom bombs were human beings. This was not true. Our predecessors were there: they were there, utterly unable to shed tears or to cry out."

Her sentiment that not only human beings but also everything else had suffered from nuclear explosion would lead to a vision of a completely desolated planet. Hayashi saw it in the ground zero created by the first nuclear blast.

How utterly irresponsible if we ever allowed such a sentiment to be realized in the near future! However, in the face of President Bush's global nuclear strategy, I am stricken by a sense of futility regarding the hope I entertained when the Cold War came to an end.

You reconfirm in your work: "there is no technical solution to the vulnerability of modern populations to weapons of mass destruction"; and "in our age of weapons of mass destruction, the logic of retaliation led only to annihilation-to 'mutual assured destruction.'"

Nothing but this painful wisdom somehow ended the Cold War, which saw the terrifying reality of nuclear weapons overflowing our planet. However, having recently presided over a debate on satellite television by young men and women in New York, Cairo and Tokyo, I suspect that this wisdom has been forgotten by the younger generation of American people.

Of course I am not in a position to make a facile criticism. That ultimate wisdom was engendered by our experience of Hiroshima. All the same, the government of Japan, while having no power to check it, agreed to President Bush's declaration of war, and passed the Emergency Defense Legislation, enabling Japan to collaborate with American military actions.

It has also been revealed, in an interpreter's memorandum, that some years after Hiroshima the Japanese emperor asked the supreme commander of the Allied Powers whether they would counteract any Communist invasion with nuclear weapons.

The Japanese people have focussed their attention not so much to nuclear weapons as to the misery that could be brought about by their use. They have been able to do so thanks to the persevering efforts of atomic bomb survivors to relate their experiences. As for me, one of the main pillars of my literary works was my report on the achievements of a medical doctor who himself experienced the bomb in Hiroshima.

However, we must ask whether the Japanese intellectuals, including myself, have ever managed to unite the attitude of the people and the state with the wisdom of atom bomb survivors who witnessed firsthand the misery brought to humankind by nuclear weapons.

The campaigns by the atom bomb survivors have been maintained at a high level. However, have they been effective on the international scale? The answer to this question is apparent from the meagerness of the information delivered from Japan in your The Gift of Time.

On the eve of the restoration to Japan of the administrative power of Okinawa, where nuclear weapons were stored on American bases, the late Prime Minister Sato was persistently questioned by the opposition party concerning the problems that might arise in the management of the U.S.-Japanese Security Treaty. It was then that he declared 'The Three Non-Nuclear Principles'. On the other hand, he had made a secret agreement that would nullify one of the principles, "never let others bring in nuclear weapons," which should have been the most urgent as it had an immediate bearing on the actual situation. However, no one could claim that the Japanese people were fooled by that. Most Japanese had been aware of the trick and even hoped that it might supplement the American nuclear strategy. The national consensus on the part of the Japanese, that they would be protected under the "nuclear umbrella," of America, has defined the attitude of the post-war Japan.

And now, for the sake of their security, the people of Japan have voiced no objection to their government taking part in the strategy of - to use the curious figure of speech - the "offensive" instead of the "defensive" nuclear umbrella; in itself a dangerous enough alignment. In Tokyo there is no demonstration against President Bush planned war against Iraq, even the threatened use of nuclear weapons.

This summer Prime Minister Koizumi went to Hiroshima to attend the memorial ceremony, but cancelled his appointment for the next morning to attend a meeting with the survivors of the bomb with the excuse that he had done it in the previous year. A renewed nuclear crisis having come to the surface, any internationally convincing proposal from a Japanese politician could only be made in terms of Hiroshima. However, when the Prime Minister goes to Washington, he never thinks of Hiroshima; and when he goes to Hiroshima, he never thinks of the world.

My dearest Jonathan Schell, I fully agree with your warning against loosening the control of the possible use of nuclear and chemical-biological weapons for mass destruction while since 11th September you have been writing to invoke the voices of the silent dead from the major ground zero.

For fifty odd years I have survived the ground zero of Hiroshima. I am not sure if I have yielded fruitful crops during all these years. With the little time I have left, I am determined to make efforts to accomplish what I have left undone. This letter is one such effort.

Yours truly,

Kenzaburo Oe

Dear Kenzaburo Oe,

Permit me to say that I was deeply stirred by your letter. The very fact of the letter, though it expressed a discouragement that I entirely share, was fortifying and sustaining. Your work on the Hiroshima survivors-both the essays about them and the fiction prompted by them-has long been unique to me in presenting the human truth of the Hiroshima catastrophe without either the slightest evasion or the slightest sacrifice of the complexity, peculiarity, and strangeness of the matter. I immediately thought of the Auden verse:

Waves of anger and fear
Circulate over the bright
And darkened lands of the earth ....

Yet, dotted everywhere,
Ironic points of light
Flash out wherever the Just
Exchange their messages

And now a new darkness spreads over the lands. You tactfully addressed mainly the ambiguities of the Japanese reactions to nuclear danger, devoting only a few sentences to the new American policies. I will follow your example and speak mainly of my own country. But first one or two other points in response to your comments.

The remark that you quoted by Kyoko Hayashi that the nuclear peril is not exhausted by the individual human victims penetrates close to the heart of the matter. Behind the threat that nuclear weapons (still 32,000 strong) pose to millions of individual human beings lies the destruction of entire species and ecosystems. Among them of course is the human species, whose potential extinction itself poses riddles of a new order for the thinking being (homo sapiens, as we optimistically describe ourselves) that poses it. For greater even than the number that would die in a nuclear holocaust are those whose birth would be foreclosed for the rest of time-a potentially infinite number. One aspect of the pathos of the Hiroshima and Nagasaki survivors, it seems to me, is that in choosing to oppose nuclear danger, they shoulder the truly measureless-this infinite-burden of speaking on behalf of these unborn and voiceless legions. It is a burden greatly increased by the silence of most of the rest of the world. The range of their voices is cut short by a world that refuses to listen, thereby foreshortening its own existence. Indifference to Hiroshima is indifference to the human future.

You ask whether Japanese intellectuals-and maybe even the survivors-have failed to get their message across to the world adequately. Failure there is-but among the hearers, not the speakers, and especially among the hearers that need the message most, the people of the United States, inventor and sole user of the bomb. No doubt the equivocal policies of the Japanese government, which you justly criticize, have had a role to play. Certainly, Japanese reliance on America's arsenal reduces the worth to the world of its anti-nuclear principles. Yet no one can seriously imagine that the United States is prevented from reflecting on it own atrocities because the government of Japan stands in the way. Nations in general hate to examine atrocities committed by themselves, and the United States is no exception. Let me give just one example. As you know (but almost no Americans know), the Japanese army photographer Yosuke Yamahata entered Nagasaki the day after the atomic bombing of the city and took photos that may well represent the fullest and most eloquent photographic representation of nuclear destruction. We live in a supposed "information age," in which pictures flash around the world at the speed of light. But the Nagasaki photos-pictures as much of the world's threatened future as of its past-took fifty years to reach the United States-being displayed for the first time only in 1995 at the Cooper-Hewitt Museum of photography in New York.

Now let me discuss the new American policies. When the Cold War ended, a question was placed before the nuclear powers. They had built their nuclear weapons in order to fight or stalemate one another. Now that the global struggle was over, would they agree to get rid of their arsenals, or would they discover some new purpose, unrelated to the Cold War, for keeping them? The question was urgent not only because nuclear danger is always urgent but because an array of other nations, including India, Pakistan, Iran, Iraq, and North Korea, among others, were considering developing nuclear arsenals and were watching to see which way the wind was blowing. Would the world, they wondered, remain nuclear-armed or otherwise? Would they "need" nuclear weapons or not?

For a decade-the careless nineteen-nineties-no clear answer was given by the nuclear powers. Nuclear weapons fell into a kind of limbo. Neither eliminated nor assigned a new role, they became characters in search of an author. As to the general public, it frankly forgot about nuclear danger. Your perception that young people in the United States have lost interest in the subject is correct. As a sometime university professor, I can testify that American students are ignorant of the most elementary facts of the nuclear age, such as the destructive power of the weapons, how many countries have them, what the Strategic Arms Reductions Talks (START) and the Nuclear Nonproliferation Treaty are. The fault is not theirs; the subject is simply no longer taught at any level of American education.

The overall political situation in the United States changed in an instant after September 11. The Bush administration gave an answer to the question about nuclear weapons that had been hanging in the air since they had lost their raison d'être through the end of the Cold War. The answer was: Yes, there is a new purpose for having nuclear weapons, and it is to prevent other countries from getting them, through the new practice of military preemption, now embodied in the proposals to overthrow the government of Iraq.

Nuclear weapons are not of course the only instruments of preemption. The United States' awesome "conventional" forces will be the first resort, with nuclear weapons held in reserve in case Saddam Hussein uses weapons of mass destruction. (It is the declared policy of the United States to respond to the use of biological or chemical weapons with nuclear retaliation, and it has asked for funds to design a new warhead for this purpose. Its name, which might have been invented by Dr. Strangelove, is the Robust Nuclear Earth Penetrator.)

And these policies, in turn, are only facets of a still broader one, spelled out in the clearest possible terms in the recently released White House document "The National Security Strategy of the United States of America" announcing the American objective of securing and preserving absolute military dominance over the entire earth. In its words, "Our forces will be strong enough to dissuade potential adversaries from pursuing a military build-up in hopes of surpassing or equaling, the power of the United States." By any definition, a program of global military dominance is an imperial program. However, there is, let me observe, a certain logic behind this policy. The world, this logic states, faces an acute danger of nuclear proliferation. It is in need of a way to stop it. The United States proposes to shoulder the responsibility single-handedly-to constitute itself as a kind of global sovereign. The danger of proliferation is by definition global-so the logic runs-therefore American military dominance must be global. The United States thus has proposed to embark on a whole series of what can be called the world's first disarmament wars.

Now as you won't be surprised to hear, I believe that this imperial logic of force is not only legally and morally unacceptable, but also constitutes a supremely perilous delusion likely to bring on the very nuclear proliferation and nuclear war it is supposed to prevent. It won't be enough, however, for those of us who reject the policy to demonstrate its failings. The fact that nuclear disarmament-formerly the aim of the peace movement-has been taken over by the promoters of war (giving new reality to Orwell's famous old words "War is Peace") is an entirely new circumstance for the peace movement to reckon with. Our most difficult job is to demonstrate that there is a different policy-a peaceful path to peace-that is fully adequate to the needs of the hour. The means of the policy would be a rejection of the logic of force and a return to the negotiations and treaties abandoned by the Bush Administration. And its indispensable foundation - do we have to say it again? - must be an unswerving commitment by all nations to the abolition of nuclear arms as well as all other weapons of mass destruction.

Jonathan Schell

Dear Jonathan Schell,

In your letter of reply, you talk about the heavy responsibility and pathos of the victims in Hiroshima and Nagasaki. I entirely share your view. They have carried out their campaign primarily to seek their own salvation, but have never failed to combine their being victimized with Japan's victimizing of people over a wide area of Asia. They have thus expressed not only their worries about the nuclear situation but also the need for Japan's reconciliation with Asia.

I was also deeply moved by your thoughts on the unborn legions of the future. I once quoted at the end of one of my novels words by Wole Soynka, a good friend of mine since my younger days: "Now forget the dead, forget even the living. Turn your mind only to the unborn."

I can never forget those people who were either killed or confined in an agonizing state of living death by the terrorists or by the unjust state authorities in our time. Whenever I come across their testimonies, I am overwhelmed by the silence of the victims and by the anger and sorrow of those who can still raise their voices. Nevertheless I find myself seeking some positive legacy for mankind engendered by the miseries of these people.

In actual fact we are currently confronted by a heap of grotesque realities which refuse to allow us to dream of such a legacy. And yet I cannot help wishing to see signs of some positive action to be taken.

For instance, I sincerely hope that the negotiations for normalizing relations between Japan and North Korea will not exclude from its agenda the abandonment of nuclear weapons development in addition to the moratorium for launching missiles as promised in the recent Pyongyang Declaration.

The situation has changed greatly as The Democratic People's Republic of Korea (North Korea) admitted its continued development of nuclear weapons, and its violation of the so-called "Agreed Framework," to Mr. Kelly, deputy assistant secretary of state, on his visit to Pyongyang.

If what you call "the American objective of securing and preserving absolute military dominance over the entire Earth" comes face to face with the line defiantly taken by Chairman Kim Jong II, we should be alarmed by the danger of an Asian version of what is about to happen in Iraq.

However, I think that there is a unique role to be played by the government of Japan, which is prepared to offer, despite its own prolonged recession, some economic assistance to North Korea provided that the parties concerned decide to step forward by extricating themselves from the American-dominated diplomacy under which they have constantly been restrained for the last 50-odd years.

Japan is in no position to talk of "nuclear weapons available," but is able to speak from its own experiences about the tremendous miseries brought by such weapons.

It would not be a matter of "offsetting" the pains caused to North Korea by the Japanese colonial rule or by the more recent "abductions" of Japanese citizens by North Korea. Should it not be rather negotiations between the two parties sharing one another's sufferings and sorrow, from which a new development, hitherto never experienced, might emerge? Should it not be a case in which sincerity on both sides for mutual reparation would go side by side with exchanging wisdom toward abandoning nuclear weapons development, which both clearly know would be a beneficial alternative?

Once this process gets into motion, the government of Japan, as a natural result, must plan to become independent from the "nuclear umbrella" of the United States. Only then will Japan play a positive role for the peace and stability of the Asia-Pacific area.

Japan should begin its response by working hand in hand with civil movements in the United States, and their now-rising European counterparts, to make the position of the United States as "a global ruler" into something of relative significance. This will be my endless, bottomless dream.

To turn to the harsh reality, however, the Senate following in the wake of the House of Representatives in the American Congress voted for the resolution to authorize President Bush to launch a military attack on Iraq. The Japanese press reports that the government of Japan, requested by the American military to expand the scale of collaboration in the Indian Ocean, has begun its preparations.

In the forthcoming week, high-ranking officials of the U. S. State Department will visit China, Korea, and, finally Japan to advise these " concerned countries " about how to cope with North Korea. The destiny of the generation who will succeed us might depend on the results of these talks.

For the past few years I have kept correspondence with intellectuals abroad. I find it particularly significant that the last of the series is with you, focussing on the theme of abandoning nuclear weapons, which has been an urgent matter to you for many years and a lifelong task for me.

In addition to these exchanged letters, I have also had opportunities to go abroad and hear what intellectuals overseas had to say at firsthand. I have found that they have different tones of voice, but share the same conviction: "There will be difficulties in the near future, but they will be resolved in the distant future, which is likely to be a bright one." These difficulties include, to begin with, economic depression, international disputes, demographic problems, food shortages, the environment, AIDS, etc.

My long-standing friend Edward Said's remark, that without this conviction of a brighter future he would not be able to be engaged in educational activities renews my respect for and trust in the genuinely authentic intellectuals, especially when I consider the reality in Palestine, Said's own leukemia, and his dedicated commitment to his work in the fields of literature and music.

Among a variety of intellectual activities, literature is destined to be created in the perilous realm of grim prospects or anticipation of the immediate future. Auden's "ironical points of light" and Orwell's pungent use of "Newspeak," which you quoted, are both rooted in this fact. Nonetheless, I will carry on my work in the faint light of the distant future.

As you have kept saying, there is the danger, both in the near and in the distant future, that nuclear weapons could render the whole of this planet Earth an utterly dark ruin. The danger periodically re-emerges, as it does now.

Dear Jonathan Schell, it is my privilege to play the intermediary between you and your young readers. In my heart of hearts I shall always keep writing my imaginary letters.

Yours sincerely,

Kenzaburo Oe

THE PRIVILEGE OF BEING ALIVE

Dear Mr. Oe,

I have never before had an exchange of letters such as ours. In the first place, we have never met. In the second, our letters are being published. Normally a letter is private-personal. Of course there is such a thing as an Open Letter, but those are usually addressed by one person or a few people to a multitude. But our letters-like the others you have exchanged in this series-are from one individual to another. I imagine that it was part of your intention in adopting this form to mingle a personal tone with a public tone. I have never heard of this being done before.

As far as I am aware, it is a new invention.

I go into all this because your letters have moved me in a personal way, and I'm wondering how to express this in front of millions of readers. Perhaps the reason is exactly your willingness to express yourself with such candor and intensity to a stranger. Perhaps it is your undimmed ardor in the thankless cause of nuclear disarmament over the decades, defying the conventional idea that idealism and passion belong to the young and fade with the passage of years, success, distinctions, honors. I'm trying to think of an eminent writer in America who would express himself as you have done and I'm having a hard time coming up with of any. Whatever the reasons, your letters have touched my heart.

Immediately following our first round of letters came the dramatic announcement by North Korea, as you mention in your last letter, that it has secretly embarked on a new program to build nuclear weapons, and may already possess some. The reaction to this news by the Bush administration was peculiar. They tended to play it down. Japanese readers, who have been hearing so much recently about the truly weird and horrifying North Korean practice of sending submarines to grab innocent Japanese people and force them to live in Korea, were no doubt startled to hear Bush spokesmen state the North Korean regime as more "conservative" than the regime of Saddam Hussein in Iraq. Perhaps people in Japan were also baffled to hear that a regime that has probably already developed nuclear weapons (North Korea) is less to be feared than one that has merely tried to develop them (Iraq).

As we have already discussed in the first round of letters, the Iraq war was to be only the first stage of a far broader American policy-one of preventing the spread of nuclear weapons by making use of the overwhelming military superiority of the United States. The North Korean announcement marks the conclusive failure of the policy. President Bush said, "The United States of America will not permit the world's most dangerous regimes to threaten us with the world's most destructive weapons." He even specifically mentioned North Korea as a member of the "axis of evil," calling it "a regime arming with missiles and weapons of mass destruction, while starving its citizens."

"Will not permit...?" Well, Caesar spoke, but the forbidden thing happened anyway. It was "permitted." That is, the United States couldn't stop it. It's interesting to note that a major reason given in this country for the difference in treatment of Iraq and North Korea is that in the event of an American attack upon it, North Korea can exact a high cost with both its conventional and nuclear forces. The city of Seoul and the American forces nearby are in immediate jeopardy. In the jargon of nuclear strategy, the United States is being "deterred." The North Koreans have explained that if they were to be assigned a place in the "axis of evil," subject to "regime change," they would defend themselves. A lesson exactly opposite to the intended one has been taught to potential proliferators by the new American policy. The lesson is: "If you want to be safe from attack by the United States, build nuclear weapons and other weapons of mass destruction, but do it secretly and quickly." Thus have nuclear weapons changed their role from a mighty club in the hands of Goliath to a lethal slingshot in the hands David.

As you can imagine, I am not one of those who hankers for an American attack on North Korea and is disappointed that the cost unfortunately has turned out to be too high. The lesson rather is that nuclear proliferation, which (together with the existing possession by nine countries of nuclear weapons) is indeed the most terrible danger that the world faces, cannot be stopped by force, not even by the force wielded by the "world's only superpower." At the root of proliferation is certain technology, certain scientific knowledge. It cannot be contained by force, any more than a mist can be dispelled by machine-gun fire. But somehow planning for the war in Iraq, immune to these lessons of experience, goes on. I am happy to report, however, that a lively antiwar movement is getting going in the United States. As you may know, more than 100,000 people showed up in Washington to protest the war. They are a minority, but the silence has been broken. Stopping the American government from continuing on its disastrous course is above all the responsibility of the American people.

How does proliferation occur? Some tankers move secretly across the oceans or a few military planes fly from one military airport to another bearing nuclear materials (in this case, the materials reportedly were sent by America's ally Pakistan to North Korea, which sent missile technology to Pakistan in exchange). Some scientists in a cave make some experiments (in this case they appear to have been North Koreans operating centrifuges that separate out bomb-grade uranium). Can the United States stop these shipments, or stay the hands of these scientists? Can it overthrow the government of every nation in which these things occur? The pretension is frankly absurd. The North Korean developments are notable in that they demonstrated its impossibility rather sooner than one might have expected. Only a political solution-only binding international treaties, of the kind already represented by the Nuclear Nonproliferation Treaty - can possibly relieve us from nuclear danger. And at the root of a political solution-I'm going to say it yet again, even though I said it in my first letter! - must be a commitment of the nuclear powers to join the rest of the world in an agreement to abolish nuclear weapons.

Dear Mr. Oe, even as you assess without illusion the dangerous trend of events facing us in the immediate future and acknowledge the unmistakable warning signs of catastrophe, you insist on taking your bearings from the faint light shed by a better distant future. Permit me to volunteer to join you in this company. Guided by dim light from that future, you set forth a moving vision of an agreement between North Korea and Japan based not on offsetting one nation's crimes against the other's but on a "sharing of sorrow" between the two countries. Certainly, the pool of common sorrow is wide and deep. Your excellent negotiating strategy (if I may put it that way) seems to me a natural consequence of the overwhelming grief you also expressed at the "silence of the victims." If these victims - with the fallen of Hiroshima and Nagasaki at the forefront - could be our representatives in Pyong Yang, Geneva, or New York, I have no doubt that the bright future would draw much nearer. And if they could be joined by the unborn generations that we threaten to shut out of existence through our nuclear folly, as Wole Soyinka said, then that future would come this very day. The question for the dead would be, "Did we die in vain?" The question for the unborn would be "Shall we come into existence or not?" Wouldn't they decide to live? Shouldn't we who now have the privilege of being alive let them?

Yours truly,

Jonathan Schell

027

ROBERT DANNIN

DEFENDING THE PASSIONATE OBSERVER
APRIL 17 2003

THE FINAL WORD IS THAT WHEN ALL IS SAID AND DONE, THERE IS, AT THE ORIGIN OR THE END ... A WORD THAT IS NOT FEIGNED, A MEANING THAT DOES NOT TRICK.
Jacques Derrida

What is the truth of war photography? How can we dispute the truthfulness of war, which is always based on deceit, without deconstructing the messenger and his/her images?

It is my belief that the public desires a reliable frame of reference to guide its political and ethical deliberations. **For example, I think that the picture essays of James Nachtwey that follow this article are a reasonable and powerful way to reconsider the events of September 11, 2001 as resulting from an imperial disregard for the lives of the world's poor and sick masses.** Put quite simply, if American is the world's superpower why does it tolerate, if not engender and then ignore, the violence and suffering depicted in these photos?

The problems of interpreting photography stem from mistrust and recognition of a corporate media empire that often works hand-in-glove with the forces of economic exploitation and political repression. Who can trust a commercially tarnished mass media? What good is served by its superior technical achievements? How authentic are its aesthetic values? As the underlying issues of resentment toward the media, these questions imply that deception lies with the photograph's occult properties. Sometimes it doesn't tell us enough, and sometimes too much. One way or another the image lacks essence, though not verisimilitude to the external events it narrates. It is insufficiently accountable for its own existence and therefore suspect as an element in our reaction to the news.

This insufficiency is an absence that does not belong to the sign itself, rather it describes a problem of the signifier, that activity, person, or thing which makes the sign. It is a problem of the frame of reference - the sum of all decisions involving the signifier - that characterizes the intent behind the image. For example, the esteemed critic Susan Sontag demonstrates that the artistic way to compensate for this insufficiency of truth in war photography lies in the photographer's choice to construct a virtual battlefield. As a means to assert puritanical intent, this solution leaves no doubt about the brutality depicted because it has no other referent but the horror of war. It eliminates the extraneous aspects of war-as-reality, and with it all the political ambiguities that could possibly adhere to the image. It does so by returning the signifier into a dispassionate manipulation of studio props. It is horrible photography yet supposedly good art.

Here, the critic summons the artist and his audience to suspend the 'normal' intentions that anonymously saturate the straightforward perception of everyday reality yet are immediately suspect for their covert role in adjusting how the image looks and where we see it. This is the logic of the true aesthete and also the kind of analysis that the critic can profess comfortably from an armchair. The image acquires greater truth when the signified becomes a simulacra of reality because the act of substitution results in a negation of doubt. It is an act that asserts the artist's privilege to replace content with pure aesthetic form and thereby re-present the image as something other than its corrupted, ideological reality. In this case, the simulation of a battlefield strewn with the dead and dying becomes a total sign whose existence no longer depends upon a sequence of other images that connects it to the manifold sources of interpretive contamination - propaganda, spin, or serendipity. Within a single frame it demonstrates, in other words, an emancipated truth about war. Its excessive dramatization challenges the particularity of a violent event by exposing the truth of violence per se. In this realm only, the insufficiency of intentions can be regulated. All the objective and subjective telemetries capable of generating doubt or confusion are suppressed in the process.

Unfortunately, there is a hidden political agenda in this view. I would call it a bureaucratic coup d'oeil (glance) that expropriates the signifier to benefit the critic who seizes a very specific authority to judge the sign for its authenticity. This is especially true in the case of an historically-conditioned criticism that reflects, unconsciously or not, the priorities of capitalist accumulation. By displacing the signifier's authority, the critic facilitates the alienation of that labor from its product and assumes a responsibility for managing its symbolism to the audience.

This type of criticism of war photography cannot be distinguished from a supervised perception of signs derived from the more familiar managed-consumption of other products that is generally called a market. As to its impact, many philosophers since Heidegger have expressed the idea that truth manifests itself through fiction. But this is not an exclusive relationship. There is science, for instance. And fiction is a form of writing. Photography lies somewhere between writing and speech as a different order of visual code. Its vision must be taken as seriously as its images. There are even reliable authors whose work, when seen integrally as is Nachtwey's in this volume, articulates an unvarnished reality.

What explains the critic's impulse to manage perceptions of war at this level? If it is not political censorship (and I don't think it is), can there be another pedagogy at work? What about the critic's responsibility to question the circumstances in which the photos are viewed? If that is an essential part of the photographic process too, then it can't be immune from criticism.

The critic's pronouncements barely engage this subject, taking it as a given that war photos are bound to appear wherever they usually appear. This presupposition fails to dislodge the quantitative value of the sign. Yet that is precisely the critic's task, to write anything but not to tamper negatively with commerce.

In fact, justifying the relative value of images has become an urgent and serious job due to the explosive quantity of photographs. Yesterday's audience was limited to newspapers, magazines, and expensive photographic books. Television and documentary cinema were somewhat separate entities governed by their own rules of profitability. The art gallery and museum remained firmly under the sway of painting and sculpture. As for print, the regular publication of individual photos and sometimes photo essays was determined by an economy of space, its price calculated along with that of advertising layouts and editorial copy, the aggregate divided by the total number of pages in a magazine's single edition. The amount of space available for pictures was thus limited by production costs, resulting not only in a scarcity of published images but also in strategic editing that subordinated them to printed commentary (cheaper, less ambiguous) and paid advertising (all profit). In the years since Reagan's colonial wars in Latin America, the media industry has coalesced into several large monopolies which, in turn, dominate the unprofitable and often anarchic photo industry. Henceforth, the rationalization of photography has proceeded hand-in-hand with advances in electronic production, always with the same goal of greater profits.

From the time of the Desert Storm (1991) until the hypocritically labeled Operation Iraqi Freedom (2003), photography has experienced unprecedented technological changes that have cheapened its costs of production. Mainly, the photojournalist's work has been digitalized, meaning faster production, higher productivity, more profit, and more work for the photographer. The introduction of the internet, powerful microprocessors, vast memories devices, and broadband cable have made pictures as ubiquitous as print and more widely disseminated than ever before.

Another pivotal development was the displacement of space by time as the ultimate measure of profit. With broadband and DVD, aided by digital printing, the question of space has practically dissolved into the more flexible dimension of time. One image-file inserted on top of another glides into sequence under control of either the viewer's mouse or a programmed slide show. Although space is no longer a constraining factor at the site of production, there remain certain limitations where is it consumed, for example, the size of the display terminal.

An illustration of the positioning or deployment of signs occurred after 1985 when the Italian textile giant, Benetton, grafted war photos onto its print advertisements in order to grab the busy consumer's attention. Once the intended effect was accomplished, however, the campaign generated more controversy than sales and gradually evaporated. Today, the price of LCD screens is falling rapidly. This enables the advertiser to display the shocker for just the few seconds required to draw the consumer toward a slide show of more conventional, though alluring, product images. Once the domain of film and TV, SPFX (special effects) is proliferating rapidly across the commercial landscape thanks to this new technology. It overcomes the limitations of space by projecting multiple images onto the same electronic poster or billboard without substantially increasing the cost. This strategy naturally demands that the consumer spend more time looking at images. We are left to contemplate how this will rebound on textual commentary, or how thinking is likely to be modified by this intense cerebral multi-tasking. The only certainty is that it will not enhance highway safety.

With such easy access to digital images, the audience can practice individual strategies for consuming them. Along with these customized uses of photography arises the element of unpredictability. This contradicts the rationalization of profits and creates unexpected consequences elsewhere in the system. For instance, images can become elements for quickly mobilizing public opinion, a phenomenon evident in the rapid consolidation of the international anti-globalization movement that followed a decade's worth of images - some published by Benetton - depicting war, genocide, and pestilence in Africa. This rallying of outraged young adults occurred under the radar of the normally vigilant media. Once aware of these developments, the powerful conglomerates responded by accelerating the hostile takeover of the traditional picture agencies. Two huge conglomerates, Getty and Corbis, seized control of entire collections of visual documentation in a relentless mergers and acquisitions blitz from 1995-2000. The media barons understood photographs not so much in terms of their accuracy of historical truth, rather as copyrighted software that could be endlessly packaged for resale.

The effect was the same in both cases, however - the blatant suppression of eyewitness history. Coinciding with the recapitalization of the picture agencies was a rationalization of editing and scanning to meet the rising demand for visual data. A strategy geared to saturate the online market addressed fear of economic risk in the world of broadband commerce. One reliable tactic was to manufacture scarcity. Corbis, owned by Microsoft founder William Gates, thus acquired and promptly sequestered the Bettman Archives in an underground bunker. A meager selection of 'meaningful' images was retained for future circulation, but the lion's share of this renowned collection of historical imagery was successfully eliminated from the public domain. Access to these immense caverns of visual knowledge will be henceforth as probable as a trip to the Vatican library.

What Gates and others call good business, Orwell described as feeding the memory hole.

Despite a near-monopoly of images, the even trickier problem lay in organizing their mass consumption. Where once there existed regular magazine subscribers, surfers now cruise the net with all the flakiness of their saltwater kin. Managing this risk is an arduous task requiring the kind of artificial intelligence that remains elusive. Consequently, there is an urgent call for a chief signifier who can administer interpretation and, by establishing value, confer desirability upon a given commodity or style. There must be a vested authority to assign value to photographs even as they are being distributed among their possible venues. From oversized prints hanging in the Metropolitan Museum and fashionable Chelsea galleries to the postage stamp vignettes appearing in newspapers and zines, the arbitration of artistic value is anything but a measure of popular acclamation or genuine political interest. Amid a blizzard of images, the chief signifier designates those believed to encase the greatest truths. The viewing public accedes to these choices, wondering why one image and not another?

During the Vietnam War, the social philosopher Herbert Marcuse coined the term, repressive tolerance, to explain the idea that we embrace all values without discriminating the virtuous from the outrageous. Repressive tolerance, he noted, has become the greatest obstacle to critical thought and a most useful tool for accommodating political will to the mass media. As quickly as images are filed into the great historical database, the chief signifier defiles them, nullifies their impact in advance by forewarning the audience of their hidden agendas, rendering them almost tolerable as profane objects yet severely lacking in truths. Functioning as agents of power, connoisseurs deconstruct the frescoes of quotidian horrors by proclaiming certain works and categories too corrupt for permanent or even momentary installation. It comes as no surprise that we are handed a revised script on how to read pictures at the precise moment of their greatest potential. For all the complaints about excessive technical precision or the beauty of war photos, is it not really the critic who aestheticizes this discourse by seasoning it with a curator's vocabulary?

Acknowledging the problematic role of the sign as a commodity, albeit a special one, restores critical insight into the editing and presentation of photographs. In resuscitating the viewer's authority, it confers a freedom to trust one's own capacity to interpret the message. But it has not yet answered some important questions. The first concerns the photograph's destination. Where is it supposed to be delivered? How will it ever get there? The second is about the unity of the signifier and signified. Is there a contract between image and reality? How does it account for the fantasies likely to blossom once the viewer sees a photo at varying distances of time and space from its origin?

To respond, we now turn to a real-time discussion.

One evening in April 2000, about 200 people crowded into a slide presentation and lecture at the Barnes & Noble bookstore in Manhattan's Union Square. The subject was a recently published book entitled Inferno (New York & London: Phaidon, 1999); the presenter was James Nachtwey, its photographer-author. The projection and the author's narrative occasioned a straightforward discussion of violence - the violence depicted in the photos and the personal risk incurred by the photographer. The audience listened respectfully to a few technical questions before eagerly returning to ones about the groups and individuals responsible for the wars and the deaths so graphically displayed. The photographer observed that it was his role to submit this evidence directly. If individuals and governments were morally indictable for these acts, then further investigation and political activism might be the expected, if not desirable, consequence.

The final question, directed at the audience instead of the photographer, asked how often they encountered similar opportunities to assemble. Very seldom, came the collective answer. Definitely, they added in response to their interlocutor's follow-up challenge: Did they think that the sponsoring corporations ought to provide more space, both printed and public, for regular viewing and discussion of such matters? This audience of after-work browsers and the curious, among them a few cognoscenti, affirmed the idea that photographs were an essential method for political deliberation.

Were the pictures of Inferno reaching the right destination?

Let us imagine a deregulated journalism. What conditions are necessary for its existence? How does it authorize the terms for a critical self-evaluation?

First, let's read what the photographer thinks about the destination of his work.

MY JOB IS TO SHARE WHAT I'VE SEEN WITH THE REST OF THE WORLD BECAUSE IT IS ONE WORLD AND THERE ARE INFLUENCES AND PRESSURES THAT CAN BE BROUGHT TO BEAR ON ANY GIVEN SITUATION ALTHOUGH VERY RARELY WITH IMMEDIATE RESULTS. BUT EVENTUALLY PRESSURE AND INFLUENCE CAN COME TO BEAR. MY JOB IS TO REACH THE MASSES, AND I THINK THAT WHEN INFLUENTIAL POLITICAL LEADERS CAN BRING SOME POLITICAL CLOUT INTO IT, WHEN THEY SEE THESE IMAGES AND READ THESE REPORTS, WHETHER IT'S ON TELEVISION OR MAGAZINES OR NEWSPAPERS, WHETHER IT'S MY WORK OR SOMEBODY ELSE'S WORK, WE ALL CONTRIBUTE TO IT. AND THEY'RE MOVED BY WHAT THEY READ AND WHAT THEY SEE. THEY HAVE AN EMOTIONAL REACTION TO IT. THEY HAVE A SENSE OF RIGHT OR WRONG ABOUT IT. THEY KNOW THAT IF THEY FEEL THAT WAY, THAT MILLIONS AND MILLIONS OF OTHER PEOPLE PROBABLY FEEL THE SAME WAY TOO. AND THERE'S A KIND OF CONSTITUENCY BUILT THAT'S IMPLICIT. THAT THERE IS SOMETHING UNACCEPTABLE GOING ON, AND IT'S THEIR JOB TO TRY AND DO SOMETHING ABOUT IT. AND THERE'S A METAPHYSICAL BELIEF IN ALL OF THIS FOR ME. IT'S ALMOST LIKE PEOPLE BELIEVING IN PRAYER. THEY SEND VIBES OUT THERE AND HOPE THAT IT HAS AN AFFECT. WELL, I'M SENDING OUT THE VIBES TO PEOPLE BECAUSE I THINK WE HAVE EACH OTHER AND THAT'S ALL WE'VE GOT. I DON'T BELIEVE IN DIVINE INTERVENTION. WE CAUSE OUR OWN PROBLEMS, AND IT'S UP TO US TO MAKE OUR OWN SOLUTIONS. AND I THINK THE BEST THING THAT I CAN DO IS TRY AND MAKE AN APPEAL TO THE BEST THAT'S IN PEOPLE AND HOPE THAT IT HAS SOME EFFECT.[1]

Digital information can be sent in various ways and can be directed to individuals or groups. On the one hand, individual readership is the dominant mode of consumption right now. We get our images through the media and view them in solitude, occasionally sharing them in the privacy of homes and offices. On the other hand, as raw materials passing through the commercial networks discussed above, war photos are studied and discussed by editors and media executives. They are mediated, properly speaking, and exposed to the errant trajectories that critics warn about. It doesn't matter too much who makes the choices or how. Anyone with the substantial experience in the magazine business, for example, will confirm that editorial proclivities have varied little over the years or among individuals. Rarely has any editor or publication succeeded in modifying the presentation or choice of images from the standards imposed by space and its commercial dictates. It is also a well known fact that stylistic variation - e.g., the use of color versus black & white - reflects the trends of product advertising. In other words, any significant change results from decisions about the best way to manipulate viewers. Similar criteria, the same individuals in some cases, govern the production of most photographic books.

We have already cited the example of Benetton as an unsuccessful attempt to reverse this process. However, it is also worth noting that the revival of black and white advertising in the early 1990s was a retaliation against Sebastião Salgado's highly-acclaimed documentary photos of the global proletariat through the expropriation of his "style."[2]

Though there are many tales purporting to account for the success of these pictures, the insider's version merits attention. On the basis of a preliminary essay about Brazilian gold miners, Salgado and his agent distributed nearly two dozen subsequent essays by offering joint-stock in his production (but not his copyright). These contracts assured simultaneous publication rights for all participating magazines. The plan bypassed the exclusive "first world rights" normally demanded by rich U.S. publications. Shares were expensive and publishers paid a steep penalty for non-publication, but this contract secured the largest audience ever worldwide for a series of still photo essays. Above all, it showed a widespread determination to fight media monopolies.

Furthermore, the method aimed deliberately to promote an unmediated correspondence between the signified and signifier. The honest depiction of class struggle has been and always will be an effort to capture space (or time) in the mass media. While only one element in the positional warfare of class conflict, it is nonetheless essential because it illustrates unity and solidarity, not simply as a possibility, but rather as a tangible reality of the sign. It implies a vantage point where the oppressed can see beyond the babble of nationalism and linguistic differences in order to summon a global common cause. Here photography attains an unprecedented level of self-directed mimesis. It manifests a potential for international revolutionary change.

Typically, this breakthrough has earned the continuing negativity of many influential critics like Sontag. Noblesse oblige. If it seems at first, an error for her to identify Salgado as a "war photographer" - since he does not generally frequent the world's killing fields - then, on second thought, the label applies after all, thanks to his strategic advance in the battle to liberate the sign from detention under the critic's watchful gaze. Perhaps it would be more accurate to call him a class-war photographer.

The publication of Nachtwey's Inferno in 1999 opened a new front in this conflict. As a gargantuan project, it assembled a decade's worth of hellish landscapes the likes of which had not been compiled in a monograph since Dante Alligheri himself. With few exceptions, the book provoked ferocious resistance, for the battleground had changed. All the potential outlets for mass publication were by now completely devoured by the predatory media conglomerates. The old editorial chain of command was gone. Efforts to serialize the book in mass market publications were met with apologies by corporate flak-catchers who regularly defer even their least consequential decisions until hearing the daily pronunciamento from the executive suite.

At Talk, a now-defunct Miramax-Hearst venture, the renown chief editor dismissed the project summarily after speed-leafing its 500 pages in less than ten minutes. On the scene were three subordinates, apparently yanked from central casting, who had no idea where Chechnya might be located or in what decade the Afghan civil war occurred. Quickly bored by the presentation, the chief escaped into the hallway where her designer-clad valets were waiting, as if in suspended animation, for the next lines of their script. Further downtown at the revered pseudo-intellectual weekly, a carefully packaged box of galley proofs was returned after a few weeks and without comment. A respectful personal letter from the photographer to the chief lay unopened. Next door at the flagship monthly, the chief expressed interest in putting the photographer's portrait on the magazine's last page. But was he sexy enough? Over at Pravda, the weekly supplement's editor-in-chief repulsed dogged efforts to place Inferno on his agenda. He order his vassals to repeat threadbare lies to the effect that their publication never recapitulated old wars (or even recently simmering conflicts) and never featured an author or his book.

Ironically, each publication was a likely venue for the musings of the critics. This is a clue to the organization of values in this milieu. It is a fact, too, that commercial priorities rule. In the rare cases when the serialization of Inferno was actually contemplated, the redesign of its presentation became a difficult issue. How would these explosive images fit onto a menu of polished automobiles and buff fashion models?

Who would be interested in shopping after seeing bombed cities and bloody children? Would advertisers withdraw because they objected to their political overtones? Similar questions arose at European publications although a few traditionalists still commanded sufficient authority to offer space. They certainly proved themselves more adept at gerrymandering and angling the class perspective within an environment of rationed editorial privileges.

These experiences teach us that multinationals cannot be entrusted to advance critical information. They pay their employees to scrutinize the contents for any trace of visual subversion. If necessary, others are hired to modify them. When challenged, they always have recourse to the chief signifier who arbitrates values not only in the board room but with equal impact upon the executive's personal art collections. In the end, to mistakenly identify these media resources as exclusive destinations is to surrender the power of historical recollection. Their only real goal is to detour the sign into the corporate dead letter office where it is disassembled, deconstructed, and shredded.

Rethinking this process necessitates better, more democratic ways to undermine the global monopolies and deliver messages to the right address. One can imagine direct boycotts that summon the media giants to open their pages and commit more bandwith to wider, unexpurgated vistas as opposed to the tunnel vision they currently offer. But that is about as likely to succeed as indirect actions toward their corporate sponsors. In passing we should also mention the tactic of mass demonstrations at media offices. This possibility was discussed in reaction to Time-Warner CNN's policy of staffing its broadcasts with dozens of army generals, a blatant exercise of military censorship. One cannot predict much luck here either, although these tactics should not be abandoned by those who favor such direct confrontations with power.

Unfortunately, there are very few public spaces left where politics can be openly engaged. The agora has been miniaturized into websites and listservs that can be useful, though not a substitute for the cashiered media, as a means of emancipating occupied zones such as schools, universities, malls, houses of worship, and other cultural institutions. It is not inconceivable that in the totally wired near-future, digital photos may be beamed directly from the field and projected to citizens forums. Interactive dialogue with photographers and indigenous correspondents will provide a new model for independent media. Larger groupings or schools of particular interest groups would reconsecrate public time and space or, possibly, revive the athenaeum where uncoerced dialogue and unfettered criticism could take place globally. Such public meeting places are not currently defined, but our imagination can seek appropriate models in the anthropology of both existing and extinct societies.

Alternatively, the existing models for active dissident can be enhanced by commandeering the electronic revolution. It is much easier to produce the samizdat (books of the Soviet underground press) with desktop publishing than when such offset manuscripts comprised the intellectual and artistic core of the anti-Soviet struggle. The essential requirement is that the dissent reject a bureaucratic, hyper-commercialized media while understanding simultaneously the appeal of an aesthetically complete work of art or literature. Like the relationship of serious musicians to Napster, some artists will acknowledge a personal responsibility to the public sphere by donating at least some of their production. (Serious photographers rarely make money on books anyway, or so publishers tell them.) The dazibao, an example from China, catalyzed the brief 1978 democracy wall movement and were instrumental again in 1989's Beijing Spring mobilizations. The low cost amplification of these and other examples is key to the sustainable development of an alternative media. The goal is proliferation and a gradual overwhelming of the repressive media apparatus.

The idea of a non-hegemonic media implies that order will emerge, nonetheless, from the chaos now typical of the web. This vision entails an interactive participation - a non-exclusivity based upon the convivial use of cameras and digital communications. Whereas there can be no rules for exclusion based on location (url), standards must still prevail. The signifier can never abandon its sense of artistic quality as the foundation of clarity and universality because it is only through terms evocative of human sensations - voice, music, movement, color, form, etc. - that representation succeeds. The problem of an alternative media comes down finally to its aesthetic dimension. No audience will give its attention to anything unless it is imbued with style. This is yet another phenomenon described years ago by Marcuse who called it repressive desublimation, meaning that we live in a world where that which is important can be described as sexy, cool, or phat. Aesthetic appeal cannot be ignored, even by those who are most determined to convey the ugly, horrible truth of war. McLuhan stated the same principle when he declared the medium to be the message. Social transformation will succeed or fail according its general appeal to the masses.

This requires a sustained emphasis on the signifier. It suggests that rethinking the impact of war photography also means debunking the shibboleths of photographic criticism. What is obvious to anyone who visits museums and art galleries is the inherent prejudice against photojournalism. Yesterday's vanguard of taste have circled their wagons around these repositories of aesthetic chic in an attempt to exclude the most democratic art form since charcoal and ocher were applied to limestone caves about twenty-thousand years ago. They instruct the uninitiated on the techniques of old masters. They recount stories of the rage and unquenchable passions of the moderns, all the while celebrating the brilliance and conceptualism of contemporary dilettantes. But when it comes to photography, they erect defensive fortifications and ready themselves for battle to protect these palaces from an intrusive public who needs them badly for the contemplative, secular refuge that they offer. If not the last bastions of elite privilege, these venerable places certainly remain exclusive temples to the symbolic reproduction of humanity. They are the workshops of high culture, as important as banks to maintaining the imperial status quo. Today, they are concerned mainly with recruiting a vigorous defense against the notion of a cultural perestroika.

How do they wage this defensive campaign?

Their refined approach betrays an underlying treachery and deceit. For deceit it is when the criteria of virtue for judging what is already inside the palace becomes the weapon of choice to negate what is outside. Planet news illustrated by photos of war, suffering, pestilence, and famines is too beautiful, they claim, too technically perfect, overly aesthetic, or distracting.

But they are institutions of culture and commerce, it could be argued. Who arrogates the right to intrude upon our business?

A right or privilege?

Neither, replies the outsider. These institutions, like public schools, are all that remains of public space. They are among the principal objectives of a low intensity turf battle waged by elements of the corporate communications empire. If lost they will surely be absorbed into some homeland security's ministry of truth.

The analogy to education is apt. Schools, like museums, are also workshops where the system of signs is manufactured. Their pedagogy determines our consciousness and its limitations on matters of morality and politics. If the aesthetic dimension is overruled by the arbiters of value, then the humanities and sciences will be one-dimensionalized in the process. The lyrical expressions of poets and writers will be tossed out the window. Dickens and Zola probed an ugly reality filled with black expectorations and dead dogs, yet their prose is magnificent. It reflects the passionate observer's desire to communicate the suffering of the nineteenth century working classes. Analogously, putrid cadavers, beautiful in their stillness, save many lives. Science and mathematics owe their development to a contemplation of idealized forms and virtuous process. Nature itself, the one we work to conserve with great passion, is but an imaginary perfection immortalized by a few lines of scripture and thereafter held beyond our reach in order to keep us striving. Its depiction - whether romantic, cubist, or realist - is constructive activity, so many attempts to fuse light, color, and form into a trustworthy sign of hope, like a prayer sent out to create an effect.

028

JAMES NACHTWEY

THE PASSION OF ALLAH
> PAKISTAN 2001

◊ **Karachi**
Heroin addicts tried to recover in
a rehabilitation center outside Karachi.

> **Peshawar**
Addicts in Peshawar begged at the
window of a passing car.

> **Karachi**
Shadows played on the ground as
addicts shot up in Karachi.

> **Quetta**
An addict in Quetta smoked heroin in a
cemetery at the rising of a full moon.

> **Peschawar**
A heroin addict died by the side of the road in
Peshawar and was readied to be
buried in a shallow grave by his fellow addicts.

028 James Nachtwey
The Passion of Allah

Page 239

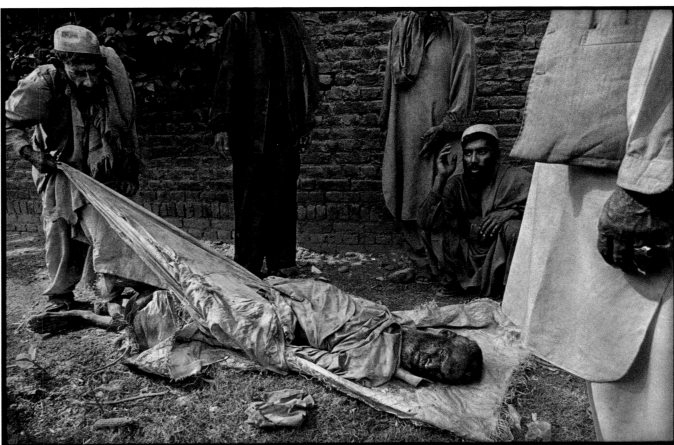

THE PASSION OF ALLAH
> KOSOVO 1999

◊ **Kosovo**
Ethnic Albanian Kosovars were forced to flee their homes during a violent campaign of deportation.

◊ **Kosovo**
Having crossed the border at dusk, a large group of deportees were too late to be admitted a camp and made shelter for the night beneath huge sheets of plastic draped over their tractors. Ethnic Albanian Kosovars were forced to flee their homes during a violent campaign of deportation, pillage and genocide carried by Serbian armed forces, police and irregulars. The deportees fled on foot, by horse-cart, tractor, car and truck. Hundreds of thousands crossed into neighboring Albania at Morini border post. Often the influx of Kosovars was made up of women, children and old people, the men having been taken captive, forced into hidden or killed.

◊ **Kosovo**
Sometimes the truckloads of Kosovars contained only men, when the women had been forced by the Serbs to stay behind.

◊ **Kosovo**
Recently arrived deportees referred to public lists in search of the location of family and friends from whom they had been separated.

> **Bellanica**
A photograph of a man who had been killed by Serbs in the town of Bellanica was found by a neighbor.

◊ **Djakovica**
The old city of Djakovica was thoroughly sacked and burned by the Serbs. As they began to return to Kosovo, the residents of the city toured the ruins and often met those whom they had been separated.

◊ **Meja**
Meja was the site of one of the innumerable massacres committed by Serb forces. Many of the victims were lined up in a field and shot point-blank. Those who managed to escape into the forest were hunted down and killed one by one.

◊ **Kosovo**
Throughout Kosovo the ethnic Albanians returned to their destroyed homesteads.

◊ **Prizren**
A political poster bearing the face of Slobodan Milosevic was smeared with mud and torn off the wall by the children of Prizren.

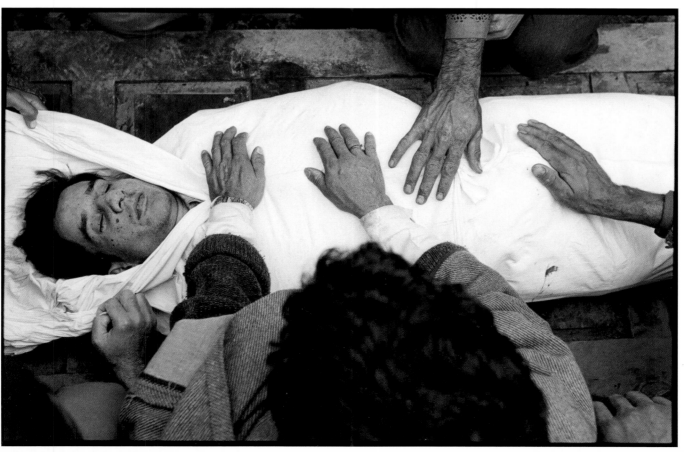

< **Srinagar**
Women mourned at the
funeral of a Moslem who was
killed by Indian
security Forces in Srinagar.

◊ **Srinagar**
In a routine search for suspected militants, an Indian soldier examined the credentials of people on a bus in Srinagar.

◊ **Kashmir**
Mourners paid their last respects to a Moslem who was killed by Indian security forces.

◊ **Srinagar**
Islamic militants shot by Indian security forces outside Srinagar were viewed by a villager.

◊ **Srinagar**
An Indian soldier lined up people at a bus station in Srinagar to search them for weapons and to examine their papers.

THE PASSION OF ALLAH
> SOMALIA 1992

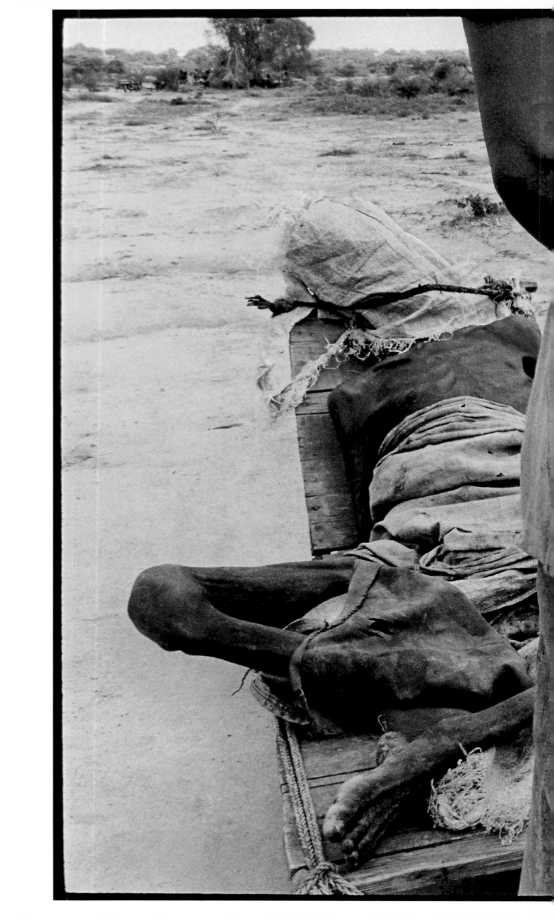

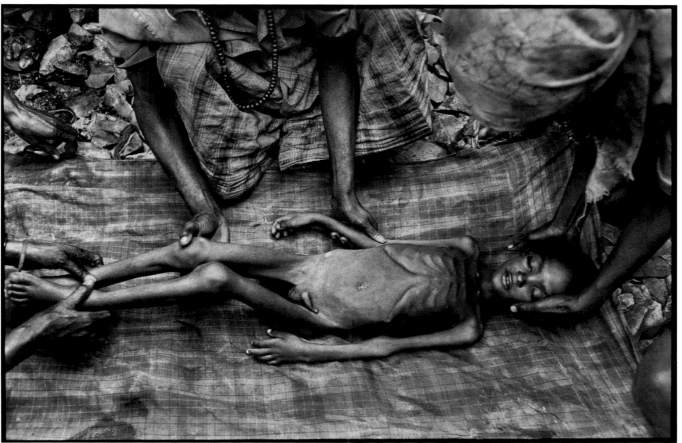

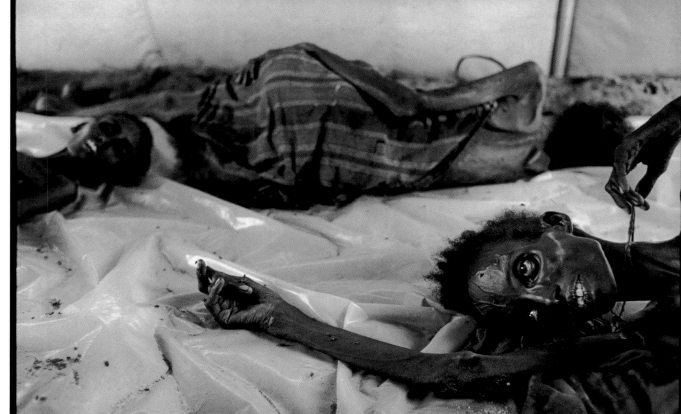

◊ **Bardera**
A mother lifted her child to carry him to his grave.

◊ **Baidoa**
The dead were sewn into shrouds made from articles of clothing or empty emergency food sacks.

◊ **Bardera**
He was transported by wheelbarrow to the burial ground.

◊ **Bardera**
Moments after the boy died, another famine victim lingered an the narrow margin between life and death.

THE PASSION OF ALLAH
> INDONESIA 1998 - 2000

◊ **Jakarta**
Students who occupied the Parliament complex in Jakarta exulted at the announcement of Suharto's resignation.

> **Jakarta**
A beggar bathed his children in the polluted canal in Jakarta.

> **Jakarta**
A beggar worked in the midst of heavy traffic in Jakarta.

> **East Java**
Miners in a sulfur pit inside a volcano in East Java labored unprotected in a dense cloud of corrosive smoke.

> Jakarta
A homeless boy slept of the effect of
drugs on the streets of Jakarta.

028 James Nachtwey
The Passion of Allah

THE PASSION OF ALLAH
> WEST BANK 2000

◊ **Bethlehem**
Family members mourned a
Palestinian man killed by Israeli soldiers
at a funeral in Bethlehem.

> **Ramallah**
Palestinian demonstrators in Ramallah
battled the Israeli military with stones during the
early phases of the second Intifada.

> **Bethlehem**
Palestinian militants marched through
Bethlehem during the funeral
of a man killed by Israeli troops.

> **Ramallah**
Palestinian pallbearers carried Ibrahim
Shahala who was killed by the Israeli army through
the streets of Ramallah.

> **East Jerusalem**
A Palestinian demonstrator placed his hands in blood of a
comrade who had been shot in the head by Israeli army troops outside
the Dome of the Rock Mosque in East Jerusalem.

THE PASSION OF ALLAH
> CHECHNIA 1995 - 1996

◊ **Chechnia**
A Chechen rebel fought from a
destroyed building on the front line.

> **Chechnia**
A woman who had ventured out to buy
supplies was killed by a mortar shell. Her neighbor
discovered her lying in the street.

> **Chechnia**
The residents of Grozny had to
brave the bombing and shelling in order to
fetch water from outdoor wells.

> **Chechnia**
Two old women tried to flee the city by foot during
the bombardment.

> **Chechnia**
The neighbor of the dead woman then found the women's husband, killed by the same shell.
A group of Chechen men passed by, tried to console the neighbor, then took the dead
man's carton of cigarettes. Later his hat was taken and he was left, frozen in the middle of the road where he died.

028 James Nachtwey
The Passion of Allah

Page 273

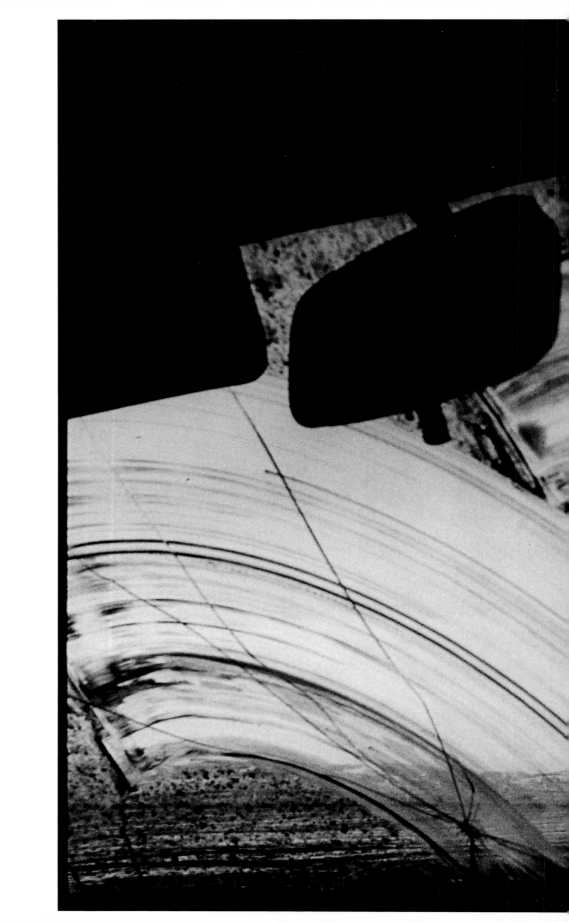

< **Chechnia**
A Chechen Muslim stopped his car for noon prayers in the middle of a road wide open to attack by Russian aircraft and artillery.

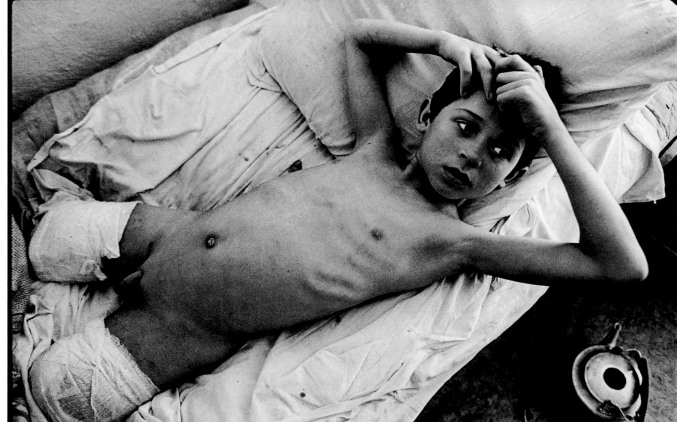

◊ **Grozny**
Boys from a orphanage played on a destroyed Russian tank and wandered through the ruins of Gronzny.

◊ **Chechnia**
Pallbearers came to a house take a woman's husband.

◊ **Chechnia**
A Chechen envoy crossed no-man's land during cease-fire negotiations with the Russians.

◊ **Chechnia**
A young boy lost his legs to the Russian bombardment.

THE PASSION OF ALLAH
> BOSNIA 1993 - 1994

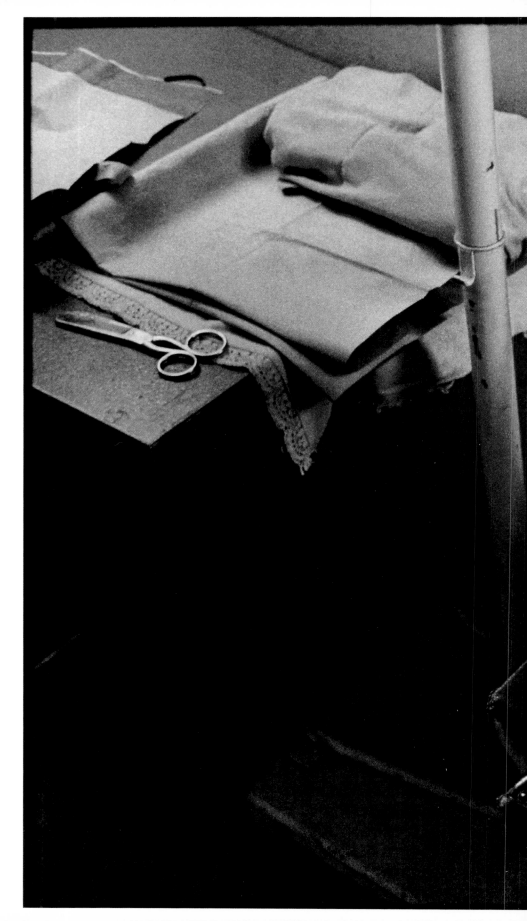

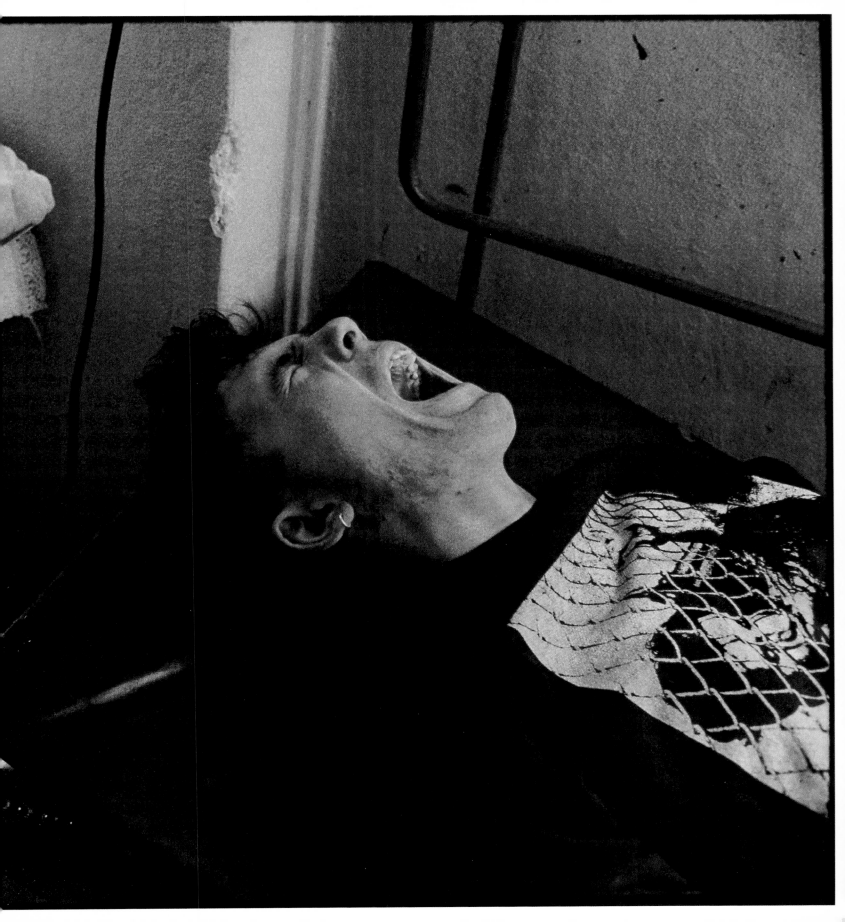

< **Brcko**
A Bosnian commando had
penetrated the Serbians lines
in Brcko. He was detected and
hit by a ritle-granade. His foot
was shredded, but he made it
back to his own lines. In a
school that had been converted
into a field hospital, surgical
preparations began before he
was anesthetized.

◊ **Bosnia**
A bedroom became battlefield as a Croatian fired at his Muslim neighbours.

◊ **Knin**
The foyer of an apartment block was covered with blood after the battle for Knin.

◊ **Rahic**
A Serbian infantry attack near the village of Rahic, outside Brcko, was successfully repulsed by Bosnian forces. The Serbs who where killed in action were collected from the battlefield and taken behind Bosnian lines. They were dumped in a farmyard, identified, and returned to their comrades the next day.

◊ **Brcko**
The Bosnian soldier killed in action were brought to the mosque in a villa outside Brcko where the were identified by their families.

> **Brcko**
The village park was converted into a cemetery for the war dead. Bosnian soldiers were laid to rest in the same field where, before the war, they had played soccer.

THE PASSION OF ALLAH
> AFGHANISTAN 1996 - 2001

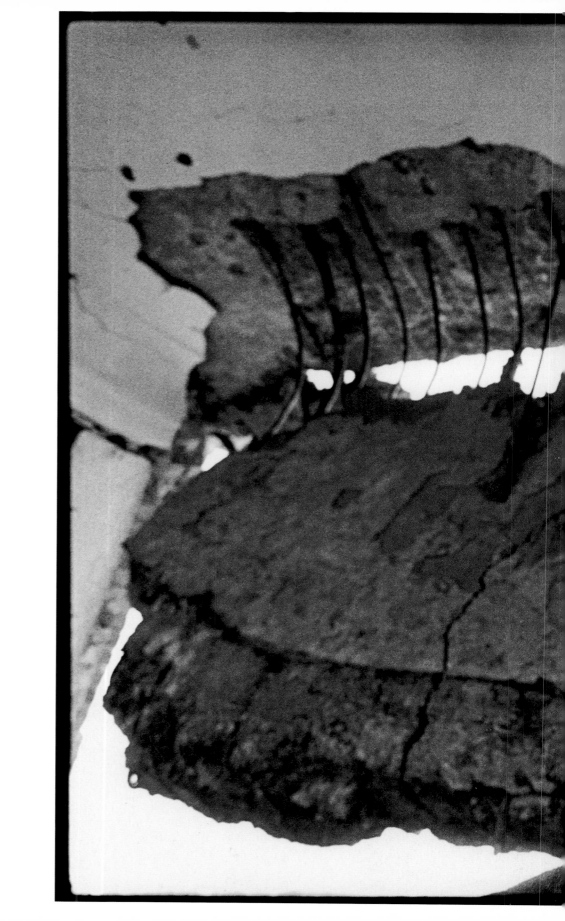

◊ **Torah Borah**
Anti-Taliban fighters prayed
during the siege
of Torah Borah, 2001.

◊ **Kabul**
A woman mourned her brother,
who was killed in a Taliban
rocket attack on Kabul, 1996.

◊ **Torah Borah**
Anti-Taliban fighters took
shelter from sniper fire in the
mountains of Torah Borah,
2001.

◊ **Kunduz**
A Taliban soldier lay dying in
the streets of Kunduz after the
city was retaken by
anti-Taliban forces, 2001.

◊ **Afghanistan**
The game of Buzkashi was brought to Afghanistan by Genghis Khan, 1996.

◊ **Afghanistan**
A mother comforted her eleven-year-old-son, who lost his leg to a land mine, 1996.

◊ **Afghanistan**
Shiites flagellated themselves on the holy day of Ashura. 1996.

◊ **Kabul**
Land mine victims learned to use prosthetic limbs at an ICRC clinic in Kabul 1996.

> **Kabul**
Sufis prayed in a trance-like state in a mosque in central Kabul 1996.

029

JOHN K. COOLEY

PROXIES AND PROXY WARS:
20TH CENTURY MISHAPS AND DISASTERS

In September 1993, almost precisely eight years before the delayed but terrible consequences of America's proxy intervention of Afghanistan in 1979-89, I found myself on a mountain road, around 15,000 feet above sea level in another remote Asian country, Tibet. The driver of the rickety tourist bus was carefully negotiating a lofty and precipitous pass. During the climb up from the rugged environs of Lhasa, we had passed gleaming glaciers and turquoise-colored lakes on the northern flanks of the Himalayas. From lonely guard posts, sentries of the occupying Chinese army watched Tibetan women in ragged but colorful clothes and headdresses do pick-and-shovel work on a patch of dirt road, perhaps earmarked by the Chinese colonial authorities in Lhasa to some day receive a tarmac.

Flying a wind-whipped Chinese banner, planted among the ubiquitous Buddhist prayer flags which adorn villages and seem to sprout from the very soil of Tibet, that guard post, marked, as we discovered later, a historical as well as a geographical milestone in the tragic timeline of Tibet's subjugation by the Middle Kingdom after World War II. The pass was near Lhatse, a tiny town sporting a café that served yak butter tea and a small shop selling canned goods, alcohol lamps, and other items useful to weary travelers and Himalayan mountaineers.

This was one of the sites where, after the Chinese Communist invasion in 1950, Tibetan Khampa tribesmen - some trained by the CIA in an ultra-secret operation at Camp Hale in the Rocky Mountains of Colorado in the early 1950s and parachuted into Tibet from the high-altitude sub-kingdom of Mustang, in a corner of Nepal, or from India - had ambushed and vainly fought the Chinese invaders, only to be later abandoned. This occurred when President Richard Nixon, vice-president under President Dwight D. Eisenhower, who had green-lighted the Tibetan operation, was told by advisors such as Henry Kissinger that a rapprochement with China, the giant of Asia, was more important than the future of Tibet.

During the 1950s and 1960s, as congressional investigators documented (Results of the 1973 Church Committee Hearings, on CIA misdeeds, and the 1984 Iran-Contra Hearings), the CIA organized proprietary airlines, known in the intelligence community as **CIA airlines**. Lines like Air America, Air Asia, Civil Air Transport, Intermountain Aviation, Southern Air Transport, and Evergreen were able to move weapons, communications gear, and other supplies to support America's proxy wars against the Soviets, their allies, and other assorted "bad guys." A huge, top-secret World War II airbase in the Arizona desert northwest of Tucson, called Marana, became for Tibet, and for many of the proxy wars before the climactic Afghanistan operation of 1979-89, a main CIA training ground for covert paramilitary air operations. In secret, and sheltered behind road signs such as "Warning: Do Not Proceed Further; Use of Deadly Force Authorized," expert paratroopers skilled in designing and packing complex chutes for dropping men and supplies in all types of weather, and mechanics and technicians capable of adapting ordinary aircraft to exotic secret missions, plied their trades.

All were sworn to total secrecy.

Marana's senior officer and future commander was Gar Thorsrude. Thorsrude supervised the recruitment and training of cadres for anti-Chinese Tibetan operations. Later, he would oversee preparations for the larger, more disastrous Bay of Pigs operation in Cuba. Once trained, over 1,000 Tibetan tribesmen, mostly Khampas, were moved to likewise secret air bases in East Asia, especially in Mustang, the forgotten, mountainous edge of Nepal controlled by a local and cooperative prince. The CIA code-named the operation "C.T. Circus."

The history of CIA intervention in Tibet, using the Khampas trained at Marana Air Base in Arizona and Camp Hale, was a sorry one for the Tibetans. Under the reign of the 13th Dalai Lama (1876-1933), an enlightened, authoritarian ruler, Tibet had attempted, unsuccessfully, to fight off the British invasion of Lhasa led by the adventurer, Colonel Younghusband in 1904. But British influence and British bureaucrats governed Tibet, to the exclusion of both Chinese and Russian influence. Near the end of the imperial Qing Dynasty in Beijing, after the Chinese Republican revolution of 1911-12, and prelude to the rise of the Kuomintang and General Chiang Kai-Shek in China, the Tibetans expelled the Chinese and made formal what had been only a tenuous independence prior to British occupation. During World War II they were wooed and pressured by both the Allies and the Axis powers. (Heinrich Harrer's book Seven Years in Tibet, and the film it inspired, is an account of a former Austrian SS officer's sojourn as a friend and informal adviser to the young 14th Dalai Lama.)

An independent government managed to function in Lhasa until 1951. But in 1947, with the independence and partition of India and Pakistan, the British withdrew from the subcontinent and Tibet lost its only real ally. In 1949, Mao Tse-Tung, victorious over Chiang Kai-Shek's Kuomintang

Nationalists in the Chinese civil war, announced the birth of the People's Republic of China and the new Communist rulers in Beijing immediately began to threaten the Lhasa government.

China overran Eastern Tibet in October 1950. The woefully under-equipped Tibetan army fought bravely but was quickly overcome, leaving only the poorly-armed resistance force of the Khampa tribes far east of Lhasa. A Tibetan delegation, pressured in Beijing in 1951, signed a treaty allowing Chinese forces to be garrisoned in Lhasa.

After a popular Tibetan uprising erupted in the capital in 1959, the Dalai Lama and his followers fled across the Himalayas into India. China began gradually incorporating Tibet into itself. In September 1995, my wife and I arrived in Lhasa as part of a group of Greek tourists from Athens, just as a senior delegation of generals and politicians from Beijing was celebrating the thirtieth anniversary of China's formal annexation in 1965 of what, to most Americans and other Westerners, was a far-off and mysterious land sheltering the mythical, paradisical monastery of flowers and longevity of James Hilton's novel, Lost Horizon - Shangri-La

Once the CIA and the Administration abandoned the hapless Khampa mercenaries they had trained, and left the country to colonization and despotic rule by Mao, China's violent Cultural Revolution spread into Tibet. Most of the cultural and religious institutions of Tibetan Buddhism were blown up with dynamite, bulldozed, or looted by the young and fanatical Red Guards. Buddhist monks, nuns, and religious and secular dissenters were imprisoned, tortured and often executed. Others were forced to undergo endless brainwashing sessions, as a monk in one of Lhasa's monasteries who survived Chinese imprisonment recounted to me on my first day in Tibet. Anyone who refused to denounce the Dalai Lama risked a long, sometimes endless, jail sentence

After Mao's death in 1976, China officially acknowledged the damage wrought by the Cultural Revolution's excesses, and the situation calmed. In the late 1970s and early 1980s, as the Soviet invasion of Afghanistan and the CIA's counter-jihad using thousands of Muslim mercenaries recruited from around the world, including those from the western region of China, Xinjiang, erupted to the west of Tibet, Deng Xiaoping's policy of relative tolerance saw the rebuilding of many destroyed monasteries and revival of religious practices. In 1979 the Jokhang Temple in Lhasa, Tibetan Buddhism's most sacred shrine, re-opened. In 1984, as the Afghanistan war raged on, China allowed Muslims to immigrate to Tibet, perhaps to weaken the Muslim demographic balance in Xinjang. Further trading and religious freedoms were restored. Tourism from abroad was sanctioned for the first time in Tibetan history, even encouraged: the Greek tour group we joined in 1995 was one of hundreds. In 1988-89, however, demonstrations by monks in Lhasa led to bloody rioting around the Jokhang, and the garrisoned Chinese army cracked down ruthlessly. Trouble spread throughout the country. Until China rescinded its order in May of 1990, Tibet was closed to foreigners. In 1963, and several times since my brief visit in 1995, further riots and demonstrations have periodically erupted, recalling for an older generation the CIA's proxy mini-war of 1958-63 using the Khampa tribesmen as mercenaries.

The fledgling CIA's flirtation with the independence-seeking Khampa Buddhists in Tibet, like its more torrid love affair with the remnants of General Chiang Kai-Shek's nationalist armies in other parts of southeast Asia, provoked countless skirmishes and battles. The agency staunchly allied itself with religious or nationalist fighters against "world Communism," personified then by the Chinese Communist forces of Mao Tse-tung and his generals. After Mao's victory in 1949, U.S. presidents and their intelligence chiefs chose a variety of allies, surrogates, and mercenary forces to help battle Moscow and Beijing in the monumental Cold War. The story of these U.S. interventions - some of which succeeded; others which, like the Khampa struggle in Tibet, failed or were abandoned by Washington - represents a progression which ultimately led to the horrors of September 11, 2001. In a very real sense, 9/11 was a consequence. The mercenaries, trained by the U.S., Pakistan, and their allies to fight the Russians in Afghanistan from 1979 to 1989, turned against their former trainers, sponsors, and benefactors. Throughout the 1990s, they wreaked a terrible toll.

The way stations toward what Usama bin Laden and his followers considered Armageddon in New York and Washington, included both secular and religious-inspired battles. Most, like Tibet, were chapters in the communist/capitalist Cold War. These include Cuba, Indo-China, Angola, and the Balkans. Largely ignoring the admonition of strategic thinker and Italian Renaissance writer, Niccolo Machiavelli to his Florentine overlord, Lorenzo de Medici, in 1517 AD against using "useless and dangerous" mercenaries and auxiliaries to fight wars, the United States employed many of both. In only in a few cases before Afghanistan - notably the overthrow of the Leftist Arbenz government in Guatemala in 1954 - did the mercenaries succeed.

Some, like the Khampas in Tibet and the native Afghan moujahiddin fighters in Afghanistan in 1979-89, were motivated by fierce patriotism and the desire to rid themselves of a hated foreign invader. Others - the foreign Muslim allies of the Afghans recruited by the CIA, the Hmong hill tribesmen in Laos during the Indo-Chinese wars, the Iraqi Kurds aided by the Shah of Iran and Israel, or the Angolan militia armies of Jonas Savimbi - were often motivated by a mixture of political and patriotic energies. In the Congo, Sierra Leone, and other African wars that have raged intermittently from the 1960s until today, this often degenerated into simple lust for loot. The United States played a leading role, as a user of proxies and mercenaries, in many of these theaters. But never, until last year, had any of them turned on their sponsors and attacked with such fury inside the continental United States as did the veterans of the Afghan war, and those trained or inspired by a tiny minority in the world of one billion Muslims who formed the legions of Usama bin Laden and Al-Qaeda.

Although the CIA's Tibetan adventure with the Khampa tribal mercenaries remained relatively unknown to most people besides the hundreds of Tibetans killed, wounded, or captured by the Chinese army, it provided a faint foretaste of future operations and future paybacks to be suffered by the United States.

There had been preludes in Central America, such as the successful CIA-supported operation in Guatemala in 1954. But it was the monumental failure of the Bay of Pigs operation against Fidel Castro's Cuba in 1961 whose foreign consequences and domestic repercussions linger in the United States to this day. Above all, the CIA's failed expedition contains lessons which the George W. Bush administration would do well to ponder in 2002, as it contemplates an operation against Iraq far greater in scope.

The facts of the Cuban fiasco are mostly undisputed. Its Cold War legacy brought heavy burdens for Americans: the near-apocalyptic U.S.-Soviet missile crisis of 1962; President Kennedy's assassination in Dallas in November 1963, and, indirectly, even the Watergate break-in of 1972 which forced Richard Nixon to become the first American President to resign from office. Nor should it be forgotten that the long civil war in Angola, fought largely by the African and Cuban proxies and mercenaries of Moscow and Washington, is also linked to the same Cuban legacy.

The facts are that on April 17, 1961, a force of about 1,400 anti-Castro Cuban exiles, organized, trained, and supplied by the CIA, landed on the Cuban coast at the Bahia de Cochinas (Bay of Pigs). The aim of the operation, for which CIA director Allen Dulles and his imaginative deputy Richard Bissell took responsibility, was to secure a bridgehead and foment a national popular upheaval to topple Castro. After three days of fighting in which President Kennedy withheld any effective American air cover or other official help, Castro's heavily armed air and land forces killed 114 of the attackers and captured the rest.

After the disaster - compressed into less than one week of history, as opposed to the generation-long Indo-China wars - Kennedy ordered an investigation of the CIA led by former U.S. Army Chief of Staff Maxwell Taylor, an advocate of covert and guerilla warfare, whose theories were soon to be tested in Indo-China. Months later, Allen Dulles, who had directed the CIA since 1953, resigned. In 1962, Richard Helms replaced Richard Bissell, deputy CIA director for the Bay of Pigs Operation. There was no outcry for reform of the CIA comparable to those which would follow the "family jewels" affair of the 1970s, nor to changes necessitated by George W. Bush's proposed creation of the Homeland Security Department following the pre-9/11 intelligence failures of 2001. After the Bay of Pigs the CIA was not fundamentally restructured. The fateful responsibility rested directly with President Kennedy and his immediate entourage, including his brother Robert, in the White House "war room."[1]

The Bay of Pigs fiasco and its background, as told by one of Kennedy's close friends and admirers, Arthur M. Schlesinger Jr., should be studied carefully by all architects of future covert operations, including those aiming at Saddam Hussein of Iraq. Just as some of the schemes to destroy Saddam were hatched during President Bill Clinton's two terms, resulting in frayed relations with friends and allies in the Middle East in the 1990s, so was the Bay of Pigs for which Kennedy and his men bore the blame in 1961, conceived by their predecessors in the Eisenhower administration.

Since the overthrow of the dictatorial Cuban regime of General Fulgencio Batista in January 1959 by Fidel Castro and his guerillas, idealists, including Kennedy who sympathized with many of Castro's declared reforms and proclaimed intentions to clean up the corrupt socio-political structures of the Batista era, had grown dismayed by Fidel's actions. He had nationalized U.S. property, and sent teams throughout Central America and the Caribbean to foment insurgencies. He had executed hundreds of "counter-revolutionaries," some of whom had originally been Castro partisans during the "heroic" phase of the revolution in the mountains of the Sierra Madre. As early as the end of 1959, schemes were being hatched in Washington to unseat, and indeed, to kill Castro. The Eisenhower administration broke diplomatic relations with Cuba in January 1961. By then, there were already over 100,000 Cuban refugees in the U.S., most of them settled in Miami, Florida.

On March 17, 1960 Eisenhower directed the CIA to collect a wide spectrum of exiled Cubans, including Batista partisans and disaffected communists, and mould them into a unified opposition. At the same time, the CIA was ordered to recruit and train a force of Cuban mercenaries for an armed attack on the Castro regime. (This in retrospect, was not too different from the various secret memos and "findings" President Jimmy Carter and his aides would craft in 1979 and 1980 for Afghanistan, first to anticipate and later to counter the Soviet invasion of December 1979.) This secret Eisenhower decision differed from President Nixon's first proposal to use exiles as proxies against Castro in the spring of 1959. At that earlier time, only Batistianos, supporters of Batista, were available. However, by March 1960, Miami and other U.S. centers were flooded with Cubans who had become disenchanted with Castro's communism. Among them many politically active professionals; doctors, lawyers, businessmen. Their objectives, as Schlesinger observed, were often similar to "the interests of North American investors [despoiled by Castro]" and to the anti-Communist "prejudices of the Eisenhower administration."[2]

The CIA soon organized an anti-Castro political front - the Frente Revolucionario Democratico, or Revolutionary Democratic Front - composed of five main groups. Three were led by former Batista men. One of these was a former prime minister, Manuel Antonio de Varona, who pledged that a post-Castro government would restore property seized by the Castro regime to their former American and Cuban owners. The other two included a liberal-minded banker and a young lieutenant, Manuel Artime, who had joined Castro in 1958, briefly heading his agrarian reform movement. After he broke with Castro in late 1959, the CIA "exfiltrated" him from Cuba and he soon became the agency's main man in the front, and their link to both political and military operations.

Artime and his CIA bosses were soon actively recruiting their secret army among Cuban refugees and émigrés in Florida and Central America. They sweet-talked President Ydigoras of Guatemala, one of the military-backed men who presided over Guatemala's perennial civil strife. (CIA involvement in Guatemala began with the overthrow the Leftist regime of Jacobo Ardenz in 1954 in favor of a repressive military regime which secured the supposedly threatened interests of the powerful United Fruit Company, and didn't end until 1996.)

Ydigoras allowed the CIA to set up a secret training camp for the exiles, together with an air base at a coffee plantation on volcanic soil 5,000 feet above the Pacific Ocean. Training was supervised by a Filipino colonel who had organized guerilla resistance against the Japanese occupation during World War II.

In August 1960, President Eisenhower approved a budget of $13 million to form small bands of trained mercenaries meant to slip secretly into Cuba and set up small centers of resistance which would be re-supplied by air drops until strong and well-armed enough to oppose Castro's regular Cuban forces. True to the philosophy applied a much larger scale in Afghanistan later on, but already on the point of violation in President George W. Bush's "war on terror" in the Philippines and elsewhere in 2002, there remained an explicit prohibition against sending U.S. military personnel into combat operations.

An important weakness in the plan soon became evident: it required cooperation between the infiltrators trained in Guatemala and several hundred guerillas inside Cuba hiding from Castro's forces in the Escambray Mountains. There existed, too, an urban underground headed by Castro opponent Manuel Ray. But Richard Bissell's men at Langley, Virginia found establishing contact with these city groups difficult. According to Schlesinger, the CIA feared that the "interior" guerillas had been penetrated by Castro's forces. The growing input of Soviet supplies and advisors, it was feared, would ultimately crush the Escambray and urban resistance. It was a classic case, seen in so many other wars and insurgencies, from the Algerian revolution of 1954-62 against the French to Cambodia in the 1970s, of the conflict between "internal" and "external" dissidents. In this instance, the "externals" - the Guatemalan brigade - won out in the contest for the favors from the CIA.[3]

By the time of the U.S. presidential elections in November 1960 and John Kennedy's triumph over Republican candidate Senator Richard Nixon, CIA planners had begun to favor landing a small force of the Guatemala-trained mercenaries on the Cuban coast to stir up an internal anti-Castro uprising. Their chosen beachhead was near the town of Trinidad, selected because its population of approximately 20,000 were thought amenable to joining the invaders. Additionally, the Escambray mountains were nearby, a good place for the invaders to regroup and prepare the internal guerilla war to unseat Castro.[4]

In 2002 such considerations were apparently in the minds of George W. Bush's planners regarding Iraq as they spun out elaborate scenarios for invasion and the overthrow of Saddam Hussein, with the autonomous and partly Allied-protected area of Kurdistan in view as both a sanctuary and launching pad.

The fatal flaw in the entire Bay of Pigs operation, as it gradually developed after Kennedy's inauguration in January 1961, was its awkward aura of deception, called by an author sympathetic to the CIA, "so grand and unwieldy that it would prove its undoing." Kennedy steadfastly insisted the operation was a purely Cuban one, the work of exiles. (In the same manner the Carter, and to some extent, Reagan administration, tried to maintain the official fiction that the Afghan moujahiddin were largely using their own meager resources in their heroic resistance of the Soviet invaders.) But "plausible deniability" of American involvement has never been a credible doctrine.

Bissell and his aides realized that victory would depend on control of the air. No beachhead assault, at Trinidad or anywhere else, could survive without it against Castro's not inconsiderable Soviet-supplied air force. They pinned their hopes on a few old B-26 bombers left over from World War II and mothballed near Tucson, Arizona which, with their U.S. insignia and other identifying marks removed, might be used to destroy Castro's planes on the ground. Some of the exhumed planes were painted with Cuban air force marks and numbers. A number of Alabama Air National Guard personnel - the last pilots to fly the B-26s, including a thirty-year-old veteran, Thomas "Pete" Ray, who was in reality a CIA officer - were recruited to train Cuban émigré commercial and cargo pilots. One of the operation's overseers was none other than the same Gar Thorsrude, godfather of the Tibet operation.

The next glitch, which helped to cripple the Bay of Pigs operation even before it started, was the same problem the CIA, the FBI, and other agencies struggled to overcome after the intelligence failures of 9/11: compartmentalization and "need to know" restrictions. Knowledge of the plan was so closely held not even the CIA's director of intelligence - as opposed to the director of operations - was in on it. In practice, this meant that the men planning the operation were also expected to assess its chances for success without any independent counsel. (This evokes another American fiasco of the new century, that of the accounting firm of Arthur Andersen which was expected to both advise and audit the Enron corporate conglomerate that ultimately collapsed amid great scandal in 2001.)

By 1960, plots to assassinate Castro were proliferating. Several of the more grotesque involved poisons: soaking Castro's favorite Cuban cigars with a depilatory to make his body hair and his beard fall out, and a box of his same favorite brand tainted with botulism toxin which the CIA delivered to Cuba in February 1961 (the same toxins are said to be stockpiled by Iraq's Saddam Hussein in 2002), which apparently never reached him.

The CIA also developed ties to organized crime as a means of recruiting possible hit men. In August 1960 Robert Maheu, an ex-CIA agent who worked for the mysterious and reclusive tycoon of aviation, the late Howard Hughes, asked John Roselli, a Mafia "soldier" to locate Cubans willing to attempt to assassinate Castro. Roselli contacted two other leading mobsters, Sam Giancana and Santos Trafficante. None of these plots panned out, but they continued fomenting until the end of Kennedy's life. On the day of his assassination in Dallas in November 1963, a CIA contact inside the Cuban government was offered a pen with a poison needle to give to Castro. The Cuban rejected the offer, calling it "too amateurish."[5]

Just as Pakistani management of the CIA's jihad against the Russians in Afghanistan in 1979-89 undermined post-war objectives of the U.S.

by giving preference in training, supplies, armament, and money to the most fanatically anti-American fighters like Gulbuddin Hekmatyar - deemed by Pakistan's ISI the most efficient and ruthless of those fighting the Russians - so did the agents and mercenaries of the CIA on the spot in Cuba shape the planned campaign to their own needs. Just as Pakistan's ISI in 1979-89 chose "reliable" fighters who would obey ISI orders, the Cubans in the field endangered the plans being laid in Langley. This was because, like the Afghans in the 1980s, they were, as Schlesinger put it, "more principled and more radical than the manageable types whom the intelligence agency preferred for operational reasons." Just as many of the royalist and conservative Afghan resistance leaders advocated the restoration of the exiled and elderly former king, Zahir Shah, the exiled Cuban leadership in the CIA's Frente began to realize that it had no real authority and didn't know what was going on the inner planning circle in Washington.

In the Guatemalan camps, the mercenary trainees were assured by their American officers that they were only one of a number of groups, perhaps ten percent of the entire force, and would get all the official U.S. support they needed.[6] The exiles likewise believed the Washington dogma that a mass landing on beaches in Cuba would touch off a general revolt, and the U.S. air force would provide cover and take out Castro's planes.

President-elect John Kennedy was not told about the impending operation until November 17, 1960. Twelve days later, CIA director Allen Dulles briefed him in detail. Kennedy okayed the plans and told Dulles to proceed with what, to Kennedy, was still only a "contingency plan." He had doubts about the whole project, just as later a few senior figures on both sides - top politburo leader and ambassador Alexander Zotov for the Soviets; and Secretary of State Cyrus Vance for the Americans - had doubts about the Afghanistan war.

The Bay of Pigs operation leaked like a sieve. On October 30, 1960, a Guatemalan newspaper, La Hora, reported that a U.S.-sponsored invasion of Cuba was in the works. Americans read about the plans in the Hispanic-American Report and The Nation, a fairly constant critic of American operations, especially overseas operations involving mercenaries. Time magazine reported in January that the Frente was being financed generously by the U.S. government at the expense of rival Cuban groups. Time also reported that when one Frente member complained about recruiting Batista supporters, a U.S. officer gave the same apology offered for the U.S. alliance with extremist Muslim groups before and after the jihad in Afghanistan: "They're anti-communists, aren't they?"

Unmarked planes began to use the officially deserted Opa-Locka airfield near Miami to shuttle mercenaries and CIA personnel to and from Guatemala. By March 1961, the CIA had assumed full control of the operation. They planned the landings to focus on Trinidad and its beaches, proposing a heavy amphibious assault at dawn, reinforced by parachute drops behind the town and simultaneous air strikes on Cuban air bases. As with the Allied landing at Anzio, Italy in 1944, full support from the population was anticipated once the beachhead was secured and slowly extended.

A series of meetings by the Pentagon and the Joint Chiefs of Staff followed Kennedy's inauguration. After inspection of the Guatemala base, the Joint Chiefs concluded that due to Castro's well-armed and motivated regular armed forces of over 200,000, success would depend upon the ability of the attackers to foment a massive anti-Castro action behind Cuban government lines. Intelligence spotted new Soviet jet planes and Cuban pilots who had been trained in Czechoslovakia to fly them.[7] (This phenomenon was later observed in Africa, when Cubans - both mercenaries and regulars - were sent in large numbers for land and aerial warfare against the CIA-backed Angolan forces of Jonas Savimbi and white-ruled South Africa.)

At a number of White House meetings, President Kennedy, heeding the caution expressed by senior advisers such as Secretary of State Dean Rusk, insisted that there must be severe limitations on the operation to preserve "plausible deniability." Kennedy remembered the 1960 U-2 disaster when Soviets shot down Francis Gary Powers' high-altitude spy flight over the USSR. The U.S. at first denied the spy mission. This had a serious impact on the U.S. position in the Cold War. Now Kennedy insisted that no American personnel have a direct role in battle (a principle observed in the infinitely larger jihad in Afghanistan in the 1980s, when Muslim mercenaries did the fighting instead.) Richard Bissell and other CIA senior officials feared Kennedy's excessive caution might emasculate the operation, all the more so when it was discovered that the well-organized anti-Castro guerilla force inside Cuba was a figment of the overheated imaginations of the Miami exiles.

The original attack plan was hastily revised. Bissell slashed the aging B-26s to be used against Castro's air force from sixteen planes to eight.

Only a few weeks before the assault, on March 15, the landing site was changed from Trinidad, which Kennedy thought would be "too noisy," to the "less spectacular" Bahia de Cochinos, the Bay of Pigs, near an existing airstrip.

On April 12, 1961, in a speech to the American Association of Newspaper Editors, Kennedy, probably in part reflecting his own and others' misgivings, and partly in an effort at conscious misdirection, pledged there would be no American military intervention in Cuba. Three days later, following the first sneak attack on Cuba by the B-26s, the pilots, posing as new defectors from Castro's air force, returned to Florida. At the United Nations, the U.S. representative, Adlai Stevenson, not knowing any better, assured the body that the U.S. had nothing to do with the bombing. Kennedy had not let him in on the secret. In what author Ted Gup refers to as the "coup de grace," Kennedy cancelled the second-wave air attack scheduled for April 16, the eve of the planned landings. The strike had been intended to destroy whatever remained of Castro's air force after the first strike the day before.

The force of nearly 1,300 exiles was now stuck on the Bay of Pigs beaches, exposed to strikes by Castro's air force. Two ships carrying ammunition and communications gear to support the beachhead were sunk; other ships withdrew out of range. The Cuban exile pilots trying to support the mercenaries on the beaches had to fly three and a half hours from a base in Nicaragua, attack, and return only to rearm, refuel and fly another mission. On April 18, at 10 pm, the brigade commander on the beach, after pleading in vain for air cover, messaged: I will not be evacuated. We will fight to the end if we have to.

In Washington, Kennedy at first refused, then grudgingly gave in to Chief of Naval Operations Admiral Arleigh Burke's pleas that Navy jets intervene to save the men. Okay, said Kennedy, but only for one hour. However, when Pete Ray and several other pilots arrived from Nicaragua over the Bay of Pigs in their B-26s, the Navy jets were not there to protect them. This, says author Ted Gup, was because the CIA had figured the hour of the strike in Cuban time, while the Navy had set its clocks by Greenwich meantime. Ray's plane was hit and crashed close to a sugar mill and Castro's headquarters. His companion Leo Baker was killed; Ray apparently died fighting Castro's men on the ground. Besides Ray and Baker, 112 other attackers were killed in the operation. The remaining 1,197 were captured and imprisoned until two years later when the U.S. paid a ransom of over $50 million worth of food and medicine. Margaret Ray, Pete Ray's widow, was warned not to contradict the White House spin doctors who were trying to deny official U.S. involvement, and would later attempt to persuade the public that the Alabama National Guardsmen lost in Cuba were "soldiers of fortune," mercenaries in it for the money. Afterward, as the official versions of the Bay of Pigs changed, "mysterious checks for $225 would arrive twice each month drawn on an account with the Bankers Trust Company of New York. There was no explanation of their origin, and none was needed."[8]

Some of the consequences of the Bay of Pigs operation were immediate; others delayed. Kennedy was so disgusted with the CIA that for a time he stopped reading its daily intelligence briefings. There was bad blood between Langley and the White House. Allen Dulles stepped down as Director in November 1961. In February 1962, Richard Bissell resigned, only to be decorated with the National Security Medal by Kennedy.

Historian Theodore Draper called the Bay of Pigs "a perfect failure." But its lessons would have to be learned over and over again: in Angola, in Bosnia, in Afghanistan.

According to Ted Gup, each president after Kennedy trying to run covert operations, alone or in parallel with public military campaigns, whether in Indo-China, Latin America or elsewhere, has had to insist on distancing himself from the covert side, especially if it contravened the law or accepted American principles. Americans as well as foreign enemies often had to be deceived, since the American public or Congress might not otherwise continue support.[9]

Among the longer-term effects of the Bay of Pigs failure was that it encouraged the Soviet Union to press home its growing advantages in Cuba, such as establishment of a Soviet electronic station to spy on the U.S. at Lourdes, Cuba. World War III almost erupted during the Cuban missile crisis in 1962 before Soviet Premier Nikita Khruschev blinked. In its dogged anti-Castro machinations, the CIA reverted to hatching more ineffectual assassination plots against the Cuban leader.

Many scenarios have been spun out in print and on the screen, suggesting that the Bay of Pigs might indirectly have led to, or contributed to, Kennedy's assassination on November 22, 1963. The bare facts were first elucidated by the seven- member investigating commission appointed by President Lyndon B. Johnson under Chief Justice Earl Warren of the U.S. Supreme Court. The Warren Report, presented in September 1964, has never been fully accepted in many of its details and even some of its crucial main points. Its findings were that a single gunman, the 24-year-old ex-Marine and ex-defector to the Soviet Union, Lee Harvey Oswald, had shot Kennedy from the book depository building in Dallas; there was no evidence of others involved; and that Jack Ruby, who later died of natural causes, shot and killed Oswald for no special reason while Oswald was in custody.

Suspicion has kept the U.S. media, Hollywood, and a large part of the American public in a state of ferment ever since. The Cuba angle came to light when, during questioning, Oswald - who denied he had shot Kennedy or a Dallas police officer who had approached him, J.D. Tippit - refused to answer questions about a U.S. selective service registration card found on him in the fictitious name of Alek J. Hiddell. This was the name Oswald had used as president of a "Fair Play For Cuba" committee branch in New Orleans, and when he bought his high-powered rifle by mail order. Soon after his arrest, the media was filled with his background as a defector to the Soviet Union, his support for Castro's government, and the Russian origin of his estranged wife, Marina.

After returning (with U.S. government financial assistance) from his unhappy stay in the USSR with his wife and baby, Oswald received aid and friendship from the Russian exile community in Dallas-Fort Worth. On April 6, 1963, he fired his rifle at Maj. Gen. Edwin Walker (resigned, U.S. Army), a prominent member of the local Right-Wing John Birch Society, and missed. Moving to New Orleans, Oswald set up the pro-Castro committee, but simultaneously tried, unsuccessfully, to join an anti-Castro group. In Mexico, on September 27, 1963, Oswald met Soviet and Cuban diplomats, but was refused a visa to visit either country. He then resumed residence under a false name in Dallas where he shot Kennedy and was killed by Jack Ruby several days later.

The Warren Commission report was at first very favorably received. Only a handful of conspiracy buffs objected. They offered a range of different views: Oswald was a tool of Castro, or the Russian KGB, of anti-Castro Cuban exiles, or extreme Right-Wing Dallas businessmen who loathed Kennedy - even that he was an innocent look-alike for a second Oswald; perhaps a Cuban or Soviet agent who disappeared. In 1966, however, two seemingly well-researched books appeared: Mark Lane's Rush to Judgment and Edward J. Epstein's Inquest: The Warren Commission and the Establishment of Truth. Both books questioned the entire report. Both became huge best sellers, sparking endless television and radio debates, and inspiring movies. In 1967 New Orleans District Attorney Jim Garrison began a sensation-seeking probe of his own. This led to indictment and eventual acquittal of a local businessman, Claw Shaw, for involvement in an alleged plot to kill Kennedy.

Long years of endless controversy followed, about ballistics; about wounds; about how many shots were fired and what vantage points supposed other shooters used, etc. The administrations following President Johnson's were adamant that the Warren Report was complete and accurate, and backed by evidence from both the FBI and the CIA.

In 1974-76, Senator Frank Church's commission revealed many CIA scandals, including the assassination plots against Castro and others, in what came to be called the "Family Jewels" affair. It came to light that from 1960 onward the CIA had contacts, as we have seen, with mob bosses Sam Giancana, Santos Trafficante, and John Roselli, with the aim of murdering Castro. Robert Maheu, who later became one of the players in the Watergate affair, was a go-between. The government and organized crime were, in a sense, literally in bed together during John Kennedy's administration. President Kennedy shared a girlfriend, Judith Campbell Exner - apparently introduced to him in 1960 by Frank Sinatra - with mobster Sam Giancana. This was despite the fact that his brother Robert Kennedy, who had shared White House war room planning activities with him before and during the Bay of Pigs operation, had earned his political reputation in an important Washington organized crime investigation in the 1950s. Exner in 1975 denied that Kennedy knew of her Mafia ties, but in a 1988 article in People magazine she admitted to arranging Kennedy-Giancana meetings in 1960-61, and to acting as a messenger. Under pressure from his brother Robert and the redoubtable FBI director, J. Edgar Hoover, who kept dossiers on the great and famous, JFK ended his relationship with Exner. After the Cuban missile crisis of October 1962, both the Mafia contacts and support for the anti-Castro Cuban groups were scaled back. Nevertheless, Castro showed that he remained aware of continued assassination plots against him up to the day Kennedy was murdered, and possibly beyond.

Many uncertainties remain about how the Bay of Pigs mercenary operation touched on President Kennedy's assassination. On the one hand, both Castro and the Mafia - used, then scorned by Robert Kennedy who continued to fight organized crime, and who the mob identified with the presidential power of his brother - had motives to kill Kennedy. There were many links between the Mafia, anxious to return to its lucrative,

Batista- era Havana casino business which Castro had wiped out, and the anti-Castro émigrés in the U.S. These exiles, especially relatives and friends of those lost and imprisoned in the Bay of Pigs disaster, believed Kennedy had betrayed them by refusing air cover during the CIA-managed invasion, abandoning them to Castro's wrath. And, following the missile crisis of 1962 with the Soviet Union, Kennedy's administration additionally pressured the exile community in the U.S. by breaking up its military training camps, effectively converting its activities into an incessant propaganda war.

In September 1976, after the Church Committee had disclosed the CIA-Mafia plots, another investigation, this time by the House Select Committee on Assassinations, began to probe the killings of President Kennedy, Robert Kennedy, and Martin Luther King. Its report essentially confirmed many Warren Commission findings, but added that shots additional to Oswald's had been fired from the so-called Grassy Knoll area in front of Kennedy's car, and that there had indeed been a conspiracy.

There were many suspicious facts about Oswald's pro-Castro and pro-Soviet activities once he had returned from the Soviet Union, which the Warren Commission and evidently the FBI had downplayed, perhaps in the conscious or unconscious determination to remove doubts from Congress and the population before the 1964 elections.[10]

IT WAS ALSO IN THE INTERESTS OF BOTH THE KBG AND THE FBI TO DIFFUSE ANY SUSPICION OF SINISTER INTERNATIONAL MOTIVES BEHIND THE ASSASSINATION, BECAUSE AFTER THE MISSILE CRISIS OF 1962 U.S.-SOVIET RELATIONS HAD ENTERED A SLOW MENDING PROCESS. THIS HAD ITS UPS AND DOWNS. IT WAS DECISIVELY SET BACK BY THE SOVIET INVASION OF AFGHANISTAN IN 1979 ON PRESIDENT JIMMY CARTER'S WATCH. THIS IN TURN SET IN MOTION THE TRAIN OF EVENTS CULMINATING IN THE TERRORISM OF AL-QAEDA AND ITS PREDECESSORS IN THE 1990S, AND FINALLY IN THE ATTACKS ON NEW YORK AND WASHINGTON ON SEPTEMBER 11, 2001.

While mercenaries, trained by and fighting for the American "side" against the Communists, played a central role in Cold War encounters like those of Tibet and Cuba, and in the final, decisive one in Afghanistan in 1979-89, it was the surrogates of both sides, the Americans and the Soviets, who nearly destroyed Angola, the former Portugese colony in Africa.

Only Angola's riches in oil, minerals like copper; and in diamonds have rescued it from the depths of abject poverty. They have also contributed to its political undoing. This same wealth helped enrich Western conglomerates, before and during the present age of economic globalization, which profited from their exploitation. Thus, the consequences of the Angolan saga, while involving no terrorist outrages inside Western countries, is nonetheless a post-colonial drama of great impact on the United States and its people.

After long centuries as a Portuguese colonial possession, in 1975 Angola finally wrested its independence from Portuguese dictator Antonio da Oliveira Salazar, a former economics professor who had applied austerity economics and secret-police iron rule for half a century. Angola's native factions were already fighting among themselves when Lisbon's rule ended. The stronger and ideologically Marxist faction, which the CIA eventually concluded was a surrogate of the Soviets, ultimately prevailed and formed a government. This was the Popular Movement for the Liberation of Angola (MPLA) of Augustinho Neto, a physician, and Marcellino Dos Santos, who was later to become president, an office he still held in 2002 after the country had been laid waste by over thirty years of "civil" war.

During my years as a correspondent in North Africa, both of the MPLA's opponents - who proclaimed their opposition to African Marxism in general, and to the MPLA in particular - operated in and out of places like Rabat and Tunis, the capitals of Morocco and Tunisia. One I met was Holden Roberto, who headed the FNLA (National Front for the Liberation of Angola). A missionary-educated Christian with a calm manner and a presence pleasing to his Western supporters who appreciated the "moderation" of his opposition to Portuguese colonialism, Roberto came from the powerful Bakongo tribe in the north of Angola, and was supported, as Henry Kissinger notes in his memoirs, by his brother-in-law, Mobutu Sese Soko, president of the Democratic Republic of the Congo (formerly the Belgian Congo, known as Zaire from 1971 to 1997). Mobutu, who ruled from 1965 until his overthrow in 1997 by army rebels under his successor, Laurent Desire Kabila, was one of the biggest and most corrupt rogues in the CIA's prodigious inventory of powerful and pliable African surrogate rulers, and was willing to offer his tribal mercenaries to almost any U.S.-backed cause in Africa.

At one of several meetings I had with Holden Roberto in Tunis in 1960, he angled for any Western support he could get. Baited by Roberto's vocal anti-Communism, the CIA soon paid him an annual stipend of $100,000. This, says Kissinger, was mainly to maintain an information channel and because Roberto was deemed most likely to succeed due to his family ties to Mobutu.[11]

In the south of Angola, the dominant tribe was the Ovimbundu. Its liberation movement was UNITA (National Union for the Total Independence of Angola) headed by Jonas Savimbi. It was not Roberto, but Savimbi and his Ovimbundu tribal mercenaries, supported by the white apartheid regime and army of South Africa, who the CIA chose as its favorite in the struggle against the Soviet and Cuban-backed MPLA government. Thus backed, UNITA succeeded in taking over Angola as it won independence in 1975, and many of the CIA's senior operatives were assigned to an Angola Task Force, designed to help Savimbi raise an army of tribal mercenaries.

Holden Roberto was soon eclipsed. Later, Moscow and Havana poured in their own mercenaries, followed by thousands of regular Cuban troops to aid the MPLA in fighting the CIA's proxies led by Savimbi. However, with defeat looming in Vietnam after the fall of Saigon in 1975, the U.S. congress and public grew gun-shy of foreign adventurism, fearing another "quagmire" in Angola and elsewhere in Africa. In June 1976 Congress' Clark Amendment banned all covert action in Angola, the first direct congressional ban on such action. It stood for the next ten years, during which time Angola, despite its untapped oil wealth in the Cabinda enclave, became one of Africa's basket cases, ravaged by the civil war between Savimbi's CIA and South African-backed UNITA and the leftist MPLA. By the early 1980s, as the CIA's jihad faced off against the Soviet forces in Afghanistan, Soviet aid in Angola is believed to have reached several billion dollars. None seemed to do much for the impoverished, often starving ten million Angolans, and only mercenaries and regular troops from South Africa prevented UNITA's total defeat by an estimated forty thousand Cuban troops.

The success of the anti-Communist coalition in Afghanistan produced an emotional high in Washington. The Reagan Administration was not prepared to see communists win anywhere. When the MPLA and its Soviet and Cuban allies began pushing UNITA back in the summer of 1985, Congress responded on August 8 by lifting its 1976 ban on the covert program in Angola. In November President Reagan signed a secret presidential "finding" authorizing anew "lethal" covert aid to UNITA. The CIA sent a senior operative to the thatched hut which served as Savimbi's headquarters, and helped supervise the flow of weapons and supplies to UNITA mercenaries.

In February 1986, Reagan's National Security Council was smelling victory in Afghanistan, a triumph due in part to the effectiveness of the Stinger anti-aircraft missiles that had helped neutralize Soviet air power. The NSC now approved the secret shipment of Stingers and TOW anti-tank missiles to Savimbi.

In the following years, the CIA continued to pump UNITA with all sorts of supplies to speed the defeat the MPLA and its Soviet-bloc backers. It relied heavily on support from Mobutu, who permitted the secret re-supply of Savimbi's mercenary forces from one of Zaire's air bases, the former Belgian air base of Kamina. There, a CIA base officer supervised the barracks and other facilities - including a movie house - for the crews manning the big cargo planes that flew the dangerous night cargo flights in and out of Angola

On the night of November 27, 1989, a Lockheed L-100-20 Hercules cargo plane was dispatched as usual to Jonas Savimbi's headquarters in Jamba, Angola. Its entire crew of six perished. The crew was a cross-section of CIA forces and surrogates. The chief officer was Jimmy Spessard of Hagerstown, Maryland, from the CIA's Science and Technology Directorate. With him was Pharies "Bud" Petty, a seasoned CIA pilot who operated under the thin cover of a CIA subsidiary he headed in Crestview, Florida called Tepper Aviaion. His mechanic was George Vincent Lacy, whose father and older brother were old CIA hands. Two Germans accompanied them; George Bensch and Gerhard Hermann Riger, both in their forties, veterans of servicing CIA aircraft. The last crew member was Michael Atkinson of Yorkshire, England, who loved adventure and had found it as a sea captain and pilot in St. Lucia in the Caribbean before joining the CIA venture in Africa. With them were seven of Savimbi's men and a planeload of supplies, primarily ammunition. Before their demiwse, they had more than once landed on Savimbi's gravel airstrip to be met by Savimbi himself, who would shake hands and present all of them with wooden African carvings.

That night the plane crashed on the final approach to Jamba. All were killed. Later, six coffins were flown to Dover Air Force Base, Delaware, a mission devoid of brass bands or ceremony. No death certificates were issued. To families and others needing to know the CIA gave "Cause of Death Unknown" notices.[12]

Throughout the 35 destructive years of its civil wars, Angola evolved despite the hardships inflicted by its mercenary armies. During the 1980s, the governing MPLA abandoned many of its Marxist principles, a process accelerated by the collapse of the Soviet Union following its withdrawal from Afghanistan at the end of the decade. In 1991 the MPLA abandoned one-party rule and won Angola's first multiparty elections the next year. This was not to the liking of Savimbi. He rekindled the dormant civil war. In Lusaka, Zambia in 1994, UNITA and the MPLA signed a peace agreement stipulating formation of a national unity government, designated by the glum acronym of GURN. Savimbi at first hesitated to join, but did so in 1997, only to be expelled in 1998 as fighting again escalated. A new MPLA-dominated government took office in 1999. It declared an amnesty in 2000 which Savimbi rejected in favor of continued resistance until his death in February 2002 - South Africa and the CIA having long since dropped out as allies - at last raised hopes for peace.

Savimbi, whom the CIA coddled on and off for thirty years, and whose tribesmen became one of the most persistent mercenary armies in Africa, was characterized shortly after his death by British author Jeremy Harding, who knew Savimbi well, as "an accomplished delinquent" who should not be pitied or mourned. "His greatest wish was to take possession of Angola, no as a common felon but as a feudal grandee," wrote Harding. With the aid of the CIA and South Africa he hoped "to stride out of the bush, fully empowered by elections or force majeure- and preside over the capital Luanda, the decadent enemy heartland of half-castes, Marxists, philanderers and oil profiteers." (Savimbi himself, with the help of a number of global companies, reputedly used murder, theft, and diamond smuggling to support UNITA, and to bust UN-imposed sanctions intended to stop the civil war.)

In his thirty-year efforts to seize power, Harding continues, he "robbed Angolan peasants of just about everything and several well-known politicians of their plausibility. Jeanne Kirkpatrick, the Reagan administration's henchperson at the UN, described him as 'one of the authentic heroes of our time.' Reagan himself is reported to have likened him to Abraham Lincoln."

Savimbi accepted help wherever he could get it; not only from South Africa and multinational corporations and the CIA, but even from Communist China. "[Savimbi] proclaimed himself a Maoist before Maoism became an anathema and a devotee of Che when fashion features in the Face [a glitzy British magazine] were still decking out pretty boys from Epping or Harrogate to look like jungle revolutionaries," Harding writes, making reference to Savimbi's prediliction, apparently catered to by his CIA handlers, for carefully-tailored battle fatigues. "Ingenuity," Harding's left-handed tribute to Savimbi goes on, "coupled with immense reserves of courage, cruelty and amour proper, was the ingredient that allowed him to continue his 'armed struggle' in Angola for so long, and to turn the country into one of the unhappiest on earth."[13]

Many of Savimbi's abuses, either supported or winked at by the CIA, have only gradually emerged. On July 6, 2002, for example, CNN reported on Savimbi's child soldiers, some as young as ten and under, many orphans of the war. Pressed into the ranks of the UNITA army, they were taught to shoot. The CNN report, quoting relief workers in Angola, named a total of 10,000 such children, including girls, who never attended school and whose lives were ruined by instructors who taught them to torture and kill their fellow Africans.[14] This phenomenon has been seen in other African wars, such as those in Sierra Leone and Liberia, in which the CIA had no direct role.

One of the best-known and most damning witnesses to the thirty-odd-year CIA operation in Angola was John Stockwell, who managed the covert program there and ran an intelligence-gathering post in Vietnam. Before ending his 13 years with the agency by resigning, he was awarded the U.S. government Order of Merit. Overwhelmed by moral indignation at the practices he observed or supervised in places like Nicaragua, El Salvador and Angola, in 1978 Stockwell published his book, Search for Enemies, which became an international bestseller. The agency prosecuted him for violation of government secrecy oaths and CIA censorship rules, and federal courts forced him to hand over all his royalty earnings to the U.S. government.

In June 1986, Stockwell delivered a lecture which was broadcast by a liberal radio station, KCSB, called The Other Americas Radio, in Santa

Barbara, California. He charged that most of the agency's operations in the world were rotten to the core, and that torture, murder, bribery, corruption, and lying to the U.S. government, Congress, and the American people, were common tools in its efforts to "defend national security." Some of Stockwell's memories of his own involvement at the top of the Angola program are graphic:

"I HAD BEEN DESIGNATED AS THE TASK FORCE COMMANDER THAT WOULD RUN THIS SECRET WAR [IN ANGOLA IN 1975 AND 1976]. IN THIS JOB, I WOULD SIT ON A SUB-COMMITTEE OF THE NATIONAL SECURITY COUNCIL. WHAT I FOUND, QUITE FRANKLY WAS FAT OLD MEN SLEEPING THROUGH SUB-COMMITTEE MEETINGS OF THE NSC IN WHICH WE WERE MAKING DECISIONS THAT WERE KILLING PEOPLE IN AFRICA. I MEAN LITERALLY. SENIOR AMBASSADOR ED MULCAHY ... WOULD GO TO SLEEP IN NEARLY EVERY ONE OF THESE MEETINGS ... THE U.S. LED THE WAY AT NEARLY EVERY ESCALATION OF THE FIGHTING. WE SAID IT WAS THE SOVIETS AND CUBANS THAT WERE DOING IT. THERE WOULD HAVE BEEN NO WAR IF WE HADN'T GONE IN FIRST. WE PUT ADVISORS IN, THEY ANSWERED WITH ADVISORS. WE PUT IN ZAIRIAN [CONGOLESE] PARA-COMMANDO BATTALIONS, THEY PUT IN CUBAN ARMY TROOPS. WE BROUGHT IN THE SOUTH AFRICAN ARMY, THEY BROUGHT IN THE CUBAN ARMY. AND THEY PUSHED US AWAY. THEY BLEW US AWAY BECAUSE WE WERE LYING, WE WERE COVERING OURSELVES WITH LIES, AND THEY WERE TELLING THE TRUTH. AND IT WAS NOT A WAR THAT WE COULD FIGHT. WE DIDN'T HAVE INTERESTS THERE THAT SHOULD HAVE BEEN DEFENDED THAT WAY..."OUR CONSUL IN LUANDA, TOM KILLORAN, VIGOROUSLY ARGUED THAT THE MPLA WAS THE BEST QUALIFIED TO RUN THE COUNTRY AND THE FRIENDLIEST TO THE U.S.. WE BRUSHED THESE PEOPLE ASIDE, FORCED NAT DAVIS [ANOTHER STATE DEPARTMENT DIPLOMAT WHO OPPOSED THE CIA PROXY WAR] TO RESIGN, AND PROCEEDED WITH OUR WAR. THE MPLA SAID THEY WANTED TO BE OUR FRIENDS, THEY DIDN'T WANT TO BE PUSHED INTO THE ARMS OF THE SOVIET UNION [SOMETHING WHICH MARCELLINO DOS SANTOS TOLD ME IN RABAT, MOROCCO, BACK IN 1961]; THEY BEGGED US NOT TO FIGHT THEM; THEY WANTED TO WORK WITH US. WE SAID THEY WANTED A CHEAP VICTORY, WE WOULD MAKE THEM EARN IT, SO TO SPEAK. AND WE DID. TEN THOUSAND AFRICANS DIED AND THEY [THE MPLA] WON THE VICTORY THAT THEY WERE WINNING ANYWAY. "THREE WEEKS AFTER WE [THE CIA OPERATION] WERE SHUT DOWN [BY THE CARTER ADMINISTRATION]...THE MPLA HAD GULF OIL BACK IN ANGOLA, PUMPING THE ANGOLAN OIL FROM THE OILFIELDS, WITH U.S. GULF TECHNICIANS, PROTECTED BY CUBAN SOLDIERS, PROTECTING THEM FROM CIA MERCENARIES WHO WERE STILL MUCKING AROUND IN NORTHERN ANGOLA."[15]

What Henry Kissinger had launched in 1975 and President Carter had scuttled was re-launched in 1981. President Ronald Reagan approved a new covert aid package for UNITA. Although the MPLA by this time was firmly established in power and working with Gulf and the other American and multi-national oil companies, UNITA was still capable of running the country. This it what they set about doing. As Jeffrey Harding reported, "Washington's financial and diplomatic backing was an immense boost...The figures for war-related deaths, and child deaths in particular, leapt dramatically in the 1980s. Towns and villages were deserted or shelled to extinction. The countryside was a living death. There were landmines and limbless people everywhere. Young men were press-ganged into the burgeoning rabble of the Angolan Army, where the discipline of the elite units could not hope to reach. Units kidnapped and abducted its fighters or picked up the homeless, traumatized survivors of government offensives. Some of them were so-called 'child soldiers'-'premature adults' is a better description. Savimbi, his white mercenaries and his black tribal ones, encouraged the practice."

CIA support for Savimbi ceased in 1993, but he fought on after the 1992 election victory of the MPLA. A new peace agreement was signed in Lusaka in 1994, but civil war erupted again in 1998, provoked largely by Savimbi. Followed a final, desperate push by UNITA in 2000 which led to Savimbi's death, a tomb-like stillness crept over the unfortunate country. The extent of the catastrophe was measured, a least in part, in a United Nations report published in June 2001.

"The humanitarian situation in Angola," it stated, "is one of the worst in the world ... At least four million persons [out of an estimated population of 12.9 million] are in a most precarious situation. The survival of about two million of them depends on international aid. Even though the end of the war has brought about a reduction in the displacing of refugees, the situation remains critical overall. The number of persons who will need urgent help during the coming months will climb to three million." The report stated that humanitarian operations between June and December 2002 required $141 million in food aid alone. The international response up to June had provided barely one-third of needs.

The figure of three million included 1.9 million Angolans who had already been placed under United Nations care before the April 4 , 2002 ceasefire. Added to this were 250,000 persons sheltered in centers near the old UNITA camps; 80,000 refugees who had returned to Angola, and 800,000 others spread among the so-called "grey zones" where no international relief organizations could reach them because of the war. The humanitarian group, "Doctors Without Borders" (Medicins sans frontieres) which received a Nobel Peace Prize in 2000 and had been working in Angola over the previous decade, accused the Angolan government and the United Nations of showing "unacceptable inertia" in their response to the crisis.

The MSF went on, "The war strategy followed by both UNITA and the Angolan government, consisting of forced displacements of people, blind violence, the burning of houses and crops, has left hundreds of thousands of people in extraordinary distress...The government's response is nearly zero."[16]

Such were the tragic results of the export of the Cold War and the intervention of the CIA and its Communist-bloc adversaries in one of Africa's largest former colonies. The Angolans and the mercenaries that served both sides in their war did not emulate the Muslim allies of the CIA and Pakistan in the 1979-89 war who exported terrorism and violence to their home countries and eventually to the United States. Nevertheless, the CIA's choice of Jonas Savimbi as an ally in a battle which the CIA was doomed to lose from the beginning, nurtured an obscene and unnecessary proxy conflict with terrible consequences for millions of Africans, and for the assorted mercenaries, spooks, and adventurers from the outside world who chose to join this unholy war in Africa, just as they would join others not unlike it in Africa, Asia ,and Latin America.

The war with the peoples of Indo-China, lost first by France, and then by the United States in its the first wartime defeat, raged in one form or another, from the end of the Japanese occupation of Southeast Asia during World War II until the last two decades of the twentieth century. It has been so well documented in the United States in print, sound, film, and in the bitter memories of so many of its surviving veterans, little of its history requires repeating. The fact is, however, that both the French and Americans used literally millions of mercenaries, sometimes as tribal allies, at other times ostensible state armies such as the national army of South Vietnam, to fight. The French vainly fought to hold on to economically valuable colonial possessions; the Americans to "stop the spread of Communism in Asia." In the end, the administrations of Presidents Eisenhower, Kennedy, Nixon, Ford and especially Lyndon B. Johnson only succeeded in spreading "communism" further - often indistinguishable from indigenous nationalism - and probably sped the rise of Communist China as well.

The lessons which arose and should have been learned from the Indo-China wars resembled in many ways those which emerged again in the 1979-89 Afghanistan War. There was, of course, the futility of using often unreliable mercenaries, and the legacy of abandoned allies whose luckier survivors often found immigrant haven in the United States. There was the spread of drugs throughout the war arena and the outside world, including America. Nor can we overlook parallels between the rise of zealots and destructive fanatics like Pol Pot's Khmer Rouge in Cambodia and the Taliban in Afghanistan. Indo-Chinese events are part of the complex tapestry of deeds and misdeeds by the United States abroad, accompanying the rise of the new American empire.

The complex story of how America came to use mercenaries in the U.S. wars in Indo-China has a simple beginning: it was a habit acquired from their colonial predecessors, the French.

One of the keenest and most far-seeing critics of the CIA's covert actions, especially their involvement in global drug trafficking to finance wars in Indo-China, Central America, and Afghanistan, was former Yale University professor Alfred J. McCoy. In his classic text, The Politics of Heroin, McCoy describes how the French in post World War II Indochina mixed the opium trade with recruiting mercenaries in order to hold their colonies in Vietnam, Laos and Cambodia. French Colonel Roger Trinquier, who I would encounter some years later running covert anti-terrorist operations against the Algerians during their ultimately successful war for independence, also helped organize a white mercenary army in the former Belgian Congo region of Katanga to fight a UN peace force during the 1961 Congo crisis. In Indochina, McCoy discovered, Trinquier organized three counter-guerilla mercenary groups which ultimately showed the way to the Americans who were to follow the French into the mire of Southeast Asian wars. These three were a local maquis beholden to the French in northeastern Laos and the Tonkin region of Vietnam in 1950-53, the Hmong (or Meo) tribal army in Laos, under the command of a notorious drug kingpin, Touby Lyfoung; the Tai tribal army, or Deo Van Long, in northwestern Tonkin; and the separate Hmong mercenaries east of the Red River in north central Tonkin.

Because growing opium poppies was the only significant economic activity in all these regions, the French incorporated opium purchasing through these groups into their pacification policy As long as the French administration bought the opium directly from these groups, they remained loyal to the French and fought the Communist Viet Minh. However, as McCoy observed during his extensive research on the scene, "when the French used non-Hmong highland minorities as brokers and did nothing to prevent the Hmong from being cheated, these same tribesmen joined the Viet Minh-with disastrous consequences for the French."

In Tonkin, northwestern Vietnam, where Dien Bien Phu was located, the local Hmong tribesmen detested the French and were instrumental in their defeat in 1954. The French in Tonkin, insead of purchasing their raw opium directly from the Hmong as in Laos, bought it from another tribal group of mercenaries, the Tai, who acted as intermediaries with the Hmong opium growers. The Tai druglords forced the Hmong to sell their opium at rock-bottom prices, embittering the Hmong toward the French, and reinforcing Hmong support for the Viet Minh communists.

In 1947 the French created the Tai Federation's first local budget, based on its only marketable commodity, Hmong opium. In 1951, French military flights began flying raw opium from the Tai area to Hanoi and Saigon for marketing, and with the pivotal French defeat at Dien Bien Phu, beginning in March 1954, the French generals discovered that they had lost the sympathies of the surrounding population who, embittered by the loss of their drug business, had permitted Viet Minh artillery gunners to bring up cannon which outgunned the French. The Viet Minh captured the French fortress on May 8, 1954. This triggered an immediate peace conference in Geneva and a joint Vietnamese, French, Russian, Chinese, British, and U.S. armistice agreement. On July 30 the war officially ended.

Colonel Trinqier nevertheless continued fighting with 40,000 hill tribe mercenaries commanded by 400 French officers. He also tried to organize 10,000 other tribesmen in the Viet Minh heartland east of the Red River. However, the bulk of French funds to pay the mercenaries was stolen. French morale collapsed and the French Expeditionary Corps began to withdraw from Indo-China in 1965. French officers approached U.S. military personnel and CIA agent Lucien Conein, offering to hand over their entire paramilitary system, including the mercenaries. The Pentagon refused, much to the regret of the CIA when years later they sent the first U.S. Green Berets into Laos and Vietnam to organize hill tribe guerilla mercenaries.[17]

The CIA had already begun to form alliances with drug traffickers early in the Cold War, which it used later in both Latin America and South Asia. In the French port of Marseilles, the Corsican Mafia became the CIA's ally in its fight against communist influence. (In much the same manner, the Roosevelt administration had used "Lucky" Luciano and other underworld figures during World War II, first to fight Axis agents intent on sabotage in the port of New York, then to undermine the Germans and Italian Fascists in Sicily before the Allied landings.) The syndicates supplying most of the heroin to the United States were protected by the alliance with the "French connection" in the Marseilles Mafia.[18]

The Southeast Asian prelude to the large-scale involvement of the CIA in hiring mercenaries and in drug trafficking came during the Truman administration, after the war's end. The fledgling CIA, inheriting the mantle of the wartime OSS (Office of Strategic Services), re-organized General Chiang Kai-Shek's Kuomintang (KMT) in northern Burma to fight the armies of Communist China. The KMT was defeated. However, while in Burma, aided by CIA logistical support, they succeeded in transforming the country into what remains one of the world's main centers of opium production.[19]

As the CIA began to inherit the old French mercenary networks and to create new ones, it soon became apparent that its clients were also main supporters of the opium and heroin business in the so-called "Golden Triangle" - Laos, Burma, and Vietnam. For example, the heroin laboratory at Nam Keung in Laos was protected by Major Chao La, commander of Yao mercenary troops for the CIA in northwestern Laos. One of the labs reportedly belonged to General Ouane Rattikone, former commander of the Royal Laotian Army. This, in a sense, was the only "mercenary" national army in the world entirely financed by the U.S. government. Later, the Shan rebel army in Burma, deeply involved in narcotics, was closely allied with the CIA. The U.S. Bureau of Narcotics, predecessor of the Drug Enforcement Administration, which vainly struggled against the CIA's nod-and-wink policy with the Afghan drug lords during the 1979-89 jihad against the Soviets, discovered that General Vang Pao, overall commander of the CIA's secret mercenary army in Laos, operated a heroin factory close to the CIA's Laos headquarters at Long Tieng. (Later, Vang Pao was given asylum in the U.S. and a new livelihood - a chicken farm in Montana).

By the late 1950s, the CIA had largely taken over the Hmong networks in Laos. From 1960 to 1974, the agency used a secret mercenary army of 30,000 Hmong tribesmen in the northern Laos mountains. Until the Afghanistan war, this was the largest covert war in the agency's history, fighting the Communist Pathet Lao guerillas who were objective allies of the Viet Minh Communists in Indo-China, christened the Viet Cong. The Hmong were a migratory hill tribe, with little loyalty to anyone outside their own chieftains. During the fifteen years they fought as U.S. allies, they took heavy casualties. The CIA ran the operation with only a handful of its officers; a ratio of one for every thousand tribal guerillas, relying mainly on its commander, General Vang Pao. The CIA planners knew that Vang Pao had to rely on support of the Hmong villagers in the northern Laos highlands. So they gave him ample resources and encouraged his alliance with tribal elites like Touby Lyfoung, the drug lord who worked with the French. Vang Pao arranged marriages of his son and daughter to children of Touby.

The austere hill tribesmen relied on two basic commodities: rice for food and opium for cash. "Since the Hmong leaders had little to gain from a French or American victory," McCoy observed, " they were free to demand air transport for their opium as partial price for tribal mercenaries. To prosecute this secret war with any efficiency, the CIA thus found that its agents, like the French paratroopers before them, had to transport the tribe's cash crop [of opium]."[20]

What happened was highly predictable. Just as in Afghanistan, where the CIA apparently adopted a French proposal to addict Soviet troops to drugs and encouraged opium production and traffic in order to help finance the anti-Russian jihad, the CIA took over from the French. In Laos, the CIA's Air America and other planes were used to transport weapons to Hmong bases, and apparently to smuggle raw opium to heroin factories. A great deal of the heroin produced from the Hmong factories was sold to American servicemen in South Vietnam. By the end of 1970, 70,000 American soldiers of the U.S. expeditionary force in Indo-China were addicted. Many who survived the wars took their addiction home with them to the U.S.. Eventually, Southeast Asian opium and its products captured one-third of the entire U.S. heroin market.[21] Later, after a decade of transition between the Indo-China wars and the notoriously un-secret CIA support under the Reagan administration for the mercenary "Contras" in Nicaraugua in the 1980s, a US government accounting office study concluded that 70 percent of all the heroin smuggled into the US and Western Europe originated from areas controlled by CIA mercenaries.[22]

One of the earliest and most adventurous of the U.S. officers organizing the U.S.-supported mercenary wars in Indo-China was Air Force Colonel Edward Geary Lansdale. Born in 1908, his reputation as a counter-insurgency leader had been established while he served as military adviser to Chiang Kai-Shek's troops in their long war against Japan; then enhanced by his tenure as adviser to President Ramon Magsaysay of the Philippines. With CIA support, in 1953 Magsaysay became president of the former American, previously Spanish colony. In the Philippines, Lansdale had considerable success against the Hukabaluk ("Huks") communist guerillas. He then moved to Vietnam and with his advice to both the outgoing French and the incoming Americans, did much to create and shore up the US satellite regime of South Vietnam. He blocked officers of the Vietnamese National Army who wanted to overthrow the pro-American president, Ngo Dinh Diem, in the fall of 1957. He then helped Diem suppress two French-subsidized mercenary armies of two religious sects, the Cao Dai and the Hoa Hao, and the soldiers of an organized crime society called the Binh Xuyen. The latter group, as Pulitzer Prize-winning newsman Neil Sheehan disclosed, had bought a franchise on the Saigon rackets, and had been given control of the police in return for suppressing the city's Viet Minh communists.[23]

During the early 1960s, the CIA delegated William Colby, later to serve as its director, and U.S. Army Colonel Gilbert Layton, to Saigon. To meet the growing Viet Cong challenge, and as a sidebar to the training of South Vietnamese Special Forces, Colby and Layton enlisted tribesmen of the high plateaus of Vietnam, called by their French name, the montagnards - or mountaineers - in mercenary groups to help them construct "strategic hamlets," another anti-guerilla tactic which the British had used against insurgents in post-World War II Malaysia, and the French had tried, unsuccessfully, in Algeria. These were "self-defense" communities of friendly tribesmen, armed and supported by Diem's civilian authorities, with the CIA and U.S. military advisors closely behind Diem. The tribal mercenaries were used to attack forces in North Vietnam, which had not yet totally come to the aid of the Viet Cong forces in the south but soon would.

President John Kennedy ignored the CIA's advice to rely more on the tribal mercenaries. Instead he accepted the advice of General Maxwell D. Taylor, who he sent as his special emissary to Saigon. He adopted a policy of relying on regular U.S. forces which were pouring into Vietnam in growing numbers. The White House either ordered or turned a blind eye to the assassination of Diem and his powerful brother by their Vietnamese opponents on November 1, 1963, only days before Kennedy's own assassination in Dallas.[24]

The Viet Cong, which organized in 1969 as the National Liberation Front of South Vietnam (NLF), gradually came to be led by the Communists and directed by Hanoi. Eventually it included all groups opposed to the Diem regime, those which followed it, and the U.S. presence.

The NLF adopted the "people's war" strategy propounded by Mao Tse-tung. The NLF guerillas used the civilian population as cover in protracted hit-and-run guerilla warfare. They avoided open combat except when the terrain gave them exceptional advantages. Men and supplies infiltrated through Laos and Cambodia along the network of rails named for Ho Chi Minh. Both sides, the Viet Minh and the Americans with their tribal mercenaries, used assassinations, urban terrorism and military action against villages and villagers.
The CIA's organization of the Montagnards in the Central Highlands failed because, as Neil Sheehan reported, Diem had failed to give the local tribes the same autonomy that minorities in the North possessed. He wished to "assimilate" them. This was the opposite of what the Montagnards wanted, because they did not wish to be "Vietnamized." (In Afghanistan the United States experienced a replay of this lesson in ethnic politics when Hamid Karzai, the U.S. choice as Afghanistan's temporary ruler after defeat of the Taliban and al-Qaeda foces in 2002, tried but did not succeed in reconciling the predominant Pushtun forces with the Tajiks of the North who assumed prominent posts after helping to bring about military victory.)

After the Kennedy assassination, President Johnson moved forces on all fronts to oppose the insurgents. He authorized the CIA, its tribal mercenaries, and U.S. Army Special Forces to start aiding the coast of North Vietnam while the U.S. Navy ran electronic intelligence missions in the Golf of Tonkin. General William Westmoreland was appointed to assist the Military Assistance Command, Vietnam (MACV). He raised the number of U.S. military "advisors" to 23,000 and sent more economic aid, warning Hanoi against its growing aid to the southern insurgents. After an attack on August 2, 1964 on a U.S. destroyer connecting electronic intelligence in international waters by North Vietnamese torpedo boats, Johnson ordered retaliatory air strikes. Congress, in the Tonkin Gulf Resolution, gave him a blank check to wage war. Following a Viet Cong attack in February 1965 on U.S. Army barracks in Pleiku, the U.S. began Operation Rolling Thunder, a massive bombing campaign against North Vietnam. Some 50,000 U.S. ground combat forces were introduced and their number soon increased.

The populations of both North and South gradually mobilized and confronted the U.S. and its allies with their full force, driven by patriotic fervor and both Soviet and Chinese aid, though far less than U.S. propaganda depicted. At the height of the war, the U.S. and allies - ultimately including 70,000 South Koreans, Thais, Australians and New Zealanders, as well as 1.5 million Vietnamese who could fairly be called mercenaries, depended on newest military technologies, including napalm, white phosphorous, and such defoliants as the notorious "Agent Orange" which spread severe illness among thousands of U.S. veterans of the war as well as among the local population. The idea of the defoliants was to deprive the Viet Cong of both cover and rice. By 1971, however, the worldwide outcry over U.S. use of chemical weapons and concern about its backlash on Americans led to its halting.

Mercenaries were not confined to the hill tribes and drug lords of Laos, or the montagnards of Vietnam. In Cambodia, as the French phased out and the Americans phased in, the minority Cambodian Buddhists in Vietnam who had migrated to Cambodia, called the Kampuchea Krom, became ardent nationalists. Both the Americans and the Khmer Republic formed them into anti-Communist fighting legions.

Another former French protectorate, Cambodia, gained independence in 1953 as a constitutional monarchy. The king Norodom Sihanouk, was French-educated and accustomed to long and luxurious exiles. In 1955 he abdicated, taking the title of Prince, but continuing to reign until deposed in 1970 by his Prime Minister, Lon Nol. From exile Sihanouk formed the Royal Government of National Union of Cambodia, backed by the Communist Khmer Rouge (Red Khmer) organization of Maoist persuasion. Lon Nol proclaimed the Khmer Republic in Phnom Penh, the capital. Working with the CIA station in Bangkok, Thailand, he tried to bolster his position by raising mercenary bands of the Kampuchea

Krom, Vietnamese immigrants, to fight Sihanouk and the Khmer Rouge communists. Leader of the mercenaries and middleman with the CIA was Son Ngoc Thanh, Cambodia's origina,l and non-Communist, independence fighter during the 1950s wars against the French. Rather than defeating Sihanouk and the Khmer Rouge, the result was to consolidate their alliance, and guarantee their support by the Chinese and Vietnamese Communists.[25]

In 1975 Sihanouk's troops caputed Phnom Penh, and Sihanouk became statutory head of state. The real power, however, was the Khmer Rouge, who soon renamed the country Democratic Kampuchea. With this defeat of America' allies and mercenaries, Cambodian society suffered one of the 20th Century's most dreadful experiments in social transformation. Under the heel of Khmer Rouge chieftain, Pol Pot, between 1975 and 1979 one-eighth of the entire population of ten million died from warfare, starvation, execution or overwork. More than half a million more fled to Thailand. Pol Pot and his cohorts destroyed the Cambodian wealthy and middle classes by taking their money and property, eliminating social distinctions. "Bourgeois" education and learning was destroyed. Peasants, soldiers of the Khmer Rouge, and a few industrial workers were officially given higher status. Professional people, including doctors, lawyers, teachers and scholars, were despoiled of their possessions and either executed or sent to perform hard labor on farmland or roads. Boys and girls over 13 were wrenched from their homes and families, indoctrinated in the tenets of the Khmer Rouge, and forced to act as executioners of all those held to be guilty of "bourgeois" crimes. Violence often exceeded even that of China's Red Guards during the Cultural Revolution.

The Vietnamese, who had triumphed over the Americans and their allies and captured Saigon, uniting the Communist North with the South in the mid-1970s, invaded Cambodia in 1979, ending Pol Pot's bloody rule. However, the Khmer Rouge guerillas continued to fight on through the 1990s, until Pol Pot's death and his followers' surrender in 1998. The United Nations mounted its biggest peacekeeping operation since is creation culminating in free elections in 1995. Trials of some Khmer Rouge leaders began in 2001. Those of the professional classes who survived often emigrated, many to the United States, Canada and France. Visitors to Cambodia during the 1990s confirmed that the effects of the revolution and war are still felt, reflected in the world's highest rate of orphans and widows.

In Vietnam, the CIA and its mercenaries, allied with a military junta in the 1960s headed by Nguyen van Thieu after he took power with CIA assistance in 1967, could not "pacify" the country with any of the tactics Washington tried. In 1967, they resorted to "Operation Phoenix," trying to wipe out the Viet Cong infrastructure through arrests, imprisonment, and assassination. Rival police and mercenary intelligence organizations fighting with the Americans were compelled to pool their information to compile blacklists and choose targets. CIA assassination squads, known as Provincial Reconaissance Units (PRU's) were the action arm. The PRU's often shot first and asked questions later, if at all. Men and women denounced and arrested in their homes or at roadblocks, or captured in fighting, were interrogated without legal process and often killed. Corrupt officials often blackmailed the innocent and took bribes not to arrest those on the target lists. CIA director William Colby would state in 1971 that under the program, 28,000 "enemies" had been captured in all of South Vietnam; 20,000 had been killed, and another 17,000 had defected to "our" side.[26]

After the Tet offensive of the Viet Cong and their North Vietnamese allies in 1968, when the Viet Minh and northern forces attacked Saigon itself and even fired upon the American Embassy, American public opinion turned decisively against the war. President Johnson, cautioned by his 42 percentage of the vote in New Hampshire's primary election for the presidency, reined in the bombing campaign against North Vietnam and withdrew from his reelection bid.

In 1971, during Nixon' first term in office, Kissinger offered to withdraw all U.S. troops within seven months after American POW's had been exchanged, but refused to abandon the Thieu regime. Nixon and Kissinger visited Beijing, but both China and the USSR increased their aid to Hanoi. However, after long negotiations conducted between Kissinger and North Vietnamese envoy Le Duc Tho in Paris, the peace accords signed there on January 31, 1972 brought about a U.S. withdrawal, and the return of many of the POW's. Vietnam was formally reunified under the victorious Communists in 1976. The ignominious retreat of the Americans and all the mercenary and allied leaders they could take with them from the roof of the American embassy in Saigon had been televised for all the world to see. In a mass exodus, one million people who had fought with or for the Americans, or who, because they were Catholics, Buddhists, or other ideological opponents of the Communists, fled the country.

Just as most commentators in the United States have shunned any serious discussion of "why they hate us" after the September 11, 2001 attacks, no one in President Gerald Ford's administration in the 1970s wanted to expose the flaws of the Indo-China wars. As Elizabeth Becker, who provided the best on-the-spot reporting of Cambodia observed, "the war had dragged on long past the height of the antiwar movement. The sharply partisan political debate in the United States was moot, once the North Vietnamese and the Khmer Rouge had fought their way into Saigon and Phnom Penh ... Americans could be jarred from their collective withdrawal from 'Vietnam' only by the most violent reminders or inescapable ironies ... by the steady staccato of a Vietnam veteran holed up in his suburban Washington house and blasting away at his neighbors' homes one wintry Sunday afternoon until the local police arrived and killed him; or by the discovery that an infamous Saigon policeman ran a fast-food café in the shadow of the Pentagon." [27]

As Becker, Sheehan and other observers such as David Halberstam have reported, the U.S. withdrawal from Southeast Asia included not only the war arena, but all non-communist states: Thailand, Singapore, Malaysia, Indonesia, and the Philippines. These member states of the Association of Southeast Asian (ASEAN) alliance were the "dominos" the U.S. administrations had sought to protect from "falling" to Communism.

Little by little, U.S. military presence in these countries shrank. But when President George W. Bush declared, after September 11, a "war on terror," American bases, troops and military advisors began to filter back to the area in various forms. In the Philippines, by the summer of 2002 several thousand U.S. troops were actively engaged in helping the Filipino army and security forces track down and, without notable success, destroy the Islamic guerilla gangs who had kidnapped and killed hostages, including Americans.

Unified Vietnam, free of Western colonial or "friendly" controls, became the Communist giant of Southeast Asia, with a population of 50 million and a huge army which fought China to a standstill in a short, sharp war. Laos became a protectorate of Vietnam, dominated by the Hanoi regime. The Hmong and other mercenaries who had fought, like the Montagnards in Vietnam, loyally for the U.S. while the CIA encouraged their drug business, were defeated by the Communist Pathet in Laos which became the Peoples Democratic Republic of Laos in December 1975. Soon, 40,000 Vietnamese soldiers were stationed in the country, more than the entire Laotian army. Vietnamese ideology and Vietnamese advisors began to dictate policy in Ventiane, the Laotian capital.

The Left in the United States, which enjoyed a brief flowering during the antiwar movement, faded soon after 1975 and the end of the war, as Elizabeth Becker and extreme critics of the war like Noam Chomsky have bitterly observed. Once the U.S. troop withdrawal of 1973 had been completed, the mass movements by students and others who had opposed American intervention in Indo-China, dissolved. Activists in other causes which had fed the antiwar movement - civil rights, feminism, gay rights - moved toward traditional lobbying activities within the American political establishment. Only a few ultra-radical and communist movements advocating revolutionary change in American society appeared, and they barely caused a ripple on the apathetic surface of American life.

For many thousands of people from Laos, Vietnam, and Cambodia who had fought for the losing American side in Vietnam, the end of the war was only the beginning of their troubles. Many fled to refugee camps in neighboring countries. Entire tribes and communities were displaced. Many who chose to stay in their homelands became the object of discrimination, persecution, or worse under the new rulers in Hanoi or Ventiane.

THERE IS A GREAT HISTORICAL IRONY IN THE VARYING FATES OF THE INDO-CHINESE MERCENARIES AND ALLIES OF AMERICA, AND OF THE MUSLIM MERCENARIES WHO FLOCKED TO THE BANNERS OF THE ANTI-SOVIET JIHAD IN AFGHANISTAN IN 1979-89. THE MUSLIM ALLIES OF THE AFGHANS, AIDED BY AMERICA, PAKISTAN, AND THEIR WEALTHY ARAB ALLIES, CHIEFLY IN SAUDI ARABIA, WON THEIR WAR, BUT THEN TURNED AGAINST AMERICA AND THOSE SAME ALLIES. THE TURNING PROCESS BEGAN IN THE LATE 1980S. ABDALAH AL-AZZAM WAS A CHARISMATIC PALESTINIAN AND ONE OF THE IDEOLOGICAL INSPIRATIONS OF THE ISLAMIC RESISTANCE MOVEMENT HAMAS IN THE ISRAELI-OCCUPIED GAZA STRIP. UNTIL HIS MYSTERIOUS MURDER IN 1989, HE SERVED THE CIA AND ITS ALLIES AS A RECRUITER AND PROVIDER OF SAFE HOUSES AND OTHER FACILITIES FOR THE MOUJAHIDDIN. AFTER HIS DEATH, USAMA BIN LADEN ASSUMED CONTROL OF AL-AZZAM'S NETWORK. BIN LADEN, ALREADY HELPING FINANCE THE ANTI-SOVIET JIHAD-AND THROUGH HIS GIANT CONSTRUCTION FIRM CREATING BASES FOR ITS FIGHTERS-SET UP AL-QAEDA (THE "MILITARY BASE" OR "COMMAND POST") AS A SERVICE CENTER FOR THE COMBATANTS. IT BECAME AN EXPANDING BASE FOR THE AFGHAN WAR VETERANS, MANY WHO CONTINUED TO BE FUNDED BY SAUDI ARABIA AND OTHER PRIVATE ARAB AND MUSLIM FINANCIERS, AND WERE TRAINED BY PAKISTAN'S ISI INTELLIGENCE SERVICE, LONG AFTER THE DEFEATED SOVIETS LEFT AFGHANISTAN.

Thus began the "privatization" of anti-Western terrorism: the use of Arab and other Islamic mercenaries, trained and battle-hardened in the Afghan jihad, to fight in Kashmir, Egypt, Algeria, the Sudan, and Far Eastern countries like the Philippines, before beginning terrorist operations in the United States with the attack on the CIA headquarters in Virginia and the first World Trade Center bombing in 1993. Bin Laden and his lieutenants expanded the Al-Qaeda concept into a widening international terrorist movement. Alone, or aided by local allies or copycat groups, it proved itself capable of such apocalyptic operations as 9/11; the Bali resort explosion of October 2002, and the Chechen rebel hostage crisis in Moscow the same month which took well over 100 lives. These events devolved directly or indirectly from the victory by "our side" in the 1979-89 Afghan war.

The Indo-Chinese allies and proxies of the CIA, on the other hand, ended up on the losing side. Their only hope for a decent post-war life, sometimes even survival, lay in emigration to the West and the protection of their American sponsors. One of the most poignant human postscripts of the Indo-Chinese was the fate of the Montagnards, from Vietnam's central highlands, numbers of whom were still arriving in the United States months after the attacks of September 11, 2001.

TIME magazine's Barry Hillenbrand recorded the arrival in Raleigh, North Carolina of hundreds of Montagnards in the summer of 2002 from two refugee camps in Cambodia. Armed with American visas and their medical records, and telling tales of their persecution by the Vietnamese, they were greeted by happy members of the 3,000-srong Montagnard community which had emigrated earlier. Some of the American Green Berets with whom they had trained and fought the war helped them to move to areas near the U.S. Army's Special Forces base at Fort Bragg, North Carolina. Glen Envil, a 34-year-old Montagnard woman who landed in Raleigh with her husband and three children, told Hillenbrand she was forced to leave Vietnam as life grew "worse and worse." The Vietnamese government seized farmland which had been Montagnard family property for generations, Vietnamese settlers and migrants were moved into their tribal lands by the government and were drawing profit from their coffee and rice crops - which had long since replaced the opium poppies of the war years. Envil and her family said they had grown so desperate that they walked for ten days through the jungle to reach a UN-run refugee camp in Cambodia.

Just as the French in African colonies, and the Americans in the Philippines, converted many "natives" to Christianity, U.S. Protestant missionaries followed the CIA and the U.S. armed forces into Indo-China to convert the "natives" there. Well more than half of the Montagnards became Christians. The Communist government in Hanoi, frowning on religion generally but tolerating the Buddhism of the Vietnamese majority, granted few government approvals for the Protestant churches of the Montagnards. One Montagnard arrival in Raleigh, 35-year-old Leh Ksor, recalled that in 2000 police used tear gas to break up a Christmas pageant in a village near the Cambodian border. Parents fleeing with their children were beaten by police. Later, about 20,000 people held a week of protests against religious persecution. Police raided the home of one 16-year-old girl who described how they seized bibles and ransacked her home. Despite Vietnamese government denials, the Human Rights Organization and the State Department authenticated the reports. The Bush administration granted special refugee status to 900 Montagnard tribesmen still in Cambodian camps in July 2002. Those remaining behind were subjected to repression and jail, splitting up families whose younger members were able to flee, but leaving behind older members to pay the price for having fought for the losing foreigners.[28]

The fact that the U.S. enlisted Muslim allies from all over the world for the Afghanistan jihad (1979-89), and subsequently allowed some of the same veterans to move to former Yugoslavia to bolster the Bosnian Muslim army in their wars against the Christian Serbs and Croats, was symptomatic of the reluctance of the U.S. after the loss of thousands of American servicemen and allies in Indo-Chinese defeats, to stop taking risks. At the end of the Cold War, with ethnic and internecine fighting breaking out in various parts of Europe, Africa, and the Far East, the U.S. and its allies tried to become peacekeepers, meaning that the United States found itself spotlighted in many regions, aspiring police chief of the world. However, the days of John F. Kennedy's exhortation that the U.S. should be prepared to "take any risks" and fight anyone's fight to put the world to rights, ended with the Cold War. President Bill Clinton's two administrations saw something like an absolute ban on anything but "tech wars" similar to the Gulf War against Iraq in 1991 where the risk of U.S. casualties was minimal. This was confirmed during the brief U.S. intervention in Somalia that began as a genuine humanitarian mission to protect emergency food supplies during that blighted country's drought and famine in 1993, but ended when 18 American soldiers were killed in a fire fight with Somali clans, one was dragged through the streets before television cameras for all the world to see.

As a result, the U.S. was happy to see Muslim volunteers, including many moujahiddin who had fought in the Afghan jihad, join the Bosnian army. **The most proxy of all the proxy wars was fought in Kosovo in 1999 by NATO air power from an altitude of 15,000 feet, where pilots were not in serious danger, but where the bombing of hostile Serb forces could not be too accurate, killing many innocent civilians. By contrast, by NATO accounts, not a single allied foot soldier was killed in the months of combat in Kosovo.**

In the mid-1990s in Bosnia, the Pentagon began "privatizing" the NATO war the way British Prime Minister Margaret Thatcher's contribution to the Afghan war was privatized using British mercenaries to train groups of moujahiddin. The U.S. did its training mainly with U.S. armed forces and CIA personnel. 29 In Yugoslavia, the U.S. wished to preserve the pious fiction of its neutrality despite sporadic intervention of NATO air power against the Bosnian Serb forces. For this reason, it could not be seen openly training and arming the Bosnian Muslims. If so, the Serbs might be driver to launch attacks on U.S. troops. The Clinton Administration pledged not to play an active role in re-arming them. Instead, the Pentagon and the CIA arranged for a private company, already quietly helping the Croats, to work with the Bosnians. Military Professional Resources Inc. (MPRI), based in Alexandria, Virginia, was founded in 1988 and boasted in one of its brochures that it was "the greatest corporate assemblage of military expertise in the world." In 1996 it claimed 160 full-time employees and about 2,000 retired generals, admirals, and other officers on call. Senior executives included retired four-star General Carl Vuono, U.S. Army commander during the Desert Storm campaign in 1991, and Crosby ("Butch") Saint, former chief of U.S. Army operations in Europe who headed MPRI's Balkan operations.[30]

There were competing bids from two other private firms, BDM, controlled by the investment firm, the Carlyle Group, headed by such luminaries as former Secretary of State James Baker, and SAIC, whose board included two former defense secretaries, William Perry and Melvin Laird, and two former CIA directors, John Deutsch and Robert Gates. The Bosnian government was headed by an avowed Muslim fundamentalist, President Alija Izetbegovic, and the $400 million program was paid largely by Saudi Arabia, the main U.S. ally in the Afghan jihad, whose National Guard has been trained by the Vinnell Corporation, an MPRI-affiliated firm, and by Kuwait, Brunei, and Malaysia. The stated aim of training the Bosnian army was to deter Serbia's better-armed forces, but it also created a useful offensive capability. MPRI had already won its spurs in Yugoslavia by supporting training and - according to some investigative reports - operations such as Operation Lightning Storm, a Croatian assault on the Krajina region where villages of the Serbian community were sacked and burned, hundreds of Serb civilians killed, and some 170,000 people driven from their homes.[31] The campaign's crimes caused several cases to be opened against Croatian officers at the International War Crimes Court in The Hague.

The roots of Muslim mercenaries fighting for the Bosnians stretch back to World War II. During that conflict, after the German invasion and occupation of Yugoslavia, several Croat and Bosnian Muslim units served the Axis armies. The Croat Ustashi became infamous for their atrocities against the anti-German Serbs, indulging in ethnic cleansing in order to convert the puppet Croat Ustahi state into a purely Croat entity. Croat volunteers, according to some historians, also manned two Nazi SS divisions as well as an elite Croat Legion which served under German command on the Russian front. In Axis-occupied Yugoslavia, the former Mufti of Jerusalem, Hajj Amine al-Husseini helped organize the Bosnian Muslims into several units under SS command, especially the largely Muslim 13th SS "Handzar" division. This was possibly intended to spearhead Hitler's drive toward Middle East oilfields in case General Erwin Rommel's German forces in North Africa were able to overrun Egypt and reach the Suez Canal (which they were not). The Bosnian Muslim units, including the Handzar division, joined the Ustashi forces in terror campaigns and ethnic cleansing against the Serbs in what is today western Bosnia-Herzogovina and the Krajina region.

Bosnian president Izetbegovic's purpose in the wars against the Croats and Serbs in the 1990 appeared to be to provoke the NATO intervention that preceded the Dayton peace accords of 1995. The building of the Bosnian Muslim army and the launching its campaigns was entrusted to Commander Ram Delic, whose plan was to precipitate Western intervention and enable the Muslim forces to conduct a major war against both Serbs and Croats. By 1993, Delic, with help and encouragement from Muslim states abroad, and certainly with the knowledge if not the active help of the CIA, was importing foreign Muslim volunteers, especially moujahiddin veterans of the Afghan war. The main Muslim bases were the Dubrave air base and heliport near Tuzla, and the Butmir airport near Sarajevo. Iran, Syria, Turkey Egypt and Saudi Arabia are believed to have pledged sophisticated weapons systems, including missiles, heavy artillery, and crews and ammunition. Iran delivered many of these supplies in C-130 cargo flights, detected by UN observers, to which the United States deliberately turned a blind eye.

By April 1994, the Bosnian regime in Serb-besieged Sarajevo had set up a professional high command. The army was organized into seven corps, each composed of one to three brigades, including special units of moujahiddin mercenaries. In May 1995, the mercenary units were formally organized as the Third Corps.

In 1993 these units had already been unleashed by the Bosnian command on the Croatian towns of Travnik and Varez, committing atrocities against Croat civilians and taking many hostages. This caused the two enemies, the Bosnian Serbs and the Bosnian Croats, to unite against what one senior Croat official, Davor Kolenda, described as "the Islamic fanatics." In the spring of 1994, following a disastrous Serbian attack on the town of Gorazde, Dutch Brig. Gen. G.J.M. Bastiaans, heading the UN Military Obsrvers (UNMO) in former Yugoslavia, declared, "It was the Muslims who provoked the Serbian attack on Goradze. The Serbs perhaps reacted excessively. But ultimately it was the Muslims who pushed the Bosnian Serb Army to the bloodbath of the civilian population of Goradze with continual provocations."

The U.S. command and the rest of NATO, even before the NATO air missions launched in late August of 1995 that helped end the war, acknowledged their support for the Bosnian Muslims, even their tacit support for violation of the arms embargo on Bosnia-Herzogovina. The U.S. and UN, as noted earlier, tolerated arms shipments from Iran and possibly other Muslim states into Croatia during 1994. These weapons found their way to Bosnian Muslim forces. In February 1995, air supply flights grew more frequent, including some flights directly into Tuzla where the Muslims were preparing an offensive. On June 30, a senior French army officer formally accused the U.S. of providing weapons, combat intelligence, and military expertise - probably the MPRI's - to the Bosnian Muslims in violation of the embargo. To European colleagues, U.S. officials privately acknowledged that C-130 flights came from Turkey and other Muslim states, but not from the U.S..

In the spring of 1995, new Islamic volunteer mercenaries closely associated with Algeria's Armed Islamic Group (GIA) began to arrive in Bosnia-Herzogovina,. Among them were some of the newly-trained Bosnian volunteers, the first suicide terrorists seen in Europe. Following the Popular Arab Islamic Conference in Khartoum, Sudan in April 1995, regional training centers, possible prototypes for Usama bin Laden's Al-Qaida movement, were set up in Tehran and Karachi, Pakistan; the later with responsibility for Albania and the Albanian Kosovar movement. The commander of the mercenary Third Corps of the Bosnian Muslim army became an Egyptian Islamist and was given the nom de guerre of "Amir Katibat al-Mujahiddin." The Third Corps was based in the Travnik and Zenica areas in central Bosnia. Secret directives of Algeria's Armed Islamic Group ordered its followers to prepare for an offensive "as a jihad to defend their religion and sacred principles against this crazed and spiteful [Christian] crusade."

Some of the planning for the spread of the Islamic jihad in the Balkans and elsewhere was done in the mid-1990s in Khartoum, the Sudanese capital, where Usama bin Lama stayed before his departure for Afghanistan in 1995 prompted by U.S. and Saudi pressure on the Sudanese military regime of General Omar Bashir. The most powerful political group, the National Islamic Front (NIF) led by Sheikh Hassan Tourabi, an urbane, well-traveled Islamic scholar educated in the West, regarded the Balkans conflicts in the same terms as it regarded Kashmir, Palestine, and other struggles pitting Muslims against the West. Therefore, the NIF under Tourabi's guidance studied legal guidelines for the type of jihad that should be waged in Bosnia. It found a fatwa, or Muslim religious decree, issued by an Islamic conference held at Al-Obayed, Sudan on April 27, 1993 that regulated jihad between Muslims and non-Muslims with specific mention of Bosnia, Palestine, and Kashmir. (Later, after the influence of Al-Qaeda declined with bin Laden's departure for Afghanistan, Tourabi's influence declined, too, enmeshed in the circumstances of the long and bloody civil war in southern Sudan between the Muslim government and the Christian animists who drew aid from southern neighbor states, Uganda, Kenya and Ethiopia,. By the year 2000, General Bashir had sidelined Tourabi, and after a December 2000 election, Bashir and his National Congress party were returned to power.)

However, in mid-May 1995, several months before the Dayton peace conference, the Algerian GIA helped complete a new camp in Bosnia called "Martys' Detachment" to receive newly arriving moujahiddin. A small number of "martyrs," or suicide terrorists, including about a dozen Bosnians trained in Afghanistan and Pakistan, arrived at the camp, which was believed by Western intelligence to be intended partly as a training camp for Islamist terrorists in Western Europe. In early June 1995, Italian authorities arrested a dozen Algerian Islamists, most of them Afghan veterans, running a terrorist network in Italy. During the same month, French security forces detained or arrested over 140 North African terrorist suspects. (New groups, run by Iran's secret service, VEVAK, have also used Afghan veterans.) A wave of terrorist bombings in the Paris metro and other at sensitive targets in France was claimed by the GIA in a September 23, 1995 communique issued in Cairo by GIA spokeman Abu Abdel Rahman Amin, explaining that the attacks in France were part of "our holy struggle ... to prove that nothing will stand in our way as long as our actions are for the sake of Allah."[32]

Such events, and the 1993 attacks on CIA headquarters in Langley, Virginia and the World Trade Center in New York by Afghan jihad veterans, should have warned everyone about the dangers of using Afghan veterans as mercenaries. In the United States intelligence community, they caused scarcely a ripple.

They did, however, in Europe - especially in France. Jean-Louis Brugiere, a Paris investigating magistrate gifted with formidable analytical powers and a dogged commitment to fight terrorism whether it directly impacted France or not, was already tracking Usama bin laden's network by the mid-1990s. Events such as the torching of a U.S. embassy building in Algiers, car bombings in Saudi Arabia, and the Paris metro attacks deepened his concern about a global threat. Soon a motley group of brigands with at least indirect links to the CIA in Roubaix, France came to his attention. Most were of Algerian descent, but their leader was a 25 year-old former French medical student named Christopher Caze, who had been raised not as a Muslim, but as a Catholic. Caze had volunteered to work as a hospital medic in Bosnia. After several months there, he returned, an apparent Muslim convert and radical Moslem, wearing white robes and black hair to his shoulders.

Caze's masked "Roubaix gang," as the French media called them, was involved in bank robberies, attacking and looting supermarkets and armored cars, and using such weapons as machine guns and grenade launchers. At the end of March 1996, French President Jacques Chirac was to preside at a meeting of the G-7 in Lille, France. On March 28, Caze's group rigged a Peugeot with explosives and bottles of compressed gas and parked it near the meeting site. French police found and defused the bomb in time, and located the gang hiding in an apartment building. Four, including Algerian ex-mercenaries who had served in Bosnia, were killed in a raid. Caze escaped only to be gunned down the next day when he attempted to crash a roadblock.

Brughiere was called in on the case. Among Caze's list of contacts was a young Algerian whom Caze had treated for his wounds in Bosnia, Fateh Kamel, a suspected Al-Qaeda member with residence in Montreal, Canada. This, as Brugiere told an investigating team from the Seattle Times newspaper, suggested that "the structure of the organization - and the targets - had changed. The targets weren't just in France or in Europe" - they were in North America as well.[33] Later, the investigation of Ahmed Ressam, the Algerian ex-GIA member captured by U.S. Customs and police as he tried to smuggle a bomb in a rental car intended to blow up Los Angeles airport at the 1999 New Year's millennium anniversary - part of an extensive global conspiracy by al-Qaeda - turned up close links between Fateh Kamel and other ex-"Bosnian Afghans," as these mercenary veterans came to be called.

Despite these multiple warnings about the Bosnian/Afghan mercenaries, they continued to pour into the Bosnian Muslim army, encouraged by President Izetbegovic. In the 1995 Dayton Peace Accords, Izetbegovic agreed with the other signatories that all of them should be out of Bosnia in 1995. Western complaints that they remained were ignored until January 2000, when U.S. law enforcement agencies, the Canadians, and others originally alerted by the investigative digging of Jean-Louis Brugiere in Paris, discovered a group of ex-"Bosnians" to be associated with the New Year's Day plots in the U.S.. One, Karim Said Atmani, was named by authorities as a document forger for a group of fellow Algerians accused of planning the bombings. Atmani was a former roommate of Ahmed Ressam, and a frequent visitor to Bosnia, from which he had returned just a few days after Ressam's arrest upon debarking from a Vancouver ferry at Port Angeles, Washington with his carload of explosives in December 1999.

The U.S. Embassy in Sarejevo and the FBI pressed the Bosnian government to search their passport and residency records. This revealed other former Afghan moujahiddin linked to the same Algerians and other terrorist groups who lived in an area 60 miles north of Sarajevo. One of them, interestingly, was a Jordanian-born American citizen, Khalil Deek, who had trained in Afghanistan before being arrested by Jordanian and Pakistani intelligence agents in December.[34] Deek was personally escorted to Jordan on a flight by the deputy chief of Jordan's redoubtable GID (General Intelligence Division) which was relentlessly pursuing al-Qaeda and other terrorists. Deek was said by Jordan media to have been arraigned with a group of similar background. The others were convicted of plotting to blow up the Radisson Hotel in Amman and of planning machine-gun attacks on American and Israeli tourists at several tourist and pilgrimage sites in Jordan. Curiously, however, Khalil Deek, whose computer was said to contain a "terrorist encyclopedia" of information like that once imparted by the CIA to anti-Russian "holy warriors" in

Afghanistan, was kept in a separate prison from the other defendants. His lawyer claimed a violation of habeas corpus and of other human rights. But Deek was quietly released and sent home to his family in California, giving rise to Jordanian suspicions that he had all along been a CIA or FBI plant, sent to infiltrate bin Laden's organization in South Asia.[34]

A third "Bosnian" suspect, an Algerian named Abu Mali, was asked to leave Bosnia in the spring of 1999 after U.S. intelligence convinced Bosnian authorities he was a terrorist threat. Still another Muslim, probably a Tunisian, named Mehrez Amdouni, was arrested by Turkish police in September 1999 in Istanbul. He had arrived on a Bosnian passport, and was charged with counterfeit and possession of stolen goods.

The center for most Muslim mercenaries in Bosnia was the town of Bocinja Donja. Washington Post correspondent Jeffrey Smith, who visited the town in March 2000, discovered a sign along the road warning visitors to "be afraid of Allah." Two NATO generals who visited the previous year were threatened or attacked by residents. In August 1999, the windshield of a visiting relief worker was shattered by the blow of an ax. Smith found that of the approximately 600 residents, 60 to 100 were former Islamic mercenary volunteers from the Middle East who had arrived to help the Bosnian Muslims in the 1992-95 war. After the war they organized a community observing a much stricter form of Islam than the one followed by the majority of Muslim Bosnians. Women wore veils and long robes; the men had beards and abstained from smoking and drinking alcohol, reminiscent of the Afghan Taliban.[35]

After the September 11, 2001 attacks in the U.S., the Bosnian government woke up and tried to clamp down on their foreign "guests." Bosnian border police reinforced border controls, and instituted landing card documents to be filled out by travelers arriving at Sarajevo airport. Bosnian security arrested such suspects as an associate of bin Laden's deputy, Abu Zubaydah (captured by the U.S. in Pakistan in early 2002). Also arrested were five Algerian GIA members. One of them, Sabir Lahmar, had made threats against NATO's SFOR security forces and U.S. interests.

Lest these measures be viewed as new cases of locking the barn door after the horse has been let out, under U.S. prompting the Bosnians did make some important anti-terrorist moves before September 11. In April 2001, authorities arrested Said Atmani, Ahmed Ressam's Canada roommate, and extradited him in July to France where Judge Brugiere had seen to an Interpol warrant. The same month, Bosnian security arrested two members of the al-Qaeda-affiliated Egyptian group, al-Gama'a al-Islamiyya. Both were extradited to Egypt in October 2001. However, as a State Department report complained, various NGO's identified as supporting terrorist activities maintained their presence in Bosnia. Having entered the region during the 1992-95 war, they "continued to provide assistance to Islamic extremists throughout Bosnia, to include procuring false documents and facilitating terrorist travel," the State Department reported. "The [Bosnian] government has taken some significant steps to freeze assets and monitor activities of some of the NGO's, but their ability to ... combat these organizations as been weakened by some residual support for those in the Islamic world that supported Bosnian wartime efforts," the report concluded.[36]

Our final consideration of the mercenary groups enlisted by the U.S. and NATO allies before the post-Afghanistan disaster of September 11, 2002, deals with Kosovo. The U.S.-led NATO war effort there in 1999 was against Serbian President Slobodan Milosevic, now on trial before the International War Crimes Tribunal in The Hague, accused of war crimes in Bosnia, Croatia and Kosovo. The force on "our side" in Kosovo, which had first been listed on the State Department's blacklist of terrorist organizations, then removed and reclassified as an "asset" for the 1999 war against Serbia, enjoying training and other CIA benefits, was the ethnic Albanian Kosovo Liberation Army (KLA).

Even before the beginning of the 1990s, the Kosovo crisis ran in tandem with the conflicts in the rest of former Yugoslavia, but was slower in developing. The year 1989 marked the 600th anniversary of the Battle of Kosovo, in which Serbia lost the province to the Ottoman Turks. Serbia still celebrates the anniversary like a national holiday, but in 1989, the vast majority of the Kosovo Albanians protested against the arbitrary actions of Serb-controlled police. Serbian leader Slobodan Milosevic initiated a severe crackdown, ending the province's former autonomy. In 1990, Milosevic and his Socialist Party were victorious in Serbian national elections. Communists also won the Yugoslav federal presidency and dominated the elections in the province of Montenegro. All this served to tighten further Belgrade's grip on Kosovo, and the repressiveness of its administration in the capital Pristina.

In 1992, in part due to pressure from Germany and Austria, the European Union recognized the breakaway republics of Croatia, Slovenia and Bosnia-Herzogovina. As the Bosnian war began and the UN imposed sanctions on the combatants, a mild-mannered and moderately-inclined ethnic Albanian politician, Ibrahim Rugova, was elected president of the self-declared "republic" of Kosovo. Rugova's moderation, however, was already being challenged by an underground ethnic Albanian force which came to be called the KLA. Closer to it politically than Rugova was Adem Demaci, who had festered in Serbian jails for 28 years, and emerged to head the Kosovo "Council for the Defense of Human Rights and Freedom." After three years of Serbian occupation, Albanian Kosovars refused to recognize the legality of the Yugoslav federal administration, dealing with it only when forced to, and boycotting all Serbian-called elections. Gradually the Albanians organized a parallel society, centered around a "makeshft private school system, " as Wes Jonasson, American journalist and close observer of the Balkans, writes in his book Dialogue With the Damned, the Balkans During a Time of Transition and Tragedy. While only Albania, recently emerged from half a century of isolation and extreme poverty under the most draconian Communist regime in post-World War II Europe, recognized the Kosovo republic, Rugova traveled in the West, strengthening ties with such leaders as Pope John Paul II. In the summer of 1993, about 90 ethnic Albanians were arrested by the Serbs on arms and subversion charges, and many were given prison terms.

During the mid-90s, the KLA was incubating in the seething unrest in Kosovo and gaining support and financial donations abroad, while the world spotlight remained on Bosnia and the Dayton peace settlement. Significant violence began to erupt in January 1998 when a Serb district council member was assassinated in his car, following an Albanian's death in a police action. The KLA began to claim credit for the ensuing attacks on Serbs, some of them fatal. By March 1998, the Serbs were using helicopters and armored vehicles and the death toll on both sides had risen to about fifty. This caused the Western Contact Group on Yugoslavia to re-impose sanctions which had been lifted after Dayton, banning credits, investments, arms trade, and freezing assets abroad. The tension and fighting continued, with Albania repeatedly asking NATO, which now had a considerable presence in the capital, Tirana, to send a peacekeeping force into Kosovo. Rugova was reelected, but when he attempted to compromise with Belgrade on the school system, the KLA warned him that he must not accept anything short of complete independence for Kosovo. The KLA took responsibility for killing six so-called Albanian collaborators. Fighting now began to develop between organized bands of KLA guerillas, many of them infiltrated from Albania, into which Kosovar refugees heading in the other direction now flowed. When strong Serb forces moved on the Drenica area in May, Albanian villagers began to fight alongside KLA units, contesting control of the border.

On June 11, 1998, 83 aircraft from thirteen NATO countries staged mock air attacks over Albania and Macedonia in an attempt to intimidate Milosevic into halting his military actions against the Albanians in western Kosovo. Planning for genuine for NATO air strikes was under way.[37]

By this time, as U.S. intelligence agents have since admitted, the CIA had begun training the KLA.

When news of this was leaked, some European diplomats were angered, suggesting it undermined political solutions to the conflict. CIA officers, newsmen on the spot reported, were ceasefire monitors assiged to Kosovo in 1998 and 1999 before the NATO war on Milosevic or the Albanian exodus from Kosovo had begun in earnest. In actuality, they developed ties with the KLA and dispensed training manuals - often not unlike those familiar to the Afghan and Bosnian moujahiddin - and field advice on how to fight the Yugoslav army and Serb police.[38] Later, eyewitnesses reported that U.S. and allied Special Forces units joined and sometimes replaced CIA officers in these functions. At about this time, one observer who visited northern Albania, found some of the CIA's raw material: young, ill-trained young men "wearing bits and pieces of uniforms, but with plentiful light arms, moving back and forth across the border with Kosovo. They seemed to have no strategy beyond wanting independence."[39]

By now, the KLA, welcoming Arab and other mercenaries from the Middle East, had long been supported by a powerful Albanian-American lobby in the United States. In February 1991, ethnic Albanian supporters and émigrés set up an office in Tirana, and lobbied Albanian President Sali Berisha, already predisposed in their favor, to play on Albanian nationalism and push for "liberation" of Kosovo. This idea had strong appeal for the approximately 400,000 ethnic Albanians and an active Rightist Albanian organization. From 1986 onward, Republican Senator Bob Dole urged Kosovo to break away from Serbia and establish independence. U.S. Representative Joseph DioGuardia helped form the Albanian-American Civic League to lobby for the Kosovar cause in Congress. Rights activist Adem Demeaci was invited to Washington and met Congressman Tom Lantos, the powerful chairman of the House of Representative's Foreign Affairs Committee.

In Europe, the largest community of ethnic Albanians, composed mainly of Kosovars, was in Germany, where there were 120,000, followed by Switzerland with 100,000. Here it was easy for the KLA to recruit mercenaries while authorities looked the other way. Wealthy Kosovars in

Switzerland were notoriously linked to drug traffic with the Balkans, a specialty of the so-called "Albanian Mafia" since the fall of the Communist regime, many of whose secret policemen, the dreaded former Sigurimi, were involved in organized crime and the flourishing arms traffic. Agence-France Presse reported on June 1, 1998 that Albanian army conscripts allowed an arms depot to be looted of hundreds of small arms. With or without Western instructors, KLA mercenaries from 1992 on were also being trained at an Albanian army camp at Labinot, near Elbasan, Albania. Some of the KLA Albanians had fought in Bosnia alongside the Arab mercenaries.[40] Evidence of these mercenaries was found in evacuated strongholds of the KLA, including paper litter pointing to Saudi Arabia, Germany and even Scotland. The death of five Arab fighters in Kosovo is said to have reported in a newspaper in Yemen.

Political leadership sat with Kosovar "prime minister" Buyar Bukoshi. Formerly close to Rugova, Bukoshi had gravitated toward the KLA. Traveling widely in Western Europe, he promoted the KLA-affiliated political organization, the People's Movement of Kosovo, and raised funds for the KLA through a three percent "tax" on the 600,000 ethnic Albanians living there. An umbrella fund called "Homeland Calling" (Vendlindja Therret) was set up in bank accounts in Switzerland and Germany.

Inside Albania, one of the biggest fund-raisers and recruiters of mercenaries was reportedly the Jashari clan, whose members were involved in an assortment of crimes. Its leader, a young man named Adem Jashari, was wanted for rape and extortion, and for smuggling arms into Kosovo from Albania beginning in 1991. He eluded capture and by 1997 had enlisted other clan leaders in the KLA cause. In early 1998 he and a brother were killed when Serb police surrounded their village. Fifty one Kosovars died in the battle, including thirty Jasharis. At this time, the U.S. State Department was still calling the KLA a "terrorist organization," although by then the CIA had probably begun its covert training program.

In the fall of 1998, the wind from Washington changed radically. The Clinton Administration began calling for an "in place" cease-fire that would permit the KLA to keep whatever territory it still controlled in the face of steadily advancing Serb forces. It also took the KLA off its terrorist list, recognizing them as a legitimate party in the conflict. Western media began to portray the conflict as David vs. Goliath. Goliath was, of course, Milosevic and his federal and Serbian forces. To strengthen his position, Milosevic played on Washington's fears of a Russian return to Eastern Europe by signing a defense pact with Russian Defense Minister Igor Sergeyev, which may have included arms supplies, although this was not affirmed publicly.

In February 1999, as both Serb repression and KLA resistance stiffened, NATO made ready for war against Milosevic. A provisional cease-fire of sorts held in Kosovo. A conference of Yugoslavs, Kosovar Albanians and NATO was called in Rambouillet, France, following failed peace missions by senior U.S. diplomats including Richard Holbrooke. This was to be a final chance for peace. But Serb and Kosovar delegates were hardly speaking to one another, let alone negotiating. Threatened by war, the Yugoslav delegation remained largely aloof and let NATO talk to the Kosovars, including the newly recognized KLA. NATO - mainly the U.S., Britain, France and Germany - began amassing over 30,000 troops. The Yugoslavs insisted that Kosovo must remain an integral part of Serbia and of federal Yugoslavia. Most odious to them was a clause in the draft agreement which gave NATO forces unlimited freedom of movement-throughout all of Yugoslavia's provinces. Milosevic was adamant: he would never agree to what he contended was a virtual NATO military occupation of his country. As NATO reinforcements poured into neighboring Macedonia through the Greek port of Thessaloniki, Milosevic mobilized 7,500 troops and 200 tanks on the Kosovo border. Allied supreme commander in Europe, General Wesley Clark, a former Rhodes scholar who participated in the Dayton accords before assuming command in 1997, firmly believed that Milosevic's forces were no match for the sophisticated weapons of the U.S. and NATO, from Tomahawk cruise missiles and Nighthawk F-117 Stealth fighters, to AWAC surveillance planes, lumbering old B-52 bombers, new B-2's, and tank-busting A-10 Warthog bombers. With NATO's 50th birthday looming, it was clear to Clark - and his chief, President Clinton - that they could not let Milosevic get the better of them.

The KLA, now being trained and assisted by the U.S., objected to the Rambouillet draft accords because they failed to grant full Kosovar independence, leaving Yugoslavia at least symbolically sovereign. U.S. Secretary of State Madeleine Albright reportedly gave the KLA assurances that a referendum on Kosovo's indepedence would be scheduled once peace was established, and the conference ended after the KLA's Thaci signed the draft agreement with NATO.

In mid-March 1999, President Clinton green lighted the massive NATO bombing of Serbia that began on the night of March 24, with an attack on about forty military targets from Belgrade to Pristina. During the 78 days of war which followed, the KLA - like most guerilla forces in large conventional wars - took a back seat as NATO's airpower slugged it out in a lopsided battle with Milosevic's forces. NATO flew a total of 37,200 missions, 200 to 300 daily, dropping some 25,000 tons of ordnance, including 1,100 cluster bomb units containing 200,000 'bomblets' which scattered, often unexploded, in civilian areas. Over 1,000 civilians were killed and thousands more wounded. Main roads and railway bridges over the Danube were destroyed, all but blocking for months to come one of Europe's most important waterways. Industrial and power-generating targets of all types were hit.

As soon as the bombing began, Milosevic's militia inside Kosovo began to move fiercely and methodically against the Albanian population of Kosovo. As of March, about 2,500 Albanians had died, with many Albanians and Serbs displaced inside Kosovo. Once the NATO bombing began on March 24, 800,000 Albanians were expelled and many more brutally killed by the Serb miltia and Yugoslav soldiers and police. The high-altitude attacks and cruise missile launches were hardly the precision bombing so widely advertised in the Western media. Television buildings, the Chinese embassy, and a number of other non-military targets were demolished in Belgrade.

When the war ended with Milosevic's surrender in June, the surviving Albanians and the refugees who came trickling back under NATO's protection began ethnic cleansing in reverse. The KLA celebrated what it considered its own victory-using NATO and the U.S., which suffered scarcely any casualties, for its air cover-by cheering General Clark in Pristina and receiving the congratulations of Madeleine Albright. [41]

What concerns us here are not the details of the war and peace, the fall of Milosevic, and the slow re-entry of the remnants of former Yugoslavia (Serbia and its junior partner Montenegro) into the democratic community of European nations. These matters are public record. Our concern is the KLA; its future, and its impact in the West, both before and after September 11, 2001.

Ironically, Mayor Rudolph W. Giuliani, one of the heroes during the September 11 attacks on New York and the physical and moral reconstruction which came afterward, had a strong preview of what the KLA was to become and what it would mean for New York. As The Wall Street Journal reported, while Giuliani was U.S. Attorney in New York City, on September 9, 1985, almost seven years to the day before the assault on New York, he and his chief assistant, William Tendy, heard an account, later confirmed by five other informants, from a defendant in a drug racketeering case he was prosecuting. It concerned an offer of $400,000 to anyone who would kill a designated US attorney and a federal drug enforcement (DEA) agent - Alan M. Cohen and Jack Delmore respectively. The two men, immediately given 24-hour bodyguards, were investigating, with intent to disrupt, the so-called "Balkan connection" heroin trade in which a group of ethnic Albanians in the New York area played a prominent role. Many Albanian immigrants to the U.S. before and after World War II had become respectable real estate managers and small business owners. An estimated 100,000 lived in the New York metropolitan area, and in other communities in Michigan, Massachusetts, and Illinois. There, a very small but dangerous minority formed an "Albanian mafia," a number with records of violent crime in places like New York's Bronx and Hamtranck, Illinois, a Detroit suburb.

According to DEA sources, heroin from South Asia was flowing through Turkey, Bulgaria and Greece into Yugoslavia. From there, it was distributed into most of Western Europe and the United States. In the U.S, ethnic Albanians and Turks were identified as the primary distributors.[42] A number of them, who the enterprising Journal reporter, Anthony M. DeStefano identified by name, had long criminal records. One of the Albanians operated a travel agency on Staten Island, which he apparently used to book drug courier trips to and from Yugoslavia. Others engaged in deadly turf or market disputes. Giuliani said he had learned of an attempt to carry out a murder contract put out on himself, Cohen, and Delmore. The conviction of over 10 Albanian-American drug traffickers followed closely.

U.S. federal authorities grew certain that the Albanian drug mafiosi were among the patrons of the KLA. Confirmation came in Europe in 1998. General Mario Mori, who commanded the Special Operations Section (ROS) of the carabinieri in Milan, succeeded in neutralizing a big drug network operating in Italy, Germany, Spain, France, and Norway operated by Kosovo Albanians. Its leader was 33-year-old Gashi Agim from Pristina. In October 1998, Agim, married to an Italian girl and living in a luxurious villa outside Milan, owned a chain of beauty parlors and perfume shops in London. In June, he and 123 other alleged drug traffickers were arrested.

Italy, General Mori announced, had been their main base. Negotiations between Kosovar bosses, of the Tirana-based Albanian gangs, and Italian operatives took place. The Italian mafia group, based in Calabria, called the 'Ndrangheta, took delivery and distributed about 50 kilograms of heroin daily. Affiliated groups were tracked down in the rest of Europe. Storehouses containing thousands of kilograms of heroin and cocaine were found in places like Bratislava and Budapest. Transport of the drugs was the responsibility mainly of Germans using cars with tanks capable of carrying 20 kilograms of drugs at a time, or long-haul trucks with "cover" loads that arrived in Milan from Austria.

The Kosovo war slowed somewhat the criminals' business because many of the Albanians had to care for their families. Many were active KLA fighters who went home to fight for a "greater Albania" (an idea enthusiastically supported by many in the U.S. Albanian community). General Mori's investigators discovered that much of their drug profits went to support families and to fund certain Albanian politicians and the anti-Serb movement. A number of those with police records demonstrated at the U.S. Embassy in Rome, demanding more American support.

The 'Ndrangheta connections in Calabria, in towns like Africo, Plati and Bovalino, purchased arms for the KLA. The Italian and Albanian main criminal arsenal was located in Calabria's Aspromonte region, and included rocket launchers, sniper rifles with telescopic sights, submachine guns, and grenades. An ROS agent told the Corriere della Sera newspaper: "The 'Ndrangheta is different from other Mafia-style organizations. It has only one objective: business. And in order to make the biggest profit it is prepared to forge alliances with anybody [especially Muslims]. The Calabrian bosses are not interested in controlling the Milanese territory. And ... the Albanian groups are free to run the prostitution racket without any interference."[43]

One of the most recent appearances of the ethnic Albanian movement, in which the militia was openly assisted by U.S.-paid contractual mercenaries for "training," was between 1999-2001 in ethnically-divided, landlocked Macedonia. (refered to officially - because of Greek sensibilities over its northern province of the same name, with its glorious past in antiquity - by the ponderous name, "Former Yugoslav Republic of Macedonia" or FYROM). About 67 percent of the approximately two million Slav Macedonians speak a Slavic language closely akin to Bulgarian. The Albanian minority claims to represent over one-third of the population, but registered only 25 percent during the last census in 1994. Before, during, and after the Kosovo war, an influx of over 100,000 Kosovar refugees threatened to upset the ethnic balance, and with it the little state's inner stability. Former Communists, holdovers from Marshal Tito's Yugoslav dictatorship or from the Milosevic era before independence in 1991, held power until the end of the 1990s. The main ethnic Albanian political party, the DPA, demanded recognition of its autonomy as a constituent "nation" within FYROM. However, it opposed other Albanian "intruders" of the former KLA, known in Macedonia as the National Liberation Army, or NLA, which emerged in 2001.

Slav-Macedonian President Boris Trajkovski was elected in December 1999 as the candidate of a nationalist Slav party, the VMRO, descended from the first-ever European terrorist organization of modern times, IMRO, or Internal Macedonian Revolutionary Organization, formed to fight Turkish domination at the start of the 20th Century.

James Bisset, a Canadian diplomat who served as a former ambassador to Yugoslavia, and became a bitter critic of what he considers NATO's wholly unjustified intervention against Yugoslavia in Kosovo, described his own observations of the upheavals in the Macedonian capital, Skopje, and the country in general, as a result of the Kosovo upheavals. During the 1999 Kosovo War, Bisset observed, the KLA realized that NATO, content to bomb the Serbs from high altitudes, was not willing to risk ground troops. This became evident after the outbreak of the war when KLA troops crossed the border from Kosovo and intruded into southern Serbia. NATO refused to send ground troops stop that aggression. Only when NATO struck a deal with the more democratic post-Milosevic regime in Belgrade to have Serbian troops restore order was the KLA advance halted.

Thwarted there, the KLA moved into Macedonia, and in March 2001 moved into FYROM. As Bisset observed, it used the "same tactics as those it used successfully in Kosovo" - i.e., ambush, assassination, and intimidation of the local [Slav] population. The Western powers armed and equipped the KLA. Macedonian government forces used the same tactics Serb forces employed in Kosovo: shelling villages harboring KLA fighters, resulting in civilian casualties and refugees. Nonetheless, the KLA continued to receive NATO help. In June 2001, when government forces were closing in on KLA fighters near the northern town of Aracinovo, a NATO protection force intervened to evacuate the KLA fighters to safety. This, according to European newsmen on the scene, was because 17 Americans from one of the U.S. mercenary groups were among the KLA forces."[44]

At one point during the summer of 2001, Albanian rebels, mercenaries, and vigilante groups controlled one-third of Macedonia. Human rights abuses, a familiar Balkan pattern, abounded on both sides. Then, in mid-August, under UN and NATO auspices, both sides signed an agreement to improve Albanian rights and observe a ceasefire. KLA/NLA rebels said they would disarm and disband in return for an amnesty. A small NATO force, led by British troops entered during the early fall of 2001 and managed to collect some Albanian weapons. The fragile country entered a period of uneasy calm.

What happened in Bosnia and Kosovo was, to some extent, repeated in Macedonia, though on a far less lethal scale. Islam - nearly all of the KLA fighters were Muslims - had entered another Balkan country in greater force. Saudi Arabia and other Arab states sent aid and charity missions, and increased their political influence in Skopje.

The arena's biggest winner was Turkey, which had the largest overseas community of ethnic Albanians in Europe. During the 1999 NATO air campaign, Turkey provided the use of air bases and 1,000 Turkish soldiers to help German troops police the Prizren area of Kosovo. Ankara was a key ally of the U.S., which supported its commercial aims in Central Asia. Paramount was the famous Baku to Ceyhan oil pipeline, cutting Iran and Russia out of the lucrative transport of Caspian and Central Asian oil to the West. For the same strategic reasons, Washington, with support of several big multinational oil and natural gas conglomerates, encouraged Turkey's takeover of leadership of the peace force in Kabul, Afghanistan in June 2002, replacing the initial British troops and officers. Albanian and other Balkan crime and drug mafias looked forward to strengthening their bases and expanding their operations in the Balkans throughout the long period of reconstruction that lay ahead.

American policy in during many of the minor wars and larger interventions since 1945 has, through use of mercenaries, frequently incurred serious consequences. In Tibet it aroused vain hopes, soon dashed, of liberating the country's ancient, tribal-based Buddhist and hierarchical society from Communist Chinese occupation and indoctrination. In Cuba the ill-starred Bay of Pigs mercenary expedition became a victory for Fidel Castro's revolution in Cuba, and a stinging setback with wide-reaching consequences for the Kennedy administration and the CIA. In Indo-China the takeover and expansion of originally French colonial concepts of proxy warfare, using druglords as pawns and drugs as a source of financing, led to defeat and (for a relative few) a new life in the West, affecting millions of American allies and supporters. In Africa's former European colonies, especially Angola, the local campaigns of the U.S.-Soviet Cold War fought by proxy by both Soviet and American sides, brought on-or aggravated-poverty, corruption and the ruin of millions of lives. Mercenaries, mostly of Afghan war origin, fought for NATO's side in the Balkans in the 1990s with mixed results.

Ultimately the international terrorist/guerilla force created by the CIA and its Pakistani and Arab allies in the 1979-89 war against the Soviets blew back against America, its people and their sense of security. The explosions of 9/11, and the ensuing spread of Al-Qaeda-type violence to many parts of the world, have underlined once again the bitter lessons of history, one of which was so well identified by Niccolo Machiavelli in his 16th-century caveat against employing mercenaries.

Analyses and post-mortems involved in plotting the Bush administration's projected "war on terrorism," - all part of an increasingly unilateral, even imperial attitude toward the militarily and economically weaker nations of the world - will reach many conclusions about the future. One of the biggest will undoubtedly be: Be wary of allies and followers. Look forward as you exercise your overwhelming power - but watch your back.

030

RON HAVIV

BLACK AND WHITE
AN UNCERTAIN JOURNEY WITH THE U.S. MILITARY

A man in a black hat enters a town, commits various evil deeds and is then confronted by a man in a white hat. They battle and time and time again the man in the white hat is victorious.

Growing up in middle class America, this seemed to be the way that the world worked. It seemed the right way, and the only way. Of course, America was supposed to be the man in the white hat, and various other rogue nations and tough guys wore the black hat in different styles.

Yet as time passed this black and white vision faded. And when I entered the world on a true level of reality, it disappeared. Over the last decade or so the United States has involved itself fighting battles of varying degrees in the world around it. Sometimes full-fledged as in the first Gulf War, then quickly backtracking, stranding thousands when the geopolitical winds shift. Other times it had to be dragged and shamed into intervention, as in Bosnia when it was determined not to fall into a quagmire with the Europeans. America has also made full use of its claim of self-defense by entering Afghanistan and Iraq. Yet in the case of Afghanistan the American attention span quickly wore out.

It is often disconcerting to be on the ground witnessing displacement, ruin, destruction and slaughter that simple policy changes might have prevented. Sitting in the desert once again, documenting another cause the United States deems imperative to its national security, raises the question — when and why intervene?

This work touches upon some of the people that were encouraged, ignored and sometimes halfheartedly helped by the United States. Hopefully in this new post — 9/11 world Americans find themselves in, we will realize that what happens thousands of miles away from our homes can and will effect us. In addition to the self-survival aspect, the people of America need to bear responsibility for our actions around the world.

< **Fort Leonard Wood**
U.S. Army conducts early morning
exercises during basic training at Ft. Leonard Wood
Missouri 1999.

030 Ron Haviv
An Uncertain Journey with the U.S. Military

Page 331

BLACK AND WHITE
> KURDISTAN

< Northern Iraq
U.S. forces hold mass in Northern Iraq
after setting up a safe zone for the Kurds
after the end of the 1st Gulf War 1991.

< Turkey
A Kurdish refugee looks at her child
who died as she fled Iraq to Turkey after
the end of the 1st Gulf War 1991.

< Turkey
A Kurdish refugee crosses from
Iraq to Turkey after the end of the
1st Gulf War 1991.

◊ Turkey
U.S. forces drop food aid to Kurds
after they fled Iraq to Turkey after the end
of the 1st Gulf War 1991.

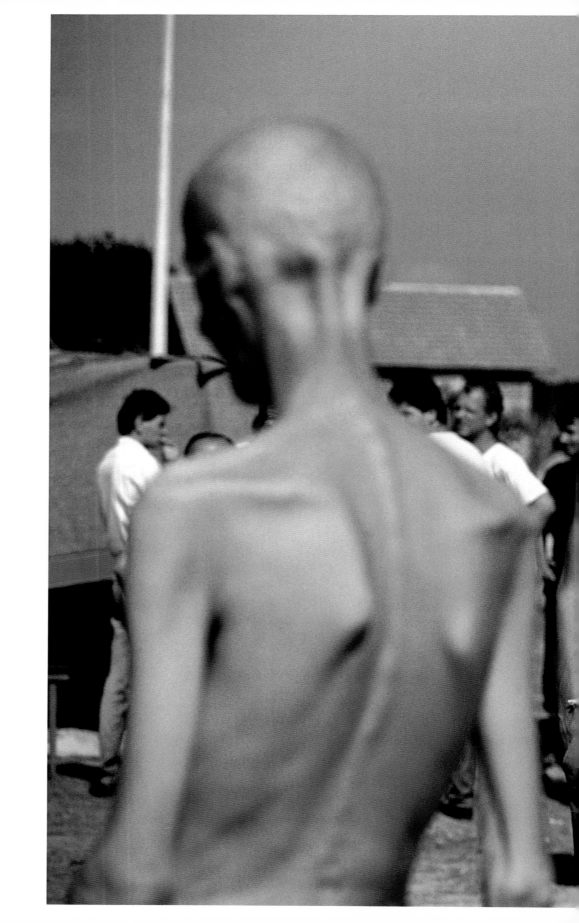

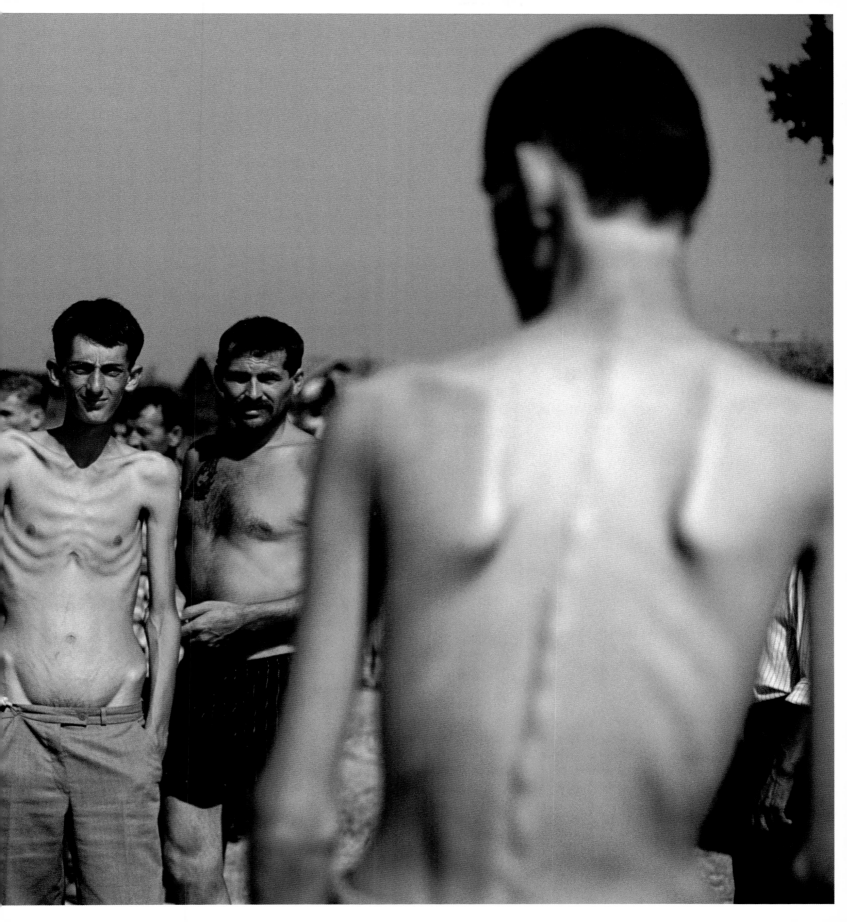

< **Bosnia**
Bosnians wait for U.S. forces
to arrive. Thirty thousand NATO
roops were deployed 1995.

< **Ahmici**
A Mosque is destroyed in
Central Bosnia 1993.

< **Trnopolje**
Prisoners at the Trnopolje
camp in Bosnia 1992.

< **Bosnia**
American peacekeepers arrive in
Bosnia to enforce the Dayton Peace Agreement
that ended the war 1995.

◊ **Bijeljina**
A Muslim in Bijeljina begs
for his life after capture by Arkan's
Tigers 1992.

> **Bijeljina**
Arkan's Tigers killing civilians
in Bijeljina, during the first battle
for Bosnia 1992.

> **Belgrade**
A torn poster of former Yugoslav President
Slobodan Milosovic on a
Belgrade wall the day of his arrest 2001.

030 Ron Haviv
An Uncertain Journey with the U.S. Military

◊ **Sarajevo**
A defaced photograph found by a Bosnian family when they returned to their home in a Sarajevo suburb. The Serbs who had occupied the house left as the city was reunified under the Muslim-led Bosnian government, taking with them the family's furniture, appliances, cabinets, sinks, and window panes. This was the sole they left behind 1996.

< **Kosovo**
U.S. soldiers work out at Camp Bond Steel, the largest US overseas field base since Vietnam, in Kosovo. 2000

< **Kosovo**
A Kosovar Albanien watches her house burn after it was struck by a Serbian artillery shell 1998

◊ **Montenegro**
Kosovar Albanians arrive in Montenegro after being expelled by Serb forces 1999.

> **Pristina**
Kosovar Albanians celebrate in the streets of Pristina 1999.

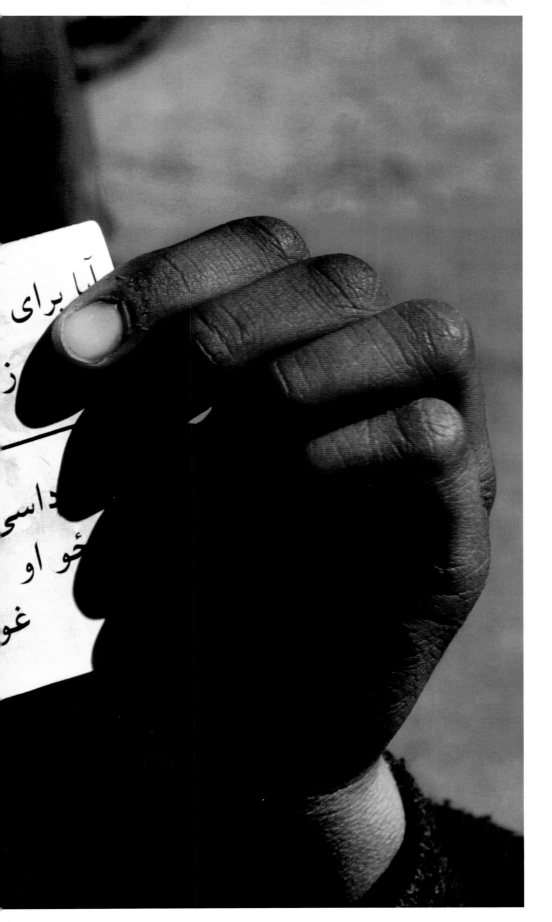

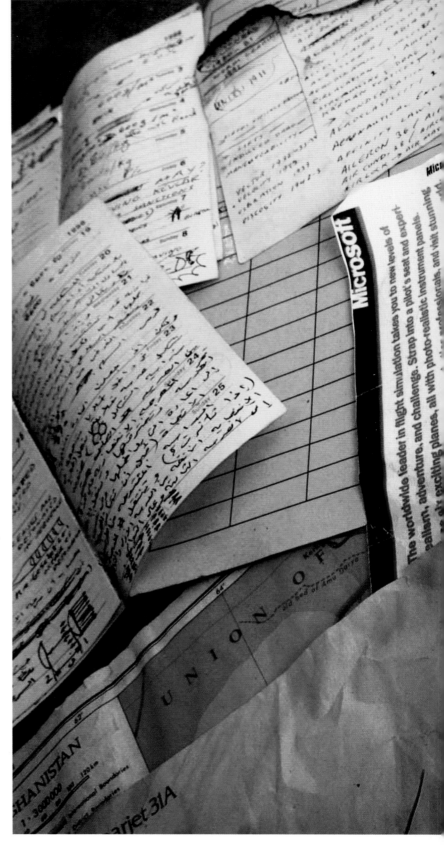

> **Kabul**
Northern Alliance soldiers
rejoice as they enter Kabul
for the first time 2001.

030 Ron Haviv
An Uncertain Journey with the U.S. Military

Page 369

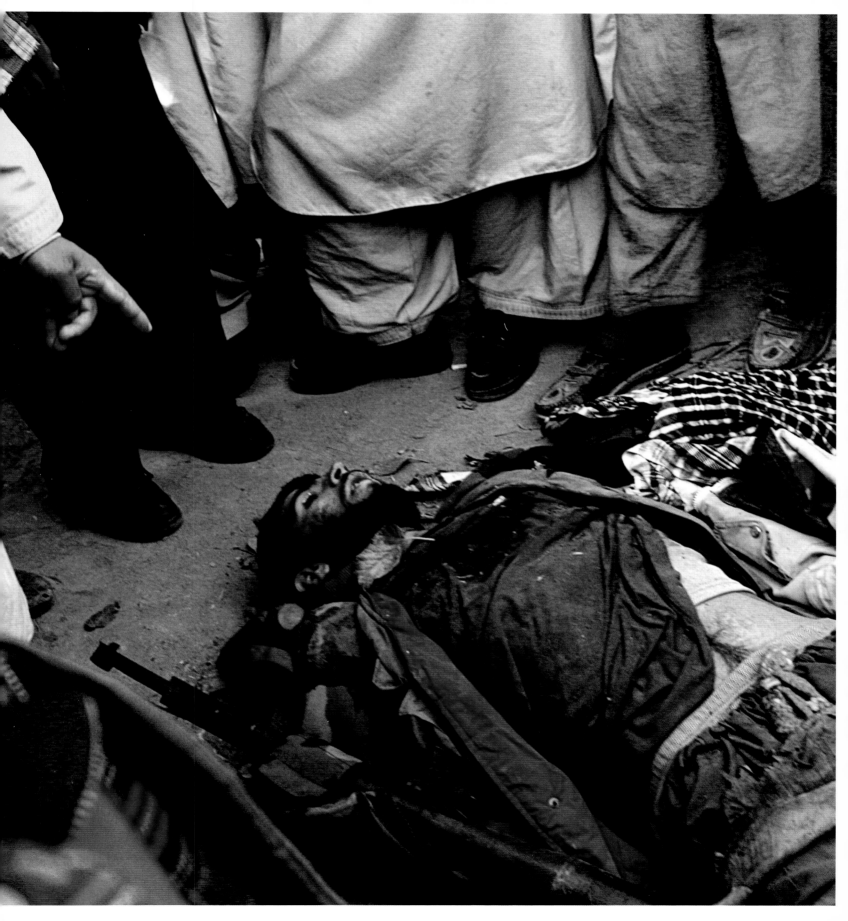

BLACK AND WHITE
> IRAQ

◊ **Basra**
Capture of an Iraqi tank by US Marines
near Basra in Southern Iraq 2003.

> **Baghdad**
U.S. Marines celebrate with the Iraqi people
as they enter the center of Bagdahd and help topple
a statue of Saddam Hussein 2003.

031

GEORGE W. BUSH

REMARKS AT THE UNITED NATIONS GENERAL ASSEMBLY
SEPTEMBER 12 2002

Mr. Secretary General, Mr. President, distinguished delegates, and ladies and gentlemen: We meet one year and one day after a terrorist attack brought grief to my country, and brought grief to many citizens of our world. Yesterday, we remembered the innocent lives taken that terrible morning. Today, we turn to the urgent duty of protecting other lives, without illusion and without fear.

We have accomplished much in the last year — in Afghanistan and beyond. We have much yet to do — in Afghanistan and beyond.

Many nations represented here have joined in the fight against global terror, and the people of the United States are grateful.

The United Nations was born in the hope that survived a world war — the hope of a world moving toward justice, escaping old patterns of conflict and fear. The founding members resolved that the peace of the world must never again be destroyed by the will and wickedness of any man. We created the United Nations Security Council, so that, unlike the League of Nations, our deliberations would be more than talk, our resolutions would be more than wishes. After generations of deceitful dictators and broken treaties and squandered lives, we dedicated ourselves to standards of human dignity shared by all, and to a system of security defended by all.

Today, these standards, and this security, are challenged. Our commitment to human dignity is challenged by persistent poverty and raging disease. The suffering is great, and our responsibilities are clear. The United States is joining with the world to supply aid where it reaches people and lifts up lives, to extend trade and the prosperity it brings, and to bring medical care where it is desperately needed.

As a symbol of our commitment to human dignity, the United States will return to UNESCO. This organization has been reformed and America will participate fully in its mission to advance human rights and tolerance and learning.

Our common security is challenged by regional conflicts — ethnic and religious strife that is ancient, but not inevitable. In the Middle East, there can be no peace for either side without freedom for both sides. America stands committed to an independent and democratic Palestine, living side by side with Israel in peace and security. Like all other people, Palestinians deserve a government that serves their interests and listens to their voices. My nation will continue to encourage all parties to step up to their responsibilities as we seek a just and comprehensive settlement to the conflict.

ABOVE ALL, OUR PRINCIPLES AND OUR SECURITY ARE CHALLENGED TODAY BY OUTLAW GROUPS AND REGIMES THAT ACCEPT NO LAW OF MORALITY AND HAVE NO LIMIT TO THEIR VIOLENT AMBITIONS. IN THE ATTACKS ON AMERICA A YEAR AGO, WE SAW THE DESTRUCTIVE INTENTIONS OF OUR ENEMIES. THIS THREAT HIDES WITHIN MANY NATIONS, INCLUDING MY OWN. IN CELLS AND CAMPS, TERRORISTS ARE PLOTTING FURTHER DESTRUCTION, AND BUILDING NEW BASES FOR THEIR WAR AGAINST CIVILIZATION. AND OUR GREATEST FEAR IS THAT TERRORISTS WILL FIND A SHORTCUT TO THEIR MAD AMBITIONS WHEN AN OUTLAW REGIME SUPPLIES THEM WITH THE TECHNOLOGIES TO KILL ON A MASSIVE SCALE.

In one place — in one regime — we find all these dangers, in their most lethal and aggressive forms, exactly the kind of aggressive threat the United Nations was born to confront.

Twelve years ago, Iraq invaded Kuwait without provocation. And the regime's forces were poised to continue their march to seize other countries and their resources. Had Saddam Hussein been appeased instead of stopped, he would have endangered the peace and stability of the world. Yet this aggression was stopped — by the might of coalition forces and the will of the United Nations.

To suspend hostilities, to spare himself, Iraq's dictator accepted a series of commitments. The terms were clear, to him and to all. And he agreed to prove he is complying with every one of those obligations.

He has proven instead only his contempt for the United Nations, and for all his pledges. By breaking every pledge — by his deceptions, and by his cruelties — Saddam Hussein has made the case against himself.

In 1991, Security Council Resolution 688 demanded that the Iraqi regime cease at once the repression of its own people, including the systematic repression of minorities — which the Council said, threatened international peace and security in the region.

This demand goes ignored.

Last year, the U.N. Commission on Human Rights found that Iraq continues to commit extremely grave violations of human rights, and that the regime's repression is all pervasive. Tens of thousands of political opponents and ordinary citizens have been subjected to arbitrary arrest and imprisonment, summary execution, and torture by beating and burning, electric shock, starvation, mutilation, and rape. Wives are tortured in front of their husbands, children in the presence of their parents — and all of these horrors concealed from the world by the apparatus of a totalitarian state.

In 1991, the U.N. Security Council, through Resolutions 686 and 687, demanded that Iraq return all prisoners from Kuwait and other lands. Iraq's regime agreed. It broke its promise. Last year the Secretary General's high-level coordinator for this issue reported that Kuwait, Saudi, Indian, Syrian, Lebanese, Iranian, Egyptian, Bahraini, and Omani nationals remain unaccounted for — more than 600 people. One American pilot is among them.

In 1991, the U.N. Security Council, through Resolution 687, demanded that Iraq renounce all involvement with terrorism, and permit no terrorist organizations to operate in Iraq. Iraq's regime agreed. It broke this promise. In violation of Security Council Resolution 1373, Iraq continues to shelter and support terrorist organizations that direct violence against Iran, Israel, and Western governments. Iraqi dissidents abroad are targeted for murder. In 1993, Iraq attempted to assassinate the Emir of Kuwait and a former American President. Iraq's government openly praised the attacks of September the 11th. And al Qaeda terrorists escaped from Afghanistan and are known to be in Iraq.

In 1991, the Iraqi regime agreed to destroy and stop developing all weapons of mass destruction and long-range missiles, and to prove to the world it has done so by complying with rigorous inspections. Iraq has broken every aspect of this fundamental pledge.

From 1991 to 1995, the Iraqi regime said it had no biological weapons. After a senior official in its weapons program defected and exposed this lie, the regime admitted to producing tens of thousands of liters of anthrax and other deadly biological agents for use with Scud warheads, aerial bombs, and aircraft spray tanks. U.N. inspectors believe Iraq has produced two to four times the amount of biological agents it declared, and has failed to account for more than three metric tons of material that could be used to produce biological weapons. Right now, Iraq is expanding and improving facilities that were used for the production of biological weapons.

United Nations' inspections also revealed that Iraq likely maintains stockpiles of VX, mustard and other chemical agents, and that the regime is rebuilding and expanding facilities capable of producing chemical weapons.

And in 1995, after four years of deception, Iraq finally admitted it had a crash nuclear weapons program prior to the Gulf War. We know now, were it not for that war, the regime in Iraq would likely have possessed a nuclear weapon no later than 1993.

Today, Iraq continues to withhold important information about its nuclear program — weapons design, procurement logs, experiment data, an accounting of nuclear materials and documentation of foreign assistance. Iraq employs capable nuclear scientists and technicians. It retains physical infrastructure needed to build a nuclear weapon. Iraq has made several attempts to buy high-strength aluminum tubes used to enrich uranium for a nuclear weapon. Should Iraq acquire fissile material, it would be able to build a nuclear weapon within a year. And Iraq's state-controlled media has reported numerous meetings between Saddam Hussein and his nuclear scientists, leaving little doubt about his continued appetite for these weapons.

Iraq also possesses a force of Scud-type missiles with ranges beyond the 150 kilometers permitted by the U.N. Work at testing and production facilities shows that Iraq is building more long-range missiles that it can inflict mass death throughout the region.

In 1990, after Iraq's invasion of Kuwait, the world imposed economic sanctions on Iraq. Those sanctions were maintained after the war to compel the regime's compliance with Security Council resolutions. In time, Iraq was allowed to use oil revenues to buy food. Saddam Hussein has subverted this program, working around the sanctions to buy missile technology and military materials. He blames the suffering of Iraq's people on the United Nations, even as he uses his oil wealth to build lavish palaces for himself, and to buy arms for his country. By refusing to comply with his own agreements, he bears full guilt for the hunger and misery of innocent Iraqi citizens.

In 1991, Iraq promised U.N. inspectors immediate and unrestricted access to verify Iraq's commitment to rid itself of weapons of mass destruction and long-range missiles. Iraq broke this promise, spending seven years deceiving, evading, and harassing U.N. inspectors before ceasing cooperation entirely. Just months after the 1991 cease-fire, the Security Council twice renewed its demand that the Iraqi regime cooperate fully with inspectors, condemning Iraq's serious violations of its obligations. The Security Council again renewed that demand in 1994, and twice more in 1996, deploring Iraq's clear violations of its obligations. The Security Council renewed its demand three more times in 1997, citing flagrant violations; and three more times in 1998, calling Iraq's behavior totally unacceptable. And in 1999, the demand was renewed yet again.

As we meet today, it's been almost four years since the last U.N. inspectors set foot in Iraq, four years for the Iraqi regime to plan, and to build, and to test behind the cloak of secrecy.

We know that Saddam Hussein pursued weapons of mass murder even when inspectors were in his country. Are we to assume that he stopped when they left? **The history, the logic, and the facts lead to one conclusion: Saddam Hussein's regime is a grave and gathering danger. To suggest otherwise is to hope against the evidence. To assume this regime's good faith is to bet the lives of millions and the peace of the world in a reckless gamble. And this is a risk we must not take.**

Delegates to the General Assembly, we have been more than patient. We've tried sanctions. We've tried the carrot of oil for food, and the stick of coalition military strikes. But Saddam Hussein has defied all these efforts and continues to develop weapons of mass destruction. The first time we may be completely certain he has a — nuclear weapons is when, God forbids, he uses one. We owe it to all our citizens to do everything in our power to prevent that day from coming.

The conduct of the Iraqi regime is a threat to the authority of the United Nations, and a threat to peace. Iraq has answered a decade of U.N. demands with a decade of defiance. All the world now faces a test, and the United Nations a difficult and defining moment. Are Security Council resolutions to be honored and enforced, or cast aside without consequence? Will the United Nations serve the purpose of its founding, or will it be irrelevant?

The United States helped found the United Nations. We want the United Nations to be effective, and respectful, and successful. We want the resolutions of the world's most important multilateral body to be enforced. And right now those resolutions are being unilaterally subverted by the Iraqi regime. Our partnership of nations can meet the test before us, by making clear what we now expect of the Iraqi regime.

IF THE IRAQI REGIME WISHES PEACE, IT WILL IMMEDIATELY AND UNCONDITIONALLY FORSWEAR, DISCLOSE, AND REMOVE OR DESTROY ALL WEAPONS OF MASS DESTRUCTION, LONG-RANGE MISSILES, AND ALL RELATED MATERIAL.

IF THE IRAQI REGIME WISHES PEACE, IT WILL IMMEDIATELY END ALL SUPPORT FOR TERRORISM AND ACT TO SUPPRESS IT, AS ALL STATES ARE REQUIRED TO DO BY U.N. SECURITY COUNCIL RESOLUTIONS.

IF THE IRAQI REGIME WISHES PEACE, IT WILL CEASE PERSECUTION OF ITS CIVILIAN POPULATION, INCLUDING SHI'A, SUNNIS, KURDS, TURKOMANS, AND OTHERS, AGAIN AS REQUIRED BY SECURITY COUNCIL RESOLUTIONS.

IF THE IRAQI REGIME WISHES PEACE, IT WILL RELEASE OR ACCOUNT FOR ALL GULF WAR PERSONNEL WHOSE FATE IS STILL UNKNOWN. IT WILL RETURN THE REMAINS OF ANY WHO ARE DECEASED, RETURN STOLEN PROPERTY, ACCEPT LIABILITY FOR LOSSES RESULTING FROM THE INVASION OF KUWAIT, AND FULLY COOPERATE WITH INTERNATIONAL EFFORTS TO RESOLVE THESE ISSUES, AS REQUIRED BY SECURITY COUNCIL RESOLUTIONS.

IF THE IRAQI REGIME WISHES PEACE, IT WILL IMMEDIATELY END ALL ILLICIT TRADE OUTSIDE THE OIL-FOR-FOOD PROGRAM. IT WILL ACCEPT U.N. ADMINISTRATION OF FUNDS FROM THAT PROGRAM, TO ENSURE THAT THE MONEY IS USED FAIRLY AND PROMPTLY FOR THE BENEFIT OF THE IRAQI PEOPLE.

If all these steps are taken, it will signal a new openness and accountability in Iraq. And it could open the prospect of the United Nations helping to build a government that represents all Iraqis — a government based on respect for human rights, economic liberty, and internationally supervised elections.

The United States has no quarrel with the Iraqi people; they've suffered too long in silent captivity. Liberty for the Iraqi people is a great moral cause, and a great strategic goal. The people of Iraq deserve it; the security of all nations requires it. Free societies do not intimidate through cruelty and conquest, and open societies do not threaten the world with mass murder. The United States supports political and economic liberty in a unified Iraq.

We can harbor no illusions — and that's important today to remember. Saddam Hussein attacked Iran in 1980 and Kuwait in 1990. He's fired ballistic missiles at Iran and Saudi Arabia, Bahrain, and Israel.

His regime once ordered the killing of every person between the ages of 15 and 70 in certain Kurdish villages in northern Iraq. He has gassed many Iranians, and 40 Iraqi villages.

My nation will work with the U.N. Security Council to meet our common challenge. If Iraq's regime defies us again, the world must move deliberately, decisively to hold Iraq to account. We will work with the U.N. Security Council for the necessary resolutions. But the purposes of the United States should not be doubted. The Security Council resolutions will be enforced — the just demands of peace and security will be met — or action will be unavoidable. And a regime that has lost its legitimacy will also lose its power.

Events can turn in one of two ways: If we fail to act in the face of danger, the people of Iraq will continue to live in brutal submission. The regime will have new power to bully and dominate and conquer its neighbors, condemning the Middle East to more years of bloodshed and fear. The regime will remain unstable — the region will remain unstable, with little hope of freedom, and isolated from the progress of our times. With every step the Iraqi regime takes toward gaining and deploying the most terrible weapons, our own options to confront that regime will narrow. And if an emboldened regime were to supply these weapons to terrorist allies, then the attacks of September the 11th would be a prelude to far greater horrors.

If we meet our responsibilities, if we overcome this danger, we can arrive at a very different future. **The people of Iraq can shake off their captivity. They can one day join a democratic Afghanistan and a democratic Palestine, inspiring reforms throughout the Muslim world.** These nations can show by their example that honest government, and respect for women, and the great Islamic tradition of learning can triumph in the Middle East and beyond. And we will show that the promise of the United Nations can be fulfilled in our time.

Neither of these outcomes is certain. Both have been set before us.

We must choose between a world of fear and a world of progress.

We cannot stand by and do nothing while dangers gather. We must stand up for our security, and for the permanent rights and the hopes of mankind. By heritage and by choice, the United States of America will make that stand. And, delegates to the United Nations, you have the power to make that stand, as well.

032

MICHAEL IGNIATIEFF

THE AMERICAN EMPIRE;
THE BURDEN

I

In a speech to graduating cadets at West Point in June, President Bush declared, "America has no empire to extend or utopia to establish." When he spoke to veterans assembled at the White House in November, he said: America has "no territorial ambitions. We don't seek an empire. Our nation is committed to freedom for ourselves and for others."

Ever since George Washington warned his countrymen against foreign entanglements, empire abroad has been seen as the republic's permanent temptation and its potential nemesis. **Yet what word but "empire" describes the awesome thing that America is becoming? It is the only nation that polices the world through five global military commands; maintains more than a million men and women at arms on four continents; deploys carrier battle groups on watch in every ocean; guarantees the survival of countries from Israel to South Korea; drives the wheels of global trade and commerce; and fills the hearts and minds of an entire planet with its dreams and desires.**

A historian once remarked that Britain acquired its empire in "a fit of absence of mind." If Americans have an empire, they have acquired it in a state of deep denial. But September 11 was an awakening, a moment of reckoning with the extent of American power and the avenging hatreds it arouses. Americans may not have thought of the World Trade Center or the Pentagon as the symbolic headquarters of a world empire, but the men with the box cutters certainly did, and so do numberless millions who cheered their terrifying exercise in the propaganda of the deed.

Being an imperial power, however, is more than being the most powerful nation or just the most hated one. It means enforcing such order as there is in the world and doing so in the American interest. It means laying down the rules America wants (on everything from markets to weapons of mass destruction) while exempting itself from other rules (the Kyoto Protocol on climate change and the International Criminal Court) that go against its interest. It also means carrying out imperial functions in places America has inherited from the failed empires of the 20th century — Ottoman, British and Soviet. In the 21st century, America rules alone, struggling to manage the insurgent zones — Palestine and the northwest frontier of Pakistan, to name but two — that have proved to be the nemeses of empires past.

Iraq lays bare the realities of America's new role. Iraq itself is an imperial fiction, cobbled together at the Versailles Peace Conference in 1919 by the French and British and held together by force and violence since independence. Now an expansionist rights violator holds it together with terror. The United Nations lay dozing like a dog before the fire, happy to ignore Saddam, until an American president seized it by the scruff of the neck and made it bark. Multilateral solutions to the world's problems are all very well, but they have no teeth unless America bares its fangs.

AMERICA'S EMPIRE IS NOT LIKE EMPIRES OF TIMES PAST, BUILT ON COLONIES, CONQUEST AND THE WHITE MAN'S BURDEN. WE ARE NO LONGER IN THE ERA OF THE UNITED FRUIT COMPANY, WHEN AMERICAN CORPORATIONS NEEDED THE MARINES TO SECURE THEIR INVESTMENTS OVERSEAS. THE 21ST CENTURY IMPERIUM IS A NEW INVENTION IN THE ANNALS OF POLITICAL SCIENCE, AN EMPIRE LITE, A GLOBAL HEGEMONY WHOSE GRACE NOTES ARE FREE MARKETS, HUMAN RIGHTS AND DEMOCRACY, ENFORCED BY THE MOST AWESOME MILITARY POWER THE WORLD HAS EVER KNOWN. IT IS THE IMPERIALISM OF A PEOPLE WHO REMEMBER THAT THEIR COUNTRY SECURED ITS INDEPENDENCE BY REVOLT AGAINST AN EMPIRE, AND WHO LIKE TO THINK OF THEMSELVES AS THE FRIEND OF FREEDOM EVERYWHERE. IT IS AN EMPIRE WITHOUT CONSCIOUSNESS OF ITSELF AS SUCH, CONSTANTLY SHOCKED THAT ITS GOOD INTENTIONS AROUSE RESENTMENT ABROAD. BUT THAT DOES NOT MAKE IT ANY LESS OF AN EMPIRE, WITH A CONVICTION THAT IT ALONE, IN HERMAN MELVILLE'S WORDS, BEARS "THE ARK OF THE LIBERTIES OF THE WORLD."

In this vein, the president's National Security Strategy, announced in September, commits America to lead other nations toward "the single sustainable model for national success," by which he meant free markets and liberal democracy. This is strange rhetoric for a Texas politician who ran for office opposing nation-building abroad and calling for a more humble America overseas. But September 11 changed everyone, including a laconic and anti-rhetorical president. His messianic note may be new to him, but it is not new to his office. It has been present in the American vocabulary at least since Woodrow Wilson went to Versailles in 1919 and told the world that he wanted to make it safe for democracy.

Ever since Wilson, presidents have sounded the same redemptive note while "frantically avoiding recognition of the imperialism that we in fact exercise," as the theologian Reinhold Niebuhr said in 1960. Even now, as President Bush appears to be maneuvering the country toward war with Iraq, the deepest implication of what is happening has not been fully faced: that Iraq is an imperial operation that would commit a reluctant republic to become the guarantor of peace, stability, democratization and oil supplies in a combustible region of Islamic peoples stretching from Egypt to Afghanistan. A role once played by the Ottoman Empire, then by the French and the British, will now be played by a nation that has to ask whether in becoming an empire it risks losing its soul as a republic.

As the United States faces this moment of truth, John Quincy Adams's warning of 1821 remains stark and pertinent: if America were tempted to "become the dictatress of the world, she would be no longer the ruler of her own spirit." What empires lavish abroad, they cannot spend on good republican government at home: on hospitals or roads or schools. A distended military budget only aggravates America's continuing failure to keep its egalitarian promise to itself. And these are not the only costs of empire. Detaining two American citizens without charge or access to counsel in military brigs, maintaining illegal combatants on a foreign island in a legal limbo, keeping lawful aliens under permanent surveillance while deporting others after secret hearings: these are not the actions of a republic that lives by the rule of law but of an imperial power reluctant to trust its own liberties. Such actions may still be a long way short of Roosevelt's internment of the Japanese, but that may mean only that the worst — following, say, another large attack on United States citizens that produces mass casualties — is yet to come.

The impending operation in Iraq is thus a defining moment in America's long debate with itself about whether its overseas role as an empire threatens or strengthens its existence as a republic. The American electorate, while still supporting the president, wonders whether his proclamation of a war without end against terrorists and tyrants may only increase its vulnerability while endangering its liberties and its economic health at home. A nation that rarely counts the cost of what it really values now must ask what the "liberation" of Iraq is worth. A republic that has paid a tiny burden to maintain its empire — no more than about 4 percent of its gross domestic product — now contemplates a bill that is altogether steeper. Even if victory is rapid, a war in Iraq and a postwar occupation may cost anywhere from $120 billion to $200 billion.

What every school child also knows about empires is that they eventually face nemeses. To call America the new Rome is at once to recall Rome's glory and its eventual fate at the hands of the barbarians. A confident and carefree republic — the city on a hill, whose people have always believed they are immune from history's harms — now has to confront not just an unending imperial destiny but also a remote possibility that seems to haunt the history of empire: hubris followed by defeat.

II

Even at this late date, it is still possible to ask: Why should a republic take on the risks of empire? Won't it run a chance of endangering its identity as a free people? The problem is that this implies innocent options that in the case of Iraq may no longer exist. Iraq is not just about whether the United States can retain its republican virtue in a wicked world. Virtuous disengagement is no longer a possibility. Since September 11, it has been about whether the republic can survive in safety at home without imperial policing abroad. Face to face with "evil empires" of the past, the republic reluctantly accepted a division of the world based on mutually assured destruction. But now it faces much less stable and reliable opponents — rogue states like Iraq and North Korea with the potential to supply weapons of mass destruction to a terrorist internationale. Iraq represents the first in a series of struggles to contain the proliferation of weapons of mass destruction, the first attempt to shut off the potential supply of lethal technologies to a global terrorist network.

Containment rather than war would be the better course, but the Bush administration seems to have concluded that containment has reached its limits — and the conclusion is not unreasonable. Containment is not designed to stop production of sarin, VX nerve gas, anthrax and nuclear weapons. Threatened retaliation might deter Saddam from using these weapons, but his continued development of them increases his capacity to intimidate and deter others, including the United States. Already his weapons have sharply raised the cost of any invasion, and as time goes by this could become prohibitive. The possibility that North Korea might quickly develop weapons of mass destruction makes regime change on the Korean peninsula all but unthinkable. Weapons of mass destruction would render Saddam the master of a region that, because it has so much of the world's proven oil reserves, makes it what a military strategist would call the empire's center of gravity.

Iraq may claim to have ceased manufacturing these weapons after 1991, but these claims remain unconvincing, because inspectors found evidence of activity after that date. So what to do? Efforts to embargo and sanction the regime have hurt only the Iraqi people. What is left? An inspections program, even a permanent one, might slow the dictator's weapons programs down, but inspections are easily evaded. That leaves us, but only as a reluctant last resort, with regime change.

Regime change is an imperial task par excellence, since it assumes that the empire's interest has a right to trump the sovereignty of a state. The Bush administration would ask, What moral authority rests with a sovereign who murders and ethnically cleanses his own people, has twice invaded neighboring countries and usurps his people's wealth in order to build palaces and lethal weapons? And the administration is not alone. Not even Kofi Annan, the secretary general, charged with defending the United Nations Charter, says that sovereignty confers impunity for such crimes, though he has made it clear he would prefer to leave a disarmed Saddam in power rather than risk the conflagration of war to unseat him.

Regime change also raises the difficult question for Americans of whether their own freedom entails a duty to defend the freedom of others beyond their borders. The precedents here are inconclusive. Just because Wilson and Roosevelt sent Americans to fight and die for freedom in Europe and Asia doesn't mean their successors are committed to this duty everywhere and forever. The war in Vietnam was sold to a skeptical American public as another battle for freedom, and it led the republic into defeat and disgrace.

YET IT REMAINS A FACT — AS DISAGREEABLE TO THOSE LEFT WINGERS WHO REGARD AMERICAN IMPERIALISM AS THE ROOT OF ALL EVIL AS IT IS TO THE RIGHT-WING ISOLATIONISTS, WHO BELIEVE THAT THE WORLD BEYOND OUR SHORES IS NONE OF OUR BUSINESS — THAT THERE ARE MANY PEOPLES WHO OWE THEIR FREEDOM TO AN EXERCISE OF AMERICAN MILITARY POWER. IT'S NOT JUST THE JAPANESE AND THE GERMANS, WHO BECAME DEMOCRATS UNDER THE WATCHFUL EYE OF GENERALS MACARTHUR AND CLAY. THERE ARE THE BOSNIANS, WHOSE NATION SURVIVED BECAUSE AMERICAN AIR POWER AND DIPLOMACY FORCED AN END TO A WAR THE EUROPEANS COULDN'T STOP. THERE ARE THE KOSOVARS, WHO WOULD STILL BE IMPRISONED IN SERBIA IF NOT FOR GEN. WESLEY CLARK AND THE AIR FORCE. THE LIST OF PEOPLE WHOSE FREEDOM DEPENDS ON AMERICAN AIR AND GROUND POWER ALSO INCLUDES THE AFGHANS AND, MOST INCONVENIENTLY OF ALL, THE IRAQIS.

The moral evaluation of empire gets complicated when one of its benefits might be freedom for the oppressed. Iraqi exiles are adamant: even if the Iraqi people might be the immediate victims of an American attack, they would also be its ultimate beneficiaries. It would make the case for military intervention easier, of course, if the Iraqi exiles cut a more impressive figure. They feud and squabble and hate one another nearly as much as they hate Saddam. But what else is to be expected from a political culture pulverized by 40 years of state terror?

If only invasion, and not containment, can build democracy in Iraq, then the question becomes whether the Bush administration actually has any real intention of doing so. The exiles fear that a mere change of regime, a coup in which one Baathist thug replaces another, would suit American interests just as well, provided the thug complied with the interests of the Pentagon and American oil companies. Whenever it has exerted power overseas, America has never been sure whether it values stability — which means not only political stability but also the steady, profitable flow of goods and raw materials — more than it values its own rhetoric about democracy. Where the two values have collided, American power has come down heavily on the side of stability, for example, toppling democratically elected leaders from Mossadegh in Iran to Allende in Chile. Iraq is yet another test of this choice. Next door in Iran, from the 1950's to the 1970's, America backed stability over democracy, propping up the autocratic rule of the shah, only to reap the whirlwind of an Islamic fundamentalist revolution in 1979 that delivered neither stability nor real democracy. Does the same fate await an American operation in Iraq?

International human rights groups, like Amnesty International, are dismayed at the way both the British government of Tony Blair and the Bush administration are citing the human rights abuses of Saddam to defend the idea of regime change. Certainly the British and the American governments maintained a complicit and dishonorable silence when Saddam gassed the Kurds in 1988. Yet now that the two governments are taking decisive action, human rights groups seem more outraged by the prospect of action than they are by the abuses they once denounced. The fact that states are both late and hypocritical in their adoption of human rights does not deprive them of the right to use force to defend them.

The disagreeable reality for those who believe in human rights is that there are some occasions — and Iraq may be one of them — when war is the only real remedy for regimes that live by terror. This does not mean the choice is morally unproblematic. The choice is one between two evils, between containing and leaving a tyrant in place and the targeted use of force, which will kill people but free a nation from the tyrant's grip.

III

Still, the claim that a free republic may sense a duty to help other people attain their freedom does not answer the prudential question of whether the republic should run such risks. For the risks are huge, and they are imperial. Order, let alone democracy, will take a decade to consolidate in Iraq. The Iraqi opposition's blueprints for a democratic and secular federation of Iraq's component peoples — Shiites, Sunnis, Kurds, Turkomans and others — are noble documents, but they are just paper unless American and then international troops, under United Nations mandate, remain to keep the peace until Iraqis trust one another sufficiently to police themselves. Like all imperial exercises in creating order, it will work only if the puppets the Americans install cease to be puppets and build independent political legitimacy of their own.

If America takes on Iraq, it takes on the reordering of the whole region. It will have to stick at it through many successive administrations. The burden of empire is of long duration, and democracies are impatient with long-lasting burdens — none more so than America. These burdens include opening up a dialogue with the Iranians, who appear to be in a political upsurge themselves, so that they do not feel threatened by a United States-led democracy on their border. The Turks will have to be reassured, and the Kurds will have to be instructed that the real aim of United States policy is not the creation of a Kurdish state that goes on to dismember Turkey. The Syrians will have to be coaxed into abandoning their claims against the Israelis and making peace. The Saudis, once democracy takes root next door in Iraq, will have to be coaxed into embracing democratic change themselves.

All this is possible, but there is a larger challenge still. Unseating an Arab government in Iraq while leaving the Palestinians to face Israeli tanks and helicopter gunships is a virtual guarantee of unending Islamic wrath against the United States. The chief danger in the whole Iraqi gamble lies here — in supposing that victory over Saddam, in the absence of a Palestinian-Israeli settlement, would leave the United States with a stable hegemony over the Middle East. Absent a Middle East peace, victory in Iraq would still leave the Palestinians face to face with the Israelis in a conflict in which they would destroy not only each other but American authority in the Islamic world as well.

The Americans have played imperial guarantor in the region since Roosevelt met with Ibn Saud in 1945 and Truman recognized Ben-Gurion's Israel in 1948. But it paid little or no price for its imperial pre-eminence until the rise of an armed Palestinian resistance after 1987. Now, with every day that American power appears complicit in Israeli attacks that kill civilians in the West Bank and in Gaza, and with the Arab nations giving their tacit support to Palestinian suicide bombers, the imperial guarantor finds itself dragged into a regional conflict that is one long hemorrhage of its diplomatic and military authority.

Properly understood, then, the operation in Iraq entails a commitment, so far unstated, to enforce a peace on the Palestinians and Israelis. Such a peace must, at a minimum, give the Palestinians a viable, contiguous state capable of providing land and employment for three million people. It must include a commitment to rebuild their shattered government infrastructure, possibly through a United Nations transitional administration, with U.N.-mandated peacekeepers to provide security for Israelis and Palestinians. This is an awesomely tall order, but if America cannot find the will to enforce this minimum of justice, neither it nor Israel will have any safety from terror. This remains true even if you accept that there are terrorists in the Arab world who will never be content unless Israel is driven into the sea. A successful American political strategy against terror depends on providing enough peace for both Israelis and Palestinians that extremists on either side begin to lose the support that keeps violence alive.

Paradoxically, reducing the size of the task does not reduce the risks. If an invasion of Iraq is delinked from Middle East peace, then all America will gain for victory in Iraq is more terror cells in the Muslim world. If America goes on to help the Palestinians achieve a state, the result will not win over those, like Osama bin Laden, who hate America for what it is. But at least it would address the rage of those who hate it for what it does.

This is finally what makes an invasion of Iraq an imperial act: for it to succeed, it will have to build freedom, not just for the Iraqis but also for the Palestinians, along with a greater sense of security for Israel. Again, the paradox of the Iraq operation is that half measures are more dangerous than whole measures. Imperial powers do not have the luxury of timidity, for timidity is not prudence; it is a confession of weakness.

IV

The question, then, is not whether America is too powerful but whether it is powerful enough. Does it have what it takes to be grandmaster of what Colin Powell has called the chessboard of the world's most inflammable region?

America has been more successful than most great powers in understanding its strengths as well as its limitations. It has become adept at using what is called soft power — influence, example and persuasion — in preference to hard power. Adepts of soft power understand that even the most powerful country in the world can't get its way all the time. Even client states have to be deferred to. When an ally like Saudi Arabia asks the United States to avoid flying over its country when bombing Afghanistan, America complies. When America seeks to use Turkey as a base for hostilities in Iraq, it must accept Turkish preconditions. Being an empire doesn't mean being omnipotent.

Nowhere is this clearer than in America's relations with Israel. America's ally is anything but a client state. Its prime minister has refused direct orders from the president of the United States in the past, and he can be counted on to do so again. An Iraq operation requires the United States not merely to prevent Israel from entering the fray but to make peace with a bitter enemy. Since 1948, American and Israeli security interests have been at one. But as the death struggle in Palestine continues, it exposes the United States to global hatreds that make it impossible for it to align its interests with those Israelis who are opposed to any settlement with the Palestinians that does not amount, in effect, to Palestinian capitulation. The issue is not whether the United States should continue to support the state of Israel, but which state, with which borders and which set of relations with its neighbors, it is willing to risk its imperial authority to secure. The apocalyptic violence of one side and the justified refusal to negotiate under fire on the other side leave precious little time to salvage a two-state solution for the Middle East. But this, even more than rescuing Iraq, is the supreme task — and test — of American leadership.

V

What assets does American leadership have at its disposal? At a time when an imperial peace in the Middle East requires diplomats, aid workers and civilians with all the skills in rebuilding shattered societies, American power projection in the area overwhelmingly wears a

military uniform. "Every great power, whatever its ideology," Arthur Schlesinger Jr. once wrote, "has its warrior caste." Without realizing the consequences of what they were doing, successive American presidents have turned the projection of American power to the warrior caste, according to the findings of research by Robert J. Lieber of Georgetown University. In President Kennedy's time, Lieber has found, the United States spent 1 percent of its G.D.P. on the nonmilitary aspects of promoting its influence overseas — State Department, foreign aid, the United Nations, information programs. Under Bush's presidency, the number has declined to just 0.2 percent.

Special Forces are more in evidence in the world's developing nations than Peace Corps volunteers and USAID food experts. As Dana Priest demonstrates in "The Mission," a soon-to-be-published study of the American military, the Pentagon's regional commanders exercise more overseas diplomatic and political leverage than the State Department's ambassadors. Even if you accept that generals can make good diplomats and Special Forces captains can make friends for the United States, it still remains true that the American presence overseas is increasingly armed, in uniform and behind barbed wire and high walls. With every American Embassy now hardened against terrorist attack, the empire's overseas outposts look increasingly like Fort Apache. American power is visible to the world in carrier battle groups patrolling offshore and F-16's whistling overhead. In southern Afghanistan, it is the 82nd Airborne, bulked up in body armor, helmets and weapons, that Pashtun peasants see, not American aid workers and water engineers. Each month the United States spends an estimated $1 billion on military operations in Afghanistan and only $25 million on aid.

This sort of projection of power, hunkered down against attack, can earn the United States fear and respect, but not admiration and affection. America's very strength — in military power — cannot conceal its weakness in the areas that really matter: the elements of power that do not subdue by force of arms but inspire by force of example.

VI

It is unsurprising that force projection overseas should awaken resentment among America's enemies. More troubling is the hostility it arouses among friends, those whose security is guaranteed by American power. Nowhere is this more obvious than in Europe. At a moment when the costs of empire are mounting for America, her rich European allies matter financially. But in America's emerging global strategy, they have been demoted to reluctant junior partners. This makes them resentful and unwilling allies, less and less able to understand the nation that liberated them in 1945.

For 50 years, Europe rebuilt itself economically while passing on the costs of its defense to the United States. This was a matter of more than just reducing its armed forces and the proportion of national income spent on the military. All Western European countries reduced the martial elements in their national identities. In the process, European identity (with the possible exception of Britain) became postmilitary and postnational. This opened a widening gap with the United States. It remained a nation in which flag, sacrifice and martial honor are central to national identity. Europeans who had once invented the idea of the martial nation-state now looked at American patriotism, the last example of the form, and no longer recognized it as anything but flag-waving extremism. The world's only empire was isolated, not just because it was the biggest power but also because it was the West's last military nation-state.

September 11 rubbed in the lesson that global power is still measured by military capability. The Europeans discovered that they lacked the military instruments to be taken seriously and that their erstwhile defenders, the Americans, regarded them, in a moment of crisis, with suspicious contempt.

Yet the Americans cannot afford to create a global order all on their own. European participation in peacekeeping, nation-building and humanitarian reconstruction is so important that the Americans are required, even when they are unwilling to do so, to include Europeans in the governance of their evolving imperial project. The Americans essentially dictate Europe's place in this new grand design. The United States is multilateral when it wants to be, unilateral when it must be; and it enforces a new division of labor in which America does the fighting, the French, British and Germans do the police patrols in the border zones and the Dutch, Swiss and Scandinavians provide the humanitarian aid.

This is a very different picture of the world than the one entertained by liberal international lawyers and human rights activists who had hoped to see American power integrated into a transnational legal and economic order organized around the United Nations, the World Trade Organization, the International Criminal Court and other international human rights and environmental institutions and mechanisms. Successive American administrations have signed on to those pieces of the transnational legal order that suit their purposes (the World Trade Organization, for example) while ignoring or even sabotaging those parts (the International Criminal Court or the Kyoto Protocol) that do not. A new international order is emerging, but it is designed to suit American imperial objectives. America's allies want a multilateral order that will essentially constrain American power. But the empire will not be tied down like Gulliver with a thousand legal strings.

VII

On the new imperial frontier, in places like Afghanistan, Bosnia and Kosovo, American military power, together with European money and humanitarian motives, is producing a form of imperial rule for a postimperial age. If this sounds contradictory, it is because the impulses that have gone into this new exercise of power are contradictory. On the one hand, the semiofficial ideology of the Western world — human rights — sustains the principle of self-determination, the right of each people to rule themselves free of outside interference. This was the ethical principle that inspired the decolonization of Asia and Africa after World War II. Now we are living through the collapse of many of these former colonial states. Into the resulting vacuum of chaos and massacre a new imperialism has reluctantly stepped — reluctantly because these places are dangerous and because they seemed, at least until September 11, to be marginal to the interests of the powers concerned. But, gradually, this reluctance has been replaced by an understanding of why order needs to be brought to these places.

Nowhere, after all, could have been more distant than Afghanistan, yet that remote and desperate place was where the attacks of September 11 were prepared. Terror has collapsed distance, and with this collapse has come a sharpened American focus on the necessity of bringing order to the frontier zones. Bringing order is the paradigmatic imperial task, but it is essential, for reasons of both economy and principle, to do so without denying local peoples their rights to some degree of self-determination.

The old European imperialism justified itself as a mission to civilize, to prepare tribes and so-called lesser breeds in the habits of self-discipline necessary for the exercise of self-rule. Self-rule did not necessarily have to happen soon — the imperial administrators hoped to enjoy the sunset as long as possible — but it was held out as a distant incentive, and the incentive was crucial in co-opting local elites and preventing them from passing into open rebellion. In the new imperialism, this promise of self-rule cannot be kept so distant, for local elites are all creations of modern nationalism, and modern nationalism's primary ethical content is self-determination. If there is an invasion of Iraq, local elites must be "empowered" to take over as soon as the American imperial forces have restored order and the European humanitarians have rebuilt the roads, schools and houses. Nation-building seeks to reconcile imperial power and local self-determination through the medium of an exit strategy. This is imperialism in a hurry: to spend money, to get results, to turn the place back to the locals and get out. But it is similar to the old imperialism in the sense that real power in these zones -- Kosovo, Bosnia, Afghanistan and soon, perhaps, Iraq — will remain in Washington.

VIII

At the beginning of the first volume of "The Decline and Fall of the Roman Empire," published in 1776, Edward Gibbon remarked that empires endure only so long as their rulers take care not to overextend their borders. Augustus bequeathed his successors an empire "within those limits which nature seemed to have placed as its permanent bulwarks and boundaries: on the west the Atlantic Ocean; the Rhine and Danube on the north; the Euphrates on the east; and towards the south the sandy deserts of Arabia and Africa." Beyond these boundaries lay the barbarians. But the "vanity or ignorance" of the Romans, Gibbon went on, led them to "despise and sometimes to forget the outlying countries that had been left in the enjoyment of a barbarous independence." As a result, the proud Romans were lulled into making the fatal mistake of "confounding the Roman monarchy with the globe of the earth."

This characteristic delusion of imperial power is to confuse global power with global domination. The Americans may have the former, but they do not have the latter. They cannot rebuild each failed state or appease each anti-American hatred, and the more they try, the more they expose themselves to the overreach that eventually undermined the classical empires of old.

The secretary of defense may be right when he warns the North Koreans that America is capable of fighting on two fronts — in Korea and Iraq — simultaneously, but Americans at home cannot be overjoyed at such a prospect, and if two fronts are possible at once, a much larger number of fronts is not. If conflict in Iraq, North Korea or both becomes a possibility, Al Qaeda can be counted on to seek to strike a busy and overextended empire in the back. What this suggests is not just that overwhelming power never confers the security it promises but also that even the overwhelmingly powerful need friends and allies. In the cold war, the road to the North Korean capital, Pyongyang, led through Moscow and Beijing. Now America needs its old cold war adversaries more than ever to control the breakaway, bankrupt Communist rogue that is threatening America and her clients from Tokyo to Seoul.

Empires survive when they understand that diplomacy, backed by force, is always to be preferred to force alone. Looking into the still more distant future, say a generation ahead, resurgent Russia and China will demand recognition both as world powers and as regional hegemons. As the North Korean case shows, America needs to share the policing of non proliferation and other threats with these powers, and if it tries, as the current National Security Strategy suggests, to prevent the emergence of any competitor to American global dominance, it risks everything that Gibbon predicted: overextension followed by defeat.

America will also remain vulnerable, despite its overwhelming military power, because its primary enemy, Iraq and North Korea notwithstanding, is not a state, susceptible to deterrence, influence and coercion, but a shadowy cell of fanatics who have proved that they cannot be deterred and coerced and who have hijacked a global ideology — Islam — that gives them a bottomless supply of recruits and allies in a war, a war not just against America but against her client regimes in the Islamic world. In many countries in that part of the world, America is caught in the middle of a civil war raging between incompetent and authoritarian regimes and the Islamic revolutionaries who want to return the Arab world to the time of the prophet. It is a civil war between the politics of pure reaction and the politics of the impossible, with America unfortunately aligned on the side of reaction. On September 11, the American empire discovered that in the Middle East its local pillars were literally built on sand.

Until September 11, successive United States administrations treated their Middle Eastern clients like gas stations. This was part of a larger pattern. After 1991 and the collapse of the Soviet empire, American presidents thought they could have imperial domination on the cheap, ruling the world without putting in place any new imperial architecture — new military alliances, new legal institutions, new international development organisms — for a postcolonial, post-Soviet world.

THE GREEKS TAUGHT THE ROMANS TO CALL THIS FAILURE HUBRIS. IT WAS ALSO, IN THE 1990'S, A GENERAL FAILURE OF THE HISTORICAL IMAGINATION, AN INABILITY OF THE POST-COLD-WAR WEST TO GRASP THAT THE EMERGING CRISIS OF STATE ORDER IN SO MANY OVERLAPPING ZONES OF THE WORLD — FROM EGYPT TO AFGHANISTAN — WOULD EVENTUALLY BECOME A SECURITY THREAT AT HOME. RADICAL ISLAM WOULD NEVER HAVE SUCCEEDED IN WINNING ADHERENTS IF THE MUSLIM COUNTRIES THAT WON INDEPENDENCE FROM THE EUROPEAN EMPIRES HAD BEEN ABLE TO CONVERT DREAMS OF SELF-DETERMINATION INTO THE REALITY OF COMPETENT, RULE-ABIDING STATES. AMERICA HAS INHERITED THIS CRISIS OF SELF-DETERMINATION FROM THE EMPIRES OF THE PAST. ITS SOLUTION — TO CREATE DEMOCRACY IN IRAQ, THEN HOPEFULLY ROLL OUT THE SAME HAPPY EXPERIMENT THROUGHOUT THE MIDDLE EAST — IS BOTH NOBLE AND DANGEROUS: NOBLE BECAUSE, IF SUCCESSFUL, IT WILL FINALLY GIVE THESE PEOPLE THE SELF-DETERMINATION THEY VAINLY FOUGHT FOR AGAINST THE EMPIRES OF THE PAST; DANGEROUS BECAUSE, IF IT FAILS, THERE WILL BE NOBODY LEFT TO BLAME BUT THE AMERICANS.

The dual nemeses of empire in the 20th century were nationalism, the desire of peoples to rule themselves free of alien domination, and narcissism, the incurable delusion of imperial rulers that the "lesser breeds" aspired only to be versions of themselves. Both nationalism and narcissism have threatened the American reassertion of global power since September 11.

IX

As the Iraqi operation looms, it is worth keeping Vietnam in mind. Vietnam was a titanic clash between two nation-building strategies, the Americans in support of the South Vietnamese versus the Communists in the north. Yet it proved impossible for foreigners to build stability in a divided country against resistance from a Communist elite fighting in the name of the Vietnamese nation. Vietnam is now one country, its civil war over and its long-term stability assured. An American operation in Iraq will not face a competing nationalist project, but across the Islamic world it will rouse the nationalist passions of people who want to rule themselves and worship as they please. As Vietnam shows, empire is no match, long-term, for nationalism.

America's success in the 20th century owed a great deal to the shrewd understanding that America's interest lay in aligning itself with freedom. Franklin Roosevelt, for example, told his advisers at Yalta in 1945, when he was dividing up the postwar world with Churchill and Stalin, that there were more than a billion "brown people" living in Asia, "ruled by a handful of whites." They resent it, the president mused aloud. America's goal, he said, "must be to help them achieve independence — 1,100,000,000 enemies are dangerous."

The core beliefs of our time are the creations of the anticolonial revolt against empire: the idea that all human beings are equal and that each human group has a right to rule itself free of foreign interference. It is at least ironic that American believers in these ideas have ended up supporting the creation of a new form of temporary colonial tutelage for Bosnians, Kosovars and Afghans — and could for Iraqis. The reason is simply that, however right these principles may be, the political form in which they are realized -- the nationalist nation-building project — so often delivers liberated colonies straight to tyranny, as in the case of Baath Party rule in Iraq, or straight to chaos, as in Bosnia or Afghanistan. For every nationalist struggle that succeeds in giving its people self-determination and dignity, there are more that deliver their people only up to slaughter or terror or both. For every Vietnam brought about by nationalist struggle, there is a Palestinian struggle trapped in a downward spiral of terror and military oppression.

The age of empire ought to have been succeeded by an age of independent, equal and self-governing nation-states. But that has not come to pass. America has inherited a world scarred not just by the failures of empires past but also by the failure of nationalist movements to create and secure free states — and now, suddenly, by the desire of Islamists to build theocratic tyrannies on the ruins of failed nationalist dreams.

Those who want America to remain a republic rather than become an empire imagine rightly, but they have not factored in what tyranny or chaos can do to vital American interests. The case for empire is that it has become, in a place like Iraq, the last hope for democracy and stability alike. Even so, empires survive only by understanding their limits. September 11 pitched the Islamic world into the beginning of a long and bloody struggle to determine how it will be ruled and by whom: the authoritarians, the Islamists or perhaps the democrats. America can help repress and contain the struggle, but even though its own security depends on the outcome, it cannot ultimately control it. Only a very deluded imperialist would believe otherwise.

033

NOAM CHOMSKY

WHO ARE THE GLOBAL TERRORISTS?
FEBRUARY 2 2002

After the atrocities of September 11, the victim declared a "war on terrorism," targeting not just the suspected perpetrators, but the country in which they were located, and others charged with terrorism worldwide. President Bush pledged to "rid the world of evildoers" and "not let evil stand," echoing Ronald Reagan's denunciation of the "evil scourge of terrorism" in 1985 - specifically, state-supported international terrorism, which had been declared to be the core issue of US foreign policy as his administration came into office.[1] The focal points of the first war on terror were the Middle East and Central America, where Honduras was the major base for US operations. The military component of the re-declared war is led by Donald Rumsfeld, who served as Reagan's special representative to the Middle East; the diplomatic efforts at the UN by John Negroponte, Reagan's Ambassador to Honduras. Planning is largely in the hands of other leading figures of the Reagan-Bush administrations.

The condemnations of terrorism are sound, but leave some questions unanswered.

The first is: What do we mean by "terrorism"?

Second: What is the proper response to the crime?

Whatever the answer, it must at least satisfy a moral truism: If we propose some principle that is to be applied to antagonists, then we must agree - in fact, strenuously insist - that the principle apply to us as well. Those who do not rise even to this minimal level of integrity plainly cannot be taken seriously when they speak of right and wrong, good and evil.

THE PROBLEM OF DEFINITION IS HELD TO BE VEXING AND COMPLEX. THERE ARE, HOWEVER, PROPOSALS THAT SEEM STRAIGHT-FORWARD, FOR EXAMPLE, IN US ARMY MANUALS, WHICH DEFINE TERRORISM AS "THE CALCULATED USE OF VIOLENCE OR THREAT OF VIOLENCE TO ATTAIN GOALS THAT ARE POLITICAL, RELIGIOUS, OR IDEOLOGICAL IN NATURE ... THROUGH INTIMIDATION, COERCION, OR INSTILLING FEAR."[2] THAT DEFINITION CARRIES ADDITIONAL AUTHORITY BECAUSE OF THE TIMING: IT WAS OFFERED AS THE REAGAN ADMINISTRATION WAS INTENSIFYING ITS WAR ON TERRORISM. THE WORLD HAS CHANGED LITTLE ENOUGH SO THAT THESE RECENT PRECEDENTS SHOULD BE INSTRUCTIVE, EVEN APART FROM THE CONTINUITY OF LEADERSHIP FROM THE FIRST WAR ON TERRORISM TO ITS RECENT REINCARNATION.

The first war received strong endorsement. The UN General Assembly condemned international terrorism two months after Reagan's denunciation, again in much stronger and more explicit terms in 1987.[3] Support was not unanimous, however. The 1987 resolution passed 153-2, Honduras abstaining. Explaining their negative vote, the US and Israel identified the fatal flaw: the statement that "nothing in the present resolution could in any way prejudice the right to self-determination, freedom, and independence, as derived from the Charter of the United Nations, of people forcibly deprived of that right ... , particularly peoples under colonial and racist regimes and foreign occupation ..." That was understood to apply to the struggle of the African National Congress against the Apartheid regime of South Africa (a US ally, while the ANC was officially labeled a "terrorist organization"); and to the Israeli military occupation, then in its 20th year, sustained by US military and diplomatic support in virtual international isolation. Presumably because of US opposition, the UN resolution against terrorism was ignored.[4]

Reagan's 1985 condemnation referred specifically to terrorism in the Middle East, selected as the lead story of 1985 in an AP poll. But for Secretary of State George Shultz, the administration moderate, the most "alarming" manifestation of "state-sponsored terrorism," a plague spread by "depraved opponents of civilization itself" in "a return to barbarism in the modern age," was frighteningly close to home. There is "a cancer, right here in our land mass," Shultz informed Congress, threatening to conquer the hemisphere in a "revolution without borders," a interesting fabrication exposed at once but regularly reiterated with appropriate shudders.[5]

So severe was the threat that on Law Day (1 May) 1985, the President announced an embargo "in response to the emergency situation created by the Nicaraguan Government's aggressive activities in Central America." He also declared a national emergency, renewed annually, because "the policies and actions of the Government of Nicaragua constitute an unusual and extraordinary threat to the national security and foreign policy of the United States."

"The terrorists - and the other states that aid and abet them - serve as grim reminders that democracy is fragile and needs to be guarded with vigilance," Shultz warned. We must "cut [the Nicaraguan cancer] out," and not by gentle means: "Negotiations are a euphemism for capitulation if the shadow of power is not cast across the bargaining table," Shultz declared, condemning those who advocate "utopian, legalistic means like outside mediation, the United Nations, and the World Court, while ignoring the power element of the equation." The US was exercising "the power element of the equation" with mercenary forces based in Honduras, under Negroponte's supervision, and successfully blocking the "utopian, legalistic means" pursued by the World Court and the Latin American Contadora nations - as Washington continued to do until its terrorist wars were won.[6]

Reagan's condemnation of the "evil scourge" was issued at a meeting in Washington with Israeli Prime Minister Shimon Peres, who arrived to join in the call to extirpate the evil shortly after he had sent his bombers to attack Tunis, killing 75 people with smart bombs that tore them to shreds among other atrocities recorded by the prominent Israeli journalist Amnon Kapeliouk on the scene. Washington cooperated by failing to warn its ally Tunisia that the bombers were on the way. Shultz informed Israeli Foreign Minister Yitzhak Shamir that Washington "had considerable sympathy for the Israeli action," but drew back when the Security Council unanimously denounced the bombing as an "act of armed aggression" (US abstaining).[7]

A second candidate for most extreme act of Mideast international terrorism in the peak year of 1985 is a car-bombing in Beirut on March 8 that killed 80 people and wounded 256. The bomb was placed outside a Mosque, timed to explode when worshippers left. "About 250 girls and women in flowing black chadors, pouring out of Friday prayers at the Imam Rida Mosque, took the brunt of the blast," Nora Boustany reported. The bomb also "burned babies in their beds," killed children "as they walked home from the mosque," and "devastated the main street of the densely populated" West Beirut suburb. The target was a Shi'ite leader accused of complicity in terrorism, but he escaped. The crime was organized by the CIA and its Saudi clients with the assistance of British intelligence.[8]

The only other competitor for the prize is the "Iron Fist" operations that Peres directed in March in occupied Lebanon, reaching new depths of "calculated brutality and arbitrary murder," a Western diplomat familiar with the area observed, as Israel Defense Forces (IDF) shelled villages, carted off the male population, killed dozens of villagers in addition to many massacred by the IDF's paramilitary associates, shelled hospitals and took patients away for "interrogation," along with numerous other atrocities.[9] The IDF high command described the targets as "terrorist villagers." The operations against them must continue, the military correspondent of the Jerusalem Post (Hirsh Goodman) added, because the IDF must "maintain order and security" in occupied Lebanon despite "the price the inhabitants will have to pay."

Like Israel's invasion of Lebanon 3 years earlier, leaving some 18,000 killed, these actions and others in Lebanon were not undertaken in self-defense but rather for political ends, as recognized at once in Israel. The same was true, almost entirely, of those that followed, up to Peres's murderous invasion of 1996. But all relied crucially on US military and diplomatic support. Accordingly, they too do not enter the annals of international terrorism.

In brief, there was nothing odd about the proclamations of the leading co-conspirators in Mideast international terrorism, which therefore passed without comment at the peak moment of horror at the "return to barbarism."

The well-remembered prize-winner for 1985 is the hijacking of the Achille Lauro and brutal murder of a passenger, Leon Klinghoffer, doubtless a vile terrorist act, and surely not justified by the claim that it was in retaliation for the far worse Tunis atrocities and a pre-emptive effort to deter others. Adopting moral truisms, the same holds of our own acts of retaliation or pre-emption.

Evidently, we have to qualify the definition of "terrorism" given in official sources: the term applies only to terrorism against us, not the terrorism we carry out against them. The practice is conventional, even among the most extreme mass murderers: the Nazis were protecting the population from terrorist partisans directed from abroad, while the Japanese were laboring selflessly to create an "earthly paradise" as they fought off the "Chinese bandits" terrorizing the peaceful people of Manchuria and their legitimate government. Exceptions would be hard to find.

The same convention applies to the war to exterminate the Nicaraguan cancer. On Law Day 1984, President Reagan proclaimed that without law there can be only "chaos and disorder." The day before, he had announced that the US would disregard the proceedings of the International Court of Justice, which went on to condemn his administration for its "unlawful use of force," ordering it to terminate these international terrorist crimes and pay substantial reparations to Nicaragua (June 1986). The Court decision was dismissed with contempt, as was a subsequent Security Council resolution calling on all states to observe international law (vetoed by the US) and repeated General Assembly resolutions (US and Israel opposed, in one case joined by El Salvador).

As the Court decision was announced, Congress substantially increased funding for the mercenary forces engaged in "the unlawful use of force." Shortly after, the US command directed them to attack "soft targets" - undefended civilian targets - and to avoid combat with the Nicaraguan army, as they could do, thanks to US control of the skies and the sophisticated communication equipment provided to the terrorist forces. The tactic was considered reasonable by prominent commentators as long as it satisfied "the test of cost-benefit analysis," an analysis of "the amount of blood and misery that will be poured in, and the likelihood that democracy will emerge at the other end" - "democracy" as Western elites understand the term, an interpretation illustrated graphically in the region.[10]

State Department Legal Advisor Abraham Sofaer explained why the US was entitled to reject ICJ jurisdiction. In earlier years, most members of the UN "were aligned with the United States and shared its views regarding world order." But since decolonization a "majority often opposes the United States on important international questions." Accordingly, we must "reserve to ourselves the power to determine" how we will act and which matters fall "essentially within the domestic jurisdiction of the United States, as determined by the United States" - in this case, the terrorist acts against Nicaragua condemned by the Court and the Security Council. For similar reasons, since the 1960s the US has been far in the lead in vetoing Security Council resolutions on a wide range of issues, Britain second, France a distant third.[11]

WASHINGTON WAGED ITS "WAR ON TERRORISM" BY CREATING AN INTERNATIONAL TERROR NETWORK OF UNPRECEDENTED SCALE, AND EMPLOYING IT WORLDWIDE, WITH LETHAL AND LONG-LASTING EFFECTS. IN CENTRAL AMERICA, TERROR GUIDED AND SUPPORTED BY THE US REACHED ITS MOST EXTREME LEVELS IN COUNTRIES WHERE THE STATE SECURITY FORCES THEMSELVES WERE THE IMMEDIATE AGENTS OF INTERNATIONAL TERRORISM. THE EFFECTS WERE REVIEWED IN A 1994 CONFERENCE ORGANIZED BY SALVADORAN JESUITS, WHOSE EXPERIENCES HAD BEEN PARTICULARLY GRUESOME.[12] THE CONFERENCE REPORT TAKES PARTICULAR NOTE OF THE EFFECTS OF THE RESIDUAL "CULTURE OF TERROR ... IN DOMESTICATING THE EXPECTATIONS OF THE MAJORITY VIS-À-VIS ALTERNATIVES DIFFERENT TO THOSE OF THE POWERFUL," AN IMPORTANT OBSERVATION ON THE EFFICACY OF STATE TERROR THAT GENERALIZES BROADLY. IN LATIN AMERICA, THE SEPTEMBER 11 ATROCITIES WERE HARSHLY CONDEMNED, BUT COMMONLY WITH THE OBSERVATION THAT THEY ARE NOTHING NEW. THEY MAY BE DESCRIBED AS "ARMAGEDDON," THE RESEARCH JOURNAL OF THE JESUIT UNIVERSITY IN MANAGUA OBSERVED, BUT NICARAGUA HAS "LIVED ITS OWN ARMAGEDDON IN EXCRUCIATING SLOW MOTION" UNDER US ASSAULT "AND IS NOW SUBMERGED IN ITS DISMAL AFTERMATH," AND OTHERS FARED FAR WORSE UNDER THE VAST PLAGUE OF STATE TERROR THAT SWEPT THROUGH THE CONTINENT FROM THE EARLY 1960S, MUCH OF IT TRACEABLE TO WASHINGTON.[13]

It is hardly surprising that Washington's call for support in its war of revenge for September 11 had little resonance in Latin America. An international Gallup poll found that support for military force rather than extradition ranged from 2 percent (Mexico) to 11 percent (Venezuela and Colombia). Condemnations of the September 11 terror were regularly accompanied by recollections of their own suffering, for example, the death of perhaps thousands of poor people (Western crimes, therefore unexamined) when George Bush I bombed the barrio Chorillo in Panama in December 1989 in Operation Just Cause, undertaken to kidnap a disobedient thug who was sentenced to life imprisonment in Florida for crimes mostly committed while he was on the CIA payroll.[14]

The record continues to the present without essential change, apart from modification of pretexts and tactics. The list of leading recipients of US arms yields ample evidence, familiar to those acquainted with international human rights reports.

It therefore comes as no surprise that President Bush informed Afghans that bombing will continue until they hand over people the US suspects of terrorism (rebuffing requests for evidence and tentative offers of negotiation). Or, when new war aims were added after three weeks of bombing, that Admiral Sir Michael Boyce, chief of the British Defense Staff, warned Afghans that US-UK attacks will continue "until the people of the country themselves recognize that this is going to go on until they get the leadership changed."[15] In other words, the US and UK will persist in "the calculated use of violence to attain goals that are political ... in nature ...": international terrorism in the technical sense, but excluded from the canon by the standard convention. The rationale is essentially that of the US-Israel international terrorist operations in Lebanon. Admiral Boyce is virtually repeating the words of the eminent Israeli statesman Abba Eban, as Reagan declared the first war on terrorism. Replying to Prime Minister Menachem Begin's account of atrocities in Lebanon committed under the Labor government in the style "of regimes which neither Mr. Begin nor I would dare to mention by name," Eban acknowledged the accuracy of the account, but added the standard justification: "there was a rational prospect, ultimately fulfilled, that affected populations would exert pressure for the cessation of hostilities."[16]

These concepts are conventional, as is the resort to terrorism when deemed appropriate. Furthermore, its success is openly celebrated. The devastation caused by US terror operations in Nicaragua was described quite frankly, leaving Americans "United in Joy" at their successful outcome, the press proclaimed. The massacre of hundreds of thousands of Indonesians in 1965, mostly landless peasants, was greeted with unconstrained euphoria, along with praise for Washington for concealing its own critical role, which might have embarrassed the "Indonesian moderates" who had cleansed their society in a "staggering mass slaughter" (New York Times) that the CIA compared to the crimes of Stalin, Hitler, and Mao.[17] There are many other examples. One might wonder why Osama bin Laden's disgraceful exultation over the atrocities of September 11 occasioned indignant surprise. But that would be an error, based on failure to distinguish their terror, which is evil, from ours, which is noble, the operative principle throughout history.

If we keep to official definitions, it is a serious error to describe terrorism as the weapon of the weak. Like most weapons, it is wielded to far greater effect by the strong. But then it is not terror; rather, "counterterror," or "low intensity warfare," or "self-defense"; and if successful, "rational" and "pragmatic," and an occasion to be "united in joy."

Let us turn to the question of proper response to the crime, bearing in mind the governing moral truism. If, for example, Admiral Boyce's dictum is legitimate, then victims of Western state terrorism are entitled to act accordingly. That conclusion is, properly, regarded as outrageous. Therefore the principle is outrageous when applied to official enemies, even more so when we recognize that the actions were undertaken with the expectation that they would place huge numbers of people at grave risk. No knowledgeable authority seriously questioned the UN estimate that "7.5 million Afghans will need food over the winter - 2.5 million more than on September 11,[18] a 50 percent increase as a result of the threat of bombing, then the actuality, with a toll that will never be investigated if history is any guide.

A different proposal, put forth by the Vatican among others, was spelled out by military historian Michael Howard: "a police operation conducted under the auspices of the United Nations ... against a criminal conspiracy whose members should be hunted down and brought before an international court, where they would receive a fair trial and, if found guilty, be awarded an appropriate sentence."[19] Though never contemplated, the proposal seems reasonable. If so, then it would be reasonable if applied to Western state terrorism, something that could also never be contemplated, though for opposite reasons.

The war in Afghanistan has commonly been described as a "just war," indeed evidently so. There have been some attempts to frame a concept of "just war" that might support the judgment. We may therefore ask how these proposals fare when evaluated in terms of the same moral truism. I have yet to see one that does not instantly collapse: application of the proposed concept to Western state terrorism would be considered unthinkable, if not despicable. For example, we might ask how the proposals would apply to the one case that is uncontroversial in the light of the judgments of the highest international authorities, Washington's war against Nicaragua; uncontroversial, that is, among those who have some commitment to international law and treaty obligations. It is an instructive experiment.

Similar questions arise in connection with other aspects of the wars on terrorism. There has been debate over whether the US-UK war in Afghanistan was authorized by ambiguous Security Council resolutions, but it is beside the point. The US surely could have obtained clear and unambiguous authorization, not for attractive reasons (consider why Russia and China eagerly joined the coalition, hardly obscure). But that course was rejected, presumably because it would suggest that there is some higher authority to which the US should defer, a condition that a state with overwhelming power is not likely to accept. There is even a name for that stance in the literature of diplomacy and international relations: establishing "credibility," a standard official justification for the resort to violence, the bombing of Serbia, to mention a recent example. The refusal to consider negotiated transfer of the suspected perpetrators presumably had the same grounds.

The moral truism applies to such matters as well. The US refuses to extradite terrorists even when their guilt has been well established. One current case involves Emmanuel Constant, the leader of the Haitian paramilitary forces that were responsible for thousands of brutal killings in the early 1990s under the military junta, which Washington officially opposed but tacitly supported, publicly undermining the OAS embargo and secretly authorizing oil shipments. Constant was sentenced in absentia by a Haitian court. The elected government has repeatedly called on the US to extradite him, again on September 30, 2001, while Taliban initiatives to negotiate transfer of bin Laden were being dismissed with contempt. Haiti's request was again ignored, probably because of concerns about what Constant might reveal about ties to the US government during the period of the terror. Do we therefore conclude that Haiti has the right to use force to compel his extradition, following as best it can Washington's model in Afghanistan? The very idea is outrageous, yielding another prima facie violation of the moral truism.

It is all too easy to add illustrations.[20] Consider Cuba, probably the main target of international terrorism since 1959, remarkable in scale and character, some of it exposed in declassified documents on Kennedy's Operation Mongoose and continuing to the late 1990s. Cold War pretexts were ritually offered as long as that was possible, but internally the story was the one commonly unearthed on inquiry. It was recounted in secret by Arthur Schlesinger, reporting the conclusions of JFK's Latin American mission to the incoming President: the Cuban threat is "the spread of the Castro idea of taking matters into one's own hands," which might stimulate the "poor and underprivileged" in other countries, who "are now demanding opportunities for a decent living" - the "virus" or "rotten apple" effect, as it is called in high places The Cold War connection was that "the Soviet Union hovers in the wings, flourishing large development loans and presenting itself as the model for achieving modernization in a single generation."[21]

True, these exploits of international terrorism - which were quite serious - are excluded by the standard convention. But suppose we keep to the official definition. In accord with the theories of "just war" and proper response, how has Cuba been entitled to react?

It is fair enough to denounce international terrorism as a plague spread by "depraved opponents of civilization itself." The commitment to "drive the evil from the world" can even be taken seriously, if it satisfies moral truisms - not, it would seem, an entirely unreasonable thought.

034

MUZAMIL JALEEL

HAUNTED BY DEATH. MY KASHMIR STRUGGLES TO LIVE
MAY 20 2003

It is a cold evening and wafts of fresh air are slapping my face. The sky is devoid of clouds and I can clearly see the snow-clad peak of Harmukh standing still like a sentry. Spring is already here, but the winter chill returns as soon as it pours for few hours.

I am sitting on the familiar stone embankment of Arin nallah, a freshwater stream, right outside the three-story mud and brick house that once was my home. I have traveled back to my village — a small hamlet in north Kashmir, forty miles from Sringar — after almost a year, and this time, memories seem to flood as I watch wave after wave wet the stone banks. It's here I used to memorize my homework from school. It's here I used to sit with friends, enjoying gossip about the day in the class, watching the rainbow trout occasionally jump out of the water. It's here, I learned to fish following the "farungs" (western tourists) who would come in droves every summer, angling trout and enjoying the beauty of the Himalayas. As the snow would melt on the arrival of spring, the lone guesthouse — a wooden hut right on the banks of the stream up in the mountains near village Shoukhbaba — would be decorated like a bride and every tourist would want to stay there. We were little kids and we all aspired to be tourist guides. It somehow seemed a license to unending fun.

Today, the hut is no longer there. It is a concrete building. It's colorful sign board is intact, but staying there is now nothing short of a curse. The guesthouse is the local camp of the Indian army and is encircled by sand bunkers. A net of barbed wire is stretched around its compound wall. This former villa of recreation is now a scary place. Trout still frolic in the stream, but there is nobody around. The tiny stretch of barren land amid mulberry trees nearby is green. It used to be the village cricket pitch, but thorny bushes have taken it over. Nobody has played here for years. **Fear seems to have replaced the laughter of the children, and venturing out of the four walls of home is no longer safe. Even a promenade along the banks of the stream is full of risks.** There are no tourists and the new generation of children does not know the "farangis," the wandering foreigners with angling rods. They have only seen men with Kalashinkovs. But if the Indian army soldiers in olive-green dominate the day - the separatist militants own the night.

I was deep in my thoughts. The memories of the past seemed a pleasant dream. The violent separatist campaign began in 1989, but the thirteen years since seem nothing less than a century of trauma. The graves of more than fifty thousand men, women, and children consumed in this war stood like a wall between me and the Kashmir of my youth. I had failed to follow my dream of becoming a tourist guide. Perhaps fate had favored me; this job would have no longer have earned me two meals a day. Instead I became a journalist - and for years now, I have been chronicling the horrors of my people: writing tearjerkers and mastering the art of obituaries. My job had taken me to almost every tragedy to have befallen Kashmir for almost a decade. Only the characters and places change; the stories are always same - full of misery and tears.

It was by now dark, and I was forced to leave for my relative's house, where I was staying overnight. It was frightening. If only the bloodshed of past thirteen years had been just a nightmare. I wanted to wake up and find Kashmir returned to its peaceful days. Those days when fear was an alien word, just a visiting ghost from a grandmother's imaginary tale. When I, along with a bunch of my friends, would forget the difference between daylight and the darkness of night. Those days when Kashmiris used to control their own lives.

As I reached my relative's house, I could feel the tension all around. The entire family had worried about me. I had broken the cardinal rule of my village: never to venture out after dusk. Dinner was served in a rush and soon the lights were switched off and the entrance door was properly bolted. Keeping lights switched on, it was said, would attract the attention of separatist militants, who would generally venture out at night in search of new hideouts, or the men of the Indian Army who occasionally patrolled the streets. The last thing the family wanted was a knock at the door.

I, too, retreated to bed, but sleep seemed miles away. I thought about the tragedy of Kashmir and its people. Whenever I looked around me, I felt guilty for being alive. I am one of those fortunate Kashmiris of my generation who had escaped physically unhurt. I recall one particular incident when I was traveling with Javeed Shah - a photographer with whom I had been covering Kashmir's tragedy for years. All across our journey of thirty miles from Srinagar (Kashmir's capital city) to Baramulla in the north, we remembered places not by their names but by whatever violent incident we had covered there. I thought about my own story, my own penchant for life, and I knew most Kashmiris want to live. Despite being completely numbed by living and working in the shadow of an unending cycle of death and mourning, I am still alive. **And somehow my own chilling, first-hand experiences of the tragedy of Kashmir explain why an immediate change in attitudes across South Asia is desperately needed so that the politics of hatred and lust for land that has consumed thousands of Kashmiri lives is replaced by a process of reconciliation and healing.**

034 Muzamil Jaleel
Haunted by Death. My Kashmir Struggles to Live

Page 399

I WAS BORN IN A SMALL HAMLET IN NORTH KASHMIR - A PLACE WHERE PEOPLE STILL HAVE TO FOOT TWO KILOMETERS TO REACH THE NEAREST BUS STOP. I GREW UP IN THE APPLE ORCHARDS AND LUSH GREEN MEADOWS, DREAMED ON THE BANKS OF A FRESHWATER STREAM. I WENT TO SCHOOL THERE, SITTING ON STRAW MATS AND MEMORIZING TABLES BY HEART. AFTER SCHOOL MY FRIENDS AND I WOULD RUSH HALFWAY HOME, TEAR OFF OUR UNIFORMS, AND DIVE INTO THE COLD WATER. THEN WE WOULD QUICKLY DRY OUR HAIR SO OUR PARENTS WOULD NOT DISCOVER WHAT WE HAD DONE. SOMETIMES, WHEN WE FELT ESPECIALLY DARING, WE WOULD SKIP AN ENTIRE DAY OF SCHOOL TO PLAY CRICKET.

My village lies in the foothills of the Harmukh peak of Himalayas. During summer breaks, we would trek to the meadows high in the mountains carrying salt slates for the family cattle, sit around a campfire, and play flute for hours. The chilling winter would turn the boys and girls of our small village into one huge family; huddled together in a big room, we would listen to stories until late into the night. Sipping hot cups of Kashmir's traditional salt tea, the village elder who had inherited the art of storytelling would transport us to the era of his tales. Rasheed Kakh had never been to school, but he remembered hundreds of beautiful folk tales by heart. He had never been to Iran but when he sang "Gul-e-Bakawali" - a famous Persian story, I remember we would not so much as blink until the end. Kashmir was like a big party, full of love and life.

Today death and fear dominate everything.

I was in Kashmir, too, when the first bomb exploded in 1988. People at first thought it was the result of a small political feud, although everyone knew the pot was boiling after years of political discontent. Then, that September a young man, Ajaz Dar, died in a violent encounter with the police. Disgruntled by the farce of decades of ostensible democracy under Indian rule, a group of young Kashmiri men decided to fight. They had dreamt of an independent Kashmir free from both India and Pakistan. Although Ajaz Dar was not the first Kashmiri to die fighting for this cause, his death was the beginning of an era of tragedy. Separatism had been the dominant sentiment among Kashmiris since 1947, when Kashmir was divided between India and Pakistan during partition and the two countries fought. But it was not until forty years later that most youngsters opted to take up guns against Indian rule in reaction to the government-sponsored rigging of the assembly polls aimed at crushing dissent. And it was no surprise that India's most wanted Kashmiri militant leader, Syed Salahudin, contested that assembly election from Srinagar, nor that, unofficially, he was ahead by a good margin. When the elections were rigged, he lost not only the contest, but faith in the process as well. His polling agents and supporters were arrested and tortured; most of them later became separatist militants.

Neighboring Pakistan, which occupies a third of Kashmir, also smelled the changing mood in Kashmir, and offered a helping hand by providing arms-training and AK-47 rifles. **The policy of "death by a thousand cuts" had worked against Soviet Union in Afghanistan, and now it was to be tried here as well.** Violence was introduced amid growing dissent against India, and hundreds of young people joined the armed movement. Kashmir was changing. I had just completed secondary school then and was enrolled in a college - a perfect potential recruit: the entire militant movement belonged to my generation. The movement was the only topic of discussion on the street, in the classroom, and at home. Soon people started coming out onto the streets. Thousands would march to the famous Sufi shrines or to the United Nations office in Srinagar, shouting slogans in favour of "Azadi" (freedom), praying at the shrines, or handing out memorandums to the UN officials. These mass protests became an everyday affair, frustrating the authorities, who began to use force to counter them. Dozens of protesters were killed by police fire.

Many of my close friends and classmates began to join. One day, half of our class was missing. They never returned to school, and nobody ever looked for them because it was understood. Although reasons for joining the militant movement varied from person to person, the majority of Kashmiris never felt that they belonged to India. What had been a relatively dormant separatist sentiment was finally exploding into a fully-fledged violent separatist uprising.

I, too, wanted to join, though I didn't know exactly why or what it would lead to. Most of us were teenagers and had not thought seriously about the consequences. Perhaps the rebel image subconsciously attracted us. Violence was by now seen as the only means, and a majority of Kashmiri youth were ready to adopt it as a way of life.

I prepared for the dangerous journey from our village in northern Kashmir to Pakistan-controlled Kashmir where all the training camps were. One didn't just have to avoid being sighted by the Indian soldiers who guarded the border round the clock, but also overcome the fierce cold and the difficulties of hiking over the snow-clad Himalayan peaks that stood in the way. I acquired the standard militant's gear: I bought the

Wellington boots, prepared a polythene jacket and trousers to wear over my warm clothes, and found some woolen cloth to wrap around my calves as protection from frostbite. Fortunately, I failed. Three times a group of us returned from the border. Each time something happened that forced our guide to take us back. The third time, twenty-three of us started our journey on foot from the hamlet of Malangam, not far from my village, only to be abandoned in a dense jungle. It was night, and the group scattered after hearing nearby gunshots, sensing the presence of Indian army men. In the morning, when we gathered again, our guide was missing. Most decided to continue on their own, but a few of us turned back. We had nothing but leaves to eat for three days. We followed the flight of crows, hoping to reach a human settlement. I was lucky. I reached home and survived.

AS THE DAYS AND MONTHS PASSED, AND AS THE ROUTES THE MILITANTS TOOK TO CROSS THE BORDER BECAME KNOWN TO INDIAN SECURITY FORCES, THE BODIES BEGAN TO ARRIVE. LINES OF YOUNG MEN WOULD DISAPPEAR ON A RIDGE AS THEY TRIED TO CROSS OVER OR RETURN HOME. THE STADIUMS WHERE WE HAD PLAYED CRICKET AND FOOTBALL, THE BEAUTIFUL GREEN PARKS WHERE WE HAD GONE ON SCHOOL EXCURSIONS AS CHILDREN, WERE TURNED INTO MARTYRS' GRAVEYARDS. ONE AFTER ANOTHER, THOSE WHO HAD PLAYED IN THOSE PLACES WERE BURIED THERE, WITH HUGE MARBLE EPITAPHS DETAILING THEIR SACRIFICE. MANY HAD NEVER FIRED EVEN A SINGLE BULLET FROM THEIR KALASHNIKOVS.

One day, I counted my friends and classmates in the martyrs' graveyards near our village. There were twenty-one of them. I could feel the smiling face of Mushtaq, whom I had known since our schooldays. He would have been thirty-two this January, but the tenth anniversary of his death was commemorated last month. He was killed in April 1993. His mother could not bear the pain and lost her mental balance. For years, she has been wandering around the villages carrying the shirt he wore on the day of his death.

Another friend, Javaid, was his parents' only son. Extremely handsome, he was obsessed with seeing change in Kashmir. The day he died, he was wearing my clothes. He had come to our house in the morning and changed there. He was twenty-three, and even six hours after his death, when they took him for burial, blood still oozed from his bullet wounds. I will never forget the moment when I lifted the coffin lid: there was that usual grin. For a moment, he seemed alive.

Today, there are more than five hundred martyrs' graveyards dotting Kashmir, and every epitaph tells a story, a tragic story, of my generation. Engraving epitaphs has become a lucrative business.

As the death toll of Kashmiris mounted, the world saw the violent movement only as the result of a territorial dispute between India and Pakistan which had its roots in the 1947 partition. India always called the rebellion a Pakistan-sponsored terrorist movement, while Pakistan projected it as a jihad - a Kashmiri struggle to join Pakistan, united by a common faith.

For India, the future of Kashmir is non-negotiable — it is an "integral part" of the country, the only Muslim majority state in the union and therefore a cornerstone of its democracy and secular credentials. For Pakistan, Kashmir is also important because the majority of its population is Muslim — it is Pakistan's "jugular vein," and an unfinished task from the subcontinent's partition which gave birth to Pakistan as a home for Indian Muslims.

With these claims on Kashmir, both countries have choked the voice of Kashmiris. The Indian government has reacted with an iron fist, deployed large numbers of security men, and turned Kashmir into one massive jail.

Pakistan's hands are not clean either. When hundreds of thousands of Kashmiris came out in support of the separatist movement in 1990, Pakistan's lust for Kashmir's land was exposed. It hijacked the separatist movement, painted it with religious fundamentalism, and introduced pro-Pakistan, and later jihadi groups, to ensure it enjoyed absolute control.

Within years, Kashmir turned into yet another battlefield in the pan-Islamic jihad, and its warriors, as well as its leaders, were now made up of non-Kashmiris whose agendas transcended the demand for self-determination. In the process, the genuine political struggle for the unification of Kashmir and the demand of the people that they should be allowed to decide their own future was forgotten.

Whatever attention Kashmir received was because it was a flash-point between two nuclear neighbors, not because Kashmiris were suffering.

034 Muzamil Jaleel
Haunted by Death. My Kashmir Struggles to Live

Page 401

India and Pakistan seem to share one common policy on Kashmir - to force Kashmiris to tow their respective lines. In fact, it seems that both countries want to fight to the last Kashmiri.

I have been a witness to all this. I have seen Kashmir change. I still remember my grandmother worrying whenever the sky turned red. "Murder has been committed somewhere," she would say. Now that suspicion can no longer be reserved for red skies: the daily death toll is twenty.

Kashmir used to be known as a crime-free state. One of my neighbors was a senior police officer in the mid-eighties; he once told me that the average yearly murder rate in Kashmir was three or four. Today, if three people perish in a day, it is considered peaceful.

TODAY WHEN I LOOK AT THE PAST THIRTEEN YEARS, I FEEL NO DISAGREEMENT WITH THE STRUGGLE AIMED AT FULFILLING PEOPLE'S POLITICAL ASPIRATIONS, BUT I REGRET NOT HAVING SENSED THE HAVOC THE GUN WOULD WREAK ON KASHMIR ONCE VIOLENCE BECAME THE MEANS TO ACHIEVE A POLITICAL GOAL. THE PROPONENTS OF KASHMIR'S ARMED MOVEMENT ALWAYS CONTEND THAT VIOLENCE IS A DESPERATE MOVE WHEN ALL THE CHANNELS OF COMMUNICATION THROUGH DEMOCRATIC MEANS ARE CHOKED. BUT OUR EXPERIENCE HAS PROVED THAT THE USE OF GUNS CAN NEVER BE CONTROLLED, AND THAT VIOLENCE ALWAYS BECOMES AN END IN ITSELF RATHER THAN A MEANS TO AN END. I AM CONVINCED THAT VIOLENCE BEGETS VIOLENCE, AND SOON TURNS INTO A VICIOUS CIRCLE WHERE EVEN GENUINE POLITICAL FIGHTS ARE DOMINATED BY SENSELESS TERROR.

I have been fortunate to have remained physically safe, even though I was assaulted by police several times. But my family and relatives have not been so lucky. My younger brother Mudabir was picked up in 1994 on suspicion of militancy, and it took us a month just to trace his whereabouts. We divided up the entire Kashmir valley among our family members. Every morning, each of us would do the rounds of the security force camps to look for him.

My mother had never been to a police station in her entire life, but by the time she finally located my brother, she knew almost every military camp around Srinagar. And by the time the security forces were convinced of his innocence and released him, he had already been tortured so badly that he spent the next two months in bed.

It is now eight years since his release, but he still has nightmares, and the mere sight of a soldier sends shivers down his spine. A late-night knock at the door gives him goose pimples and sends his heart rate soaring. But this is no longer exceptional in Kashmir.

A cousin's husband bled to death after he was caught in a crossfire while coming out of a mosque one evening. He could have been saved had he reached the hospital in time. But the security forces did not allow his family out of their house and take him to the hospital, and there was no other medical help. He bled to death crying for help, and his wife, mother, and younger brother could do nothing but watch. A boy was born in the family four months after his death.

By 1992, there were hardly any young men left in the few villages around my home in north Kashmir. Many had joined the militant movement. Some had died, while others had gone underground; some had surrendered and become counterinsurgents, and were part of the pro-government militias. Many had migrated to the urban area of Srinagar city, which was then deemed comparatively safe.

The complexion of the separatist movement was changing fast; it no longer represented merely the genuine political aspirations of the people. The pro-Pakistan jihadi groups who dominated the movement tried to impose their radical religious, social, and cultural agendas, ignoring the fact that their extremism was alien to the very ethos of Kashmir.

Kashmir has a history of composite culture and religious tolerance. In fact, Islam did not arrive in Kashmir through the clatter of the sword. It was introduced by mystics and Sufis who conquered the hearts of the people. In the centuries that followed, Kashmir turned into a melting pot of ideas and a meeting ground for Buddhism, Hinduism, and Islam; there was no place for religious extremism. Now, fear had forced Kashmir's minority Hindus - Kashmiri pandits - to leave their homes and hearths and run to the plains of India for safety. Neighbors for centuries, Hindus and Muslims began suspecting each other. Kashmiri Hindus had always been the segment of Kashmiri society most loyal to India. And when Kashmir's struggle to fulfill their political aspirations were colored by religion, they no longer felt

at home in their own land. Kashmir began to see an unprecedented intolerance to political differences from both warring sides. On one hand, the Indian government used its military might to suppress the voices of dissent. The separatist militants responded in the language of bullets to any disagreement with their ideology and goals.

Now, as fanaticism began to dominate, utilizing the power of the gun, the militant movement fast became a mere tool in Pakistan's plan to bleed its arch-rival India.

I decided to leave my village to move to Srinagar and enroll at Kashmir University. I was so desperate to leave, I applied to almost every department. It was by mere chance that I got into journalism. But when I started writing about the war later that year, I felt that I had been part of this tragic story from the beginning. I knew the militants and the mukhbirs (the police informers); those who surrendered and those who did not; those who faced death because they had a dream and those who were sacrificed by mere chance, neither knowing nor understanding the issues at stake; those who believed they were fighting a holy war and those who joined for unholy reasons. But, as it turned out, there was more to the story.

My first assignment as a reporter was to visit a city police station and collect information regarding some corpses there. I accompanied a few local photographers, who began taking pictures as I stared at the six bullet-riddled bodies. They were in terrible condition: blood-soaked clothes, entrails exposed, faces unrecognisable.

That evening, I was haunted by the picture of bodies lying in a pool of blood — even a drink of water reminded me of blood. I couldn't sleep for days; corpses haunted my dreams. A few months later I arrived at the site of a massacre to find wailing women and unshaven men sitting in huddles. Bodies lay scattered like rag dolls discarded by careless children. I felt a lump growing in my throat, my legs felt heavy. I was incredibly tired, and wanted to throw down my notebook and sit silently with the mourners. The noise of the camera shutters invaded my private thoughts, forcing me to think about the story I had to write.

I wrote that day, continued writing similar stories for years, and now I seem to have lost count. One day I rush to the funeral of a group of Muslim youth shot dead by Indian security forces, and watch mothers wail and cry as their loved ones are carried away for burial. The next day, I find myself amid a family of a militant's victim. The mourning has same phrases and a similar sound.

Then, once in a while there are those mysterious massacres — where dozens of Hindus (who had not left with the wave of minority migration at the start of the separatist violence) are mowed down in the darkness of night by unidentified assassins, or those mysterious bomb blasts in a market place or village courtyard, killing innocent villagers. Both sides condemn such killings, call them gruesome, and blame each other.

Here are few recent examples:

It was March 24, 2003. I received a call early in the morning from a journalist friend. He informed me about a massacre in Nadimarg village. For me, it was yet another milestone on Kashmir's blood-drenched road. Unidentified armed men wearing olive-green fatigues had sneaked into this remote village in south Kashmir at midnight, dragged out the sleeping minority Hindus, eleven men, eleven women, and two infants, and sprayed them with bullets.

One more massacre pushing Kashmir once again to its familiar brink. After two hours, I reached Nadimarg. The massacre was so gruesome that even in a place where trauma and tragedy have become cliche, everyone was searching for adjectives.

This is what happened that night: Suraj had gone to sleep after celebrating his third birthday. His mother, among those asked to come out and fall in line, tried to hide him behind her. The first bullet got the mother, the second the father, then another crushed Suraj's right toe, and sheared off three fingers. An hour and a half later, he died crying.

034 Muzamil Jaleel
Haunted by Death. My Kashmir Struggles to Live

Page 403

Monu was just two years old. The bullets made a sieve of his chest. His three-month-old brother is the family's only survivor. His parents were killed next to him.

Pritima, a twenty-three-year-old woman who was disabled and could not walk, was dragged out and shot dead.

Mohan Lal Bhat, nineteen, spent the next day looking at his father, mother, sister, and uncle all covered in white, their names scrawled in blue ink on the cotton.

The first two bullets hit Chunni Lal in his thigh and arm. He fell down and found himself in a pile of bodies. As the guns fell silent, the gunmen came to check for survivors. In a pool of blood, he held his breath, and played dead, surviving to tell the story.

Phoola Devi, sixty, had slipped away from the line and hidden in the bushes just meters from the massacre site. Gripped with fear, she watched her husband, Bansilal, and her twenty-two-year-old daughter, Rajni, die crying for help.

Eyewitnesses told me that the killers carried AK rifles and were attired in olive-green uniforms, bullet-proof vests, and helmets. They told the villagers that they were soldiers, and that they had to search the houses. They then asked everybody to come out. Those who didn't obey were dragged. Everybody was asked to line up, only to be showered with bullets. The few people who survived had somehow managed to hide themselves and escape being spotted by the killers.

The most ironic aspect of this tragedy was that both government functionaries as well as separatist leaders arrived in the village to condemn the massacre and show solidarity with the survivors. Both sides accussed the other. If the history of such massacres in Kashmir reveals anything, it is that the identity of these midnight assassins will never be established.

On April 22, 2003, another village was scarred by violence, perpetrated by the same invisible hand, visited on innocent people. In fact, it had taken just one blast to change the lives of about a thousand villagers, including the seventeen injured. The six dead, at least, had nothing to worry about anymore. The blast hurled this hamlet, about twenty-five miles south of Srinagar (Kashmir's capital) into silent mourning. I arrived a few hours after the blast, and this time there were no VIPs, no government officials, or separatist leaders. Just people wounded and aggrieved. One woman, who was lucky to escape the blast with just a few splinter cuts on her thigh and shoulder, winced in pain as she tried to walk to the local dispensary. An old man leaned against a walnut tree as he watched the village boys wash the blood stains on the road. I knew that the ending might again be the same, but the story needed to be fleshed out and told. Not that it would make any difference here. The villagers who had assembled around 8 a.m in the morning near a narrow culvert a few meters from their cattle, waiting for the shepherd, didn't know their pastoral setting would soon be dabbed with red. Suddenly, there was a deafening blast. The stone wall on the road was blown to pieces. "I could see only dust and smoke," Mushtaq Ahmad Sofi, who had watched it all from the balcony of his house nearby, told me. "It seemed as if there was a rain of shrapnel and pieces of stone on the tin roof of our house. I rushed downstairs and ran towards the culvert. It was like a flood of blood. There were bodies scattered all around."

Sofi said they evacuated the injured for almost an hour. "There were around fifteen men, women, and children hit by the shrapnel,'' he said. Five died on the spot, while the sixth victim was rushed to the hospital where he died. The villagers say an improvised explosive device had been hidden in the stone wall. Nodody had a clear idea as to who was the actual perpetrator. An Indian security force camp was nearby and there were whispers that militants might have planted the bomb to attack the men from the camp who used to patrol the street every morning. But why the bomb would explode when there were no Indian security force men around, nobody knows.

I was trying to check the details when the sound of wailing women drifted over the air from a small shack. It was here that thirty-five-year-old Aftab Ahmad Mir had lived until that morning. A laborer, Mir had stepped out, only to be blown to bits. A white shroud, which would have otherwise covered his body, became a receptacle of the parts. At home, his wife, Raja, who was expecting their second child later that same day, was waiting for him. "He had to take me to admit in the hospital at around ten a.m.," Raja told me. Mir could not keep the promise; he was dead by then. Mir had a brother, as well - Nazir Ahmad Mir, who went missing five years ago. Now there are two widows Mir's wife and his aged mother, besides his son and the one yet unborn.

On the other end of the village lived Bashir Ahmad Mir. A twenty-eight year-old graduate, he was unemployed and had to work as a laborer to feed his two younger sisters and mother. When the villagers laid him down in his grave that day, his mother lay unconscious on the verandah of their mud and brick house.

And then there was the horse who bled to death as its fifty-year-old owner, Ghulam Mohammad Khan, who had been on his way to the village for work, lay motionless in a pool of blood.

Over the years, chronicling the horrors of Kashmir has become routine. In fact, when violence rules the day, there is nothing but tears to jerk out of the reader's soul. If I avoided writing about the gory details of death, I would end up either writing about orphans or widows, or those unfortunate women called "half-widows" whose husbands went missing after being arrested.

My reactions to such incidents also changed. Kashmir had become a news pasture. Every evening, I would wait for the police bulletin that provided the daily death statistics. Much as a shopkeeper counts his cash before calling it a day, I would count the dead before leaving the office. I once used a calculator to count the hundred and five men and women who were killed across twelve districts in twenty-four hours. My newspaper wanted a breakdown and I found myself lost in numbers.

I could no longer relate to these tragedies as strongly as I wanted to. I am witness to this same metamorphosis in the Kashmiri community, who have become virtually insensitive to their own traumas.

I BELONG TO KASHMIR'S CURSED GENERATION — THE YOUTH OF THE NINETIES. I HAVE LIVED ALL THESE TROUBLED YEARS IN KASHMIR AND I AM LUCKY TO BE ALIVE AND WELL. BUT IN THE PROCESS MY TEARS HAVE DRIED UP. I HAVE LOST NORMAL HUMAN FEELINGS. I FEEL IMMUNE TO THE DEATH OF MY OWN PEOPLE; I HAVE DEVELOPED AN INABILITY TO MOURN. AND I KNOW THE SAME IS SILENTLY HAPPENING TO MOST OF US. EVERY KASHMIRI TODAY HAS A STORY, AND MOST OF THEM ARE MUCH MORE TRAUMATIC, TRAGIC, AND UNTOLD.

The decades' long history of hostility between India and Pakistan has not left the two countries untouched. They, too, have become hostage to a culture of deep hatred, animosity, and suspicion towards each other — so much so, that all the saner voices of reason and logic are now lost in the din of jingoism and false national pride. In fact, in both countries, domestic electoral politics are actually driven by this hatred for each other, and both use Kashmir as an instrument to raise the pitch of their respective hate campiagns. In the process, the plight of Kashmiris goes unnoticed.

Kashmir has long been the bone of contention between India and Pakistan. If concrete steps are taken to end violence and to resolve this problem peacefully, Kashmir can actually become a bridge of friendship between the two nuclear neighbors, ushering a new dawn of peace and prosperity across the sub-contnent. It is, however, only possible if both countries sincerely accept the need to heed the genuine political aspirations of Kashmiri people, and try to address it democratically rather than using this political discontent to achieve their own vested interests and fulfill their respective agendas.

Like every Kashmiri, I want to see peace again - I want to write happy stories. I want to go out in the evenings and walk under streetlights without any fear. Now, I am burdened by constant uncertainty. I want to plan my days. I dream of a Kashmir where sons give shoulder to the coffins of their old fathers, instead of elderly parents leading dirges for their beloved sons.

034 Muzamil Jaleel
Haunted by Death. My Kashmir Struggles to Live

Page 405

035

GARY KNIGHT

KASHMIR
JANUARY - JUNE 2002

< Kashmir
Dal Lake, Srinigar, Kashmir.

◊ Kashmir
Fishermen and traders on
Dal Lake, Srinagar, Kashmir.

> Kashmir
A farmer ploughs his rice paddy using two oxen and a wooden plough in a
village between Sopore and Bandipore. The mountains in the background are used by
pro-independence militants to evade the Indian security forces.

> Kashmir
Worshippers return home after a day of festivities
at Hazrat bul Mosque after the
anniversary of Prophet Mohammeds birthday.

> Uri
A border security policeman patrolling the indian
side of the line of control that separates
the indian and pakistani controlled parts of Kashmir.

035 Gary Knight
Kashmir

Page 409

◊ **Srinagar**
A woman begs in Srinagar. Kashmir's primary
source of income was tourism
that has been devastated by the civil war.

> **Srinagar**
Workers along a canal, Srinagar.

> **Srinagar**
The Special Boat Patrol of the Indian Army
cruise around the canals of Dal Lake, Srinagar
looking for pro-independence militants.

> **Srinagar/Bandipore**
Soldiers of the Indian Raiput Rifle Regiment patrol the
main road between Srinagar and Bandipore. This
regiment is consistently accused of human right abuses.

> **Srinagar**
An Indian Border Security Force Officer
searches a vehicle for weapons
on a night patrol in Srinigar, Kashmir.

035 Gary Knight
Kashmir

Page 417

< Kashmir
Bereaved Kashmiris mourn the death
of two family members.

< Srinagar
The funeral of slain Kashmiri Militant Fayaz Ahmed Lone (25) of Doba Village at the Masjid Siddiari Mosque in Srinagar. Local journalists and Human Rights Workers
claim that Lones death was a custodial execution by the Indian security forces. He was apparantly being transported from his place
of capture to Srinagar in a truck full of Indian soldiers when he tried to escape. He was shot 6 times at point blank range. The Indian military deny the charge.

◊ **Srinagar**
The martyrs graveyard, Srinagar.
Many foreign and Kashmiri militants
are buried here.

＞ **Srinagar**
Women at a suffi shrine,
Srinagar. Kashmir May 2002.

＞ **Srinagar**
Hazratbal mosque
on the edge of Dal Lake,
Srinagar.

036

PANKAJ MISHRA

THE OTHER FACE OF FANATICISM
FEBRUARY 2 2003

On the evening of January. 30, 1948, five months after the independence and partition of India, Mohandas Gandhi was walking to a prayer meeting on the grounds of his temporary home in New Delhi when he was shot three times in the chest and abdomen. Gandhi was then seventy-eight and a forlorn figure. He had been unable to prevent the bloody creation of Pakistan as a separate homeland for Indian Muslims. The violent uprooting of millions of Hindus and Muslims across the hastily drawn borders of India and Pakistan had tainted the freedom from colonial rule that he had so arduously worked toward. The fasts he had undertaken in order to stop Hindus and Muslims from killing one another had weakened him, and when the bullets from an automatic pistol hit his frail body at point-blank range, he collapsed and died instantly. His assassin made no attempt to escape and, as he himself would later admit, even shouted for the police.

Millions of shocked Indians waited for more news that night. They feared unspeakable violence if Gandhi's murderer turned out to be a Muslim. There was much relief, also some puzzlement, when the assassin was revealed as Nathuram Godse, a Hindu Brahmin from western India, a region relatively untouched by the brutal passions of the partition.

Godse had been an activist in the Rashtriya Swayamsevak Sangh (National Volunteers Association, or R.S.S.), which was founded in the central Indian city of Nagpur in 1925 and was devoted to the creation of a militant Hindu state. During his trial, Godse made a long and eloquent speech claiming that Gandhi's "constant and consistent pandering to the Muslims" had left him with no choice. He blamed Gandhi for the "vivisection of the country, our motherland" and said that he hoped with Gandhi dead "the nation would be saved from the inroads of Pakistan." Godse requested that no mercy be shown him at his trial and went cheerfully to the gallows in November 1949, singing paeans to the "living Motherland, the land of the Hindus."

Now, more than half a century later, many Indians feel that the R.S.S. has never been closer to fulfilling its dream. Its political wing, the Bharatiya Janata Party (Indian People's Party, B.J.P.), the most important among the "Sangh Parivar" — the "family" of various Hindu nationalist groups supervised by the R.S.S. — has dominated the coalition government in New Delhi since 1998. Both Atal Bihari Vajpayee, India's prime minister, and his hard-line deputy and likely heir, L.K. Advani, belong to the R.S.S., and neither has ever repudiated its militant ideology.

IN THE LAST FIVE YEARS, THE HINDU NATIONALISTS HAVE CONDUCTED NUCLEAR TESTS AND CHALLENGED PAKISTAN TO A FOURTH AND FINAL WAR WITH INDIA. THEY HAVE TAKEN A MUCH HARSHER LINE THAN PREVIOUS GOVERNMENTS WITH THE DECADE-LONG INSURGENCY IN THE MUSLIM MAJORITY STATE OF KASHMIR, WHICH IS BACKED BY RADICAL ISLAMISTS IN PAKISTAN. AFTER A TERRORIST ATTACK ON THE INDIAN PARLIAMENT IN DECEMBER 2001, THEY MOBILIZED HUNDREDS OF THOUSANDS OF TROOPS ON INDIA'S BORDER WITH PAKISTAN. THE TROOPS WERE PARTLY WITHDRAWN LAST OCTOBER, BUT A WAR WITH PAKISTAN — ONE INVOLVING NUCLEAR WEAPONS — REMAINS A TERRIFYING POSSIBILITY AND IS IN FACT SUPPORTED BY POWERFUL, PRO-HINDU NATIONALIST SECTIONS OF THE INDIAN INTELLIGENTSIA.

The Hindu nationalists' attempts to stoke Hindu fears about Muslims also appear to be succeeding among many of India's disaffected voters.

In December, the B.J.P. won elections in the western state of Gujarat, despite being blamed by many journalists and human rights organizations for the vicious killings of more than 2,000 Muslims there early last year.

According to a report by Human Rights Watch, the worst violence occurred in the commercial city of Ahmedabad: "Between February 28 and March 2 the attackers descended with militia-like precision on Ahmedabad by the thousands, arriving in trucks and clad in saffron scarves and khaki shorts, the signature uniform of Hindu nationalist — Hindutva — groups. Chanting slogans of incitement to kill, they came armed with swords, trishuls (three-pronged spears associated with Hindu mythology), sophisticated explosives and gas cylinders. They were guided by computer printouts listing the addresses of Muslim families and their properties ... and embarked on a murderous rampage confident that the police was with them. In many cases, the police led the charge, using gunfire to kill Muslims who got in the mobs' way."

The scale of the violence was matched only by its brutality. Women were gang-raped before being killed. Children were burned alive. Gravediggers at mass burial sites told investigators "that most bodies that had arrived ... were burned and butchered beyond recognition. Many were missing body parts — arms, legs and even heads. The elderly and the handicapped were not spared. In some cases, pregnant women had their bellies cut open and their fetuses pulled out and hacked or burned before the women were killed.''

Narenda Modi, the chief minister of Gujarat, who is also a member of the R.S.S., explained the killings as an ''equal and opposite reaction'' (a statement he later denied) to the murder in late February of almost sixty people, most of whom were Hindu activists, by a mob of Muslims. The Human Rights Watch report disputed this defense, charging that the Hindu nationalists had planned the Gujarat killings well in advance of the attack on the Hindu activists. It cited widespread reports in the Indian media that suggest that a senior Hindu nationalist minister sat in the police control room in Ahmedabad issuing orders not to rescue Muslims from murder, rape, and arson.

Many secular Indians saw the ghost of Nathuram Godse presiding over the killings in Gujarat. In an article in the prestigious monthly Seminar, Ashis Nandy, India's leading social scientist, lamented that the ''state's political soul has been won over by [Gandhi's] killers.'' This seems truer after Hindu nationalists implicated in India's worst pogrom won state elections held in Gujarat in December — a fact that Praful Bidwai, a widely syndicated Indian columnist, described to me as ''profoundly shameful and disturbing.''

Not much is known about the R.S.S. in the West. After September 11, the Hindu nationalists have presented themselves as reliable allies in the fight against Muslim fundamentalists. But in India their resemblance to the European Fascist movements of the 1930's has never been less than clear. In his manifesto "We, or Our Nationhood Defined" (1939), Madhav Sadashiv Golwalkar, supreme director of the R.S.S. from 1940 to 1973, said that Hindus could "profit" from the example of the Nazis, who had manifested "race pride at its highest" by purging Germany of the Jews. According to him, India was Hindustan, a land of Hindus where Jews and Parsis were "guests" and Muslims and Christians "invaders."

GOLWALKAR WAS CLEAR ABOUT WHAT HE EXPECTED THE GUESTS AND INVADERS TO DO: "THE FOREIGN RACES IN HINDUSTAN MUST EITHER ADOPT THE HINDU CULTURE AND LANGUAGE, MUST LEARN TO RESPECT AND HOLD IN REVERENCE HINDU RELIGION, MUST ENTERTAIN NO IDEAS BUT THOSE OF GLORIFICATION OF THE HINDU RACE AND CULTURE ... OR MAY STAY IN THE COUNTRY, WHOLLY SUBORDINATED TO THE HINDU NATION, CLAIMING NOTHING, DESERVING NO PRIVILEGES."

Fears about the rise of militant Hindu nationalism, present since the day Godse killed Gandhi, have been particularly intense since the late 1980's, when the Congress — the party of Gandhi and Nehru that had ruled India for much of the previous four decades — was damaged by a series of corruption scandals and allegations of misrule. The B.J.P., which began under another name in 1951, saw an opportunity in the decay of the Congress Party.

In 1989, it officially began a campaign to build a temple over the birthplace of the Hindu god Rama in the northern town of Ayodhya. (The Hindu activists whose train was attacked last February had been assisting in the construction of the temple.) Hindu nationalists have long claimed that the mosque that stood over the site was built in the 16th century by the first Mogul emperor, Babur, as an act of contempt toward Hinduism. The mosque was a symbol of slavery and shame, B.J.P. leaders declared, and removing it and building a grand temple in its place was a point of honor for all Hindus.

In December 1992, senior B.J.P. politicians watched as an uncontrollable crowd of Hindus, armed with shovels, pickaxes and crowbars, and shouting ''Death to Muslims,'' demolished the mosque. It is estimated that at least 1,700 people, most of them Muslim, died during the riots that followed. In March 1993, Muslim gangsters, reportedly aided by the Pakistani intelligence agency, retaliated with simultaneous bomb attacks that killed more than 300 civilians.

The struggle over the construction of a Rama temple on the site continued throughout the nineties, inflaming both sides. Muslims (who form twelve percent of India's population of more than one billion) and secular Indians protested the Hindu nationalist attempt to rewrite history. But the nationalists fed on a growing dissatisfaction among upper-caste and middle-class Hindus. In March 1998, facing a fragmented opposition, the B.J.P. emerged as the single strongest party in the Indian Parliament, and Vajpayee and Advani took the top two jobs in the federal government.

After the massacres in Gujarat last year, the Hindu nationalist response was shockingly blunt. "Let Muslims understand," an official R.S.S. resolution said in March, "that their safety lies in the goodwill of the majority." Speaking at a public rally in April, Prime Minister Vajpayee seemed to blame Muslims for the recent violence. "Wherever Muslims live," he said, "they don't want to live in peace." Replying to international criticism of the killings in Gujarat, he said, "No one should teach us about secularism."

Vajpayee has worked hard to build close ties with the United States. Recent joint naval exercises in the Indian Ocean and frequent visits by Colin Powell seem to confirm Washington's view of India as a long-term ally against radical Islamism and China. But Vajpayee's efforts can also be seen as part of R.S.S.'s millenarian vision of India as a great superpower — and not just in Asia. A clearer sense of his worldview can be had from a long discourse K.S. Sudarshan, the present supreme director of the R.S.S. and an adviser to Vajpayee and Advani, delivered to R.S.S. members in 1999.

In the address, he described how a new epic war was about to commence between the demonic and divine powers that forever contended for supremacy in the world. Sudarshan identified the United States as the biggest example of the "rise of inhumanity" in the contemporary world.

He claimed that India exercised the "greatest terror" over America, a theme he had touched on in his praise of India's nuclear tests in 1998 when he said that "our history has proved that we are a heroic, intelligent race capable of becoming world leaders, but the one deficiency that we had was of weapons, good weapons." He ended his speech by predicting the "final victory" of Hindu nationalism.

"THE HINDU NATIONALISTS ARE ESPECIALLY CAUTIOUS AT PRESENT," AN INDIAN JOURNALIST TOLD ME THIS FALL. "THEIR FASCISTIC NATURE HAS BEEN OBSCURED SO FAR IN THE WEST BY THE FACT THAT INDIA IS A DEMOCRACY AND A POTENTIALLY LARGE CONSUMER MARKET. THEY HAVE MANAGED TO SPEAK WITH TWO VOICES, ONE FOR FOREIGN CONSUMPTION AND THE OTHER FOR LOCAL. BUT THEY KNOW THAT RELIGIOUS EXTREMISTS ARE UNDER CLOSER SCRUTINY WORLDWIDE AFTER 9/11, AND THEY KNOW THAT THEY DON'T LOOK TOO GOOD AFTER THE KILLINGS OF 2,000 MUSLIMS IN GUJARAT."

When I arrived at the R.S.S.'s media office in Delhi, I was told by the brusque young man in charge, "The R.S.S. is not interested in publicity." Sudarshan declined my request for an interview. Deputy Prime Minister Advani also declined to be interviewed on his connection with the R.S.S. Other members bluntly refused to talk to what they described as an "anti-Hindu" foreign newspaper.

One person who would talk was Tarun Vijay, the young editor of an R.S.S. weekly who was described as the "modern face of Hindu nationalism." Vijay shows up frequently on STAR News, India's most prominent news channel, and speaks both Hindi and English fluently. He is known as one of Advani's closest confidants.

When I ask Vijay about the R.S.S.'s role in the killings in Gujarat, his normally suave manner falters. "Westerners don't understand," he says agitatedly, "that the R.S.S. is a patriotic organization working for the welfare of all Indians."

It must be said that his own career seems to prove this. He was so impressed by the "selflessness" and "patriotism" of the R.S.S. members he met as a young man, he says, that he left his home and went to work in western India protecting tribal peoples from discrimination. "Some of my best friends are Muslims," he says. "My wife wears jeans, and she wears her hair short. We eat at Muslim homes. There are reasonable people among Muslims, but they are afraid to speak their minds. We are trying to have a dialogue with them. We are trying to talk with Christians also. After all, Jesus Christ is my greatest hero. But the left-wing and secular people are always portraying us as anti-Muslim and anti-Christian fanatics."

"The superior organization of the R.S.S., which now reaches up to the highest levels of the Indian government, is its strength in a chaotic country like India. Christophe Jaffrelot, a French scholar and the leading authority on Hindu nationalism, says he believes that the mission of the R.S.S. is to "fashion society, to sustain it, improve it and finally merge with it when the point [is] reached where society and the organization [are] co-extensive." Bharat Bhushan, a prominent Indian journalist, agrees. The R.S.S., he says, is "the only organization which has consistently geared itself to micro-level politics.'' Its members run not just the biggest political party in India but also educational institutions, trade unions, literary societies and religious sects; they work to indoctrinate low-caste groups as well as affluent Indians living in the West.

The scale and diversity of this essentially evangelical effort is remarkable. Highly placed members of the R.S.S. conduct nuclear tests, strike a belligerent attitude toward Muslims and Pakistan and push India's claims to superpower status, while other members are involved in almost absurd small-time social engineering.

I was startled, for instance, when Vijay triumphantly showed me the headline in his magazine about the patenting of cow urine in the United States. Western science, he said, had validated an ancient Hindu belief in the holiness of the cow — yet further proof of how the Hindu way of life anticipated and indeed was superior to the discoveries of modern science.

This was more than rhetoric. Forty miles out of Nagpur, at a clearing in a teak forest, I came across an R.S.S.-run laboratory devoted to showcasing the multifarious benefits of cow urine. Most of the cows were out grazing, but there were a few calves in a large shed that, according to the lab's supervisor, had been ''rescued'' recently from nearby Muslim butchers. In one room, its whitewashed walls spattered with saffron-hued posters of Lord Rama, devout young Hindus stood before test tubes and beakers full of cow urine, distilling the holy liquid to get rid of the foul-smelling ammonia and make it drinkable. In another room, tribal women in garishly colored saris sat on the floor before a small hill of white powder — dental powder made from cow urine.

The nearest, and probably unwilling, consumers of the various products made from cow urine were the poor tribal students in the primary school next to the lab, one of 13,000 educational institutions run by Hindu nationalists. In gloomy rooms, where students studied and slept and where their frayed laundry hung from the iron bars of the windows, there were large gleaming portraits of militant Hindu freedom fighters.

I sat in the small office of the headmaster, a thin excitable young man. From the window, above which hung a large fantastical map of undivided India, I could see tribal women who had walked from their homes and now sat on the porch examining the sores and calluses on their bare feet, waiting to meet their children during recess. The principal explained to me how the R.S.S. member in charge of the federal government's education department was making sure that the new history textbooks carried the important message of Hindu pride and Muslim cruelty to every school and child in the country. His own work was to make the students aware of the glorious Hindu culture from which tribal living had sundered them. The message of the R.S.S., he said, was egalitarian and modern; it believed in raising low-caste people and tribals to a higher level of culture.

According to John Dayal, the vice president of the All India Catholic Union, the R.S.S. has spent millions of dollars trying to convert tribal people to Hindu nationalism. Dayal, who monitors the missionary activities of the R.S.S. very closely, claimed that in less than one year the R.S.S. distributed one million trishuls, or tridents, in three tribal districts in central India.

B.L. Bhole, a political scientist at Nagpur University, saw a Brahminical ploy in these attempts. ''The R.S.S. can't attract young middle-class people anymore, so they hope for better luck among the poor,'' he said. ''But the basic values the R.S.S. promotes are drawn from the high Sanskritic culture of Hinduism, which seeks to maintain a social hierarchy with Brahmins at the very top. The united Hindu nation they keep talking about is one where basically low-caste Hindus and Muslims and Christians don't complain much while accepting the dominance of a Brahmin minority.

''The R.S.S. has been most successful in Gujarat, where low -caste Hindus and tribals were indoctrinated at the kind of schools you went to. They were in the mobs led by upper-caste Hindu nationalists that attacked Muslims and Christians. But the R.S.S. still doesn't have much support outside Gujarat. This is a serious setback for them, and the only thing they can do to increase their mass base is keep stoking anti-Muslim and anti-Christian passions and hope they can get enough Hindus, both upper caste and low caste, behind them.''

The consistent demonizing of Muslims and Christians by Hindu nationalists may seem gratuitous — Christians in India are a tiny and scattered minority, and the Muslims are too poor, disorganized and fearful to pose any kind of threat to Hindus — but it is indispensable to the project of a Hindu nation. The attempt to unite low- and upper-caste Hindus in a united front against Muslims and Christians has certainly

worked in the state of Gujarat. Ashok Singhal, the president of the Vishwa Hindu Parishad (World Hindu Council, V.H.P.), yet another R.S.S. affiliate, seemed to accept proudly the charge of inciting anti-Muslim hatred when he described last year's pogrom in Gujarat as a "victory for Hindu society." Whole villages, he said, had been "emptied of Islam." "We were successful," he said, "in our experiment of raising Hindu consciousness, which will be repeated all over the country now."

This sounds like an empty threat, but the B.J.P.'s gains in the recent elections in Gujarat, where it did best in riot-affected areas, may have encouraged hard-liners to think that they can win Hindu votes by whipping up anti-Muslim hysteria elsewhere in India. Narendra Modi is to be the star campaigner for the B.J.P. in the local elections later this month in the north Indian state of Himachal Pradesh, an area with almost no Hindu-Muslim tensions to date. Virbhadra Singh, a senior opposition leader from the Congress, wonders if the Hindu nationalists have hatched an "ill-conceived plan to stage-manage some terrorist incident in the state." John Dayal fears that Hindu nationalists may also target Christians. "They have never been more afraid," he told me. "I have been expecting the very worst since the B.J.P. came to power, and the worst, I think, may still be in the future."

The worst possibility at present is of a militant backlash by Muslims. In the villages and towns near Ayodhya, I found Muslims full of anxiety. They spoke of the insidious and frequent threats and beatings they received from local Hindu politicians and policemen. At one mosque in the countryside, a young man loudly asserted that Muslims were not going to suffer injustice anymore, that they were going to retaliate. His elders shouted him down, and then a mullah gently led me out of the madrasa with one arm around my shoulders, assuring me that the Muslims were loyal to India, their homeland, where they had long lived in peace with their Hindu brothers.

Saghir Ahmad Ansari, a Muslim social activist in Nagpur, told me that the Muslims he knew felt "that the Hindu nationalists, who were implacably opposed to their existence in India, now controlled everything, the government, our rights, our future." He said he worried about the Muslim response to Gujarat. "When the government itself supervises the killing of 2,000 Muslims, when Hindu mobs rape Muslim girls with impunity and force 100,000 Muslims into refugee camps, you can't hope that the victims won't dream of revenge," he said. "I fear, although I don't like saying or thinking about this, that the ideology of jihad and terrorist violence will find new takers among the 130 million Muslims of India. This will greatly please the Islamic fundamentalists of Pakistan and Afghanistan."

HIS FEARS ABOUT VENGEFUL MUSLIMS WERE PROVED RIGHT IN SEPTEMBER, WHEN TERRORISTS, REPORTEDLY FROM PAKISTAN, MURDERED MORE THAN THIRTY HINDUS AT THE FAMOUS AKSHARDHAM TEMPLE IN GUJARAT IN OSTENSIBLE RETALIATION FOR THE MASSACRES LAST WINTER. IT WAS THE BIGGEST ATTACK IN RECENT YEARS BY MUSLIM TERRORISTS OUTSIDE OF KASHMIR, AND THE HINDU RAGE IT PROVOKED FURTHER ENSURED THE VICTORY OF HINDU NATIONALIST HARD-LINERS IN DECEMBER'S ELECTIONS.

The growth of religious militancy in South Asia is likely to excite many Hindus. As they see it, Gujarat proved to be a successful "laboratory" of Hindu nationalism in which carefully stoked anti-Muslim sentiments eventually brought about a pogrom, and a Muslim backlash seemed to lead to even greater Hindu unity. A few months ago, I met Nathuram Godse's younger brother, Gopal Godse, who spent sixteen years in prison for conspiring with his brother and a few other Brahmins to murder Gandhi. He lives in Pune, a western city known now for its computer software engineers. In his tiny two-room apartment, where the dust from the busy street thickly powders a mess of files and books and the framed garlanded photographs of Gandhi's murderer, Godse, a frail man of eighty-three, at first seems like someone abandoned by history.

But recent events seem to Godse to have vindicated his Hindu nationalist cause. Gujarat proved that the Hindus were growing more militant and patriotic and that the Muslims were on the run not just in India but everywhere in the world. India had nuclear bombs; it was growing richer and stronger while Pakistan was slowly imploding. Only recently, Godse reminds me, Advani advocated the dismemberment of Pakistan.

India has turned its back on Gandhi, Godse claims, and has come close to embracing his brother's vision. Nathuram did not die in vain. He asked for his ashes to be immersed in the Indus, the holy river of India that flows through Pakistan, only when the Mother India was whole again. For over half a century, Godse has waited for the day when he could travel to the Indus with the urn containing his brother's ashes. Now, he says, he won't have to wait much longer.

037

BETH BARON

WAVES OF ISLAMIC RADICALISM
APRIL 14 2003

Debates on the causes for September 11th have pivoted around two positions:

America was attacked because of what we stand for, or America was attacked because of what we have done abroad, particularly in the Middle East.

BOTH POSITIONS MINIMIZE DEVELOPMENTS INTERNAL TO THE MIDDLE EAST AND FAIL TO TAKE ACCOUNT OF THE HISTORY OF RADICAL ISLAMIST MOVEMENTS.

While not belittling the impact of American foreign policy on Middle Easterners, this essay focuses on the history of Islamist movements and their roots in a period when other imperial powers proved dominant.

Experts on Islamism have offered two models for understanding the contemporary phenomenon. The paradigm preferred by many French academics is one of expansion and decline. To these authorities, recent acts of international terrorism, and even the events of September 11, are a last gasp of a failed movement. This movement, they claim, had its heyday in the seventies and eighties. Since then it has met with little success in its primary objective of overthrowing regimes in Saudi Arabia, Syria, Egypt, Algeria, and elsewhere, and setting up Islamic states. That Muslims did not mobilize in large numbers at the pivotal moment to oppose the American invasion of Afghanistan, they argue, points to the weakened condition of Islamism. And that large numbers did not enlist in the defense of Iraq would be another sign.

The "expansion-decline" model focuses on the most radical elements in the Islamist movement and ignores the gains made by more "moderate" Islamists on the ground. The difference between the former and the latter is one of methods rather than goals. While the "moderates" also strive for an Islamic state, they have worked at Islamicizing from below and have used a variety of methods, including the ballot box where possible, to increase their influence.

Both "moderate" and radical Islamists can be accommodated in a model that sketches waves of Islamic activism to explain major transitions in the movement. There may be disagreement on the exact timing of the crests and troughs of waves, but this analysis incorporates a broad spectrum of Islamist activity over a long period of time. Here I stress activism in the Sunni Arab world, as the actors in the attack of September 11th came out of that context, and in particular, the development of that movement in Egypt. **Egypt is important as it has often provided the brains of the movement, while Saudis and others have contributed the money and the brawn.** This was so for

the events of September 11. The influences of Pakistani and other Sunni Islamists, and their relationship to the Shi`i radicalism of the Islamic Republic of Iran, need separate analysis. I will return to Shi`i radicalism briefly below.

The first wave of Islamic radicalism came in the 1920s through the 1940s. Under the charismatic leadership of Hasan al-Banna, the Muslim Brotherhood (MB) emerged as the largest and most durable of a cluster of likeminded organizations in Egypt. In this phase, the MB operated in the open, often as an ally of the leading nationalist party, the Wafd. It espoused an anti-imperialist agenda directed at the British (who still occupied parts of Egypt and had a hand in Egyptian politics), fought against importation of Western culture and habits, and strove for a re-Islamicization of the individual and society. They often claimed to want to return to the practices of the early Muslims, but that past never existed as they imagined. The MB recruited widely in Egyptian cities and towns as well as in Syria, Palestine, and beyond, mostly among the middle strata. They propagated their message in mosques, cafes, clubs, and other locales, and set up a number of women's branches as well. By the 1940s, they had over a million members and sympathizers in Egypt alone, a hefty figure.

The second wave of Islamic radicalism began after revolutions toppled monarchies and the old order in major Arab states (Egypt, Iraq, and Syria) and ran roughly from the 1950s through the early 1980s. These regimes soon showed their secular colors. Thereafter, the Muslim Brotherhood and similar groups shifted the focus of their attack from the British or the French to the new military regimes. Those regimes increasingly saw the MB and its offshoots as threats, especially when they launched kidnappings and assassinations, challenging the authority and ideology of the state. Islamic radicals were driven underground as the new Arab states banned Islamist organizations, publications, and activities, and imprisoned many male and female members. There in prison, Islamists honed their arguments and produced tracts and splinter groups that further radicalized the movement and its methods.

Now at war, Islamists increasingly sought to take over the state and Islamicize from above, a top-down approach rather than the bottom-up one favored in the past. Yet in clashes with the military and police, the Islamists consistently came out on the losing side. This was so even when Islamists assassinated Sadat in Egypt in 1981. Egyptians did not rise up to overthrow the officers who ran the state.

By the end of the second wave, the radical Islamists had either been destroyed by the state, as in Syria (with the shelling by government forces of Hama which left some 20,000 Islamists, sympathizers, and citizens dead in 1982) and Iraq (with the execution by Ba`thi agents of Shi`i leaders and their families); severely crippled, as in Egypt; or were in a bloody stand-off, as in Algeria (which faced a long civil war). Saudi Arabia stood out, having used a different strategy. It attempted to buy off Islamists with the oil wealth of the 1970s, shape the movement in its own Wahhabi image, and at the same time, keep the radicals at bay and outside its borders. Only in Iran, Sudan, and Afghanistan did Islamists take the reigns of power, though Shi`i Iran remains a separate case. In the third wave, from the 1990s, the centers and modes of activity shifted. Unsuccessful at toppling regimes at home, radicals took their battles abroad and found refuge in weak states. These included Afghanistan, where many had already flocked to fight the Soviets after their invasion of the country in 1979, and with the blessing of the Taliban, came to training camps. (In another weak state, or state in the making, Islamists in the West Bank and Gaza challenged Arafat and the secular Palestinian Authority which had been given power under the Oslo accords.) Other Islamist sympathizers took shelter in Europe, where anonymity served them well. To their ranks were added new recruits, Muslims radicalized by the experience of exile or growing up in a non-Muslim country.

In this mobile world, the Islamist movement became transnational as disparate groups coalesced, combined causes and resources, and found new targets. Once committed to overthrowing regimes at home, they turned their discontent toward the West. Their anti-imperialism was a return to the roots of the movement, but the culprits were no longer the same. The French and British had by then been replaced by the Americans and their close allies. The injustices they listed included: U.S. bases in Saudi Arabia expanded after the first Gulf War in 1991; Israeli occupation of Palestine (by which they meant the West Bank, Gaza and Israel proper); Russian soldiers in Chechneya; and so on. In this third wave, Islamists created a new fusion: Egyptian radicals teamed up with Saudi funders, Afghani fighters, Pakistani students, and recruits from elsewhere. They used new technologies and methods such as suicide bombing perfected among radical Shi`i in Lebanon and Palestinians.

Meantime, states such as Egypt sought to buy off or accommodate the more "moderate" Islamists.

They thus yielded on certain issues such as women's, gay, and minority rights. Leaders sought legitimization by ca-tering to clerics and religious conservatives. This encouraged a trend in the 1990s of increased Islamization, as the Islamic discourse predominated.

THE ATTACKS ON THE WORLD TRADE CENTER IN 2001 AND THE SUBSEQUENT AMERICAN RIPOSTE - WAR IN AFGHANISTAN - IS PART OF THIS THIRD WAVE. AMERICANS HAVE THUS JOINED REGIMES IN EGYPT, SYRIA, AND IRAQ IN COMBATING AND ROUTING ISLAMIST RADICALS.

But the U.S. war in Iraq, one of the most secular states in the region, does not fit easily into these waves. The Bush administration tried to make linkages between the Islamists and the Iraqis (the Czech connection, anthrax scare, pockets of Qaeda, and possible future sharing of weapons of mass destruction). Although the case was not convincing, many Americans may have been persuaded by the juxtapositions.

The linkages may come, however, in the unintended consequences of this war (just as U.S. support for fighters in Afghanistan against the Soviet Union produced its unintended consequences - strengthening the very Islamists who later turned on the U.S.) While Sunni Islamists drew inspiration and support from Wahhabi fundamentalists in Saudi Arabia, Shi`i Islamists in Lebanon and elsewhere have looked to Iran and received guidance and aid. The Shi`i form sixty percent of Iraq's population, and some Iraqi Shi`i leaders fled Ba`thi rule and took refuge in Iran under the Islamic Republic. Iran's 1979 Revolution brought clerics to power and proved quite unique. Whether the Shi`i of Iraq will opt for an Iranian blueprint or, like Shi`i in Lebanon, participate in a sectarian politics, or find their own political path remains to be seen. Other questions arise: Will a U.S. presence in Iraq fuel anti-imperialism and push the population toward Islamism? And now that demonstrations of American power have confirmed an Islamist worldview, will the numbers of recruits to their movements outside of Iraq escalate?

Richard Mitchell, an authority on the early Muslim Brotherhood, observed in the late 1960s that the movement was losing ground to secular nationalism. His book was meant to be an autopsy. It was not the first, nor will it be the last, obituary of Islamism in either its radical or less radical manifestations. The movement thrives for a variety of internal and external reasons. Opposition to corrupt authoritarian military or monarchical regimes, and Western power, can take few other forms.

As the power of the West looms large, and after two military excursions into the region even larger, discontent may flourish.

038

JACQUES MENASCHE

FENCED UP TO HEAVEN
EIGHT STOPS ON THE ISRAELI/WEST BANK FRONTIER

LEBANON

SYRIA

HAIFA

NAZARETH

SALEM • •RAM-ON
                  •JENIN
HADERA •   •BARTA

TULKARM

QALQILYA •   •NABLUS

                 WEST BANK

HOLON •

                •RAM ALLAH
                •JERICHO

JERUSALEM •GILO
                •BETHLEHEM

GAZA •   •HEBRON

GAZA STRIP

                  •RAFAH

                •BEERSHEBA

                ISRAEL   JORDAN

EGYPT

Another bomb just went off in Tel Aviv.

You'd think people get used to it after two years.

They don't. They get used to the pattern, maybe - the sudden adrenaline jolt of news, the video loops on TV, the hospital number flashed on the screen, the call ups - but in some basic way the bombing itself is always grimly novel.

So it was this time.

A pair of young Palestinians reached Tel Aviv but apparently didn't realize it was Tisha B'Av, Judaism's dark day commemorating the destruction of the Holy Temple, that all the stores and restaurants closed at sundown. They wandered around in the seedy section of the old central bus station for awhile, looking for someone to blow up. One was propositioned by a prostitute; he begged off, saying he was "going to die tonight."

Finally on Solomon Street they found an open coffee shop, one of those cigarette, candy, newspaper joints frequented by foreign workers, and with no better target detonated, killing a Romanian, a Chinese, an Israeli, and of course themselves.

Each bomb has the effect of inaugurating a new round of discussion on the Israeli talk shows.

The talk goes in circles. Nobody believes much in a political solution these days. Nobody believes in a military one, either. Instead, in a land of diminished expectations, with more than 600 Israelis and 1800 Palestinians dead, the best hope according to the overwhelming majority of Israelis is separation, the grave of the peace process marked by fence posts.

There are many different maps of Israel - biblical, political, architectural, military - but the map of fences, scratched on the landscape with barricades, checkpoints, ditches, concrete, wire and chains, combines them all. On it, the country grows smaller and the borders longer, until it almost seems as if the country is nothing but borders, the Gaza Strip and the sea to the west, Egypt south, Lebanon and Syria north, Jordan east.

All these frontiers have had troubles, but for the last two years it has been the porous north-south axis dividing Israel from the Occupied Territories, the border within the border, that's caught fire. Israelis calls it the seam. And like Ebb and Flow - their moniker for the second intifada - there is an uncanny poetry in the term. A faint echo of the nation's Eastern European origin, of seamstresses and sweatshops, the schmata business, the language of tailors.

AFTER SEVENTY SUCCESSFUL SUICIDE BOMBINGS, ISRAEL HAS DECIDED TO STITCH IT UP. DRIVEN BY PUBLIC PRESSURE, A 225 KILOMETER FENCE IS TO BE CONSTRUCTED ALONG THE DANGEROUS THIN PART BETWEEN JERUSALEM IN THE SOUTH AND AFULA IN THE NORTH. IT IS A DECISION MOST ISRAELIS SUPPORT, AND WHICH ALMOST NO ONE SEEMS TO THINK WILL WORK. AT BEST, IT'S A PROFOUNDLY PESSIMISTIC ACT, ANOTHER ENOUGH-IS-ENOUGH GESTURE, RELYING ON THE SAME BRUTISH TOOLS THAT HAVE CHARACTERIZED OPERATION DETERMINED PATH: METAL AND CONCRETE. AT IT'S WORST, IT AROUSES AN ALMOST EXISTENTIAL ANXIETY FROM A PEOPLE TRAUMATIZED BY THE MEMORY OF CONCENTRATION CAMPS, NOW BECOME GUARDS AND INMATES AT THE SAME TIME.

> JERUSALEM

The 1949 Armistice line, the "Green Line," with one exception, does not digress from tracing a line around the Judea and Samarian Mountains, separating them from the populous coastal plain of the Mediterranean. The exception is Jerusalem. Jerusalem is a pleat in the fabric, a pinch to the east, a black hole on the map sucking up land. Claimed by Arabs, Jews and Christians, neither able to fuse or divide, without solution, it is the unhealable wound, the juggernaut against which every hope crashes, not only the new fence's geographic origin, but its ideological epicenter.

It's an oppressive place, and in summer, hot as hell. At a café on Hillel Street a woman, seven months pregnant, looks at her sonogram pictures while chain-smoking. A motorcycle starts up and she jumps out of her seat.

Night is calmer. The temperature drops thirty degrees Fahrenheit, a breeze blows in off the desert, and a giant orange moon rises behind the Mount of Olives. One of the most serene places, ironically, is at the absolute ground zero of the conflict: inside the Old City, at the Wailing Wall. There, under a black, quiet sky, two hundred men in black twist before the flood-lit stone, caressing it with a muted gurgle of Hebrew, Yiddish, English. Like a raging sea, all the men are in motion, each in their own pantomime - one twisting left to right, feet stationary; another bobbing forward, hands spread against the Wall as if he was being arrested.

The Wall was once part of the Temple Court's defensive ramparts. And two thousand years later, the holiest shrine in the Jewish world remains a barrier, the alpha and omega of barriers, dividing the Old City's Jewish Quarter from the Dome of the Rock, the fault line of a global religious schism. It's strata have been charted - the wide Herodian stones at the bottom, the tapering stones of the Byzantines, Arabs and Turks - but has anyone mapped it's face? Like the face of the moon? The Sea of Tranquility? Does the broken stone two-thirds of the way up in the center, a five-foot chunk, have a name? Is every crack, crevice, and pock mark, every flowering tuft of green, white and lavender flower sprouting through the crannies, documented?

> GILO

Such minutia dominates debate around the new security fence's proposed course around Jerusalem. Construction has begun at two points, near the city's major checkpoints in the north and south, but the fate of East Jerusalem in the middle remains undecided, and hardly does the fence begin its meandering journey at Gilo down south before it's immediately dogged by the presence of the Tomb of Rachel, a Jewish pilgrimage site, on the Palestinian side.

A middle-class suburb ten minutes from the Old City, Gilo was built following Israel's victory in the Six Day War and marks modern Jerusalem's southern border with the West Bank. Ten minutes and you're there, a sliver of land between Jerusalem and the Arab "beits" - Beit Safafa, Beit Jala, and Bethlehem. Often shot at over the valley, the town has protected every exposed road or school with lined-up concrete slabs painted with pastoral scenes of bicycles and fish. But they didn't stop the bomber who got in a few weeks ago, got on a bus and killed nineteen people.

The new fence construction site is on a nearby plateau. On one side, a valley with a figure-eight dirt road ripping through a grove of olive trees, livened every so often by a truck, an army jeep, or wild dog; on the other, the Tunnels Road leading to settlements in the territories, a strip of black asphalt and raw concrete that looks like the Autobahn. But then everything in Israel looks like something else: fantastic Arabian villas, Chicagoan office towers, malls from Tennessee - all of it roamed over by big-bearded Hasidim from Brooklyn, Thai flower workers, Romanians construction workers, Coptic priests, Ethiopians, Russians, Arabs.

It's hard to tell what Yad is. The site's foreman, he is wearing an Australian field hat and has a big bushy moustache. He looks like a Prussian general. But for troops he only has a few Arab workers, for weapons only a handful of bulldozers and cranes, and the one with the mechanical arm with the finger attached seems to be broken.

"It's all bullshit," he says.

The fence, he explains, was inaugurated with great fanfare. "Three weeks ago, we were very popular," Yad says. "Television cameras ... even the Minister of Defense." Little since seems to have been accomplished. Just a few hundred meters of ditch and a patrol road. The equipment silent. The pill box guarding the site is empty. Inside, a drawing of a soldier, stapled to a stick and propped against the square look-out, keeps watch.

Yad reconsiders; it's not all bullshit after all. "It's all money," he says.

> QALQILYA . A

The effect of the fence's $200 million price tag on a wartime economy dead to tourists isn't negligible, and is at least part of the reason the fence, some kind of fence, isn't already built. (A Florida land developer, faced with 225 completed homes on one square mile tracts of land, would probably have it up in a month.)

Instead construction is proceeding on an ad-hoc, need-to basis. Like the three hundred mobile check-points, fences are military props that go where they need to. And right now they need to go up the skinny, populous part of the country, especially where the seam skirts the three major Palestinian cities, Jenin, Tulkarm, and Qalqilya.

Forty kilometers up the road from Jerusalem, Qalqilya is the closest to Tel Aviv. Under the Oslo Accords it developed a long roadside market and prospered, buoyed by bargain-hunting Israelis. But with the start of the Al-Aksa intifada, proximity turned toxic, turned Qalqilya into a suicide bomber's launch pad, and brought down the full wrath of Determined Path.

Now an Israeli army camp sits at the head of a giant snaking concrete wall. The 30-foot high barrier was erected last month, ostensibly to protect the new, nearly-completed Trans-Israel Highway it parallels. Now it protects everything.

"Everyone in my unit knows someone killed in the last twenty months," Major Ohad says. "We don't have any dilemma about what we are doing here."

Like the rest of his men at the camp, Ohad is a reservist called up and told to report the next day for emergency mobilization. All the men have other lives. One does marketing for Intel, another teaches martial arts. Today, after thirty-one days of operations in Qalqilya, patrolling the border, guarding construction, and sleeping in the oven-hot air, they are going home.

A patrol sweeps up the dirt road beside the wall spewing dust and crashes to rest at the gate. The back door opens. Two Palestinian prisoners, wanted men, are bundled out by half-a-dozen soldiers. One prisoner is wearing a business suit. Both are blindfolded, hands behind their backs. They are swept through the gate and spirited into a white trailer.

The blindfolds, made of black cloth, leave a chilling impression. What is there to see?

The thirty-foot tall concrete wall?
The watchtower?
Maps, papers?
The soldiers strewn in their cots, languishing in the big tent's heat?

After the prisoners are safely dispatched to Security, the reservists pack their rucksacks, unload and disassemble their weapons, fill the camp with the great noise of unclicking. Then they head out into the scorching sun, lingering at the gate with the churning exhaust of the buses, waiting for a ride back to the base, from there back home, back to work.

> QALQILYA . B

A few have volunteered to stay on. For some it's a matter of ideology, a call to protect the country. For others, given the ten percent unemployment rate in Israel, there just isn't any work to go back to.

But if the overall economic impact of the second intifada on Israelis has been bad, for Palestinians it has been seismic. Really there is no West Bank economy left. Four years ago, 100,000 people used to cross the fields every morning to go to their agricultural jobs in Israel. Now they are locked up in a stranglehold of the closures. Movement between cities in the West Bank is frozen. Curfews have made normal working days, schedules, budgets, supplies impossible. Nothing gets made and nothing gets bought.

Directly across from the army camp on the Palestinian side of the wall is a citrus grove. By West Bank standards it used to be fairly prosperous one, ten dunem (2.5 acres) bursting with orange, lemon, and avocado saplings sold in Nablus and Hebron, even Amman, Jordan. Now its owner, Asad, eats grass. Just picks up handfuls and munches it like a rabbit.

He and his brothers and uncles and cousins sit on plastic chairs on the cement porch of their ramshackle house in the grove, the monster white wall behind them marking the edge of their property. There is something epic about this sweep of concrete, the way it interrupts the tedium of flat earth, the way its creates a space, the green citrus trees, blue sky, white wall. One day about a month ago when Asad was away, he says, the Israelis came, confiscated two-thirds of his property, and put it up.

A cassette of Arab music is playing. Tea is poured. Then you are served up the story, a disastrous story - the death of Asad's father in a car accident seven years ago, the twelve younger brothers to support, the wall, the closure of the roads, the shut-down business. The whole season going to waste.

The saplings are growing, getting too big, he laments. They are already shooting roots. In a month they'll be worthless. Asad points to a man in one of the greenhouses, a forlorn figure at the end of a row of crew-cut lemon trees lit by the tent's muted light, shearing off the tops, a snaking green trail of lopped-off sprigs at his feet.

"We don't hate Israelis," his Uncle Nasim says.

"Before I had a boss in Israel, in Kfar Saba. When he got cancer, he was divorced and had only one child.

So I sat with him in the hospital for one month.

This man he used to call me up when there was problems.

He would say, 'Nasim, what news from the crazies on your side and mine?"

Now the man is dead.

Nasim stares to the west at the sun is setting over the wall, over at the beach twenty kilometers away.

We used to get the breeze from the ocean," he says.

"Now the wall blocks it."

A tank passes on the other side. The wall rumbles, snorts, roars, comes alive, a wave.

> TULKARM

In a sense it is alive. For as every military commander here will tell you, a fence is only any good backed by force of arms. In the absence of the sealed border the security fence promises to create, the helicopters, armored jeeps, informers, AK-47s, and tanks are the fence.

Asad and his family keep silent as the lethal machine passes, keep silent before the awesome military might of the Israelis, who only a few days ago unleashed an F-4 fighter jet and a one-ton bomb to assassinate Mahmud Abu Hunud, a Hamas mastermind, killing in the process thirteen civilians, including nine children.

Israelis, though, often take great pains to play down this superior force.

"Oh they look ferocious," Avi, a nineteen year-old Israeli soldier says, patting the gun barrel of a tank, "but really they're just big babies."

Avi stands in the broiling sun twenty kilometers north, between the wall and the army base at the edge of Tulkarm, guarding a parking lot of modified American M-4 tanks. Half-way up the West Bank, at the foot of the Samarian Mountains, Tulkarm is another volatile bomber-laden launch pad city, only sixteen kilometers from the coast. From here the Israeli Defense Forces coordinates all its operations for the central command.

Avi is trying to tap into that old Israeli underdog mentality, a small people with inferior arms but great cunning, intellect, and moral superiority able to triumph against insurmountable odds. David and Goliath. "Do you know how old these are? They are from World War Two!"

A tank just returning from a mission in town rumbles up to the gate in a swell of dust, grinds to a stop. Soldiers pop out of the hatch, strip off their helmets, and walk on the top as if they were on parade float. They speak in excited tones. One of the men, the tall one with the curly hair and glasses, was hit in the face by a Coke bottle full of gasoline that was thrown off a balcony.

The soldier was lucky, the Molotov cocktail didn't explode. But climbing off the tank, he looks hot and humiliated, his green fatigues, bullet-proof vest, helmet, all stained dark with sweat and gasoline, his face dirty-streaked, stinging red. He couldn't do anything. The street was too narrow to turn the gun turret.

> BARTA

A weapon too big. Imagine. Not only can't you ride to the moral high ground in an M-4, you can't even get through the alleys of Tulkarm.

For some Israeli soldiers the result is rage, the rage of impotence, and consequently, overkill. Ten kilometers north there is a check-point between two towns, Baqa Gharbiya in Israel, and Baqa Sharqiya on the West Bank. On both sides of it the streets are deserted, stalls locked-down, the potholed road crawling with military vehicles. Israeli Intelligence received a report of a suicide-bomber coming this way and the area has been put under immediate curfew. When an Arab shop owner tarries, a soldier throws a canister of tear gas in front of his shop. A plume of white smoke stinks up the street, settles on the pyramid of green melons.

And this on the Israeli side.

But something unexpected happens when you cross into the West Bank. It gets beautiful. A path ambles north. The border is lined with fences, walls - but the more meaningful delineation is this passage into Beauty, from gas stations, agricultural grids, and strip malls, to narrow white villages tiered to the roll of the desert, submissive to it, never letting you forget where you are, that this is where the Bible happened, brown hills spotted by clusters of olive trees, the wadis, the cypress forest, the rock and sand.

And out of this, suddenly, Barta.

Unlike the Baqas, Barta, further up the border, is a single town divided in half. In the center there is dip, and at the bottom of that dip, down the hill past the shops, a trench. Part of the 1949 Armistice line, the trench separating Palestinian Barta from Israeli Barta is filled with garbage. There is a bridge in between. On the bridge stands a date seller. The odor there is powerful, sickening.

It remains unclear just which side of Barta the new security fence will run. On the Palestinian side they haven't even heard about it. Those who have couldn't care less. "They can put up a hundred fences," says Abu, the radiator repairman. "It will make no difference."

In his shop, Abu sits on a vinyl seat from a car. Like most around here he readily equates the Israelis with the Nazis. He also believes the Mossad, Israel's secret service, blew up the World Trade Center. But his twelve year-old son, Said, is the real hard-liner of the family. Said hates Israel, supports the "martyrdom" operations. He doesn't believe in peace, two lands, two peoples. Agreement or no he will fight Israel until it is gone. "Let the Jews go back where they came from," he says, "- to Germany, Holland, USA, Belgium."

Abu is more circumspect. He doesn't want any trouble.

There are fences around words, too.

"I don't know from where he hears this," he says.

> SALEM

We might be slow to grasp it, but it's a new world in the Middle East. The moral and political inevitability of peace, of two states side by side, which five years ago seemed a far-gone conclusion, is now just gone. Instead, the fence seeks a border without the nation.

From Barta the road veers ten kilometers east toward the northern tip of the West Bank, to Salem at the foot of the Jezreel Valley. Here, the security fence will end - or begin, depending on how you look at it.

Salem is also the major check-point in and out of Jenin, and a few weeks ago it was hopping: the flood-lit Defense Minister surrounded by cameras conducting a tour of the first new stretch of fence up on the hill, below all the tanks and men coming and going from Jenin, transporting prisoners, conducting operations.

Now it's like the circus has left town. The fence, having never gotten further than the 120 foot strip the minister showed off a month ago, is free-standing in the sand like a piece of sculpture. The unit in charge of moving equipment is moving equipment, rolling tanks onto flat bed trailers and driving away.

The only people left look like gas station attendants, two teenage girls wearing uniforms with no stripes or insignia, and a boy in a white t-shirt. It's the end of the day. The fiery sun is beginning to set behind the town's minaret. They goof around, struggle to get something out of each other's hands. There's no big hurry. It's someone's birthday. There's a cake in the shed with the gear.

Every few minutes a jeep sweeps past, on its way to Jenin to enforce the curfew.

> RAM-ON

Which isn't to say the new fence won't get built. It will, eventually. But Israel is digging in for the long-term, and a few months here or there isn't going to make a difference

For Elan and Galia it will make no difference at all. The couple live up in Ram-on, an agricultural settlement on the northern border of the West Bank, opposite Jenin. The new security fence won't come up this high. Instead the moshav has their own electronic fence, and a white surveillance balloon flying overhead.

They have Friends on. Their living room looks like every other living room in Israel, Van Gogh prints and framed photographs of their son in uniform - with the difference that their son died in a helicopter crash eleven years ago. He's the background against which to weigh Elan's sparkling blue-eyed exuberance, his flood of talking, and the way Galia is the opposite. Galia who seems frozen, like it happened yesterday. Eleven years of yesterdays, bloodshot eyes like she just stopped crying five minutes ago.

Do they feel safe? Elan laughs and tells about the night last month a terrorist came through the fence and shot into their neighbor's bedroom. Galia chews a finger, terrified just thinking about it. The terrorist got through, but he was killed - so it helps and it doesn't.

Elan is happy to drive visitors to the perimeter. Besides growing onion bulbs, he moonlights as a biblical tour guide and has some thoughts on fences in the bible, how a particular verse in the story of the Rehab, the whore of Jericho, proves that even thousands of years ago, fences and gated communities like this one were already part of the landscape.

The truck takes a dirt path through the fields. "Here, this is the electric fence," Elan says, reaching an intersection. It's about seven feet tall and made up of straight white posts, twenty-five perfectly-spaced wires stretched between. It looks brand new. On the other side of the road is a ditch - the Green Line. Beyond that, fields turning green to brown, then sloping up into the white bric-a-brac of Jenin.

It's not hard to think of ways over: jump from a friend's shoulders, make an incline with two boards, pole vault. One thing is clear right away - what every child probably knows - you see a fence and your natural reaction is to get to the other side. Because this fence is not seamless, the easiest way would be to go around it until you reach the gap.

What would happen if you started walking across the field to Jenin right now?

Elan says he's not sure ... but he doesn't advise it.

039

CHRISTOPHER ANDERSON

THE STONE THROWERS
GAZA STRIP

< Eres
A Palestinian boy launches
a rock toward the Israelis at
Eres in the Gaza Strip.

> Martyrs' Square
Young Palestinians gather for a
demonstration in Martyrs' Square
in the Gaza Strip.

> Gaza Strip
At a school, pictures of classmates
killed during clahes hang on the walls,
praising them for giving their lives.

> Gaza Strip
Young boys break large rocks to make
more accurate ammunition during clashes.

This war always seemed stranger than most. Geopolitical rhetoric, religious sovereignty, refugees, occupation, etc., were cast in the usual lofty ideals. This, unfortunately, was nothing new. Even the horrible violence that strikes the innocents is the same sinister byproduct of all wars. Yet, what made the conflict in the Middle East so different (I am referring to the early months of the second Intifada when these pictures where taken) was that much of the fighting, on the Palestinian side at least, was being carried out by children. Pre-teenagers and mid-teenagers and boys as young as five were dying with shocking frequency while waging "battle" against one of the most highly trained armies on earth. In the first three months of the Intifada, 68 boys under the age of eighteen were killed in clashes with soldiers.

They were armed with rocks and slingshots.

The violence did not deter them; quite the opposite, in fact.

I traveled to the Gaza Strip in October of 2000 to meet these boys.

I went to learn who they were and why they were doing what they were doing. It was not my intention to make a political statement on who was right or wrong, or who was justified or guilty in relation to the question of Israel. I simply wanted to know who they were, and to photograph them as human beings rather than statistics in a newspaper. Some will see the pictures as pro-Palestinian propaganda. Others will see it as exactly the opposite. Certainly both voices have made themselves known to me. What I did see was shocking, and very confusing. I saw young children shot. On the other hand, I also saw a system that encouraged these children to their deaths.

Both sickened me.

The whole process seemed designed-on both sides-to ensure the misery of all peoples in the future.

At the time the extent to which this anger and frustration could spill out of the barbed wire fences of the Gaza Strip didn't occur to me. But as I watched the live footage of the World Trade Centers on September 11, my thoughts were on Gaza. I felt as if I was watching an extension of the very anger and frustration I had witnessed there.

What had spilled over the Gaza fence was now a flood in lower Manhattan. Again, I felt sickened, not just by the horrible violence of the event, but also by the fact that this terrible design flaw could send us all into a process of defense and retaliation that would only guarantee our own future misery.

> **Jenin**
The home of a boy who was killed the day before in the Gaza strip is covered by graffitti from Palestinian political parties praising him a sa martyr. His brother and sister play out front.

> **Gaza Strip**
A young boy brandishes his grandfather's AK-47 assualt rifle during a funeral for a young boy in the Gaza Strip.

◊ **Khan Yunis**
A boy is gravely wounded in the head during clashes with Israeli Troops in Khan Yunis, The Gaza Strip.

◊ **Martyrs' Cemetery**
Funeral for young man killed during clashes with Israeli soldiers in the Gaza Strip. The body is paraded through the streets from the hospital to the Martyrs' Cemetery. Here, a father of this boy screams in anguish.

> **Karny Crossing**
Palestinian youths throw rocks at Israeli soldiers during clashes at Karny Crossing in the Gaza strip.

◊ **Khan Yunis**
Clashes at Khan Yunis
in the Gaza Strip.

> **Karny Crossing**
Palestinian youths throw rocks at
Israeli soldiers during clashes at Karny
Crossing in the Gaza strip.

> **Ramallah**
Taking a break during clashes at the front
lines. Often, lunch is even brought to the boys
in the afternoon by adults .

> **Khan Yunis**
Palestinian boys try to cover their faces from
the tear gas shot by Israeli forces. Khan Yunis
refugee camp in the Gaza Strip.

> **Ramallah**
At the front lines of clashes in
Ramallah, The West Bank.

> **Ramallah**
A Palestinian dressed in a Palestinian flag like a cape takes shelter
behind an overturned car and covers his face until tear gas passes by during
clashes in Ramallah, the West Bank.

039 Christopher Anderson
The Stone Throwers

Page 485

040

EDWARD W. SAID

WHO IS IN CHARGE?
MARCH 7 2003

The Bush administration's relentless unilateral march towards war is profoundly disturbing for many reasons, but so far as American citizens are concerned the whole grotesque show is a tremendous failure in democracy.

AN IMMENSELY WEALTHY AND POWERFUL REPUBLIC HAS BEEN HIJACKED BY A SMALL CABAL OF INDIVIDUALS, ALL OF THEM UNELECTED AND THEREFORE UNRESPONSIVE TO PUBLIC PRESSURE, AND SIMPLY TURNED ON ITS HEAD.

IT IS NO EXAGGERATION TO SAY THAT THIS WAR IS THE MOST UNPOPULAR IN MODERN HISTORY. BEFORE THE WAR HAS BEGUN THERE HAVE BEEN MORE PEOPLE PROTESTING IT IN THIS COUNTRY ALONE THAN WAS THE CASE AT THE HEIGHT OF THE ANTI-VIETNAM WAR DEMONSTRATIONS DURING THE SIXTIES AND SEVENTIES. NOTE ALSO THAT THOSE RALLIES TOOK PLACE AFTER THE WAR HAD BEEN GOING ON FOR SEVERAL YEARS: THIS ONE HAS YET TO BEGIN, EVEN THOUGH A LARGE NUMBER OF OVERTLY AGGRESSIVE AND BELLIGERENT STEPS HAVE ALREADY BEEN TAKEN BY THE US AND ITS LOYAL PUPPY, THE UK GOVERNMENT OF THE INCREASINGLY RIDICULOUS TONY BLAIR.

I have been criticised recently for my anti-war position by illiterates who claim that what I say is an implied defence of Saddam Hussein and his appalling regime. To my Kuwaiti critics, do I need to remind them that I publicly opposed Ba'athi Iraq during the only visit I made to Kuwait in 1985, when in an open conversation with the then Minister of Education Hassan Al-Ibrahim I accused him and his regime of aiding and abetting Arab fascism in their financial support of Saddam Hussein? I was told then that Kuwait was proud to have committed billions of dollars to Saddam's war against "the Persians", as they were then contemptuously called, and that it was a more important struggle than someone like me could comprehend. I remember clearly warning those Kuwaiti acolytes of Saddam Hussein about him and his ill will against Kuwait, but to no avail. I have been a public opponent of the Iraqi regime since it came to power in the seventies: I never visited the place, never was fooled by its claims to secularism and modernisation (even when many of my contemporaries either worked for or celebrated Iraq as the main gun in the Arab arsenal against Zionism, a stupid idea, I thought), never concealed my contempt for its methods of rule and fascist behaviour. And now when I speak my mind about the ridiculous posturing of certain members of the Iraqi opposition as hapless strutting tools of US imperialism, I am told that I know nothing about life without democracy (about which more later), and am therefore unable to appreciate their nobility of soul. Little notice is taken of the fact that barely a week after extolling President Bush's commitment to democracy Professor Makiya is now denouncing the US and its plans for a post-Saddam military-Ba'athi government in Iraq. When individuals get in the habit of switching the gods whom they worship politically there's no end to the number of changes they make before they finally come to rest in utter disgrace and well deserved oblivion.

But to return to the US and its current actions.

In all my encounters and travels I have yet to meet a person who is for the war. Even worse, most Americans now feel that this mobilisation has already gone too far to stop, and that we are on the verge of a disaster for the country. Consider first of all that the Democratic Party, with few exceptions, has simply gone over to the president's side in a gutless display of false patriotism. Wherever you look in the Congress there are the tell-tale signs either of the Zionist lobby, the right-wing Christians, or the military-industrial complex, three inordinately influential minority groups who share hostility to the Arab world, unbridled support for extremist Zionism, and an insensate conviction that they are on the side of the angels. Every one of the 500 congressional districts in this country has a defence industry in it, so that war has been turned into a matter of jobs, not of security.

But, one might well ask, how does running an unbelievably expensive war remedy, for instance, economic recession, the almost certain bankruptcy of the social security system, a mounting national debt, and a massive failure in public education?

Demonstrations are looked at simply as a kind of degraded mob action, while the most hypocritical lies pass for absolute truth, without criticism and without objection.

The media has simply become a branch of the war effort. What has entirely disappeared from television is anything remotely resembling a consistently dissenting voice. Every major channel now employs retired generals, former CIA agents, terrorism experts and known neoconservatives as "consultants" who speak a revolting jargon designed to sound authoritative but in effect supporting everything done by the US, from the UN to the sands of Arabia. Only one major daily newspaper (in Baltimore) has published anything about US eavesdropping, telephone tapping and message interception of the six small countries that are members of the Security Council and whose votes are undecided. There are no antiwar voices to read or hear in any of the major medias of this country, no Arabs or Muslims (who have been consigned en masse to the ranks of the fanatics and terrorists of this world), no critics of Israel, not on Public Broadcasting, not in The New York Times, the New Yorker, US News and World Report, CNN and the rest. When these organisations mention Iraq's flouting of 17 UN resolutions as a pretext for war, the 64 resolutions flouted by Israel (with US support) are never mentioned. Nor is the enormous human suffering of the Iraqi people during the past 12 years mentioned. Whatever the dreaded Saddam has done Israel and Sharon have also done with American support, yet no one says anything about the latter while fulminating about the former. This makes a total mockery of taunts by Bush and others that the UN should abide by its own resolutions.

THE AMERICAN PEOPLE HAVE THUS BEEN DELIBERATELY LIED TO, THEIR INTERESTS CYNICALLY MISREPRESENTED AND MISREPORTED, THE REAL AIMS AND INTENTIONS OF THIS PRIVATE WAR OF BUSH THE SON AND HIS JUNTA CONCEALED WITH COMPLETE ARROGANCE.

Never mind that Wolfowitz, Feith, and Perle, all of them unelected officials who work for unelected Donald Rumsfeld at the Pentagon, have for some time openly advocated Israeli annexation of the West Bank and Gaza and the cessation of the Oslo process, have called for war against Iraq (and later Iran), and the building of more illegal Israeli settlements in their capacity (during Netanyahu's successful campaign for prime minister in 1996) as private consultants to him, and that that has become US policy now.

Never mind that Israel's iniquitous policies against Palestinians, which are reported only at the ends of articles (when they are reported at all) as so many miscellaneous civilian deaths, are never compared with Saddam's crimes, which they match or in some cases exceed, all of them, in the final analysis, paid for by the US taxpayer without consultation or approval. Over 40,000 Palestinians have been wounded seriously in the last two years, and about 2,500 killed wantonly by Israeli soldiers who are instructed to humiliate and punish an entire people during what has become the longest military occupation in modern history.

Never mind that not a single critical Arab or Muslim voice has been seen or heard on the major American media, liberal, moderate, or reactionary, with any regularity at all since the preparations for war have gone into their final phase. Consider also that none of the major planners of this war, certainly not the so-called experts like Bernard Lewis and Fouad Ajami, neither of whom has so much as lived in or come near the Arab world in decades, nor the military and political people like Powell, Rice, Cheney, or the great god Bush himself, know anything about the Muslim or Arab worlds beyond what they see through Israeli or oil company or military lenses, and therefore have no idea what a war of this magnitude against Iraq will produce for the people actually living there.

And consider too the sheer, unadorned hubris of men like Wolfowitz and his assistants. Asked to testify to a largely somnolent Congress about the war's consequences and costs they are allowed to escape without giving any concrete answers, which effectively dismisses the evidence of the army chief of staff who has spoken of a military occupation force of 400,000 troops for 10 years at a cost of almost a trillion dollars.

DEMOCRACY TRADUCED AND BETRAYED, DEMOCRACY CELEBRATED BUT IN FACT HUMILIATED AND TRAMPLED ON BY A TINY GROUP

OF MEN WHO HAVE SIMPLY TAKEN CHARGE OF THIS REPUBLIC AS IF IT WERE NOTHING MORE THAN, WHAT, AN ARAB COUNTRY? IT IS RIGHT TO ASK WHO IS IN CHARGE SINCE CLEARLY THE PEOPLE OF THE UNITED STATES ARE NOT PROPERLY REPRESENTED BY THE WAR THIS ADMINISTRATION IS ABOUT TO LOOSE ON A WORLD ALREADY BELEAGUERED BY TOO MUCH MISERY AND POVERTY TO ENDURE MORE. AND AMERICANS HAVE BEEN BADLY SERVED BY A MEDIA CONTROLLED ESSENTIALLY BY A TINY GROUP OF MEN WHO EDIT OUT ANYTHING THAT MIGHT CAUSE THE GOVERNMENT THE SLIGHTEST CONCERN OR WORRY. AS FOR THE DEMAGOGUES AND SERVILE INTELLECTUALS WHO TALK ABOUT WAR FROM THE PRIVACY OF THEIR FANTASY WORLDS, WHO GAVE THEM THE RIGHT TO CONNIVE IN THE IMMISERATION OF MILLIONS OF PEOPLE WHOSE MAJOR CRIME SEEMS TO BE THAT THEY ARE MUSLIMS AND ARABS? WHAT AMERICAN, EXCEPT FOR THIS SMALL UNREPRESENTATIVE GROUP, IS SERIOUSLY INTERESTED IN INCREASING THE WORLD'S ALREADY AMPLE STORES OF ANTI-AMERICANISM? HARDLY ANY I WOULD SUPPOSE.

Jonathan Swift, thou shouldst be living at this hour.

041

GÜNTHER GRASS

THE INJUSTICE OF THE MIGHTIER
MARCH 25 2003

A war has begun, one which has for a long time been desired and planned. Against all the concerns and warnings from the United Nations, an internationally illegal order for a preventive attack has been issued to an overwhelming military apparatus. No objections helped.

The vote of the Security Council was ignored and scorned as irrelevant. As of March 20, 2003, only the right of the stronger applies. And based on this injustice the stronger has the power to buy and reward those who favour war, to disregard or even punish those who are against war.

The words of the current American president who says 'those who are not for us are against us' weighs as a burden on everything happening today in an echo from barbaric periods. So it does not come as a surprise when the aggressor's choice of words more and more resembles that of his enemy.

Religious fundamentalism empowers both sides to abuse the term 'God' as used by all religions and to take 'God' - according to their individual fanatical understanding - hostage. Even the passionate warning of the Pope, who is cognizant of the continuing damage of the mentality and practice of Christian crusading, had no effect.

AGITATED, POWERLESS, BUT ALSO FILLED WITH RAGE, WE HAVE TO WATCH THE MORAL DECLINE OF THE SOLE RULING WORLD POWER, SENSING THAT ONE THING WILL RESULT FROM THE ORGANISED INSANITY: MOTIVATION FOR A SWELLING TERRORISM, FOR FURTHER VIOLENCE AND COUNTER-VIOLENCE.

Are these the United States of America, who for many reasons have a good place in our memory? The generous providers of the Marshall Plan? The patient masters who taught the subject of democracy? Who forthrightly criticised themselves? The country which once was helped by the process of European Enlightenment in overcoming colonial rule, gave itself an exemplary Constitution and to whom the freedom of expression was an inalienable human right?

Not only is it we who are experiencing how this picture, which in the course of the years became more and more one of wishful thinking, has faded and become a distortion of itself. There are also many Americans who love their country and are appalled at the decay of their innate values and at the hybris of their own power.

I regard myself as allied with them. On their side, I am avowedly pro-American. With them, I protest against the brutally executed injustice of the mightier, against restrictions on freedom of opinion, against an information policy which in its practice compares only with that of totalitarian states, and against any cynical calculation in which the death of many thousands of women and children is accepted when it comes to the preservation of economic and power interests.

No, it is not anti-Americanism which is damaging the reputation of the USA, not dictator Saddam Hussein and his largely disarmed country which are endangering the strongest power in the world; it is President Bush and his government who are pushing the decay of democratic values, who are inflicting damage on their country, who are ignoring the United Nations and who now, in an internationally illegal war are inflicting horror on the world.

We Germans have often been asked whether we are proud of our country. It was difficult to answer. And there were reasons for our hesitation. I can say that I am a little bit proud of Germany because of the rejection by the majority of citizens of my country of the preventive war now begun. After the responsibility for two world wars with criminal results, we have, though it was difficult, learned from history and grasped the lessons meted to us.

Since 1990 the Federal Republic of Germany has been a sovereign state. For the first time the government has made use of this sovereignty in that it had the courage to contradict the powerful ally and preserve Germany from falling back into the position of a minor.

I thank Federal Chancellor Gerhard Schroeder and his Foreign Minister Joschka Fischer for their steadfastness; they maintained their credibility despite all the internal and external attacks.

Many people might currently be disheartened. There are reasons for it. Nevertheless our 'no' to war and 'yes' to peace should not fade away. What has happened? The rock which we rolled uphill is now back at the foot of the mountain.

And so once again we roll it back up, even if we sense that, scarcely up on top, it will be awaiting us again at the foot of the mountain. This, in any event this - the never-ending protest and counter-protest - is and remains humanly possible.

042

DAVID RIEFF

THE GREAT DIVORCE
EUROPE AND AMERICA IN POST-SEPTEMBER 11TH ERA

For once, the media and the pundits are not exaggerating. While there has not yet been a final parting of the ways between the great powers of Western Europe, above all, France and Germany – the nations that the American defense secretary, Donald Rumsfeld, rather mysteriously called the "Old" Europe – and the United States, relations between Washington and the European Union countries are at their lowest ebb since the beginning of the Cold War. In academic and policy circles, the talk is of 'the end' of the Atlantic alliance. Meanwhile, long latent antipathies are being rubbed alight on both sides of the ocean. Anecdotes abound. In the United States Senate, French fries have been renamed "Freedom fries", and on the radio talk shows in which the American id routinely expresses itself, the tenor is one of contempt for European 'cowardice' in refusing to join the good fight against Saddam Hussein, mixed with indignation that Europe is not more "grateful" to America for its actions in the twentieth century's two world wars and, hence, willing to go along with America's plans in Iraq.

It is a tone that owes as much to secondary school hurt feelings as to objective appraisals of national interest. From the perspective of many, though obviously not all ordinary Americans, Europe owes the U.S. support and loyalty. Even as worldly and cosmopolitan a figure as John Kornblum, the former U.S. ambassador to Germany who now heads the Berlin office of the banking house Lazard Freres, has observed that "an ally is a friend who sticks with you when you have a problem." But of course, that is precisely not what an ally does when she disagrees with you – at least not an ally who is your equal. It is what a friend does in private life, whether that friend thinks you are right or wrong. But in international relations, such fealty, when it involves signing on to a course of action that you feel is not in your own interests – which is what most members of the Western European elite feels about America's intent to topple Saddam Hussein by force – is only appropriate for a subordinate.

The fact that the public at large, most of the media, not to mention the Bush administration itself, does not see this and tends to view those European leaders like Blair, Aznar, and, to a lesser extent, Berlusconi, as loyal friends, while Schroeder, Chirac and the other opponents of U.S. action are seen as false friends, testifies to the irrational character of the debate on the American side. Again, it is the world as refracted through the schoolyard, not the chancellery, that is being evoked. Or, to put it another way, America is behaving like the proverbial Jewish mother complaining of being abandoned by her ungrateful children after all she has done for them. And while both different in form and substance, the anger toward the United States and the accounts of the motives behind its actions, are equally irrational, personalized, and hysterical in Europe.

One does not have to believe, to cite Lord Palmerston's axiom so well-loved by international relations 'realists' like myself, that states do not have permanent friends, they only have permanent interests, to see that such personalization of the dispute over Iraq can only make the crisis worse. As long as the dialogue is one between European angst and American bellicism, there cannot be an accommodation – even if that accommodation turns out to be, as I believe it will, to a new reality in which the post-World War II order – a peace and security system ostensibly based on the United Nations Security Council, the North Atlantic Alliance, American tutelage and European vassalage, etc. – is seen as having outlasted its sell-by date. In any case, there should be nothing shocking about the fact that an international system that lasted more than fifty years should have to be radically overhauled. Looking back, no one thinks the structure of Europe in 1745 – of Louis XV in France and the Jacobite wars in the British Isles – was appropriate to the Europe of 1803 and Napoleon, or that the international system incarnated in the reactionary Holy Alliance of 1815 was appropriate to the bourgeois Europe of 1873. Or, to use a Mexican example, it is as if the political order of Francisco Madero had been expected to last into the era of Miguel Aleman. **Why should anyone have believed that the World War II settlement was eternal, or its structures anymore immortal than any other set of political arrangements?**

OF COURSE, RATIONALLY PEOPLE DO NOT BELIEVE THIS. AND IT IS PERHAPS ONLY HUMAN NATURE NOT TO WANT TO CONTEMPLATE THE END OF THE POLITICAL ORDER IN WHICH ONE HAS COME TO MATURITY, JUST AS IT IS ONLY HUMAN TO NOT WANT TO CONTEMPLATE THE WORLD PROCEEDING ON ITS MERRY WAY AFTER ONE HAS ONESELF BEEN FOREVER EXTINGUISHED. IN THIS

CONNECTION, IT IS SIGNIFICANT, I THINK, THAT IT IS THE VERY YOUNG, WHETHER THEY ARE AMERICANS WHO SUPPORT THE RUSH TO WAR IN IRAQ, OR EUROPEANS WHO ARE COMING TO LOATHE THE UNITED STATES AND TO SEE IT AS A FAR GREATER THREAT TO GLOBAL STABILITY THAN SADDAM HUSSEIN, WHO ARE MOST COMFORTABLE WITH THE IDEA OF THE END TO THE CURRENTLY ESTABLISHED ORDER OF THINGS. STILL, VIEWED COLDLY, WHAT IS MOST SURPRISING IS NOT THAT THERE HAS BEEN A FALLING OUT AMONG POST-WORLD WAR II WESTERN ALLIES, NOR THAT THE UNITED NATIONS (THE UNITED NATIONS OF ALL INSTITUTIONS! THIS AFTER THE BALKANS AND RWANDA) IS NO LONGER SEEN AS A SOLUTION THE GLOBAL PROBLEMS OF PEACE AND SECURITY, BUT RATHER THAT THE OLD SYSTEM LASTED AS LONG AS IT DID. THE SALIENT POINT, AGAIN, IS THAT STRUCTURES OF INTERNATIONAL ORDER ARE NOT FOUNDED ON SENTIMENT, BUT ON INTEREST, AND INTERESTS ARE SITUATIONAL AND HISTORICALLY DETERMINED. IN OTHER WORDS, UNLIKE FRIENDSHIP OR FAITH, THEY ARE NEITHER SENTIMENTAL NOR PERMANENT.

Viewed from this perspective, the rift between the United States and Europe was probably inevitable. It is true that the widespread European opposition to the Bush administration's determination to go to war to unseat the Saddam Hussein tyranny in Iraq, whether its European allies approved of the decision or not, is overwhelming among the educated classes and young people, especially, polling data suggests, in those countries like Britain, Spain, and Italy, whose governments have supported Washington. But Iraq is at most an emblem of this estrangement and a catalyst for what otherwise might have been a more delayed and, perhaps, subtler playing out of the trans-Atlantic divorce. It should not obscure the fact (as, alas, it has in most of the public debate over the issue on both sides) that deeper beliefs and emotions, and, most importantly, historical forces that have been in operation for some time, lie at its heart.

Not that these "atmospherics" are trivial. To the contrary, the spleen and suspicion with which, from their respective plinths, Western Europeans and Americans now view one another, has made any kind of cool-headed dialogue virtually impossible. It is a dialogue of the deaf, a battle of reductionist clichés. **For many, if not most Western Europeans, George W. Bush seems to incarnate all the left wing clichés of the American yahoo-the moronic cowboy, the irresponsible barbarian whose vision of the world is purely and woefully Manichean, the religious fanatic, the man of violence.** A cartoon in the left French weekly, Charlie Hebdo, pictured Bush in full regalia-six-shooter, moronic grin, and cowboy hat, mounted astride the globe like a rodeo bull-rider. "Master of the Universe and Kings of Cretins," read the caption, "'no' to such a dual mandate!"

It is an old European trope, this conviction that when all is said and done what is essential about the United States is its barbarous id. In this fantasy, anything cultivated in the United States is an extension of Europe (and, these days, of Latin America and East Asia), whereas it is the uncouth, the uncivilized, and the naïve that is, as it were, natively American. Hence, French aesthetes reveled in heaping lavish praise on the asinine antics of Jerry Lewis movies while being dismissive of American seriousness. The idea dates back at least as far as the nineteen-twenties when D.H. Lawrence, ensconced in New Mexico and contemplating nineteenth century American literature, could insist with serene confidence that the quintessential American was "hard, isolate, and a killer."

Of course, these attitudes are complicated. At the same time that Western Europeans felt superior to America, they were also in love with America.

And the love affair transformed them far more than it transformed Americans. Perhaps this was for no other reason than that, for most of the twentieth century, the modern and the American seemed to go hand in hand. To anyone who remembers Europe even as recently as the nineteen-sixties, what is remarkable about the last four decades is the continent's Americanization. During the recent mass demonstrations against the looming American campaign against Saddam Hussein that overwhelms the city centers of most major Western capitals, the durability of this Americanization was everywhere in evidence. To watch young demonstrators in U.S. High School 'letter jackets,' cowboy boots, and denims, chanting anti-U.S. slogans was, to put the matter charitably, a textbook illustration of the theory of cognitive dissonance.

That said, there is no reason why young Europeans should not be culturally Americanized and politically anti-American. Such paradoxes are scarcely unheard of in cultures, particularly modern cultures, which are so fundamentally marked by paradox. And after all, European ambivalence toward the United States, both culturally and politically, was always a significant element of the trans-Atlantic dynamic.

During the Cold War, such feelings tended to be more muted. The generation that had lived through the Second World War tended to be grateful to the Americans – in most countries for their liberation, and in the German case for their democratization and moral rehabilitation. Even the so-called generation of May '68, particularly in Germany, inherited these attitudes to some degree. As the German Foreign Minister, Joshka Fischer, put it recently, "We're a democracy, and because we have America to thank for this, my sympathy and solidarity with that country is unshakable."

Fischer is in many ways emblematic of the European Left in this regard. It is noteworthy that while many bitterly opposed the U.S. war in Vietnam, and, later, the deployment of missiles in Europe in the early nineteen-eighties, most still tended, at least tacitly, to concede or take for granted that American military guarantees to Europe were essential to Europe's security and prosperity. The proof of this is that while there were mass demonstrations against American actions in Vietnam, and against basing of certain specific weapons systems on European soil, there was never a mass movement calling for the withdrawal of U.S. forces. During those years, the Americans were resented, but they were also viewed as indispensable. That consensus fractured with the end of the Cold War.

In U.S. policy circles today, the reigning view is that the U.S. is, if anything, more indispensable than ever. It was Madeleine Albright, Bill Clinton's Secretary of State, who coined the term "the indispensable nation" to describe the U.S. role in the post-Cold War World, a fact that should give pause to those Europeans and U.S. liberals who think they discern a fundamental difference between the Clinton and Bush approaches to foreign policy and American hegemony. But in Europe, doubts about whether the U.S. needs to exercise that kind of hegemony for the common good, which was the Cold War consensus, however grudging, among America's European allies, are increasingly in evidence. Such hegemony, once seen as essential to the maintenance of peace and order, is now viewed by many Europeans as constituting an almost existential threat to it. Better to tolerate a Muamar Khaddafi, a Kim Jong II, or a Saddam Hussein (or, in the nineteen-nineties, a Slobodan Milosevic) than to endanger international peace and security by going to war with all the unpredictable and dangerous consequences that war entails. At the very least, most Europeans insist, war should be a last resort, undertaken only when the offending tyrant has proved he will not stop – as many Europeans would say Milosevic did when, having been let off the hook in the aftermath of Bosnia, he refused to mend his ways and, indeed, provoked a crisis in Kosovo.

But policy disagreements pitting American absolutism versus European pragmatism (and what a philosophical switch that is!) are only part of the dynamic that is at play. The simple fact is that Europe more than a decade after the Cold War is not the same place that it was a generation ago. The cohorts that were viscerally grateful to the U.S. for what it did both during World War II and the Cold War are passing from the scene. For their part, the younger generations do not see why they have to remain eternally both morally indebted and politically subordinate to the United States, even if that was the only viable option for their parents and grandparents. And, again, the arrangement suited Europeans at the time. The French, the Germans, the Italians, even the still bellicose British did not want to spend the kind of money on defense that would have been necessary to act autonomously, and get out from under U.S. tutelage. They were sick of war, engaged in the radical project of decolonization (one of the most radical peaceful transformations in human history), and eager to restart their own economies. No proud state likes being something of a vassal, but under the circumstances most Europeans judged it the least bad choice open to them.

No longer.

At the root of the French and German governments' willingness to openly break with Washington over the question of Iraq is a Western Europe with far less interest in doing nothing to upset the American-dominated security system of the Cold War era. American commentators, particularly neo-conservative writers close to the Bush administration like Robert Kagan, whose recent bestseller, Of Paradise and Power, made the case that Europe and the U.S. had diverged because Europe is weak and America strong and each is behaving accordingly, are, at most, only partly right. Europe is very strong economically; in some sectors, stronger than the United States. To cite only one obvious example, when it decided that it no longer wished to be dependent on U.S. commercial aircraft makers like Boeing – and, indeed, wished to take their markets – it created a continental champion, Airbus, which has done just that. Europe is also willing to exercise its commercial power to block initiatives supported in Washington, as the recent decision by the European Union to block the merger of two American firms, General Electric and Honeywell, demonstrated clearly. A continent comfortable asserting its economic independence was bound to assert its political independence sooner or later.

Neo-conservative American thinkers tend to dismiss these developments as secondary. There is something strangely Spartan about their thinking, as if the only poems in their heads are poems of force. And that, when all is said and done, is the deepest problem with the neo-conservative vision of the U.S.-Europe divide. Even at its best, as in the work of writers like Kagan or Max Boot, while it claims to be cool-headed and realistic (at its worst, it boils down to the assertion that the Europeans are "ungrateful" for what the U.S. has done for them, as if the U.S. had had no interests but only values at stake during World War II and the Cold War and accrued no benefit from its victories), in fact, it is, on the one hand, floridly ideological and utopian, and on the other makes the bizarre assumption that power and military power are essentially inseparable. And this, historically, is anything but self-evident – as neo-conservatives, who so often cite him, should have learned from Clausewitz, if from no one else.

"War," the great military philosopher famously said, "is the extension of politics by other means." The lesson American neo-conservatives draw from this is that is that without great military power, states are reduced to impotence. But for Europeans, the lesson of the past several decades shows something quite different. With the possible exceptions of Britain and France, most European nations have renounced their martial pasts and any future military ambitions. The Belgian minister of defense spoke for many when, answering a mocking piece in The Wall Street Journal about his country's military capacities, he insisted indignantly that Belgium's armed forces were well prepared for humanitarian and peacekeeping roles and for assisting the civilian population. Why such a force needed advanced fighter aircraft, since he was describing a kind of paramilitary emergency relief organization, the minister never made clear. But behind this kind of official incoherence and thick self-righteousness lies something far more serious-something the American policy elite (and not just conservatives, but liberals as well) has trouble taking in: **The Western Europeans have come to the radical conclusion that they can impose their will by peaceful means.**

For a continent steeped in blood, it is the most radical of conclusions. And the jury is very much still out about whether such an approach, however consoling morally, will work geo-strategically. Robert Kagan believes that the Europeans are living in a fool's paradise. For him, their Kantian commonwealth of perpetual peace, a universe governed by law, not force, is only sustainable because the United States, like Moses watching the Israelites entering the Promised Land, not only forswears the possibility of entering itself, but accepts the burden of serving as a rampart between Europe's privileged Kantian island and the Hobbesian world of blood, fire, and defiance that is to be found everywhere else in our world.

The self-congratulation implicit in this vision is noteworthy, but need not long detain us. What is significant is the extent to which the best and the brightest in the European and US policy elites differ over the role of force in the post-Cold War world. The reigning American view is that force remains at the center of human affairs, just as it always has. And conservative voices in the U.S. are joined in this by a surprising number of human rights activists and humanitarian aid workers who, in despair over the weakness of the [law-based] international system, have come to the reluctant conclusion that in a Rwanda, a Bosnia, or an East Timor, human rights must be imposed-by military force, if necessary. And while most do not quite go so far as to make the point explicitly, the only credible imposer of such human rights norms is the U.S. military. It alone has the capacity to stop genocide, if only it can muster the will and moral courage to do so.

The same left-liberal activists in the U.S. who were begging the U.S. to act in defiance of the UN Security Council and international law to reverse ethnic cleansing in Kosovo now complain when the Bush administration acts on exactly the same unilateralist premises in Iraq. Because of this, their complaints carry little conviction. To the contrary, it can be argued that they prepared the ideological ground for the Bush administration's recourse to unilateralism and disdain for, or at least impatience with the post-World War II system of international order. If intervention was right in Kosovo against the Milosevic regime, why is it not right in Iraq against Saddam Hussein and his cronies, who the American Human Rights group, Human Rights Watch, has claimed are guilty of genocide? The American human rights movement, like the Bush administration, is also finally the champion of force – of imposing democracy, to use the old May '68 phrase, 'by whatever means necessary.' The imperial visions may differ in important respects, but they are both imperial visions nonetheless, and that commonality is what, in the final analysis, is most salient.

Given the immense power of the United States, and the equally impressive determination of the Bush administration, above all of the President himself, who is one of the most under-rated figures in recent U.S. political history, to pursue its quite revolutionary agenda – in effect, the thwarting of America's enemies by conquest if necessary combined with an effort to democratize the world in America's image – it is hard to see what Europe could do to restrain the U.S. In any case, while European disenchantment with America transcends national boundaries, the political leadership of the major European powers is more divided than they seem at present. A recent editorial in the French newspaper, Le Monde, noted acerbically that France faced a geopolitical reality in which it had a neighbor across the Channel that could not relinquish its dream of vanished imperial glory and a neighbor across the Rhine that could not relinquish its dream of remaining a vast Switzerland. The upshot of this (correct) calculation is that on matters of foreign policy Europe continues to be unable to speak with one voice. And, of course, until it does it can constitute no break to U.S. power or U.S. principle.

The likeliest outcome over the short term is, indeed, the further fraying of the international system, the marginalization of the UN – which now risks becoming little more than the colonial authority in post-conflict situations, to the newly refounded American empire – and, if not a trans-Atlantic divorce between Europe and the United States, then, as matrimonial lawyers like to say, a trial separation.

This may not be a bad thing.

What those who are nostalgic for the passing international order cannot or do not choose to face is that its time has passed. One may welcome the American empire, or hope for its failure, but one should not mourn for a status quo that could not continue because it had lost its reason for being. To do so is simply sentimental, and about the destructive role of sentiment in politics it is not possible to say too much.

043

ARUNDHATI ROY

THE ORDINARY PERSON'S GUIDE TO EMPIRE

APRIL 1 2003

Mesopotamia.

Babylon.

The Tigris and Euphrates.

How many children, in how many classrooms, over how many centuries, have hang-glided through the past, transported on the wings of these words?

And now the bombs are falling, incinerating and humiliating that ancient civilization.

On the steel torsos of their missiles, adolescent American soldiers scrawl colourful messages in childish handwriting: For Saddam, from the Fat Boy Posse. A building goes down. A market place. A home. A girl who loves a boy. A child who only ever wanted to play with his older brother's marbles.

On the 21st of March, the day after American and British troops began their illegal invasion and occupation of Iraq, an 'embedded' CNN correspondent interviewed an American soldier. "I wanna get in there and get my nose dirty," Private AJ said. "I wanna take revenge for 9/11."

To be fair to the correspondent, even though he was 'embedded' he did sort of weakly suggest that so far there was no real evidence that linked the Iraqi Government to the September 11th attacks. Private AJ stuck his teenage tongue out all the way down to the end of his chin. "Yeah, well that stuff's way over my head," he said.

ACCORDING TO A NEW YORK TIMES/CBS NEWS SURVEY, 42% OF THE AMERICAN PUBLIC BELIEVES THAT SADDAM HUSSEIN IS DIRECTLY RESPONSIBLE FOR THE SEPTEMBER 11TH ATTACKS ON THE WORLD TRADE CENTRE AND THE PENTAGON. AND AN ABC NEWS POLL SAYS THAT 55% OF AMERICANS BELIEVE THAT SADDAM HUSSEIN DIRECTLY SUPPORTS THE AL-QAEDA. WHAT PERCENTAGE OF AMERICA'S ARMED FORCES BELIEVE THESE FABRICATIONS IS ANYBODY'S GUESS.

It is unlikely that British and American troops fighting in Iraq are aware that their governments supported Saddam Hussein both politically and financially through his worst excesses.

But why should poor AJ and his fellow soldiers be burdened with these details? It doesn't matter any more, does it? Hundreds of

thousands of men, tanks, ships, choppers, bombs, ammunition, gas masks, high protein food, whole aircrafts ferrying toilet paper, insect repellent, vitamins and bottled mineral water, are on the move. The phenomenal logistics of Operation Iraqi Freedom make it a universe unto itself. It doesn't need to justify its existence anymore. It exists. It is.

President George W Bush, Commander in Chief of the US army, navy, airforce and marines has issued clear instructions "Iraq. Will. Be. Liberated". (Perhaps he means that even if Iraqi people's bodies are killed, their souls will be liberated.) American and British citizens owe it to the Supreme Commander to forsake thought and rally behind their troops.

Their countries are at war.

And what a war it is.

After using the 'good offices' of UN diplomacy (economic sanctions and weapons inspections) to ensure that Iraq was brought to its knees, its people starved, half a million of its children killed, its infrastructure severely damaged, after making sure that most of its weapons have been destroyed, in an act of cowardice that must surely be unrivalled in history, the 'Allies'/'Coalition of the Willing' (better known as the Coalition of the Bullied and Bought) - sent in an invading army!

Operation Iraqi Freedom?

I don't think so.

It's more like Operation Let's Run a Race, but First Let Me Break Your Knees.

So far the Iraqi army, with its hungry, ill equipped soldiers, its old guns and ageing tanks, has somehow managed to temporarily confound and occasionally even out-maneuver the 'Allies'. Faced with the richest, best equipped, most powerful armed forces the world has ever seen, Iraq has shown spectacular courage and has even managed to put up what actually amounts to a defence. A defence which the Bush/Blair Pair have immediately denounced as deceitful and cowardly. (But then deceit is an old tradition with us natives. When we're invaded/colonized/occupied and stripped of all dignity, we turn to guile and opportunism.)

Even allowing for the fact that Iraq and the 'Allies' are at war, the extent to which the 'Allies' and their media cohorts are prepared to go is astounding to the point of being counter-productive to their own objectives.

When Saddam Hussein appeared on national TV to address the Iraqi people following the failure of the most elaborate assassination attempt in history - 'Operation Decapitation' - we had Geoff Hoon, British Defence Secretary deriding him for not having the courage to stand up and be killed, calling him a coward who hides in trenches.

We then had a flurry of Coalition speculation -

Was it really Saddam Hussein, was it his double?

Or was it Osama with a shave?

Was it pre-recorded?

Was it a speech?

Was it black magic?

Will it turn into a pumpkin if we really, really want it to?

After dropping not hundreds, but thousands of bombs on Baghdad, when a market place was mistakenly blown up and civilians killed - a US army spokesman implied that the Iraqis were blowing themselves up! "They're using very old stock. Their missiles go up and come down."

If so, may we ask how this squares with the accusation that the Iraqi regime is a paid up member of the Axis of Evil and a threat to world peace?

When the Arab TV station al-Jazeera shows civilian casualties it's denounced as 'emotive' Arab propaganda aimed at orchestrating hostility towards the 'Allies', as though Iraqis are dying only in order to make the 'Allies' look bad. Even French Television has come in for some stick for similar reasons. But the awed, breathless footage of aircraft carriers, stealth bombers and cruise missiles arcing across the desert sky on American and British TV is described as the "terrible beauty" of war.

When invading American soldiers (from the army "that's only here to help") are taken prisoner and shown on Iraqi TV, George Bush says it violates the Geneva convention and "exposes the evil at the heart of the regime". But it is entirely acceptable for US television stations to show the hundreds of prisoners being held by the US government in Guantanamo Bay, kneeling on the ground with their hands tied behind their backs, blinded with opaque goggles and with earphones clamped on their ears, to ensure complete visual and aural deprivation. When questioned about the treatment of prisoners in Guantanamo Bay, US Government officials don't deny that they're being being ill-treated. They deny that they're "prisoners of war"! They call them "unlawful combatants," implying that their ill-treatment is legitimate! (So what's the Party Line on the massacre of prisoners in Mazar-e-Sharif, Afghanistan? Forgive and Forget? And what of the prisoner tortured to death by the Special Forces at the Bagram Airforce Base? Doctors have formally called it homicide.)

When the 'Allies' bombed the Iraqi Television station (also, incidentally, a contravention of the Geneva convention), there was vulgar jubilation in the American Media. In fact Fox TV had been lobbying for the attack for a while. It was seen as a righteous blow against Arab propaganda. But mainstream American and British TV continue to advertise themselves as 'balanced' when their propaganda has achieved hallucinatory levels.

Why should propaganda be the exclusive preserve of the western media? Just because they do it better?
Western journalists 'embedded' with troops are given the status of heroes reporting from the frontlines of war. Non 'embedded' journalists (like the BBC's Rageh Omaar, reporting from besieged and bombed Baghdad, witnessing, and clearly affected by the sight of bodies of burned children and wounded people) are undermined even before they begin their reportage: "We have to tell you that he is being monitored by the Iraqi Authorities."

Increasingly, on British and American TV, Iraqi soldiers are being referred to as "militia" (ie: rabble). One BBC correspondent portentously referred to them as "quasi-terrorists." Iraqi defence is 'resistance' or worse still, 'pockets of resistance', Iraqi military strategy is deceit. (The US government bugging the phone lines of UN Security Council delegates, reported by the London Observer, is hard-headed pragmatism.) Clearly for the 'Allies', the only morally acceptable strategy the Iraqi army can pursue is to march out into the desert and be bombed by B-52s or be mowed down by machine gun fire. Anything short of that is cheating.

And now we have the siege of Basra. About a million and a half people, forty percent of them children. Without clean water, and with very little food. We're still waiting for the legendary Shia 'uprising', for the happy hordes to stream out of the city and rain roses and hosannahs on the 'liberating' army. Where are the hordes? Don't they know that television productions work to tight schedules? (It may well be that if the Saddam Hussein regime falls there will be dancing on the streets of Basra. But then, if the Bush regime were to fall, there would be dancing on the streets the world over.)

After days of enforcing hunger and thirst on the citizens of Basra, the Allies have brought in a few trucks of food and water and positioned them tantalizingly on the outskirts of the city. Desperate people flock to the trucks and fight each other for food. (The water we hear, is being sold. To re-vitalize the dying economy, you understand.) On top of the trucks, desperate photographers fought each other to get pictures of desperate people fighting each other for food. Those pictures will go out through photo agencies to newspapers and glossy magazines that pay extremely well. Their message: The messiahs are at hand, distributing fishes and loaves.

As of July last year the delivery of 5.4 billion dollars worth of supplies to Iraq was blocked by the Bush/Blair Pair. It didn't really make the news. But now under the loving caress of live TV, 450 tonnes of humanitarian aid - a miniscule fraction of what's actually needed (call it a script prop) - arrived on a British ship, the "Sir Galahad". Its arrival in the port of Umm Qasr merited a whole day of live TV broadcasts. Barf bag, anyone?

Nick Guttmann, Head of Emergencies for Christian Aid, writing for Independent on Sunday said that it would take thirty-two Sir Galahad's a day to match the amount of food Iraq was receiving before the bombing began.

We oughtn't to be surprised though. It's old tactics. They've been at it for years. Consider this moderate proposal by John McNaughton from the Pentagon Papers published during the Vietnam War:

STRIKES AT POPULATION TARGETS (PER SE) ARE LIKELY NOT ONLY TO CREATE A COUNTERPRODUCTIVE WAVE OF REVULSION ABROAD AND AT HOME, BUT GREATLY TO INCREASE THE RISK OF ENLARGING THE WAR WITH CHINA OR THE SOVIET UNION. DESTRUCTION OF LOCKS AND DAMS, HOWEVER - IF HANDLED RIGHT - MIGHT ... OFFER PROMISE. IT SHOULD BE STUDIED. SUCH DESTRUCTION DOES NOT KILL OR DROWN PEOPLE. BY SHALLOW-FLOODING THE RICE, IT LEADS AFTER TIME TO WIDESPREAD STARVATION (MORE THAN A MILLION?) UNLESS FOOD IS PROVIDED - WHICH WE COULD OFFER TO DO "AT THE CONFERENCE TABLE."

Times haven't changed very much. The technique has evolved into a doctrine. It's called 'Winning Hearts and Minds'.

So, here's the moral math as it stands: Two hundred thousand Iraqis estimated to have been killed in the first Gulf War. Hundreds of thousands dead because of the economic sanctions. (At least that lot has been saved from Saddam Hussein.) More being killed every day. Tens of thousands of US soldiers who fought the 1991 war officially declared 'disabled' by a disease called the Gulf War Syndrome believed in part to be caused by exposure to Depleted Uranium. It hasn't stopped the 'Allies' from continuing to use Depleted Uranium.

And now this talk of bringing the UN back into the picture.

But that old UN girl - it turns out that she just ain't what she was cracked up to be. She's been demoted (although she retains her high salary). Now she's the world's janitor. She's the Philippino cleaning lady, the Indian jamadarni, the postal bride from Thailand, the Mexican household help, the Jamaican au pair. She's employed to clean other peoples' shit. She's used and abused at will.

Despite Tony Blair's earnest submissions, and all his fawning, George Bush has made it clear that the UN will play no independent part in the administration of post-war Iraq. The US will decide who gets those juicy 're-construction' contracts. But Bush has appealed to the international community not to 'politicize' the issue of humanitarian aid. On the 28th of March, after Bush called for the immediate resumption of the UN's Oil for Food programme, the UN Security Council voted unanimously for the resolution. This means that everybody agrees that Iraqi money (from the sale of Iraqi oil) should be used to feed Iraqi people who are starving because of US led sanctions and the illegal US led war.

Contracts for the 're-construction' of Iraq we're told, in discussions on the business news, could jump-start the world economy. It's funny how the interests of American Corporations are so often, so successfully and so deliberately confused with the interests of the world economy. While the American people will end up paying for the war, oil companies, weapons manufacturers, arms dealers, and corporations involved in 're-construction' work will make direct gains from the war. Many of them are old friends and former employers of the Bush/Cheney/Rumsfeld/Rice cabal. Bush has already asked Congress for 75 billion dollars. Contracts for 're-construction' are already being negotiated. The news doesn't hit the stands because much of the US corporate media is owned and managed by the same interests.

Operation Iraqi Freedom, Tony Blair assures us is about returning Iraqi oil to the Iraqi people. That is, returning Iraqi oil to the Iraqi people via Corporate Multinationals. Like Shell, like Chevron, like

Halliburton. Or are we missing the plot here? Perhaps Halliburton is actually an Iraqi company? Perhaps US Vice-President Dick Cheney (who was a former Director of Halliburton) is a closet Iraqi?

As the rift between Europe and America deepens, there are signs that the world could be entering a new era of economic boycotts.

CNN reported that Americans are emptying French wine into gutters, chanting "We don't want your stinking wine." We've heard about the re-baptism of French fries. Freedom fries they're called now. There's news trickling in about Americans boycotting German goods. The thing is that if the fallout of the war takes this turn, it is the US who will suffer the most. Its homeland may be defended by border patrols and nuclear weapons, but its economy is strung out across the globe. Its economic outposts are exposed and vulnerable to attack in every direction. Already the internet is buzzing with elaborate lists of American and British government products and companies that should be boycotted. Apart from the usual targets, Coke, Pepsi and McDonalds - government agencies like USAID, the British DFID, British and American banks, Arthur Anderson, Merrill Lynch, American Express, corporations like Bechtel, General Electric, and companies like Reebok, Nike and Gap - could find themselves under siege. These lists are being honed and refined by activists across the world. They could become a practical guide that directs and channelizes the amorphous, but growing fury in the world. Suddenly, the 'inevitablity' of the project of Corporate Globalization is beginning to seem more than a little evitable.

It's become clear that the War against Terror is not really about terror, and the War on Iraq not only about oil. It's about a Superpower's self-destructive impulse towards supremacy, stranglehold, global hegemony. The argument is being made that the people of Argentina and Iraq have both been decimated by the same process. Only the weapons used against them differ: In one case it's an IMF cheque book. In the other, cruise missiles.

Finally, there's the matter of Saddam Husseins's arsenal of Weapons of Mass Destruction.

(Oops, nearly forgot about those!)

In the fog of war - one thing's for sure - if the Saddam Hussein regime indeed has Weapons of Mass Destruction, it is showing an astonishing degree of responsibility and restraint in the teeth of extreme provocation. Under similar circumstances, (say if Iraqi troops were bombing New York and laying siege to Washington DC) could we expect the same

of the Bush regime? Would it keep its thousands of nuclear warheads in their wrapping paper? What about its chemical and biological weapons? Its stocks of anthrax , smallpox and nerve gas? Would it?

Excuse me while I laugh.

In the fog of war we're forced to speculate: Either Saddam Hussein is an extremely responsible tyrant. Or - he simply does not possess Weapons of Mass Destruction.

Either way, regardless of what happens next, Iraq comes out of the argument smelling sweeter than the US government.

So here's Iraq - Rogue State, grave threat to world peace, paid up member of the Axis of Evil.

Here's Iraq, invaded, bombed, besieged, bullied, its sovereignty shat upon, its children killed by cancers, its people blown up on the streets.

And here's all of us watching. CNN-BBC, BBC-CNN late into the night. Here's all of us, enduring the horror of the war, enduring the horror of the propaganda and enduring the slaughter of language as we know and understand it. Freedom now means mass murder (or, in the US, fried potatoes). When someone says 'humanitarian aid' we automatically go looking for induced starvation. 'Embedded' I have to admit, is a great find. It's what it sounds like. And what about 'arsenal of tactics?' Nice!

In most parts of the world, the invasion of Iraq is being seen as a racist war. The real danger of a racist war unleashed by racist regimes is that it engenders racism in everybody - perpetrators, victims, spectators. It sets the parameters for the debate, it lays out a grid for a particular way of thinking. There is a tidal wave of hatred for the United States rising from the ancient heart of the world. In Africa, Latin America, Asia, Europe, Australia. I encounter it every day. Sometimes it comes from the most unlikely sources. Bankers, businessmen, yuppie students, and they bring to it all the crassness of their conservative, illiberal politics. That absurd inability to separate governments from people: America is a nation of morons, a nation of murderers, they say, (with the same carelessness with which they say, "All muslims are terrorists"). Even in the grotesque universe of racist insult, the British make their entry as add-ons. Arse-lickers, they're called.

Suddenly, I, who have been vilified for being 'anti-American' and 'anti-West', find myself in the extraordinary position of defending the people of America. And Britain.

Those who descend so easily into the pit of racist abuse would do well to remember the hundreds of thousands of American and British citizens who protested against their country's stockpile of nuclear weapons. And the thousands of American war resistors who forced their government to withdraw from Vietnam. They should know that the most scholarly, scathing, hilarious critiques of the US government and the 'American Way of Life' comes from American citizens. And that the funniest, most bitter condemnation of their Prime-minister comes from the British media. Finally they should remember that right now, hundreds of thousands of British and American citizens are on the streets protesting the war. The Coalition of the Bullied and Bought consists of governments, not people. More than one third of America's citizens have survived the relentless propaganda they've been subjected to and many thousands are actively fighting their own government. In the ultra-patriotic climate that prevails in the US, that's as brave as any Iraqi fighting for his or her homeland.

While the 'Allies' wait in the desert for an uprising of Shia Muslims on the streets of Basra, the real uprising is taking place in hundreds of cities across the world. It has been the most spectacular display of public morality ever seen.

Most courageous of all, are the hundreds of thousands of American people on the streets of America's great cities - Washington, New York, Chicago, San Francisco. The fact is that the only institution in the world today that is more powerful than the American government, is American civil society. American citizens have a huge responsibility riding on their shoulders. How can we not salute and support those who not only acknowledge but act upon that responsibility?

They are our allies, our friends.

At the end of it all, it remains to be said that dictators like Saddam Hussein, and all the other despots in the Middle-East, in the Central Asian Republics, in Africa and Latin America, many of them installed, supported and financed by the US government, are a menace to their own people. Other than strengthening the hand of civil society (instead of weakening it as has been done in the case of Iraq), there is no easy, pristine way of dealing with them. (It's odd how those who dismiss the peace movement as utopian, don't hesitate to proffer the most absurdly dreamy reasons for going to war: To

stamp out terrorism, install democracy, eliminate fascism, and most entertainingly, to "rid the world of evil-doers.")

REGARDLESS OF WHAT THE PROPAGANDA MACHINE TELLS US, THESE TIN POT DICTATORS ARE NOT THE GREATEST THREAT TO THE WORLD. THE REAL AND PRESSING DANGER, THE GREATEST THREAT OF ALL IS THE LOCOMOTIVE FORCE THAT DRIVES THE POLITICAL AND ECONOMIC ENGINE OF THE US GOVERNMENT, CURRENTLY PILOTED BY GEORGE BUSH. BUSH-BASHING IS FUN, BECAUSE HE MAKES SUCH AN EASY, SUMPTUOUS TARGET. IT'S TRUE THAT HE IS A DANGEROUS, ALMOST SUICIDAL PILOT, BUT THE MACHINE HE HANDLES IS FAR MORE DANGEROUS THAN THE MAN HIMSELF.

Despite the pall of gloom that hangs over us today, I'd like to file a cautious plea for hope: In times of war, one wants one's weakest enemy at the helm of his forces. And President George W Bush is certainly that. Any other even averagely intelligent US President would have probably done the very same things, but would have managed to smoke up the glass and confuse the opposition. Perhaps even carry the UN with him. George Bush's tactless imprudence and his brazen belief that he can run the world with his riot squad, has done the opposite. He has achieved what writers, activists and scholars have striven to achieve for decades. He has exposed the ducts. He has placed on full public view the working parts, the nuts and bolts of the apocalyptic apparatus of the American Empire.

Now that the blueprint (The Ordinary Person's Guide to Empire) has been put into mass circulation, it could be disabled quicker than the pundits predicted.

Bring on the spanners.

"PERPETUAL PEACE IS A DREAM, AND NOT EVEN A BEAUTIFUL DREAM, AND WAR IS AN INTEGRAL PART OF GOD'S ORDERING OF THE UNIVERSE. IN WAR, MAN'S NOBLEST VIRTUES COME INTO PLAY: COURAGE AND RENUNCIATION, FIDELITY TO DUTY AND A READINESS FOR SACRIFICE THAT DOES NOT STOP SHORT OF OFFERING UP LIFE ITSELF. WITHOUT WAR THE WORLD WOULD BECOME SWAMPED IN MATERIALISM."

General Helmuth von Moltke

044

LEWIS H. LAPHAM

PAX AMERICANA
APRIL 14 2003

More than once during the decade of the 1990s I attended a national security conference in Washington at which the senior statesmen seated on the dais could be counted upon to say – always with a note of regret, of course, and wishing they didn't have to be so blunt – that America wasn't likely to come to its senses unless or until something really awful happened. The citizenry was drifting into moral relativism and cultural decline, the schools all but fully submerged in the swamp of materialism, and somehow the country needed to be re-awakened to the fact that the world was a far more dangerous place than had been dreamed of in the philosophy of Jerry Seinfeld or the World Wildlife Fund.

Because the gentlemen on the dais had served the administrations of presidents Ronald Reagan and George H. W. Bush as secretaries of defense or state, sometimes as chiefs of naval operations or directors of the Central Intelligence Agency, their remarks were understood to bear the stamps of selfless patriotism. They had signed enough weapons contracts to know that America was always and everywhere surrounded by ambitious and resentful enemies; like General von Moltke, they endorsed the proposition that war was good for business and the soul.

Invariably their remarks were received with approving murmurs of wise assent, which wasn't surprising because the meetings invariably had been called to order by one or another of the neo-conservative think tanks dedicated to the cause of an assertive American foreign policy. The high-end intellectuals in the room (sometimes Richard Perle, often William Bennett accompanied by a smirk of columnists from The Weekly Standard) never tired of telling the travelers from New York (over coffee between the morning's first and second power point, while investigating the poached salmon before the luncheon speech) that the ideas of government made to the measure of a provincial democratic republic (America in 1941) no longer could

accommodate the interests of a global nation state that deserved to wear the crown and name of empire (America, circa 1995).

It wasn't that anybody had intended so impressive a metamorphosis, but how could it be otherwise? The Russians had lost the Cold War, their weapons gone to rust, their economy in ruins, and the statues of V. I. Lenin reduced to a rubble of broken stones. From the Chinese not even Henry Kissinger expected anything but a supply of cheap labor for another thirty years. If not America, "the world's only surviving super-power," who else could lift the imperial burden once carried on the back of Rome? Now that history was at an end, America embodied "the single model of human progress"; the American way was the only way, and where else except in Washington to kiss the kindly hand of power?

Conference participants unsure of the answers to the questions were invited to consult a Pentagon's policy paper, "Defense Strategy for the 1990s," composed by Dick Cheney and Colin Powell while serving as senior counselors to the first President Bush. Drafted and revised in 1992 before its publication in 1993, the document acknowledged and accepted America's mission to rule the world – for the good of all mankind, of course, and by way of setting a proper example for foreign heads of state who otherwise might stumble into the temptation of joyous despotism. Assisted in their labors by Paul Wolfowitz (then as now an under-secretary of defense) Messrs. Powell and Cheney had revealed the doctrines of preemptive strike, forward deterrence, absolute domination. Let any lesser nation anywhere on earth even begin to think of challenging the American supremacy (moral, military or economic), and America reserved the right to strangle the impudence at birth – to bomb the peasants or the palace, block the flows of oil or bank credit, change the unsanitary regime.

The soundness of the policy was perfectly obvious to everybody in the room, as plain to see as the salmon under the mustard sauce. Unhappily (and here was the purpose of the conference, also the topic of the evening's keynote address) the truth was not so obvious to those of their fellow-countrymen too often and too easily misdirected by the lying liberal news media into the swamps of materialism. The times were much too prosperous, the stock market going nowhere but up, President Bill Clinton's behavior (emotionally indulgent, ethically slack) corrupting the minds of adolescent girls and debasing the art of middle-aged saxophonists.

The after-dinner conversations never failed to unearth fond remembrances of the Cold War with the Russians. The Russians had served as the essential enemy, world-class and operatic, and what was one to do without them? It was all very well and good to write strong-minded op-ed pieces calling for the invasion of Iraq or the death of Yasir Arafat, but absent a reliable threat of nuclear annihilation, who would rally to the bugles and the drums? The newspapers were doing their patriotic best to float the rumors of Armageddon – a few terrorists here and there in the deserts of Arabia, some bandits in the mountains of Afghanistan and the jungles of Colombia, six or seven mercenary armies wandering in the mists of equatorial Africa. Dangerous people one and all, clearly hostile and probably unshaven, but none of them a match for the dear departed Russians who, for nearly half a century had furnished the military and foreign policy bureaucracies in Washington with a world-encircling menace as precious to the American economy as General Motors and Iowa corn. An enemy by no means easy to replace, but without such an enemy, how then to maintain the Pentagon's weapons budget at combat strength, or press forward to the glory of an empire made in the image of the Westchester Country Club?

The question formed the sub-text of almost every discussion of grand geo-political strategy that I can remember overhearing in a Washington conference room during the decade of the 1990s. **I haven't spoken to any of the panelists or keynote speakers since the cautionary signs from heaven appeared in the sky on September 11, 2001, but I wouldn't be surprised to hear them say that although the attacks were abominable, a criminal outrage, and certainly a lot more destructive than might reasonably have been expected, sometimes people needed harsh reminders to recall them to the banners of noble virtue under which von Moltke's German army invaded Belgium in 1914 and massacred every man, woman and child in the city of Dinant. General Tommy Franks' army didn't achieve as brilliant or as complete a success in Baghdad in April 2003, but it made a good beginning-set the proper tone, established the necessary precedent, opened the road to the American Rome.**

045

CHRISTOPHER MORRIS

COUNTER TERRORISM AND THE WAR IN IRAQ
2001 - 2003

◊ **Washington D.C.**
U.S. President George W. Bush with his national security team in the Oval Office at the
White House moments after announcing to the world that the United States will withdraw from the 1972
Anti-Ballistic Missile Treaty and press ahead with a missile defense system. December 13 2001.

> **Washington D.C.**
U.S. President George W. Bush in a home security meeting at the
White House. Present are the FBI director and the CIA director Tenet.
December 13, 2001.

> **Washington D.C.**
United States President George W. Bush in the Oval Office
of the White House. Washington DC. December 2001.

045 Christopher Morris
Counter Terrorism and the War in Iraq

Page 517

◊ **Andrews Air Force Base**
U.S. President George W. Bush at Andrews
Air Force base. After returning from Norfolk
Naval Air Station. December 2001.

> **Tampa**
Commander Franks & Vice Commander Delong with their staff hold
their daily satellite hook up with forces under their control during the war in Afghanistan.
HQ CENTCOM MacDill Tampa Florida February 25 2002.

> **Tampa**
General Franks holds his morning Briefing with
Generals on his staff in the War trophy room.
HQ CENTCOM MacDill Tampa Florida February 2002.

> **Tampa**
General Tommy Franks late in the day
in his office at MacDill.
HQ CENTCOM February 25 2002.

> **Tampa**
General Tommy Franks late in the day
in his office at MacDill.
HQ CENTCOM February 25 2002.

045 Christopher Morris
Counter Terrorism and the War in Iraq

◊ **Northern Kuwait**
Charlie Company. First of the 30th, Third Infantry
Division. South of the Iraqi Border
depart for their attack position on March 20 2003.

> **Northern Kuwait**
Charlie Company. First of the 30th, Third Infantry
Division. South of the Iraqi Border
depart for their attack position on March 20 2003.

> **An Nasiriya**
U.S. troops from Charlie Company, break down
the door at the Tallil military Air Base on
the outskirts of An Nasiriya Iraq March 22 2003.

> **An Nasiriya**
Charlie Company on the Morning of
March 22, 2003. Seize of the Tallil Airbase
outside An Nasiriyah Iraq.

> **An Nasiriya**
Charlie Company on the Morning of
March 22, 2003. Seize of the Tallil Airbase
outside An Nasiriyah Iraq.

> **An Nasiriya**
U.S. Soldiers from Charlie Company search
Iraqi military buildings outside the Tallil military airbase.
March 23 2003.

045 Christopher Morris
Counter Terrorism and the War in Iraq

Page 533

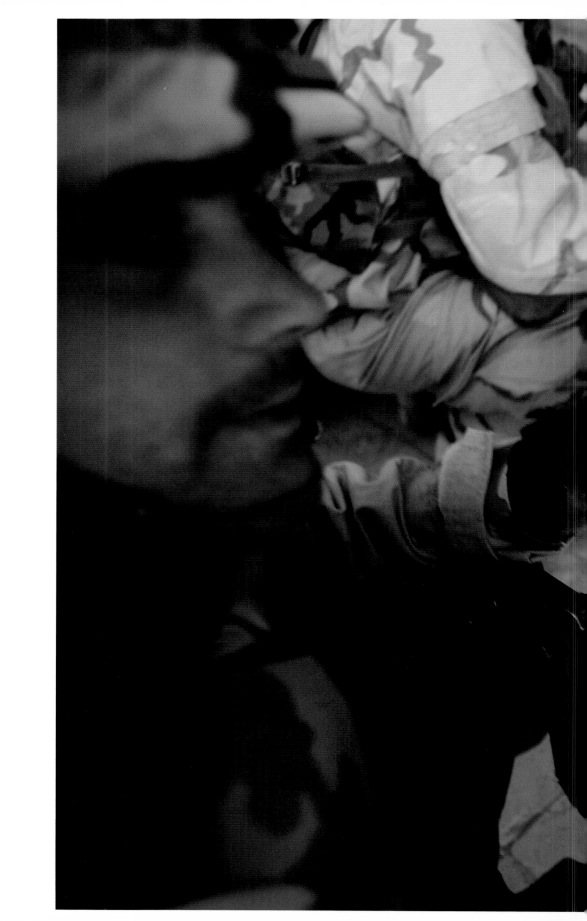

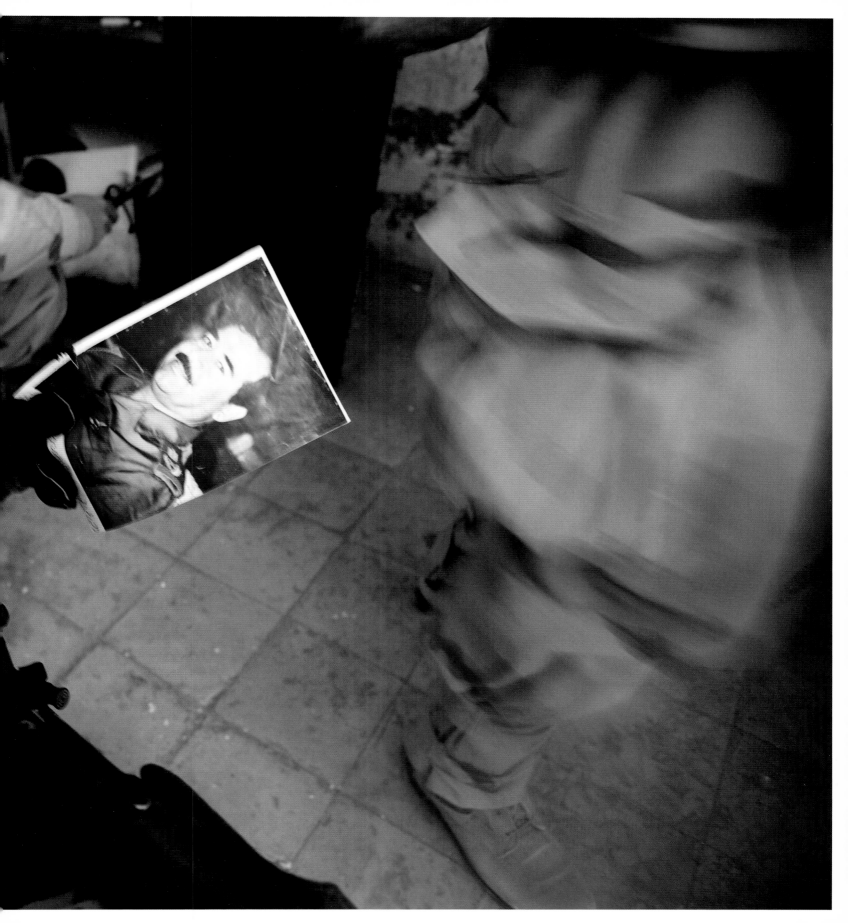

< Al Samawah
U.S. troops from Charlie Company search
Iraqis near the town of Al Samawah.
During a major sandstorm. March 25 2003.

< Al Samawah
Charlie Company in pursuit of an Iraqi
RPG team, they detain and examine a car with father
and small boy. March 25 2003.

◊ **Al Samawah**
Charlie Company in pursuit of an Iraqi RPG team, they detain
and examine a car with father and small boy during apocalyptic sand storm.
March 25 2003.

◊ Karbala
U.S. troops from Charlie Company open fire on a truck that is not stopping.
Warning shots were fired over vehicle, then directly into the cab killing one civilian.
Karbala, The Karbala Gap, Iraq April 2 2003.

> Karbala
Civilian victim who made the mistake of not
stopping his truck in time.

> Karbala
Body bag of Iraqi farmer who failed to stop in time.

> **Al Samawah**
U.S. troops from Charlie Company
search Iraqis near the town of Al Samawah.
Iraq March 24 2003.

> **Baghdad**
U.S. troops from Charlie Company on the move towards the
center of Baghdad on April 8 2003.

045 Christopher Morris
Counter Terrorism and the War in Iraq

Page 551

046

JON LEE ANDERSON

THE PROBLEM WITH DREAMS
BAGHDAD APRIL 26 2003

In October 2002, during the run-up to the American and British-led war against Iraq, a man in a Baghdad bazaar approached me.

"Why does Bush want to make war with Iraq?"

he asked rhetorically. His name was Muhammad Abdullah Ahmed, and he was a forty-nine year-old former civil servant.

"Bush is not crazy," he said. "No, it is because he is directed by the Zionist organizations, and they want to destroy the earth."

Muhammad went on for several minutes, trying to convince me, as a "a representative of America," that the Jews were responsible for pretty much anything that had ever gone wrong (including the September 11 attack on the World Trade Center), and that the Christians of the United States should realize that they were stooges in a Jewish plot to kill everybody else and take over the world. This was not an unfamiliar argument, and Ahmed was not a nut case; these views are commonplace amongst Iraqis, and were, more or less, the official position of Saddam Hussein's Ba'ath party.

For many years, such fantastical views of history have gone mostly unchecked by coherent counter-arguments. The reason is simple: from the end of the 1991 Gulf War until Saddam's recent ouster, all forms of positive U.S. influence in Iraq were nearly non-existent. For an entire generation of Iraqis, "the West" has meant little more than UN sanctions, onerous daily over-flights of U.S. and British warplanes, and bombs. It is hardly surprising, then, that many Iraqis are suspicious about the motives behind the U.S. and British invasion.

IN APRIL 2003, IN THE IMMEDIATE AFTERMATH OF THE FALL OF BAGHDAD, ALMOST ALL IRAQIS I SPOKE TO – EVEN THOSE HAPPY AT SADDAM'S DOWNFALL – BELIEVED THE AMERICANS HAD LAUNCHED OPERATION IRAQI FREEDOM NOT BECAUSE OF ALLEGED WEAPONS OF MASS DESTRUCTION, OR TO BRING ABOUT DEMOCRATIC CHANGE, BUT BECAUSE THE UNITED STATES WANTS TO CONTROL IRAQ'S VAST OIL RESERVES, AND TO TURN THEIR COUNTRY INTO AN AMERICAN COLONY.

Even if the Americans intend to do "the right thing" in Iraq – to rebuild what they have destroyed, to install a democratic government, and then leave – they will only be able to do so with the trust and goodwill of the Iraqi people. And it would be in the U.S. interest to do the right thing, and quickly, because the removal of Saddam and the military occupation of Iraq has provided a rallying point for the country's previously-suppressed Islamic radicals. It would be a bitter irony of history indeed if the overthrow of Saddam Hussein led, after all, to a new Iraqi battleground in the "War on Terror."

This is more or less what happened after the U.S.-backed mujahedin succeeded in ousting the Soviet army from in Afghanistan: the United States lost interest and relinquished its role to Islamic extremists like the Taliban and Osama Bin Laden. And the rest, of course, is history.

Or is it?

Since driving the Taliban from power in Afghanistan in 2001, the U.S. has done little to strengthen the fledgling Karzai government it installed. The country remains an insecure patchwork of separate fiefdoms ruled by opium-growing warlords and their militias; fugitive remnants of the Taliban have joined forces with other anti-Western Islamists who periodically attack and kill American troops. Huge swatches of the countryside remain under the authority of xenophobic mullahs who preach hatred of the West, and decry all forms of outside influence as the devilish meddling of kafirs, unbelievers. The influence of America's chosen man, Karzai, extends not much further than the capital of Kabul.

If the United States wishes to see Afghanistan pacified and united, it must provide Karzai the means of becoming the country's most powerful figure. The surest way to do this, in my view, would be to create a mini-Marshal Plan for Afghanistan – paid for by the United States but contingent on Karzai's authority – which would rebuild Afghanistan's roads, factories, hospitals, and schools over the next five years. By opening up the country and providing employment to hundreds of thousands of former refugees and destitute people in rural areas, such a program would reduce the power of the warlords and mullahs and, most importantly, allow for the free flow of new ideas throughout Afghanistan. Then, when Karzai is strong enough to defend himself, the U.S. should withdraw its forces. By paying for this program in toto, making it work, and not asking for a penny in return, the United States would send an important message to Muslims around the world that it actually cares about the democratic values it preaches, that it is not, as so many Muslims nowadays believe, embarked on a latter-day "Crusade" against Islam. If the U.S. additionally helped restore the rule of law in Iraq, and used its influence to secure a Middle East peace acceptable to both Israelis and Palestinians, then much of the poisonous alchemy of ideas and hatreds which brought about September 11 might dissipate, perhaps even vanish altogether.

It is astonishing to see how quickly political change can transform people's minds. In Kabul, for instance, a few weeks after the fall of the Taliban, I became friends with Fridoun, a young medical student. Fridoun had come of age under the Taliban's strict rule, and like all young men his age – he was then twenty-three – he wore a beard, appropriately Islamic garb (a loose-fitting tunic and pantaloon outfit called a shalwar kameez) and continued to pray devoutly five times a day. Islam, clearly, remained at the core of Fridoun's existence, and he was not yet ready, in those tense early days after the Taliban's ouster, to question its place in his life.

When I returned to Kabul a few months later, in the spring of 2002, the city had acquired a more relaxed atmosphere. Fewer unruly Kalashnikov-toting mujahedin roamed the streets, commerce had rebounded, and thousands of refugees had begun to pour back into the city. Hundreds of Western expatriates working for aid agencies, scores of journalists, and several thousand international peacekeeping troops had also arrived. Fridoun had relaxed considerably. He joked with me, saying that he realized he must have seemed "a bit of a Taliban" during my last visit. He still retained his Islamic faith, he assured me, but sometimes, instead of rushing off to the mosque when the muezzin called the faithful to prayer, he merely murmured his prayers silently to himself. He was still wearing his beard, I noticed, but had clipped it shorter. Some days, as if trying out a novelty, Fridoun dressed in a pair of newly-bought Western-style jeans and a button-down shirt, although he clearly felt more comfortable in the loose-fitting shalwar kameez. Given the oppoprtunity, he had begun to realize that his faith, and the way he chose to observe it, was a matter of free choice rather than obligation.

He told me that he felt like he was emerging from a long trance.

047

MATT MCALLESTER

AMMAN JORDAN
APRIL 4 2003

In the early morning of March 25, 2003 — the fifth day of the U.S. bombing campaign against Baghdad — Matthew McAllester, Newsday correspondent in the Iraqi capital, was taken into custody by Iraqi security forces along with three other journalists and a peace activist.

THREE DAYS AGO I WAS RELEASED FROM ABU GHRAIB PRISON TO THE WEST OF BAGHDAD AFTER BEING HELD BY THE IRAQI INTELLIGENCE SERVICES FOR EIGHT DAYS WITHOUT CHARGE OR EXPLANATION. AS MY FOUR FELLOW WESTERN INMATES AND I MADE OUR FINAL WALK THROUGH THE LONG CORRIDORS OF ABU GHRAIB, HUNDREDS OF EYES FOLLOWED US. WE WERE LEAVING BUT HUNDREDS OF IRAQI PRISONERS WERE STAYING BEHIND IN THE MOST FEARED PRISON IN IRAQ. NO DOUBT, MOST OF THEM ARE STILL THERE AS I WRITE. NONE OF THEM, I AM QUITE SURE, HAS A LEGION OF JOURNALISTS, RELATIVES, FRIENDS, POLITICIANS, RELIGIOUS FIGURES, AND PRIVATE CITIZENS WORKING FOR THEIR RELEASE ALL OVER THE WORLD. WE DID. FOR THAT, I KNOW I SHALL NEVER BE ABLE TO FIND ENOUGH WORDS OF GRATITUDE. BUT COULD I PUSH MY LUCK A LITTLE AND PRESUME TO ASK JUST ONE MORE THING OF ALL OF THOSE PEOPLE WHO HELPED SECURE OUR RELEASE? LET US NEVER FORGET THOSE WHO ARE IMPRISONED, TORTURED, AND EXECUTED WITHOUT DUE PROCESS, WHEREVER THEY ARE IN THE WORLD. AS OUR CASE SHOWS, INTERNATIONAL PRESSURE CAN WORK.

048

GENERAL WESLEY K. CLARK

A NEW KIND OF WAR
MAY 2 2003

The worst breakdown of U.S. national security in American history occurred more than twenty months ago. Some three thousand people died in New York and at the Pentagon. The United States has done much in response.

The real question is, are we safer, now and in the long run.

America struck back quickly, taking down the Taliban government in Afghanistan, invading Iraq to compel regime change, and pursuing the Al Qaeda group around the world. American forces are now more widely committed than ever before, everywhere from detachments in Central Asia, nine thousand in Afghanistan, to more than a hundred thousand on the ground in Iraq. And at home, thousands have been detained and investigated; many were deported. New procedures are in place to redress the conventional balance between individual rights and the public's need for security. And the war continues.

In our battles, to date, our military has been superb. With a minimal ground presence, we knocked off the Taliban regime in less than two months. With about a third the force of Desert Storm, we captured Baghdad and ran off Saddam's regime. Thousands of Iraqis were killed – though we aren't counting – while our own losses were comparatively light.

Most of the bad things that worried many people about invading Iraq never happened. Israel wasn't struck by SCUD missiles, a new wave of warfare didn't engulf the Middle East, and no terrorist strikes hit us anywhere, not in the U.S. nor abroad. If Saddam had weapons of mass destruction – and all the intelligence has suggested that he did – then he wasn't able to use them against us, if he ever intended to.

If you believe that we were struck on 9/11 because terrorists thought they could get away with it, then we have conclusively refuted that idea. In both Afghanistan and Iraq, U.S. forces were incredibly successful militarily, and struck with a ferocity that should remove any doubt about either American capability or will to retaliate – or strike preemptively.

BUT WE ALSO KNOW THAT THE WAR CAN'T BE WON SIMPLY BY MILITARY FORCE. WAR HAS TO BE ABOUT CONVINCING PEOPLE TO CHANGE THEIR MINDS – TO STOP TARGETING US. AND BY THIS STANDARD, THE ANSWER TO THE QUESTION, "ARE WE SAFER?" IS, THAT WE DON'T KNOW YET.

Terrorist campaigns take years to develop: years of recruitment, organizational development, nurturing grievances, planning strikes. By all public commentary, the Al Qaeda network is still talking about attacking us, still nurturing grievances, and still looking for recruits. Striking Iraq may have pleased the majority of Americans, but every opinion poll suggests that these same actions displeased most of the rest of the world. In much of the Arab world, there was a sense of humiliation. The relatives of those who died in Iraq and Afghanistan will certainly not forget what we have done. And the impoverished, angry, and uneducated may have learned more reasons to hate America.

Winning in this campaign will require going beyond conventional military action. It is not simply about changing regimes in the Arab world. Police action and the sharing of information among many governments will be necessary. But even beyond all this, we are going to have to help promote a new set of understandings, and a new web of support to help "drain the swamp" in which terrorism grows.

We should be asking, do we really understand the motivations and sources of the terrorism directed against us? Were we struck because we were perceived as vulnerable, because we were perceived as strong, or for other reasons? Will we be safer when others fear us more, or when they like us more, or simply when we are less intrusive?

We should be asking, are we using international institutions most effectively to reduce these sources of conflict and hatreds? Can more be done with agencies like the World Bank, and the United Nations to promote development and foster international understanding? Do we need to create other institutions to help us protect ourselves?

And we should be asking, are American actions abroad conveying the correct image, understanding, and support for Americans?

Certainly we must be strong, and we must not shirk from defending ourselves or our allies, but is that enough? Have we emphasized the right humanitarian programs? Are we promoting the kinds of cultural exchanges that will best deter other actions against us? Are our representatives, both governmental and commercial, promoting policies and behaving in ways which will actually improve our security?

The war on terror is a different kind of war. And we are well equipped to win it militarily. But conventional military victory is a necessary, though insufficient, condition for success. More will be required. **The challenge now is to understand more clearly just what that "more" is, and then to put it into practice.** And by this standard, the war is a long way from over.

049

ANNA CATALDI

THOUGHTS ABOUT A JUST WORLD
APRIL 29 2003

I'm sitting here at the computer, thinking about the assurance I gave you (could it really have been over a year ago? ...) to write something for the new book.

I feel guilty for having done nothing about it before now, but the events that followed in the wake of 11 September 2001 all happened in such quick succession that I found it increasingly difficult to make sense of them.

Now I shall try to explain why.

During the last twelve years I have traveled to many war-zones. Over longer or shorter periods of time I have been witness to the conflicts of this world. I have seen things that were unacceptable not only to me but to those having to endure them. Then, when I returned to my own peaceful, modern, and technologically advanced country, it seemed of no consequence to anyone that I had left behind me, only a few hours' flight away, mothers, wives, and children mourning those whose names we did not know, those killed by our modern and technologically advanced weapons.

As has already been said countless times, when New York was attacked it was not only that the Twin Towers and those inside them went up in flames, but the sense of the invulnerability of American soil. A right that had seemed inviolable to her people was shaken to its foundations.

But now in the name of this outrage, and for the sake of pre-empting others in the future, how many innocent lives have already been sacrificed? In Afghanistan? In Iraq? – where bombs rained down on a defenseless population, nearly half of whom were children?

For anyone concerned with the problem of what is ethically justifiable, 9/11 signaled a watershed: there could be no return to the slipshod values into which we had had somnolently strayed.

Since then we have been watching the day-to-day development of situations that have become increasingly disquieting despite the clumsy rhetoric of demagogic statements from those who govern our world these days. **We struggle to understand what is happening around us, but confusion grows daily. We find ourselves overwhelmed by a dialectic that leaves us increasingly perplexed. The flag of democracy is waved by the same superpower that coincidentally on another 11 September, this time in 1973, helped overthrow the democratic government of Allende in Chile and replace it with the bloody dictatorship of Pinochet.** And today this same superpower, claiming to export democracy, is attacking innocent civilians with weapons of mass destruction, such as the terrible cluster bombs that every military convention has declared illegal. Then we find the same government – which in an unprecedented move had signed on to the International War Crimes Tribunal – invoking the Geneva Convention, the repository of all the rules that limit and ban war crimes, the very rules which it had just flouted.

How many times since the tragic attack on the Twin Towers have we heard the justifiable condemnation of Islamic fanaticism and its terrible consequences? On that, we all agree. Nothing, in our view, justifies the killing of a single human being in the name of God. Whoever that person might be. And yet, from the very lips of the president of a secular, modern and democratic nation, we have heard the name of God invoked to justify a war considered illegal by a large proportion of the world's population. The memory of marching in Paris in protest against an exaggeratedly militaristic president is still fresh in my mind. Today that same president, putting himself forward as a leader of the anti-war brigade, is being attacked by those who, having founded Médecins Sans Frontières in the cause of human rights, have fought to help war victims for over thirty years.

Humanitarian aid seems to have shed its identification with compassion and become big business and a tool for political propaganda.

In 1915, in his essay, "Timely Thoughts on War and Death," Sigmund Freud expressed the distress he was suffering as a result of the tragic events of the First World War. "We are experiencing the bitter awakening from a dream of civilization. It appears that no event has ever managed to destroy so great a part of humanity's common heritage, plunged the most lucid minds into greater confusion, so profoundly debased all that was most noble."

The shamefulness of the Holocaust and the butchery of the Second World War still lay in the future.

But afterwards the world seemed to react positively. **For half a century it inspired the hope that by means of a series of conventions and the institution of international organizations, it had built a forum for debate that would make the flagrant violation of the rights of sovereign states a thing of the past.**

We deluded ourselves yet again.

9/11, and the use to which it has been put, appears to have legitimized the demolition of everything in which we believed. This I say in the name of my colleagues – the journalists, photo-reporters, humanitarian aid workers, and others – who, putting their lives at risk, and in many cases sacrificing them, believed that through their words, their pictures, their work, they could make the world rethink the horror and uselessness of armed conflict.

Convinced of the superiority of our civilization, we threw ourselves into wars believing that our motives were noble. We were the good guys hurling ourselves against the bad ones ... And now where do we think we stand? Did 9/11 create an entirely new situation, or has the event and its aftermath forced us to confront ambiguities we were always reluctant to face? We need only think of how Europe comported itself during the Balkan war, the genocide in Rwanda, the massacre we dared not protest in Chechnya.

I believe it is time we examined our conscience, honestly confronting the weakness, cowardliness, and opportunism we have chosen to ignore so as not to compromise the easy life enjoyed by our own privileged society.

We are facing grim times, but perhaps it is only at times like this, when every tyranny seems to have become legitimate, that we can find the moral strength to begin, yet again, to lay the foundations for a more just world.

050

MICHAEL PERSSON

THE BIG PICTURE
APRIL 9 2003

> A flag flickered in the breeze that day ... caught my eye from all the hundreds of other signs hoisted about.

Why I noticed had nothing to do with the quick-moving material drawing me in ...

no, that wasn't it ...

it was the image, the image of planet earth.

Amongst the slogans, colorful parodies, and shocking real-life photographs, **Earth stood out, alone**. I hadn't seen the planet in a while.

It looked the same as when I'd seen it last, and doubtless no different from the time when it's picture was first taken, some thirty-five, forty years ago. Much had changed since the sixties. Almost everything. And yet here, February 16th, 2003, in San Francisco, at a demonstration intended to stop a war I felt as if nothing had changed, nothing but the gadgets and mod-cons attaching themselves to me, the twenty thousand others here, and most of the country's population. Many had rallied before against armed aggression...they remembered those occasions like the soldiers doing battle remembered, both were veterans ... different roles ... same conflict. Joan Baez sung Lennon's "Imagine" in Tibetan ... she'd sung at a few of these in her time ... my mind kept a picture of her young face next to Dylan's from one of those appearances. Like the old hands in the crowd, she was here again.

Since the last war in the Gulf, life had moved on. Beside my ex-girlfriend, her five-month old baby, in a city that had once been home I thought back to the bus ride I'd taken in 1991 from Turkey to its border with Iraq. From the bus to where I stood: twelve years, three different lives on three separate continents, four girlfriends and one marriage later. Yeah, life had moved on. I was a news photographer on that bus then ... part of what later went down in history as Desert Storm, although at the time it hadn't been christened. This time, in Operation Iraqi Freedom, I was part of something else. This time I was a protester doing my bit to prevent something that even for those in attendance knew would go-down in spite of this showing and the many others like it.

Inside the Trans-bay bus, that morning, talk filled every little space as we made our way to the assembly point across the Golden Gate Bridge. A guitar played, smiles appeared, songs and rainbows were all in tow. This could have been 1964, the bus, Ken Kesey's psychedelic harvester, and some of the folks on board members of the original Merry Pranksters en route to reconfigure American society along with the rest of us: the vanguard. All we needed was a little LSD to break through the conformity, and whoosh: we'd have it licked. "It's about the hundred year suppression of technology," said one. "It's the dark ages, man." "We're filling up our prisons with kids from our failing schools," came from another. "Conspiracy theory? It's called a theory because it works." I was comfortable in this, felt part of a tradition ... felt a cord had me tied to the last Gulf War protests, the ones against Vietnam and even beyond. I was a link: someone who'd offer this experience to the next in-line, making up society's ever-changing opinions. The bus stopped, "Civic Center, everyone off," said the chubby driver wearing his union button like others wore their peace signs.

At the demonstration we sat on the lawn reading: Free Palestine, No Blood For Oil, Presidents Bush and Hussein dressed as cowboys shooting it out, Corporate Media Lies, Who Would Jesus Bomb?, Fuck Bush, and I Feel Good. Seemed everyone had something on their minds. There were more, many more, good and clever too. They reminded me of bumper stickers, and we the people: individuals gathered for a single cause; united in our differences, and as it goes in the Constitution: E pluribus Unum. Life had moved on, and yet this gathering felt too primitive, too time honored to have come about just here and now. We the people were holding council. The United States and its allies had moved towards another showdown, something we'd been told at every outset would never happen again. Our leaders' actions, said the spokesman on TV, were the people's will. Funny, no one had asked me.

Leaving, the police lined the periphery around Civic Center, beside them kids dressed in black ... jackboots, balaclavas, and body language that told you all you needed to know: there would be shit kicking. They looked young, not necessarily poor, but perhaps not privileged either, yet they appeared to have had enough of this life without having gotten involved in the first place. A message told us "The march is now over.

Please leave the area in an orderly fashion, so that other marchers may complete their march as you have done. Thank you." Someone mentioned Kent State and Berkeley, maybe that was true, maybe the whole day was nothing but a repeat, a re-run. Planet earth appeared again. That flag sure looked good even from this distance. It was hard to look away. My companion said goodbye, she needed to get home; the kid was tired and tomorrow was a busy day. Cell phones began ringing again as out of respect they'd been silent all afternoon. The setting sun ushered us back to our everyday lives, and the day, the day that had meant so much had finished.

> March 22nd, five weeks later war had begun. Bombs fell, their blasts out of earshot from those living "from sea to shining sea." I added myself to another march in New York City. "Out of the stores, into the streets," "Hell no, we won't go, we won't fight for Texaco." The mood wasn't the same as San Francisco's jamboree; perhaps the previous demos had done little to halt our government's need for victory in the Arabian Peninsular: a desire stronger than their fear of domestic dissent. "Look at these fucking people," said a guy holding five bottles of assorted beer, directing himself towards the marchers, "Who's gonna save you when they come for yaaaaa!!! Huh?"

I'd come alone, but my friends were here, as many as forty thousand of them. "Whose streets! Our streets!" rose out of me. It felt good to be a part of this, let out a little steam. I shouted it over and over to the point where my normal reserve turned to a pack attitude with every reprise of that chant, the one that felt louder than all those crosses on those ballots in that 2001 election, the campaign that saw the president take office from a recount of a recount of an initial miscalculation in the numbers in the state which his brother governed. "NO WAR, NO WAR, NO WAR," bounced off the buildings down the streets and all about those wanting war to end, corporate media dead, the oil-based Western economy shifting tack, and demonstration to remain a fundamental right. Would the old people singing, "Give Peace a Chance" prove to their children marching beside them that this would work? What about the silent majority ... the ones whose windows had become galleries of the Stars and Stripes? What about their children? I thought back to an image I'd first taken when I'd just picked up a camera. It was of a demonstrator looking into the face of a riot cop. This was London, 1990, and it was the Poll-Tax Riots. Another image ... the same image ... shot later in my career, showing a bleeding, defiant Muslim student raising his fist at a Turkish riot cop. This was Istanbul, 1991, the first Gulf War. Nothing had changed, although that didn't matter now, all that mattered was we were making a difference. Things would surely be different.

Broadway stretched further than I could see, it was spring and warm, and the sun sliced down the high-rises making its magic. The week before had seen snow here, and even though we wore t-shirts, winter hadn't been gone long enough for anyone to believe-people carried over-coats and umbrellas just in case, even the cops wore rain jackets; though some stood uncomfortably over-heating in their winter uniforms. They hadn't banked on this. None of us knew what the weather would do. We were all victims of its whimsy, all of us, united by the planet's indifference towards our existence, the one truth that would never change.

A guy leaned on his pick-up truck on the corner of Washington Square. He had on jeans, a sweatshirt with a Bald Eagle on it, workman's boots, and wrap-around shades. He watched us. "These colors don't run" was on display from his rear windshield; the truck had its engine on. The communal clutch I'd been in a second ago was gone. Peeling off from the crowd, I was an individual again, just another solitary member of my society. I'd done my bit: my voice was horse; my body sweaty, my conscience clear, and my political family were again nothing more than the faceless bunch I dumbly brushed by everyday.

> Boston Common was different. I was here to see ... take pictures. During Desert Storm I'd photographed Iraqi soldiers, Kurdish refugees and Western military build-up. But here I was aiming at a concept, something that San Francisco, New York City, and now Boston would all share. Red, white, and blue flashed in front of me as I exited the station — plenty of it, held upright by people wearing camouflage. This was the side I'd been looking for: those protesting the protesters. A line separated both parties as I approached. To my eye, the white, male dominated, working class group were in harmony lashing out at the splintered opposition with one voice. "GET A JOB" "USA, USA." When the other side replied "No War, No War" the patriots shot back with "9/11, 9/11! MORE HUMAN SHIELDS, MORE HUMAN SHIELDS!" Defending the country

sounded easier than attacking it. And for the flag bearers, national sentiment seemed to create greater emotion, compared to the reasoned protestation by the new-world citizenry. But in the end volume won out; the vocal mob took effect with communication turning to hoots and hollers of tribes that sounded out around the common. Things got heated but never violent: deep-seated ideology made compromise impossible for everyone-and on closer inspection each stereotype: a person who confirmed my theory, another who looked like they belonged on one side, in fact, belonged on the other. The stereotypes were in my head, and the assumptions I so wanted to prove didn't exist.

Eric, a retired infantry sergeant, who'd fought in Desert Storm, told me the scenario: those who worked and those who didn't. The kids on the other side of the imaginary line existed in privilege without the responsibilities working people had, he said, hell, they just went to college. Eric now worked as a biologist in disease research. His studies in this field saved at least ten American children a year. He was proud of this. After his tour of duty and commission ended he needed work. "Went to college. Took three years, but in the end I got my degree."

The patriots moved on, flags heralding their loud one-liners mocking those on the wrong side. "NO WAR, NO WAR" they chortled at a peace-group walking by. A father looking on bent down by his child, pointing to the noisy mob, making a face, "No war, no war," he said, returning the compliment. Everybody was talking, and in the strangest ways.

The facts, the facts: the goddamned facts were at work.

Everywhere I turned-the facts. Talking on that Saturday to the members of the Falun Gong, the marching Islamists, the ascetic communalists whose teachings and codes emerged from ideas and stuff you couldn't touch; it was facts that ruled. It sort of felt like the Dalai Lama had started a software company: it made no sense. They, me, everybody, couldn't see the big picture. Maybe because everything that sounded the same, looked the same, and ultimately appeared the same, making all the differences setting everyone apart — the same. The anti-war protesters seemed not to want to think about their part in the whole, just the bit they played here today. It all made sense. They worked. Some went to church. They socialized; vacationed, drank Starbucks, and were now performing their civic duties in accordance with their beliefs: stopping imperialism by demonstrating against the system that had created all that they shared in, in the first place. A retired school-teacher, holding "Shame On You America," whispered she was glad the World Trade Center was hit, since the people in that building were nothing but plunderers, sackers of poor countries, profiteers. And she? What did she and her husband have? A couple of cars and two homes, why she asked? A Vietnam vet sitting on a bench, beside her said that to his mind this war was "for thems with things that wanted more, against those with nothing." He had nothing he said, didn't want anything either, and had his wife leave him because of it. "In the Bible it says it's the love of money that is the root of all evil, not money on its own," he revealed pointing to the sky. "The world's gone, man, definitely gone." Police choppers monitored the human flow; on the rooftops men watched with binoculars. Someone screamed "Big Brother!" as two cops walked amongst the crowd videotaping faces no one knew. Was the screamer right? Had the police in 2003 become that of 1984? The man who wrote "Corporate Media: Government Monkeys" in chalk with an arrow pointing to the TV cameras and anchor men interviewing jolly owners of cute dogs with anti-war slogans tied to their tails, was he right like the Vietnam veteran was right? Had the world gone mad? In Iraq there was a battle raging with bullets and bombs. Here it was information, tons of it. I for one held enough to fill most of my pockets from it all. Seemed everyone was busy with information, donation, application, manifestation and maximum circulation. "Hey ..." said the Vet, "... wanna know something? Wanna know the definition of a bayonet? A piece of steel with two poor boys on each end. That's a fact."

A man I'd met on the common, that day, told me of the terrible confusion he'd lived in, twenty years ago, riding society's merry-go-round. He'd stepped off, turning his back on it all for the simple life: one, he said, had meant he never carried more than a hundred dollars with him, ever. He called himself Kharash, although he'd been William Smith before his "revelation," as he called it. Kharash had long mousey hair, blue eyes, a beard, and an ease that set him apart from the thousands that day. He and his family group ran a café and bakery, "Common Ground," and described how they made just enough, but were happy. "The people here with all their opinions aren't bad people. They're doing what they believe in," he said. "America is a good country, no different from any other, with an incredible power that has the potential to create unbelievable good and unimaginable bad. I fear another 9/11 will turn this country's human energy in on itself. It'll implode." Kharash wasn't preaching; he had little desire in persuading me of anything - he was just talking. He offered his card ... told me to look him up when I was in Boston next. The picture on it was of a king and a pauper sitting at a table drinking coffee, the pauper wore the king's crown and both had smiles on their faces. I put the card in my pocket along with the others I'd amassed, and watched Kharash walk away.

> Today, April 9th, 2003 the war in Iraq is almost over, the military objectives nearly complete.

And history, as we like to say, has once again been made.

And the demonstrators in the United States, and all over the world? What of them? And all those in support of Shock and Awe? Where did they go? What happened with the marches, the return to the bye-gone days, the tribes, the facts, and the confusion that moved us so?

I thought I'd been part of something, thought I had an idea that would describe all I'd seen. Had I been fooled?

Was it important, or was all the activity just a slice of time made to stand out from all the others by those who lived in it, here and now? I could have stayed at home and hit my head with a hammer for all the good I'd done. Was the picture on the gentle man's card the ideal? Was he the ideal: the man who only wanted enough? In the end the war confirmed the gap between what those on the streets wanted and what they'd get.

I couldn't help thinking that if democracy really worked, why would the people be allowed to have it?

In times of war groups come together be it for one cause, or another. In times of war there is an obligation to do something, no matter what. And during war what appears to be a contest of those with differing opinions is perhaps only a desire to communicate, be less alone. Man's history of forgetting helps him move into the future self assured and righteous with whatever new God fits the times.

Only earth remains as it holds us in its sway as we its occupants continue, living, dying, fighting, thinking and proclaiming the instant unique until it happens all over again. The image of planet earth struck a note that day in San Francisco.

It was the big picture.

NOTES

WHAT YOU NEED TO KNOW ABOUT THE ESSAYS

© 2002 His Holiness The Dalai Lama

Page 156 - 157

017 THOMAS L. FRIEDMAN > Noah and 9-11

© 2002 by the New York Times Co. Reprinted with permission

Page 158 - 159

018 ROBERT FISK > A Year on. A View from the Middle East

© 2002 Robert Fisk. First Published by The Independent September 2002

Page 160 - 165

019 CHRISTOPHER HITCHENS > Appointment in Samarra?

© 2002 Christopher Hitchens

Page 166 - 167

020 SUSAN SONTAG > Of Courage and Resistance

© 2003 Susan Sontag. Reprinted with permission of the Wylie Agency Inc.

Page 168 - 173

021 EYAD SARRAJ > They Never Promised Heaven. Reflections on September 11

© 2002 Eyad Sarraj M.D.

Page 174 - 175

022 ALEXANDRA BOULAT > Terror Against Terror

Photographs © 2002 Alexandra Boulat . VII

Text © 2002 Alexandra Boulat . VII

Page 176 - 207

023 URI SAVIR > Glocalization: A New Balance of Power

© 2003 Uri Savir

Page 208 - 211

024 JOSEPH S. NYE > America is not an Empire

© 2002 Joseph S. Nye

Page 212 - 215

025 WILLIAM F. SCHULZ > I don't Even Want to Speak English Again: Terrorism and the Challenge to Human Rights

© 2002 William F. Schulz

Page 216 - 219

026 SCHELL - OE A Letter Exchange: October 2002

© 2002 Jonathan Schell. Kenzaburo Oe letters translated from Japanese by Hisaaki Yamanouchi

Page 220 - 229

027 ROBERT DANNIN > Defending the Passionate Observer

© 2003 Robert Dannin

Page 230 - 237

[1] James Nachtwey, Interview with author, 11 January 1999

[2] Workers, New York: Aperture, 1993.

028 JAMES NACHTWEY > The Passion of Allah

© 2003 James Nachtwey

Page 238 - 297

029 JOHN K. COOLEY > Proxies and Proxy Wars: 20th Century Mishaps and Disasters

© 2002 John K. Cooley

Page 298 - 327

[1] F.J. Harper, in Political Scandals and Causes Since 1945: An International Reference Compendium (London, Longman Current Affairs, 1991), pp. 348-349.

[2] Arthur M . Schlesinger Jr., A Thousand Days, John F. Kennedy in the White House (London, Andre Deutsch, 1965), pp 204-205.

[3] Ibid, pp.206-207

[4] Ibid, p. 206.

[5] Harper, op. cit., p. 417

[6] Haynes Johnson, The Bay of Pigs (New York, Dell, 1964), p. 56.

[7] Schlesinger, op.cit. pp. 216-219.

[8] Ed Gup, The Book of Honor, (New York, Doubleday, 2000), pp. 114-120.

[9] Ibid., page 121.

[10] Hunter, pop. Cit., pp. 350-51.

[11] Private interview, concerned US diplomat, Washington, DC, January 1980.

[12] Gup, op.cit. pp. 320-326.

[13] Jermey Harding, Diary column, London Review of Books, March 21, 2002, p. 34.

[14] CNN International TV news report, July 6, 2002.

[15] Internet transcript "John Stockwell: The Secret Wars of the CIA," undated.

[16] Jean-Pierre Tuquoi, "Une desastre humanitaire menace plusieurs millions d'Angolais," Le Monde, Paris, June 20, 2002, p. 2.

[17] Alfred J. McCoy, The Politics of Heroin: CIA complicity in the global drug trade (Brooklyn, Lawrence Hill Books, 1991), pp. 141-144.

[18] Ibid, p. 491.

[19] Christopher Robbins, Air America (New York, GP Putnam, 1979), p. 230.

20 McCoy, op.cit., p. 290.

21 McCoy, pp. 289-92 and p. 491 Robbins p. 276.

22 National Reporter magazine, Washington DC, Winter 1986.

23 Neil Sheehan, A Bright Shining Lie (Picador Books and Jonathan Cape, London and Fil River, Mass. 1988), pp. 138-139

24 Roger Faligo and Remi Kauffer, Les Maitres Espions, Histoire Mondiale du Renseignement, Tome 2 (Paris, Robert Lafont, 1994), pp.223-224.

25 Elizabeth Becker, When the War Was Over, Cambodia's Revolution and the voices of its People (New York, Simon and Schuster, 1986), p. 55 and p. 120.

26 Sheehan, op.cit., pp. 732-733.

27 Becker, op.cit., pp.372-373.

28 "Settling Old Scores," TIME international edition, July 8, 2002, pp.43-45.

29 See John K. Cooley, Unholy Wars, Afghanistan, America and International Terrorism (London and Sterling, Va., Pluto Books, third revised edition, 2002), Chapter 5, "Recruiters, Trainers and Assorted Spooks," pp. 64-85.

30 Mark Thompson, "Generals for Hire," TIME, January 15, 1996, pp. 10-12.

31 Ken Silverstein, "Privatizing War," The Nation, July 7-August 8, 1997, online.

32 Yossef Bodansky, Offensive in the Balkans, The Potential for a Wider War as a Result of Foreign Intervention in Bosnia-Herzogovina (Alexandria, Va., The International Strategic Studies Association Inc., 1995), passim. See also John K. Cooley, Unholy Wars, op.cit., pp. 163-176.

33 Special report by Hal Bernton, Mike Carter, David Heath and James Neff in the Seattle Times, June 23-July 7, 2002, Part 5.

34 Personal interviews and research by the author in 2001.

35 R. Jeffrey Smith, "A Bosnian Village's Terrorist Ties," Washington Post Foreign Service, March 11, 2000, internet, pp. 1-3.

36 "Bosnia and Herzegovina," in Patterns of Global Terrorism, US State Department annual report, May 21, 2002, online version.

37 Wes Jonasson, Dialogue With the Damned, The Balkans During A Time of Transition and Tragedy (London, Minerva Press, 2002), pp. 251-255.

38 Sunday Times, London, March 12, 2000.

39 Jonasson, op. cit.,note, p. 256.

40 Ibid., note, p. 257.

41 Ibid., pp. 448-466, personal interviews and general media coverage.

42 Interviews.

43 Roberto Ruscica, in Corriere della Sera (Milan), October 15, 1998.

44 James Bisset, "We Created A Monster," Toronto Globe and Mail July 31, 2001, internet.

O30 RON HAVIV > Black and White: An Uncertain Journey with the U.S. Military

© Photographs 2003 Ron Haviv . VII

© Text 2003 Ron Haviv . VII

Page 328 - 377

031 GEORGE W. BUSH > Remarks at the United Nations General Assembly

© 2002 George W. Bush

Page 378 - 381

032 MICHAEL IGNIATIEFF > The American Empire: The Burden

© 2003 Michael Igniatieff distributed by The New York Times Special Features/Syndication Sales

Page 382 - 391

033 NOAM CHOMSKY > Who are the Global Terrorists?

© 2002 Noam Chomsky. First published in World in Collision: Terror and the Future of Global Order (Palgrave Macmillan 2002)

Page 392 - 397

1 New York Times, Oct. 18, 1985.

2 US Army Operational Concept for Terrorism Counteraction (TRADOC Pamphlet No. 525-37), 1984

3 GA Res. 40/61, 9 Dec. 1985; Res. 42/159, 7 Dec. 1987.

4 See my Necessary Illusions (Boston: South End, 1989), chap. 4; my essay in Alex George, ed., Western State Terrorism (Cambridge: Polity/Blackwell, 1991)

5 Shultz, "Terrorism: The Challenge to the Democracies," June 24, 1984 (State Dept. Current Policy No. 589); "Terrorism and the Modern World," Oct. 25, 1984 (State Department Current Policy No. 629). Shultz's congressional testimony, 1986, 1983; the former part of a major campaign to gain more funding for the contras; see Jack Spence and Eldon Kenworthy in Thomas Walker, ed., Reagan versus the Sandinistas (Boulder, London: Westview, 1987).

6 Shultz, "Moral Principles and Strategic Interests," April 14, 1986 (State Department, Current Policy No. 820).

7 New York Times, Oct. 17, 18, Kapeliouk, Yediot Ahronot, Nov. 15, 1985. Foreknowledge, Los Angeles Times, Oct. 3; Geoffrey Jansen, Middle East International, Oct. 11, 1985. Bernard Gwertzman, New York Times, Oct. 2, 7, 1985.

8 Boustany, Washington Post Weekly, March 14, 1988; Bob Woodward, Veil (New York: Simon & Schuster, 1987, 396f.).

9 Guardian, March 6, 1985. For details and sources, see my "Middle East Terrorism and the American Ideological System," in Pirates and Emperors, Old and New (Cambridge: South End Press, 2002.

10 For details, see my Culture of Terrorism (Boston: South End, 1988), 77ff.

11 Sofaer, The United States and the World Court (State Dept. Current Policy 769), Dec. 1985.

12 Juan Hernández Pico, Envío(Universidad Centroamericana, Managua), March 1994.

13 Envío, Oct. 2001. For a judicious review of the aftermath, see Thomas Walker and Ariel Armony, eds., Repression, Resistance, and Democratic Transition in Central America (Wilmington: Scholarly Resources, 2000).

14 Envío, Oct. 2001; Panamanian journalist Ricardo Stevens, NACLA Report on the Americas, Nov/Dec 2001.

15 Patrick Tyler and Elisabeth Bumiller, New York Times, Oct. 12; Michael Gordon, New York Times, Oct. 28, 2001; both p. 1.

16 Jerusalem Post, Aug. 16, 1981.

17 For extensive review, see my Necessary Illusions and Deterring Democracy, updated ed. (Hill and Wang, 1992) (Nicaragua); Year 501 (Boston: South End Press,

1993) (Indonesia).

18 Elisabeth Bumiller and Elizabeth Becker, New York Times, Oct. 17, 2001.

19 Foreign Affairs, Jan/Feb 2002; talk of Oct. 30. See Tania Branigan, Guardian, Oct. 31, 2001.

20 For a sample, see George, op cit. Exceptions are rare, and the reactions they elicit are not without interest.

21 Foreign Relations of the United States, 1961-63, vol. XII, American Republics, p. 13ff., 33

034 MUZAMIL JALEEL > Haunted by Death. My Kashmir Struggles to Live

© 2003 Muzamil Jaleel

Page 398 - 405

035 GARY KNIGHT > Kashmir

© 2002 Gary Knight . VII

Page 406 - 445

036 PANKAJ MISHRA > The Other Face of Fanaticism

© 2002 Pankaj Mishra distributed by The New York Times Special Features/Syndication Sales

Page 446 - 451

037 BETH BARON > Waves of Islamic Radicalism

© 2003 Beth Baron

Page 452 - 455

038 JACQUES MENASCHE > Fenced Up to Heaven. Eight Stops on the Israeli/West Bank Frontier

© 2002 Jacques Menasche

Page 456 - 465

039 CHRISTOPHER ANDERSON > The Stone Throwers

© Photographs 2002 Christopher Anderson . VII

© Text 2002 Christopher Anderson . VII

Page 466 - 495

040 EDWARD SAID > Who is in Charge?

© 2003 Edward W. Said

Page 496 - 499

041 GÜNTHER GRASS > The Injustice Of The Mightier

© 2003 Günther Grass translated from German by dpa

Page 500 - 501

042 DAVID RIEFF > The Great Divorce. Europe and America in Post September 11th Era

© 2003 David Rieff

Page 502 - 507

043 ARUNDHATI ROY > The Ordinary Person's Guide to Empire

© 2003 Arundhati Roy. First published by The Guardian, 2003. Will appear in the Second Edition of Arundhati Roy War Talk (Cambridge: South End Press 2003)

Page 508 - 513

044 LEWIS H. LAPHAM > Pax Americana

© 2003 Lewis H. Lapham

Page 514 - 515

045 CHRISTOPHER MORRIS > Counter Terrorism and the War in Iraq

© Photographs 2003 Christopher Morris . VII

Page 516 - 561

046 JON LEE ANDERSON > The Problem with Dreams

© 2003 Jon Lee Anderson

Page 562 - 563

047 MATT MCALLESTER > Amman Jordan April 4 2003

© 2003 Matt McAllester

Page 564 - 565

048 GENERAL WESLEY K. CLARK > A New Kind of War

© 2003 General Wesley K. Clark

Page 566 - 567

049 ANNA CATALDI > Thoughts About a Just World

© 2003 Anna Cataldi translated form Italian by © 2003 Avril Bardoni

Page 568 - 569

050 MICHAEL PERSSON > The Big Picture

© 2003 Michael Persson

Page0 570 - 575

RETHINK

Conceived Designed and Edited by Giorgio Baravalle . de.MO
Text Editor Jacques Menasche
Graphic Design Intern Sebastian Gröbner

Printed and bound in Italy by Grafiche Milani Segrate Milano.

Published in 2003 by de.MO > design.Method of Operation Ltd. 123 Nine Partners Lane Millbrook New York 12545   **www.de-mo.org**

Distributed in the United States by de.MO Millbrook New York and in Europe by Vice Versa Verlag Berlin Germany.

First edition . Library of Congress Control Number 2003092215

ISBN 0-9705768-6-2

Thank you to my wife Elizabeth for giving some of her immense talent to this project and for her patience and inspiration throughout this long process. Our editorial and political discussions were always constructive. To Cari, my great regret that you were unable to complete this project with us. de.MO misses you. Thank you to all the contributors that made this book possible.